If you're looking for a trustworthy guide through the financial maze, consider what these respected leaders have said about Austin Pryor and *Sound Mind Investing*.

"I have known Austin Pryor for over 25 years now, and I regard him as a good friend. I have found his counsel to be both biblical and practical. I know of no other individual with whom I would consult with more confidence on the subject of mutual fund investing than Austin. If you will spend the time to read carefully the counsel Austin provides in this book, you will find it both time and money well spent."

Larry Burkett
Founder and President / Christian Financial Concepts

"I have had the privilege of knowing Austin Pryor since the beginning of my Christian life. There are few that I have as much respect for and confidence in than Austin. His counsel in the investment area has proven to be extraordinarily wise and discerning over a long time period. I can recommend this book without hesitation as a 'must read' for anyone interested in investing in very uncertain economic times. I consider it a privilege to be able to make this recommendation."

Ron Blue
Founding Partner / Ronald Blue & Co.

"When I wrote *The Glorious Journey*, I had to include a quote by Austin Pryor in my book. Here is a man of great insight who has the ability to make difficult subjects easy to comprehend. It is obvious that *Sound Mind Investing* combines biblical wisdom with very practical and understandable application. Anyone would profit from reading this book."

Dr. Charles F. Stanley
Senior Pastor / First Baptist Church of Atlanta

(Turn the page for more comments from Christian leaders and teachers.)

"Austin Pryor's book, *Sound Mind Investing,* is a masterpiece on the subject of Christian economics. It is clearly a comprehensive hand-book for any person seeking professional guidance in investments. As a minister, of course, I am especially appreciative of the godly orientation manifest throughout this important work, and of the powerful testimony presented in Section Six, 'Investing That Glorifies God.'"

D. James Kennedy, Ph.D.
Senior Minister / Coral Ridge Presbyterian Church

"I have known Austin personally since 1973, and find him to be a man of integrity who is committed to serving our blessed Lord and Savior. His book is an outstanding compendium of helpful investment information. It is thorough, easy-to-understand and has a uniquely appealing style and readability. But most important, it incorporates Scriptural principles to help the reader be a better steward of God's resources."

Bill Bright
Founder and President / Campus Crusade for Christ

"*Sound Mind Investing* gives important steps to help you prepare before you invest. You'll learn how to set priorities, avoid risk, and develop reasonable long-term financial goals. It will tell you everything you need to know to make wise financial choices for your family. And Austin does it without getting bogged down in complex financial terms that might make things confusing for lay people like you and me. This is a vital tool that you'll want to refer to again and again as you make your financial decisions."

Beverly LaHaye
Founder / Concerned Women of America

"I have never outgrown the enjoyment of a book with lots of pictures. This book clearly explains what before was difficult to understand. A true expert knows his field well enough to explain it in simple terms yet with profound insights. Austin Pryor deciphers the bewildering jargon of the investment world for the first-time investor, yet also provides profound insight for the seasoned money manager. As a book that applies biblical principles to an area of great need, I highly recommend *Sound Mind Investing.*"

Howard Hendricks
Chairman, Center for Christian Leadership / Distinguished Professor, Dallas Theological Seminary

"I am grateful for *Sound Mind Investing*.
Many of us have failed to be the stewards we ought, and most
of us are too busy to give quality attention to these matters.
That is why this book is so significant.
May God bless it for the welfare of the saints."
Adrian Rogers
Senior Minister / Bellevue Baptist Church

"If you're looking for an attractive easy-to-follow investment guide
written in plain English, look no further. Austin Pryor writes without
vested interests in any specific plan or fund. This means greater candor
and objectivity. I'm frankly skeptical of a lot of stuff coming out of the
financial realm with its short-term 'for this life only' perspective. Austin is
a man with a larger and better perspective. May every reader seek to make
wise investments of money and time in God's kingdom, investments that
will pay off not only in this life, but in the eternal life to come!"
Randy Alcorn
Director of Eternal Perspective Ministries / Author of Money, Possessions & Eternity

"One of the main reasons I wrote *Wake Up, Women!* was to
encourage the endless number of Christian women who seem to know
little or nothing about finances. I included Austin's excellent book in my
bibliography because it's an inviting, easy-to-understand, step-by-step
primer for anyone who finds the subject difficult (if not terrifying).
If you're in the process of 'waking up' in this area, I heartily
recommend you pick up a copy of *Sound Mind Investing*."
Florence Littauer
Author and Speaker

"I have known Austin Pryor personally for over two decades, and have
found him to be not only a knowledgeable investment consultant, but a
man with a deep relationship with the Lord Jesus Christ. In this world,
where distrust seems to prevail, it is very encouraging to know that in the
Christian community there is a man with integrity that is backed up by
years of professional experience. I 100% endorse *Sound Mind Investing*."
Bob George
President of People to People / Author of Classic Christianity

A road map that includes what you

need to know and where to find it.

AUSTIN PRYOR

SOUND MIND

REVISED AND UPDATED

INVESTING

A Step–By–Step Guide to Financial Stability & Growth

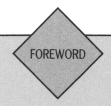

BY LARRY BURKETT

I have known Austin Pryor for over 25 years now, and I regard him as a good friend. As I have observed him over the years, I have found his counsel to be both biblical and practical. I know of no other individual with whom I would consult with more confidence on the subject of mutual fund investing than Austin.

I believe the true character of an investment adviser is not only the degree of success he has achieved, but the integrity that is maintained in the process. Austin has achieved success in the business world, but, more important, he has done so with truth and honesty.

When Austin began his monthly investment newsletter, he asked for my help in getting the word out to Christians. Since I regard the reputation of the ministry I represent as more important than any friendship, I imposed some conditions for helping. First, Austin had to agree to forego building his investment advisory business (which was his primary source of income). I felt that to sell an investment newsletter while accepting investors' money would be a potential conflict of interest. Because he felt it was more important to teach Christians investment strategies, Austin readily agreed to cease accepting new clients.

My second condition was perhaps even more restricting since it required him to submit his newsletter to our editorial staff for review and critique every month. Without hesitation, Austin also agreed to this condition. We soon found this review to be unnecessary and discontinued it.

I say this only to emphasize that I endorse the integrity and honesty of Austin Pryor. Obviously you, the reader, must evaluate his advice yourself. No one individual has the right advice for everyone, and anyone can, and will, be wrong in the changing economy we live in. But if you will spend the time to read carefully the counsel Austin provides in this book, you will find it both time and money well spent.

SPECIAL
THANKS!

FROM THE AUTHOR

To Larry Burkett . . .
. . . the idea of offering investment help especially for Christians was yours to start with, and without your gracious support, the monthly newsletter would never have gotten off the ground. Thanks for believing in me, and for helping me launch a new career in writing that has proven so very gratifying. How proud we are of you and Judy, and grateful for our friendship these 25+ years!

To Doug and Gena Cobb . . .
. . . for your help in teaching me the ropes of desktop publishing. Your consistent interest and personal prayer support was, and continues to be, immensely appreciated.

To Catharine Smith . . .
. . . a lot of people have good secretaries, but you're definitely off the top of the scale when it comes to getting things done. Your loyalty, hard work, and unselfish spirit have blessed me and our family for going on two decades. Thank you!

To Vicki Mosher . . .
. . . you've come alongside to help grow our ministry. The genuine interest you have shown in the welfare of our readers is evidence that you have been heaven-sent. Thank you for praying the Jabez prayer for us. You are appreciated!

To my sons and their wives . . .
. . . What wonderful gifts you are to us! To have three terrific sons who have given their lives to the Lord Jesus, and for you to have married precious young women who love Him as well. Tre, Andrew, and Matthew—thanks for the work you each have done at various times in contributing to this book and the work here at SMI, furthering, we trust, the reach of the gospel of Christ.

To Mark and Cindy Biller . . .
. . . Thank you for surrendering your lives to the Lordship of Christ, even if it meant moving to Kentucky! We appreciate your obedience to the call and your servants' spirits. And Mark, the Lord knew I'd need your help in carrying the editing and researching load on this third edition—your contributions made a real difference!

And to all my newsletter readers . . .
. . . who have shown their support and prayed so faithfully that the Lord would give His blessing to our work. To get anything of value accomplished, there's no substitute for people who are willing to pray!

How to Know
If This Book Has
Been Written for You

"C'mon, Herb. We've got to go.
Are you going to buy the book or not?"

The foundation of every successful investment program begins with a clear understanding of one's motivation: "What's my purpose in investing?"

For the Christian, the answer is two fold: (1) to provide financially for the needs of your household, and (2) to increase your assets in order to serve God more fully. This book was written to help you do both.

If you're like most Americans these days, you look with bewilderment at the flood of investment opportunities passing before you. You're not only being encouraged to invest in mutual funds, but also to day trade stocks, IPOs, commodities futures, stock and index options, and other complicated securities. You're even told to invest by borrowing against the equity in your home.

During the past twenty years, the variety of financial opportunities available to the average investor multiplied greatly. For most people, it's too much of a good thing—this "option glut" often serves to paralyze them. Many of the alternatives seem very complicated. Strategies that used to occupy only the wealthy now appear to be urged on everyone. Even everyday economic decisions that should be routine seem to require as much research and planning as a takeover of one major corporation by another!

Finding your way is not made any easier by the investment industry.

To a large degree, any intimidation felt by the average investor is the result of the way the industry conducts itself. For one thing, investment "experts" make your task of learning more difficult because everything they say sounds so complicated. They create the impression that investing is very hard, and that it might be best if it were not entrusted to amateurs (like you).

And then there's the matter of the industry's preoccupation with making forecasts. It's one thing to help investors make more informed decisions by giving out economic data, corporate profiles, historical trends, and the like. But then to use that information as the basis for market predictions is quite another. The fact is that nobody knows for sure what's coming next year, next month, next week, or even tomorrow. Forecasts from the brokerage community and investment media, at best, are conflicting and confusing. At their worst, they're totally misleading and eventually will prove extremely expensive to any investor who takes them seriously.

Most people have only vague notions as to what their long-term investment goals are. As a result, they move through life as responders . . .

. . . deciding on a case-by-case basis whether to say yes to the various investment opportunities that randomly come to their attention. Their thinking is short-term. Depending on their mood that day, or the advice of a friend

---

Why does this book already have yellow highlighting in it?

Because I went through and highlighted the points that I especially wanted to impress upon you or bring to your attention. It's another of the ways I've tried to make the book user-friendly and visually interesting.

(Underlining added for emphasis in all verses.)

For God hath not given us the spirit of fear hath: but of power, and of love, and of <u>a sound mind</u>.
2 Timothy 1:7 (KJV)

<u>If any of you lacks wisdom, he should ask God</u>, who gives generously to all without finding fault, and it will be given to him. But when he asks, he must believe and not doubt . . .
James 1:5–6

who's in on a "good thing," or even how persuasive a salesperson is, they make a decision whether to invest. Often, they give little thought as to exactly where that particular investment fits in fulfilling their long-term goals.

Responders feel a need to "do something" when a major news story hits. Because they're not quite sure where *they're* going, they tend to watch the crowd to see where *it's* going. They begin listening for the hot tips, taking the gurus seriously, and putting too many eggs in the same basket. They might realize they're going somewhat out of bounds, but they're looking for that extra edge. The problem is they're drinking from "broken cisterns." The crowd and the experts don't know what's coming next any more than they do.

In order to find peace of mind in your investment decisions, you need to become *an initiator* **rather than** *a responder.*

Initiators have a concrete game plan in mind. They have made the effort to develop a strategy that specifically takes into account their long-term financial goals as well as their own personal investment temperament. It is shaped around what they hope to accomplish in the future, and it fits who they are "inside."

Make it your goal to become an initiator! Be like a shopper at the food market who buys only those ingredients needed to prepare a specific recipe. Before she goes to the supermarket, Cindy knows what she's looking for. When she is confronted with special promotions for products that aren't on her shopping list, she readily passes them by. Cindy won't need to spend any time at all considering whether to buy them *because her shopping is purposeful.* Similarly, before you begin to invest, put together a strategy that takes into account the risk of loss you can comfortably carry both financially *and* emotionally.

The plans of the diligent lead to profit as surely as haste leads to poverty.

Proverbs 21:5

Suppose one of you wants to build a tower. Will he not first sit down and estimate the cost to see if he has enough money to complete it? For if he lays the foundation and is not able to finish it, everyone who sees it will ridicule him, saying, "This fellow began to build and was not able to finish."

Luke 14:28–30

If you're ready to spend a little time learning a few basics, you can be of good cheer! This book is written especially with your needs in mind . . .

. . . to equip you to have the confidence to take charge of your financial life—to become an initiator. I plan to help you do this in five primary ways.

❶ **I'm going to teach you only what you** *need to know,* **not all that there** *is to know.* (That should be pretty good news, right there!) I don't take the "complete guide" approach.

THE "COMPLETE GUIDE" APPROACH TO TEACHING

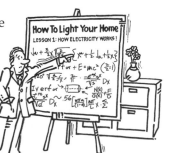

THE "ONLY WHAT YOU NEED TO KNOW" APPROACH TO TEACHING USED IN THIS BOOK

The Daredevil

"There's a lot of money to be made by people who aren't afraid to go for it! I may be overly optimistic (and a tad impulsive), but I don't usually worry about my investment decisions once they're made."

The Explorer

"To be successful in investing, you've got to keep in step with the latest trends. I'm open to new investment opportunities with potentially large returns even if they are a little more risky."

The Researcher

"I don't believe in investing in something just because everyone else is doing it. Once I make a decision, I have a lot of confidence in it, even if other investors around me are changing their minds."

The Preserver

"You can't be too careful when it comes to investing your money. I am much more interested in minimizing my chances for losses than I am in taking greater risks to earn possibly higher returns."

Instead, I assume that you just want the basic essentials for now. And put that way, there really isn't all that much for you to learn. Just as you can throw a wall switch and enjoy the benefits of electricity without understanding how it all works, so it is with mutual funds. I will cover just enough information here to teach you to "throw the switch" that will enable you to establish a practical (and relatively easy to supervise) long-term investment strategy.

❷ I'm going to give you a framework for setting priorities on how to spend (or invest) your monthly surplus. It's based on working your way through Four Levels toward financial security. If you have consumer debt outstanding (Level One) or lack a sufficient contingency fund (Level Two), I believe it's best to apply your surplus in those areas. However, that doesn't mean you are free from making important investment decisions in connection with stock, bond, and money market securities. If you have an IRA, you've got the responsibility for managing it. Or perhaps you have a pension plan at work, like a Keogh, SEP-IRA, or 401(k), where you are allowed to make decisions as to how your account is invested. Perhaps you've purchased a variable annuity, which offers you similar choices. These retirement investments represent money that was set aside in the past, and although you may not be adding to them at present, you still must decide how best to invest the money that's already there. To one degree or another, you will do a better job of making these decisions if you have a basic understanding of the investment markets. Even if you're still at the first two levels, you can use this time productively to build your understanding of investing principles. Then, when you have larger amounts to manage in the future, you won't need a crash course—your knowledge and confidence levels will be up to the task!

❸ I'm going to introduce you to four basic investment temperaments—four approaches to risk-taking. They're represented by the cartoon images you see on the left. In chapter 17, I'll lead you through a process of discovering which of the four is most appropriate for your basic emotional makeup and financial situation. Once you learn this, you'll have a yardstick for measuring risk that will be helpful to you for years to come.

❹ I'm going to teach you in an extremely user-friendly way. The lessons are worded in everyday "plain-English" language, and come in small, easy-to-digest portions. Also, I've put lots of extra time into making the layout and design of these pages as clear, interesting, and easy-to-follow as possible (as I hope you're beginning to notice by now).

❺ **I'm going to base all of the above on the time-tested principles taught in Holy Scripture.** There's nothing new under the sun, so you should not be surprised to learn that the underlying values and priorities that shape the very practical strategies taught in this book are merely the outworkings of concepts taught in God's Word for centuries. Investing at the beginning of the twenty-first century, we may be tempted to feel we have grown too sophisticated for biblical lessons. In truth, the current census and economic statistics reveal that our need for biblical truth is more serious than perhaps we realize. Individually, and as a nation, we have built our financial houses on the sand and are reaping the consequences. We dare not ignore God's wisdom any longer.

I have devised this book to serve as a tool to help you follow through and build on the biblical principles that Larry Burkett, Ron Blue, and others . . .

. . . have written about so well. Where they usually stay with general principles, I want to take you the next step—showing you how to apply those principles in specific ways out in the financial marketplace. I've often used the analogy of learning how to "dress for success." Books that teach fashion concepts (including information about fabrics, color coordination, fit, and style) help build an understanding of the basics. But you still need to get in your car, travel to the local mall, and purchase your wardrobe.

I think of myself as the person who goes with you, helps you pick the clothes out, watches you try them on, and offers you opinions on whether the style, color, and fit

LET ME TELL YOU HOW THIS THIRD EDITION OF SOUND MIND INVESTING DIFFERS FROM EARLIER ONES.

If you read an earlier edition of this book, you may be wondering if there is a sufficient difference in this new version to make its purchase worthwhile. Naturally, as the author, I've no doubt there is! If you'll check out the improvements cited below, I believe you'll agree.

❶ All the stock market and fund performance data has been updated to include the dynamic changes of the past few years. As a result, I've made some adjustments in the guidelines I offer for how to allocate your investments between stocks and bonds (see the "controlling your risk" table in chapter 17), and beefed up the chapter on systematic strategies that can help guide your investing in an era of volatile markets (chapter 19).

❷ All the tax law regulations and strategies have been revised to reflect the latest information. This has led to some important strategic changes in investment strategy, such as when investing for college (chapter 8) where the new 529 savings plans have become the investment vehicles of choice. Or in planning for retirement where the question of funding priorities (401(k) or Deductible IRA or Roth IRA?) have been addressed more thoroughly in chapters 22 and 23.

❸ I've added dozens of suggestions on where to go on the Internet to find helpful financial information linked to the topics in each chapter. The Web is growing in importance as a source of information for savers and investors, and I point you to some of our favorite sites.

❹ Finally, the material has been reorganized so as to conform with the Four Levels for setting priorities which is so foundational in the SMI newsletter. In the process, I've added new chapters on budgeting (chapter 2), credit cards (chapter 3), and investing your accumulation fund (chapter 7). This new arrangement simplifies things for beginners.

Austin

Web Sidebars

Financial information is constantly changing, and while the principles taught in this book won't change, the details will. Wherever you see this computer graphic throughout the book, you'll find the best resources that were available on the Web as of the book's publishing date.

For an update to the Web resources found in this book, check our website. The links and content there are continually improving as new sites offer better alternatives. It's an ongoing revision to this book's Web material, and you'll find us online at www.soundmindinvesting.com.

is a good one for *you*. I also know a few things about the reputations of various stores and clothing manufacturers, and steer you away from the bad ones.

In order to avoid information overload, you need to develop a sense of proportion. Everything doesn't have to be learned or done yesterday. There's no such thing as "wealth without risk," so accept that you'll make a few mistakes along the way. But that's OK. You'll do fine over the long haul if you follow the basics, exercise self-discipline, and stay the course.

Before you begin your stock and bond market investing, however, you need to achieve a certain level of financial fitness. It's like those exhortations . . .

. . . to see your doctor for a physical exam before launching out on a new exercise program. Think of it as practicing financial aerobics. Now, I know working out isn't any fun. Personally, I haven't gone to work out at the fitness center in several months. Not once. *Nada*. Zero. Zip. I'm too lazy.

My workout schedule usually goes something like this. I work out faithfully for three months, starting in early March, to get ready to go out in public in my beachwear. Then, it's off to the beach where I have a great time with family and friends. Upon my return, I carefully avoid the fitness center until the following March. During the recurring nine-month periods of well-deserved rest from exercising, I've made a discovery. It's tedious, hard work to get in shape, but getting out of shape is remarkably simple. All you have to do is . . . nothing. Just relax. Stop investing time in it. It's amazing how easy it is to get out of shape. I wish it weren't like that, but it is. Being in shape, it turns out, has a very short shelf life.

We all would like great health and physical fitness, but only the people with self-discipline achieve such goals. Other areas of life are the same way. Invest time, commitment, and sacrifice in your marriage or dating relationship, and it grows stronger by the month. Replace that with neglect and making decisions just to please yourself, and the relationship weakens. The same is true of your career and a host of life's other activities—including your financial affairs. They also need time, commitment, and sacrifice in order to be healthy and grow. Are you in shape financially?

If you're not, I'm writing this book with the assumption that you're serious about making progress. At the very least, you've got good intentions. I'm hoping that this book will help those good intentions lead to determined action. Now, let's get started with your financial fitness tests to see just what kind of shape you're in! ◆

SECTION

1

THE FIRST LEVEL OF FINANCIAL FITNESS

Getting Debt-Free

The rich rules over the poor,
and the borrower becomes the lender's slave.

Proverbs 22:7

"It's from the credit card company.
Says it's our final notice."

CHAPTER PREVIEW

Laying The
Proper Foundation

I. **Before you begin investing your surplus funds in the markets, you should pay off any outstanding consumer-type debts.**

   A. Debt is defined as that which one is bound to pay or perform. It is a financial obligation that must be met.

   B. For purposes of this book, consumer debt includes credit card debt, local charge accounts, auto loans, and home equity loans. First mortgage loans on one's home will be covered separately in chapter four.

II. **Aside from the practical advantages of getting debt-free—less financial stress and huge savings on interest expense— there are biblical ones as well.**

   A. To be obedient. "Let no debt remain outstanding, except the continuing debt to love one another, for he who loves his fellowman has fulfilled the law" (Romans 13:8).

   B. To maintain your integrity. "The wicked borrow and do not repay, but the righteous give generously" (Psalm 37:21).

   C. To preserve your allegiance to Christ alone. "The rich rule over the poor, and the borrower is servant to the lender" (Proverbs 22:7).

   D. Debt is especially dangerous when it tempts us to violate our convictions, to rob our primary Creditor (God) to pay our secondary creditors (men), or when our monthly payments strap us to the point that we have little freedom to respond to the Holy Spirit's promptings to give generously.

III. **A thoughtful and workable plan for getting debt-free is a sign of maturity.**

   A. Goal setting is important. Your goals should be consistent with God's Word and reflect His guidance. They should also be set with your spouse (if married) and in writing.

   B. Many helpful resources exist to help you in your efforts to get debt-free. Several are suggested for your consideration.

   C. Getting debt-free requires self-control but is attainable by everyone.

The <u>wicked borrow and do not repay</u>, but the righteous give generously.
Psalm 37:21

<u>Give everyone what you owe him</u>: If you owe taxes, pay taxes; <u>if revenue, then revenue;</u> if respect, then respect; if honor, then honor. <u>Let no debt remain outstanding,</u> except the continuing debt to love one another, for he who loves his fellowman has fulfilled the law.
Romans 13:7–8

We begin our journey toward financial security and peace of mind by making it a priority to . . .

. . . pay off those credit cards, car loans, and other short-term debts. That's right, the first fitness test you need to pass is the "debt" test. Webster's says that debt is anything you're "bound to pay or perform; the state of owing something." Using that definition, very few Americans are free of debt.

Why place an emphasis on getting debt-free as the first step toward a sound *investing* strategy? Because it's unwise to take on the risks that come with investing unless you have staying power. That means you don't want to be in a position where circumstances unrelated to your investment strategy force you to sell your holdings and use the money elsewhere, such as for interest and debt payments. Also, for Christians, debts are moral as well as legal obligations and they must be honorably met no matter the circumstances.

Have you ever wished you could "begin again" financially?

I once heard a sermon by a noted pastor in which he read a poem called "The Land of Beginning Again." The pastor then presented the claims of Christ, explaining that He is King in the Land of Beginning Again. Each of us has experienced his share of errors, failures, and missed opportunities. We all have things that we would do differently if given a second chance. What wonderful news to know that, in Christ, the slate is wiped clean and we do have the opportunity of beginning again.

In a similar fashion, many who have become weighed down by debt wish they could get free. They have learned that the satisfaction that comes with spending is brief indeed compared to the pressure of making monthly payments which often go on for years. For some, it seems hopeless. You may sometimes feel this way yourself.

If so, take heart! You can make great strides this year. It will require planning, discipline, sacrifice, and singleness of purpose, but there are some excellent books on the market that can help. Two of my favorites are:

• *Debt-Free Living* by Larry Burkett. For the couple facing financial crisis, this book offers a scriptural way back. In addition, it provides a layman's guide to consumer rights and summarizes federal codes and acts covering credit agencies, credit reports, debt collection agencies, and bankruptcy.

• *Taming the Money Monster* by Ron Blue. This book offers expert advice on how to get out of debt, stay out of debt, and experience true financial freedom. It shows why we tend to slip into debt, how we're manipulated into making unwise borrowing decisions, and how to evaluate the opportunities when borrowing seems the right thing to do.

A friend of mine likes to say that the most powerful force in the universe (humanly speaking, of course) is singleness of purpose. Individuals or groups, no matter how determined, disciplined, or talented, will never realize their potential for growth and accomplishment without singleness of purpose. Their time, money, and energies must be focused on common goals. One thing that successful people seem to have in common is an emphasis—perhaps that's putting it too lightly, make that *an obsession*—concerning setting goals.

Without singleness of purpose and specific goals, we can become like the person described in Scripture as double-minded. "That man should not think he will receive anything from the Lord; he is a double-minded man, unstable in all he does" (James 1:7-8). So let me encourage you to engage in a meaningful goal-setting exercise as you work to get debt-free. Here are some suggestions for effective goal-setting in any area of life; adapt them to your financial situation.

• **Set goals that are consistent with God's Word.** Many successful people have accomplished much, yet remain unhappy. Having singleness of purpose toward the wrong goals only leads to wrong results. Examine your motivations, as well as your actions, in the light of God's wisdom.

• **Ask God for His guidance.** This is not the same as having scripturally sound goals. This has more to do with having the wisdom needed to set the right personal priorities. God promises to guide us if we're willing to submit to Him. It's not: "Show me Your will, Lord, so I can decide if I'm willing." Rather, it's: "Before You even reveal Your will to me, Lord, the answer is yes."

• **If married, set your goals together.** If two have become "one flesh," how critical that they have a singleness of purpose in their commitment toward common goals. Few areas will so quickly affect a couple's relationship as a financial plan that limits their spending freedom because it brings mutually conflicting goals into the open. If you can't reach a meeting of the minds on what your priorities should be, perhaps the marriage relationship itself needs some work.

• **Put your goals in writing, signing your name and date.** This act helps cement in your thinking that you really have made a firm commitment of your will to achieving your goals. It is also helpful to have your goals posted where you will see them daily as additional motivation to stay the course when the inevitable temptations to compromise arise.

Aside from the practical advantages of getting debt-free—less financial stress and huge savings on interest expense—there are biblical ones as well. Here are three that seem compelling to me:

• **To be obedient.** "Give everyone what you owe him: If you owe taxes, pay taxes; if revenue, then revenue; if respect, then respect; if honor, then honor. Let no debt remain outstanding, except the continuing debt to love one

Recommended Resources
These books contain helpful advice in the area of goal-setting and communicating.

First Comes Love, Then Comes Money
by Roger Gibson
The author explores (often humorously) several aspects of the money pitfalls in marriage, including debt management, discovering your money personality, and balancing the differing spending habits of spouses. A good nuts and bolts book for learning to avoid crippling confrontations.

Money Before Marriage
by Larry Burkett
This financial workbook for engaged couples is an invaluable guide based on the author's decades of experience in counseling hundreds of couples in financial trouble. It explains how to apply to your marriage what God's Word says about finances, understand your personality profile and that of your future mate, and prepare your new family's first spending plan.

another, for he who loves his fellowman has fulfilled the law" (Romans 13:7-8). God's word is just as binding on the conscience of the follower of Christ when it instructs us to pay our debts as it is when it tells us to love others, avoid sin, preserve our marriage, and a host of other moral guidelines that we take seriously.

• **To maintain your integrity.** "The wicked borrow and do not repay, but the righteous give generously" (Psalm 37:21). Americans are increasingly looking at bankruptcy as a "fix" for their debt problems. In 1981, 360,000 bankruptcy petitions were filed. By 1999, it had skyrocketed to 1.3 *million* households. Obviously, more and more people are faced with debt that they believe to be unconquerable. However, bankruptcy can never be more than a temporary solution for the Christian. When we borrow, we are making a vow to repay under the agreed-upon conditions of the loan. Unless the lender releases us, we are obligated to pay the debt back. In some forms of bankruptcy, the courts establish a repayment plan based on the amount of debt that you can afford to pay and directs the creditors to operate within this plan. These arrangements, rather than help you avoid responsibility for your debts, make it possible for you to honor your vow and maintain your integrity and witness to the faithfulness of Christ.

• **To preserve your allegiance to Christ alone.** "The rich rule over the poor, and the borrower is servant to the lender" (Proverbs 22:7). To be in subjection to those from whom we borrow makes it impossible to serve Christ with our undivided energies. Is it possible we may have missed exciting and rewarding opportunities for serving Him because we weren't available? Those who love Christ want to be available to be used by Him in His kingdom work, but how can He use us in a new vocation or field of ministry when our debt obligations make it impossible to say "Yes!" to the call? We want to conduct our lives so that, to the greatest extent possible, we're free to serve Christ.

12 WARNING SIGNS OF EXCESSIVE DEBT

How about a financial health checkup? If any of these twelve warning signs describe your current state of affairs, you are "past due" to get on the road to recovery. Be honest.

❑ You are unable to pay each month's bills on time.

❑ You routinely receive overdue notices because of late or missing payments.

❑ You pay only the minimum amounts required on your credit card bills.

❑ You've reached the credit limits on your credit cards.

❑ You've applied for more credit cards to keep up your spending.

❑ You have used a cash advance from one credit card to make payments on others.

❑ You regularly take cash advances on your credit cards to pay routine living expenses such as food, rent, or utilities.

❑ You owe more on your car than it is worth as a trade-in.

❑ You postdate checks and cover them on payday or with new borrowings.

❑ You don't know the total amount of installment debt you owe.

❑ You no longer contribute to a savings account.

❑ You have no savings at all!

Building on this theme of the dangers of debt in relation to our spiritual lives, Randy Alcorn writes:

"God doesn't promise to bail us out of unwise financial decisions. Many Christians have learned valuable but extremely painful lessons through losing their houses, businesses, and other valued assets for not knowing the difference between presuming upon God and trusting in him. God disciplines his children, and one way he does that is in making us face the consequences of unnecessary debt. Though I don't believe debt is always wrong, I have become acutely aware of its dangers. Here are some of the most serious ones:

"Debt is especially dangerous when it tempts us to violate our convictions. A Christian couple assumed a large home mortgage based on both their incomes. But when the wife became pregnant, they realized that in order to keep the house they would have to violate their convictions against leaving their child in a day-care center while the mother worked. Once they realize their dilemma, it would be better to confess their error, ask God's forgiveness, and take whatever losses they might need to take in order to get out of their house and into one appropriate for a single income.

"Debt is especially dangerous when we are tempted to rob our primary Creditor (God) to pay our secondary creditors (men). I know Christians who cut back on their giving in order to make their monthly payments on this item and that. If by giving to God I can no longer afford to make payments, then I need to liquidate my assets, take losses where I must, and cut all spending to a minimum to eliminate the payments once and for all. But never should I rob God.

"Debt is especially dangerous when our monthly payments strap us to the point that we have little freedom to respond to the Holy Spirit's promptings to give generously to meet others' needs. Here I am talking not just about the tithe but the freewill giving, that which is above and beyond the minimum. If my indebtedness leaves me unable to respond to God in this way, I have robbed myself and others of incalculable blessings."

An emphasis on our faithfulness in tithing is one I appreciate. If you're encumbered by debt, however, you may be thinking that you can't tithe at this time.

Debt payments, generally speaking, are a poor reason for not tithing. It's true that I don't know your circumstances. It helps to have walked in others' shoes in understanding the challenges they face. Fortunately, God does this better than anybody. He knows the pressures you're under, the desires you have, and the temptations you face. And knowing all of that, He still wants you to be generous in your giving.

In my own life, I have used 2 Corinthians 8-9 as a guide when making

Recommended Resource

Adapted from <u>Money, Possessions, & Eternity</u> by Randy Alcorn

Copyright 1989 by Randy C. Alcorn

Randy Alcorn has provided a fresh mining of the biblical texts regarding money and possessions. His work is well-researched and painstakingly biblical. Christians who want a balanced survey of the Bible's teaching on wealth will not be disappointed. Highly recommended!

Take A Longer View

Randy Alcorn provides solid teaching on stewardship and many other topics on the Eternal Perspective Ministries website. Visit it at www.epm.org.

Surety – What is it?

Surety must be one of the least taught and least understood principles in God's Word. It's hard to understand why when you consider the number of references to surety in Proverbs. In a literal sense, surety means to deposit a pledge in either money, goods, or part payment for a greater obligation. Surety means taking on an obligation to pay later without a "certain" way to pay. "A man lacking in sense pledges, and becomes surety in the presence of his neighbor" (Proverbs 17:18).

Obviously, surety is not a biblical law—it is a principle. A principle is a biblical guide to keep you on God's path and out of the world's traps. You don't get punished for violating a principle unknowingly; you suffer the consequences. The consequences of violating the principle of surety is that you presume upon the future. In other words, when you sign surety for a debt, you pledge your future. Since only God has omniscient insight into the future, when you sign surety, you presume upon God's will. "Come now, you who say, 'Today or tomorrow, we shall go to such and such a city, and spend a year there and engage in business and make a profit.' Yet you do not know what your life will be like tomorrow. You are just a vapor that appears for a little while and then vanishes away" (James 4:13-14).

Does that mean that a Christian should never borrow? No, God's Word does not prohibit borrowing—although it doesn't encourage it either. But scriptural borrowing would be limited to contracts where the means to pay is certain. That means that the lender agrees to accept pledged collateral (like a house) in total payment of the outstanding debt at any time. Therefore, if ever you couldn't continue to pay the mortgage note, the house would be surrendered and the debt canceled.

The question is often asked when discussing surety, "What if I am already signed as surety?" You can only do what you can do. Fortunately, God doesn't expect more out of us than we are capable of doing. If you can get out of surety, you should. But if you cannot, then work at reducing the liability and paying off the debts early. If you never decide to be debt free, then most probably you never will be.

Adapted from <u>Using Your Money Wisely</u>
by Larry Burkett

Copyright 1985
by Christian Financial Concepts

life-style decisions that affect my ability to give. The people praised in these passages were not wealthy, but nevertheless "their overflowing joy and their extreme poverty welled up in rich generosity. For I testify that they gave as much as they were able, and even beyond their ability" (8:2-3). From God's perspective, giving is an affair of the heart:

• "For you know the grace of our Lord Jesus Christ, that though he was rich, yet for your sakes he became poor, so that you through his poverty might become rich..." (8:9). God is pleased when we give with grateful hearts. I trust that at whatever level you are giving at the present time, you are doing so out of gratitude for God's unspeakable generosity towards you. When we give in this way, we are worshipping.

• "Each man should give what he has decided in his heart to give, not reluctantly or under compulsion, for God loves a cheerful giver..." (9:7). God is pleased when we give with happy hearts, simply for the joy of expressing our love for Him. It is a tangible way of showing that He truly holds first place in our lives. Many families justify not giving by saying they need private Christian educations for their children, a second family car, a savings reserve for rainy days, or funding for their retirement plan. These are all good and worthwhile things . . . unless they crowd our wonderful God out of His rightful place.

• "And God is able to make all grace abound to you, so that in all things at all times, having all that you need, you will abound in every good work..." (9:8). God is pleased when we give with trusting hearts, counting on Him to provide for the daily necessities of life. God made the tithe proportional—if one's income is small, the tithe is small. Yet, it's also large in the sense that it releases His giving back to us so that we will "have all that we need."

Have you considered what would happen if your income suddenly dropped 10%? Would you make it through, albeit with some sacrifice needed? Of course. In all likelihood, you can tithe (even though you may think you can't).

We are not *commanded* to give generously. Rather, our giving is a test of the sincerity of our love (8:8) and our willingness to trust in God's utter faithfulness (9:8). When you pray about your giving, may I encourage you to give to the full measure of your gratitude and cheerfulness. And continue to ask God to enlarge the capacity of your heart toward Him so you can eagerly embrace the sacrifice needed to give all the more.

A S O U N D M I N D B R I E F I N G

Ten Motivating Reasons to Get Debt-Free

by Wilson J. Humber

Before we examine ten warnings against debt, let's look at the opposing theological positions concerning debt. One extreme is to assume that the passage "Owe nothing to anyone except to love one another" (Romans 13:8 NASB) is a command to avoid all debt at all times. A few even label debt as a sin. The opposite extreme assumes that debt is acceptable, normal, and often God's way of meeting our needs as He promised to do.

My view is that debt is not a sin to avoid, but a dangerous tool which must be used with extreme caution due to its potential for enslaving people in financial bondage. Following are ten reasons I believe debt is extremely dangerous and should be used, if at all, with great care and after much prayer.

1. Debt presumes on the future. Scripture clearly says, "Do not boast about tomorrow, for you do not know what a day may bring forth" (Proverbs 27:1 NASB). When you commit yourself to payments over time, you are presuming: no pay reductions, no loss of job, and no unexpected expenses. That is a dangerous and improbable assumption.

2. Debt lowers your standard of living in the future. Money that you borrow today must be repaid over time along with the cost of renting the money, which is interest.

3. Debt avoids facing life-style decisions. It allows you to make the decision of whether you can afford to buy an item by focusing on the low payment rather than on the cost of the item. The question of whether you can afford it should include all the cost: purchase price, operational expense, and finance charges. Credit is dangerous because it is too easy to say yes to low payments over time and ignore the real decision—can I afford it, and do I need it?

4. Debt places the awesome power of compound interest at work against you. Here is an example for credit card debt. If you borrow $100 on your credit card and make only minimum payments, do you know how long it will take to repay the loan? Would you believe up to thirty years? Items charged on your MasterCard can cost you seven to eight times the purchase price!

5. Debt may delay God's plan for your life. Or it might cause you to forfeit a blessing God had planned to give. Before you obligate yourself to payments give God a chance to provide your needs.

6. Debt evades the necessity of distinguishing wants and desires from real "needs". In our home we have what we call the "I want list." The "I want list" has two rules. First, not more than five items are allowed on the list at one time. Second, we have to wait thirty days after the item is entered on the list before it can be purchased. You would be amazed how many wants and desires fade over the thirty days and the amount of impulse buying that is eliminated. This simple idea has helped to transform me from a chronic impulse buyer into a much better steward of His assets.

7. Debt encourages impulse buying and overspending. The chief financial officer of a national credit card company said that consumers will spend 27% more on plastic than they would with cash or check. Any merchant who accepts plastic will verify that consumers will spend 25% to 30% more with plastic. That is why businesses pay a fee of 1% to 7% of every purchase you make on plastic for the privilege of accepting your credit cards.

8. Debt and credit cards stifle creativity and resourcefulness. If we want something today, we charge it rather than "make do" with what we have. We feel entitled to what we want, when we want it, so we automatically head to the mall, never considering a simpler, less expensive choice: "doing without." It is not fashionable today to resole our shoes, repair our cars, or mend whatever wears out; we simply replace them.

9. Debt and credit cards eliminate margin in our lives. Plastic becomes our margin. Rather than planning what we need and allowing a margin for errors or overruns, we "charge" ahead and spend, thinking that if we must write a check that we don't have sufficient funds to cover, we have overdraft protection with our credit line. Your credit card is not an asset but a potential future liability which becomes a liability when you use it.

10. Debt teaches your children bad habits. Your children will have a casual regard for using credit cards, obtaining car loans, and applying for student loans. When I began counseling young people, I was astounded by the size of the debt load many had accumulated. They had graduated from college by borrowing the costs and living to the limit of their credit cards. They had never considered paying cash for transportation or anything else, and began adult life with a mountain of debt that creates years of financial bondage.

As appeared in the Sound Mind Investing newsletter. Wilson Humber is a certified financial planner and registered investment adviser with more than two decades of experience as a tax, investment, and estate counselor. Adapted from The Financially Challenged: A Survival Guide for Getting Through the Week, the Month, and the Rest of Your Life by Wilson J. Humber. Published by Moody Press. Copyright 1995. Used with permission.

The problem we face in attempting to get completely debt-free is that we are our own worst enemies.

Most debt problems result from an excess of spending, not a lack of income. It's not hard to spend money. With a little practice, most of us get really good at it. Advertisers show us things that (they say) will make our lives more fun, exciting, and fulfilling. And if our eyes are bigger than our wallets, lenders shower us with credit cards and encourage us to pamper ourselves. It may be expensive, but after all "we're worth it." For the most part, we're all prone to being tempted by the neat stuff we see around us.

If you've made more than your share of past mistakes, it's never too late to correct poor spending habits! The solution is deceptively simple: You need a plan to keep you on course. To remind you where you want to go and help you get there. To assure that you spend less than you earn. To help you actually live out your priorities. Then you'll have a monthly surplus that can be applied to gradually eliminating your debts. In chapter 2, we'll discuss spending plans and how to put one together that fits your situation. ◆

2

CHAPTER PREVIEW

Your Spending Plan: Don't Leave Home Without It!

I. **A winning financial strategy begins with your monthly surplus. And making sure you have a monthly surplus begins with a workable budget. A good spending plan can help you in many ways.**

    A. To apply your current income more strategically as you reduce frivolous or irresponsible spending and gradually but steadily eliminate your debt.

    B. To reach financial goals that would otherwise be unattainable as you raise your standard of living and are equipped to withstand economic downturns.

    C. To increase your giving to the Lord and His work.

    D. To stay motivated by giving you a sense of accomplishment as you measure your progress.

II. **To develop a successful spending plan with your spouse, you should:**

    A. Be truthful in your communications and thorough in your preparations.

    B. Be willing to change your lifestyle.

    C. Be consistent in monitoring your spending.

    D. Be disciplined in staying within your agreed upon limits.

    E. Be mutually supportive.

III. **If you presently have the means to pay part or all of a debt but are investing in the stock market with those funds instead, you are playing a very dangerous game. There are only three possible outcomes:**

    A. You could lose part or all of your investment money, in which case you are worse off than ever.

    B. You could make a profit, but the profit could be less than the interest you are paying on your debt. You are still worse off.

    C. You could *consistently* make profits, after taxes, that exceed the interest payments you are making on your debt. For an amateur investor, this is *extremely* unlikely.

IV. **A tried-and-true five step formula for using your monthly surplus to wipe out your debt in the fastest possible time is presented.**

Recommended Resources
These books contain helpful instruction on how to set up a workable spending plan.

The Financial Planning Workbook
by Larry Burkett
This workbook offers practical advice about managing your finances and provides a series of easy-to-follow worksheets that allow you to structure and maintain your own family's budget. Larry shows you where to start, how to stay on track, and even addresses special budgeting problems. To order call (800) 722-1976.

Master Your Money
by Ron Blue
Popular financial advisor Ron Blue has combined the Bible's timeless teachings on stewardship and responsibility with up-to-date advice on financial management and cash control. The many charts, worksheets, and a handy glossary of terms make this a practical guide.

Money Talks, and So Can We
by Ron and Judy Blue
A book for those who want to begin with the basics. The Blues provide a framework through which couples can successfully communicate about their finances. By specifically addressing some of the most common conflicts, this book provides practical advice and valuable tools couples can use to strengthen their marriages and secure their financial future.

So you want to be be a millionaire? Okay, here's what you do.

Starting when you're 30, save $264 a month. Invest it in a tax-deferred account like an IRA, and earn an average return of 10% per year. When you turn 65, *voilà*, you'll have a million bucks (or so).

Of course, how much that will buy when you reach retirement is another story. Assuming 3% inflation, it will be worth about one-third as much as it is today. I throw that in only to impress you with the fact that, while $264 is a nice starting point, you'll probably want to set aside much more.

For now, however, the question is this: Do you *have* an extra $264 each month? Or let me put it this way: If your family were a business, would you be showing a profit of at least $264 a month? After all the income is counted and all the bills are paid, is there money left over? There better be, because that monthly surplus is the key to building your financial security.

If you're not sure you even have a monthly surplus (let alone how much it is), then you've got two choices. One, you can continue your "easy come, easy go" approach, spending your money according to your moods and whims of the day. That's a fun way to go through life—until you begin drowning in a sea of debt. Meanwhile, you're robbing yourself of the opportunity to move toward financial stability and security. By the time you come to your senses, it could be too late to redeem the situation.

Or, two, you can buckle down and develop a plan to guide your spending decisions. In other words, act like a grown up. Sure, creating and living by a budget is a hassle. But if you're tempted to skip this chapter, you do so at your peril. For 99.9% of us, living by a budget is absolutely essential if we're to progress financially. It certainly was for me and my family (more on that shortly). A winning and gratifying financial strategy begins with your monthly surplus. And making sure you have a monthly surplus begins with a workable budget and—there's no sense kidding ourselves—a healthy dose of self-discipline. A good spending plan can help you:

- Apply your current income more strategically as you reduce or eliminate frivolous or irresponsible spending.
- Improve communication with your spouse as you set priorities.
- Gradually but steadily eliminate your debt.
- Raise your standard of living and equip you to withstand economic downturns.
- Increase your giving to the Lord and His work.
- Stay motivated by giving you a sense of accomplishment as you measure your progress.
- Reach financial goals that would otherwise be unattainable.
- Invest for the long-term with regularity.

There are many excellent resources available that will guide you through the process of putting together a workable spending plan (see the sidebar on page 30). They generally follow an allocation-type strategy where all your expenditures are categorized and budgets assigned to each category. Spending is monitored weekly (or monthly) to make sure that you're staying within the amounts allotted.

For several years during the late 1980s, my wife Susie and I used this kind of rigorous approach to control our spending . . .

. . . and it worked pretty well. I didn't keep a diary at the time, but looking back on it now, these are the "keys to success" that come to mind.

1. Be truthful in your communications. I keep track of the money in our family, and I was the first to realize we were facing a serious financial challenge (see chapter 30 for background). Susie knew that we were experiencing some financial disappointments, but didn't know how difficult it had become to balance our income and outgo. Even though some of the events that had caused the problem were beyond my control, I felt like a failure in my role as the financial provider in the family. I hated the idea of telling her our situation, but knew it would take both our best efforts to deal with it responsibly.

2. Be thorough in your preparations. As I began working on our spending plan, I listed not only every category of spending I could think of, but also every anticipated item within

A SOUND MIND BRIEFING

One Young Couple's Budgetary Journey

by Andrew Pryor

It's December. My wife Angie and I have begun working on a spending plan for the coming year. We've been using the Financial Planning Organizer, a great cash management tool by Larry Burkett. The basic focus in the opening section is on helping us think correctly about the importance of living within our means. Having the ability to separate our needs (life's basic requirements), wants (degree of quality of goods purchased), and desires (spending from our surplus after meeting all other obligations) is critical as we begin to formulate a budget.

Fortunately, Angie and I have a very similar understanding of what we "need," including freedom from debt. Proverbs 22:7 says, "The rich rule over the poor, and the borrower is servant to the lender." I think about my debt quite a bit. I think how wonderful it would be to be debt-free. I used to think that a job would present itself after college, and the money to pay back my debts would be readily available. But "after college" is here and I still have quite a long way to go. I'm now facing up to the challenge of putting into day-to-day practice all that I know about the dangers of debt and the importance of paying it off.

The Organizer also provides an overview of the four primary uses of income: tithing, paying our taxes, providing for our family, and retiring our debts. Whatever is left after we've met these requirements is our surplus. Tithing is a commitment Angie and I share. I haven't always been good about this. It's easy to say we're going to tithe, but when the bills come in, or I get a desire confused with a need, it's difficult to put into practice. We need to learn to give to God first and trust Him to provide. I really believe He will bless us for our faithfulness.

We can't come up with a realistic budget for the future until we know where all our money is going now. The Organizer offers suggestions on how we can begin tracking our spending. Angie and I know for sure how much we spend on rent, electricity, car insurance, gas, debt retirement, and our phone bill each month. These were easier because we paid by check and have a paper trail. For example, our electric bill over the past nine months has averaged $57.33. It's trickier to keep track of our cash spending (e.g., food, drug store, entertainment). Over the past month, one thing that has become apparent is that we spent quite a bit on eating out. It's easy to be persuaded by friends and family to do this on the spur of the moment, and it sure adds up. This kind of spending should probably be included in our "entertainment" category, since it is a form of recreation for us, and it isn't a "need" but a "desire." Budget-breakers are everywhere, and they almost always come in appealing packages.

January: With sweat dripping from my forehead from the burning heat of the conversation, sparks flying, blood flowing, muscles tensed, we did it. We forged out a budget. After taking into consideration our spending, tithing, savings goals, and some 29 subcategories of spending, we have come up with our budgeting guidelines for this

the saga continues >

As appeared in the Sound Mind Investing newsletter. Andrew Pryor is the webmaster for soundmindinvesting.com. He sometimes doubles as a contributing author to the SMI newsletter who reports on the never-particularly-pleasant battle of the budget.

each category. For example, I didn't just put down $500 for family birthdays—I listed each person on the gift list and how much we typically spent on that person. The more categories you have, the better idea you'll have of where all the money's going and, consequently, the more ideas you'll get on where you can save. Furthermore, I didn't just put down round numbers that "seemed right." I used my cancelled checks, Visa bills, and old tax returns to see what I'd actually spent in the past.

3. Be willing to change your lifestyle. All of my work only gave us a picture of where our money had gone in the past. Then it was time to go over the spending categories and discuss what we could do to lower (or temporarily eliminate) the spending in each one. Savings are possible in almost every category if you're willing to make changes in your lifestyle and shopping habits.

The trendiness of frugal living has given rise to several helpful newsletters on how to live well on less money. Here are two that I've found to be worthwhile. I'd suggest sending for samples of each to see which ones best fit your needs and lifestyle.

• *The Cheapskate Monthly.* With wit and humor, editor Mary Hunt makes saving money almost a pleasant experience. The design is great, and the content is even better. Mary has gained national recognition by appearing on such programs as "Good Morning America" and "Focus on the Family." There's a wealth of money-saving information and encouragement in this publication. The Cheapskate Monthly, P.O. Box 2135, Paramount, CA 90723-8135 or call (800) 550-3502. The cost is $18.00 for a twelve-page newsletter that is published monthly. A free sample issue will be sent upon your request.

• *The Pocket Change Investor.* Cleverly written by Marc Eisenson and Nancy Castleman, this newsletter offers you a smorgasbord of money saving strategies. In addition to saving on routine budget items, you'll learn how to save thousands of dollars on your home mortgage and credit cards. There's a nice variety of topics featured in each issue. For an example of the Eisenson style, see "Big Savings Through Mortgage Pre-payments" on page 55. For a sample issue, send $1 to: The Pocket Change Investor, P.O. Box 78, Elizaville, NY 12523. Or, get four quarterly, eight-page issues for just $12.95.

4. Be consistent in monitoring your spending. My goal was to account for 100% of our spending (an almost impossible task, as I was to find out!). It's amazing how much money is spent a few dollars here and a few dollars there. This was more of a burden on Susie than on me because the wife typically handles the majority of the routine spending. We used old reliable—the envelope system—to help us stay within our budget. Here's how we did it.

Each week, I would write a check to Susie for the amount of her spending. She would cash it and carry the money in her purse in a small envelope that was just slightly larger than a dollar bill. If she went to Kroger's and spent $48.24,

Budgeting Tools

Larry Burkett and Crown Financial Ministries have several easy to use tools available at their website at www.cfcministry.org.

Newsletters

The organizations recommended nearby also have helpful material available on their websites: www.cheapskatemonthly.com, www.goodadvicepress.com.

she'd write "Groceries $48.24" on the front of the envelope at the time she withdrew the money. Ditto the drug store, gas, school lunch money . . . whatever. There were two advantages to doing it this way. First, she was reminded to keep track of her spending because she was pulling the cash from the actual envelope. Second, she could pace herself as the week went along and she saw her cash begin to dwindle. At the end of the week, she'd give me the old dog-eared envelope so I could track her spending in a computer worksheet. Any unspent money was transferred to a new envelope and the process would start over.

An area of confusion for many couples is how to handle the spending that occurs periodically rather than weekly. The way that worked best for us was to divide those items into two groups. I took responsibility for the expenses that were somewhat automatic with respect to the amount and date due—for example, monthly mortgage, life insurance premiums, utilities, and tuition payments. These were typically paid by check. Susie took those categories where purchasing decisions were involved—birthdays, clothing, household items and repairs—and we set aside an amount in an envelope for each one. These were handled like the weekly envelope system except she typically didn't need to carry them with her every time she went out.

5. Be disciplined in staying within your agreed upon limits. The reason you need to closely monitor your spending is so you will know if you're on target on whether mid-

One Young Couple's Budgetary Journey
...continued from page 31...

year. It took prayer, some tough decision making, lots of patience, and a reliance on God to provide. There may need to be some modifications made along the way, but we're ready to put it into practice.

The table below shows our budgeting percentages (along with those suggested by Larry Burkett for young couples as well as families of four). Unfortunately, we have a large amount of our income going toward debt, the majority of which is related to getting my college degree. Another tough fact to deal with is that taxes and Social Security take one-fourth of our income. I'm sure we're not the only family that finds this very discouraging. (I stand by my thinking that election day should fall on April 15th.)

The most difficult aspect in putting this together was estimating Angie's income. Only about $30,000 of our gross income is "guaranteed." Angie's job is commissioned-based, so we're forced to make some educated guesses. So as not to presume on God's generosity, however, we tried to be conservative in our estimate.

Midway through the year, I'll be back with an update to let you know how we're doing. Meanwhile, we'll be trying our best to live by this budget day-by-day in the same way we challenge and encourage you to live by yours.

	Pryor Household	Young Marrieds	Family of Four
Gross Income	100.0%	100.0%	100.0%
- Tithe	10.0%	10.0%	10.0%
- Taxes/SocSec	25.1%	24.5%	19.0%
Net Spendable	64.9%	65.5%	71.0%
Housing-Related[1]	28.9%	28.5%	27.0%
Food	9.3%	11.5%	12.0%
Automobiles	13.9%	12.0%	12.0%
Insurance	0.5%	5.0%	5.0%
Debts	21.1%	5.0%	5.0%
Entertainment/Rec.	8.3%	6.5%	7.0%
Clothing	2.2%	5.5%	6.0%
Savings	6.6%	5.0%	5.0%
Medical/Dental	2.7%	4.0%	4.0%
All Other/Misc.	6.5%	7.0%	8.0%
Investing[2]	0%	10.0%	9.0%
School/Child Care[3]	0%	0%	5.0%

[1]These are calculated as a percentage of the Net Spendable. [2]If there is a surplus, then it should be used for long-term needs such as college education or retirement. [3]If needed, then other categories must be adjusted accordingly.

July: The moment I have dreaded has finally arrived. It's time to let you in on how Angie and I fared in following the spending plan I disclosed to the masses about six months ago. The world's largest accountability group is now in session.

Thankfully, when it comes to budgets, there is room for second chances . . . and thirds . . . and fourths. If our experience is any indication, an effective budget needs constant refinement. And keeping track of the cash flow is no picnic, either! But, it's necessary if we're to understand what we did right and what we did wrong.

A key component in our budget was the estimates we made on Angie's income. The income projections concerning her real estate commissions were pretty much wild guesses, albeit conservative ones. Real estate is a tough business and Angie tried her best (which is all I could ask). Fortunately, her tenacity along with God's blessing resulted in income for the first six months which was slightly higher than we had projected.

For those of you who live off commission-based incomes, I feel for you. Speculative budgeting is definitely challenging. Each "deal" needs to happen for budgets to be met, and this adds stress to your business life as well as your personal life. This kind of budgeting makes the whole cash flow process a lot more difficult. >

How To Mess Up
Your Spending Plan

In his book Christians and Money,
financial consultant Donald Joiner
lists these stumbling blocks that
often keep families from
successfully implementing a
spending plan:

• Failure to communicate.
Many times, husbands and wives
don't take the time to honestly
talk about their true financial
situation. It's the husband's
responsibility to keep his wife
informed. If she is not aware that
they are having trouble paying all
the bills, she will continue to
spend as if everything is all right.

• Failure to plan for emergencies.
No matter how well you plan,
emergencies (or at least
unplanned financial expenses) are
guaranteed to happen. If you do
not make any provision for
emergencies, they have the
potential of destroying you, your
finances, and all you care about.

• Failure to control impulse
buying.
Without a plan, when you see
something that looks good and
credit is available, what's to keep
you from purchasing it?

• Failure to say no to children.
I have seen more financial plans
lead to panic situations because
"we want the best for our
children." Children will ask, and
we will want to give them all they
want. But when they know the
financial limits, creative solutions
can come from painful situations.

• Failure to keep records.
Records of what you spend and
how much you earn are essential
to controlling any financial plan.
They will enable you to be
prepared for whatever comes up.
With records you will discover
that there are really very few
surprises. As a bonus, thorough
records and good planning may
help reduce your taxes.

course adjustments are needed. This gives you a certain degree of flexibility. If you go over in one area, you'll need to cut back in another. For example, an unexpected dental bill of $200 may have to come out of your "recreation" envelope if the "medical" envelope is already empty. Or, you might prefer to take $20 out of ten different envelopes to spread the shortfall around and lessen the impact on any one category.

6. Be mutually supportive. Susie was great! She wasn't critical or complaining in any way. In fact, she continually reminded me that God was our source of supply, and we would just need to do the best we could while waiting on Him to send a solution. Her positive attitude was a tremendous encouragement to me as we "tightened our belt." It was key to have her cooperation. If you and your spouse aren't of one mind as to the importance of developing and living out this kind of lifestyle, conflicts will arise frequently.

Here are some additional pointers on setting up a workable plan. They come from Stephen and Amanda Sorenson in their book *Living Smart, Spending Less*:

• On the income side, be conservative in your expectations. If you earn more than expected, you'll progress even faster.

• Set money aside for taxes when your income first comes in. We deposit all income into an account, but we set aside a percentage for taxes and don't consider that money to be "usable funds." Other people put tax money into a special savings account.

• Reflect the needs of individual family members in the spending plan. One child may need more money for sports equipment, for instance; another may need money for camp.

• Give each responsible family member a little money to spend that doesn't have to be accounted for.

• Stick with your plan until you have your income and expenses well in hand and can follow the basic plan naturally. If at any time you begin to lose control of your spending, return to the basics again.

The point of all this feverish effort is to make sure you have a monthly surplus. Assuming you're successful in that regard . . .

. . . what's the best use for it? At the outset of this chapter, I pointed out how a $264 monthly investment over 35 years of saving and investing could grow to a $1 million retirement nest egg. Later in the book, we'll look at the specifics of just how to set up an effective and easy to maintain long-term strategy. For now, however, I want to pick up on the theme I introduced in chapter one: Getting debt-free is foundational to your financial growth and security. I encourage you to *initially* use your monthly surplus toward accomplishing this crucial (and God-given) goal. Once that's done, all the money that was previously going toward monthly debt payments can then be profitably redirected to your investment portfolio.

Now, it's at this point that many readers rebel. Why defer a potentially rewarding (and exciting!) investing program in favor of (ugh) paying off debts? My answer is two-fold. First, the best way to assure that you enjoy stock market success is to lay a strong financial foundation beforehand. That's because a strong foundation is what *gives you the luxury of investing in the markets with a long-term commitment.*

Bear markets, where stock prices drop 20%-40% and more, are only a threat to those who *have* to sell at the lower prices. Long-term investors can wait for the inevitable recovery (and scoop up stocks at bargain prices in the meantime). What group is most likely to be forced to sell their holdings rather than wait out the storm? Those who experience financial setbacks in their spending plans—perhaps through a lost job, an unexpected pregnancy, a medical emergency, or major car or home repairs. Lacking other financial reserves and shackled by ongoing monthly debt payments, they must sell their stocks and use the proceeds to help remedy the setback.

The second main reason is that it's surprisingly difficult to earn more in the markets than the interest you're paying on your debt. If you have the means to pay your debts off now but

One Young Couple's Budgetary Journey
...continued from page 33...

So it really wasn't on the income side that we had any problems. It was (surprise!) on the spending side. I suppose this is typical for most people in debt. You can see from the table below how our actual spending compared to our projected spending. A few items require special mention:

- **Net Spendable Income.** No, we didn't actually find a way to make our income jump the way it looks. Instead, we made two bookkeeping errors. First, we didn't think to have taxes withheld from Angie's commission checks. Oops! Second, the amount set aside for our tithe was sometimes computed on the amount of a paycheck rather than on the gross. To remedy this, we'll have to set aside larger-than-normal amounts for these two areas over the remainder of the year. That'll be an uphill climb!

- **Food.** We ate out too much with our friends. What can I say? We're social animals.

- **Clothing.** We got nothing but great deals, but obviously you can't save money by spending money. No more outlet malls.

- **Medical.** I needed chiropractic visits for my back. I tore the ACL in my knee while volunteering to help with a Young Life activity and have surgery coming up this month—that'll be a great way to end the summer. We needed new glasses/contacts for Angie and me (a truly unforeseen expense!). Although the doctor visits were (and still are) essential, it required a lot more money than we had allocated to our "medical" category. Who knew I'd fall apart at 28?

Cash Flow Categories	Jan-June As Projected	Jan-June Actual
Gross Income	100.0%	100.0%
· Tithe	10.0%	7.0%
· Taxes/SocSec	25.1%	16.2%
Net Spendable	64.9%	76.8%
Housing-Related	28.9%	26.9%
Food	9.3%	13.6%
Automobiles	13.9%	9.2%
Insurance	0.5%	0.9%
Debts	21.1%	18.9%
Entertainment/Rec.	8.3%	7.5%
Clothing	2.2%	7.2%
Savings	6.6%	–2.9%
Medical/Dental	2.7%	7.9%
All Other/Misc.	6.5%	10.8%

- **The Mysterious "Other."** Too many trips to the A T M resulted in a higher "miscellaneous" category than expected because we did a poor job of tracking where that money was going. There were also some unbudgeted pet and computer expenses.

- **Savings.** Since we spent more than we took in, the deficit was paid for out of our savings. This is no way to build a savings reserve!

So, where does this humbling experience leave us financially going into the next six months? As a result of what I've learned, my record keeping and cash flow tracking will be much improved. Obviously, we're going to have to tighten our belts in the problem areas. We now know where we need to be more conservative and where we need to allocate more. We have tried to be consistent in our tithing, and have good records of what we still need to put towards our tithe over the remainder of the year to get back on track. As always, we're trusting God to help us through.

January the following year: Growing pains. What I thought of as part of adolescence has followed me into adulthood. At the age of 28, I find they're as much a part of my life experiences as ever before. There are physical challenges, like when my knee rotated (and didn't tell my foot!) during a basketball game last spring. There are emotional adjustments as I grow into being the husband and provider I want to be. I experience spiritual growing pains as I continue to mature in my walk with Christ. And (did you see where this was leading?) drawing up a budget and trying >

are investing with that money instead, there are only three possible outcomes from a money management point of view. First, you might lose part—or even all—of your investment money. It does happen, you know. Then, how will you meet your obligations? The anxiety, pressure, and embarrassment this could cause you would be nightmarish. In fact, the leading reported cause of divorce is financial pressures. Yes, it could even destroy your family.

Second, you might make a profit, but the profit could be less than the interest you are paying on your debt. The prevailing interest rate charged by banks for major credit cards is 14%–18% per year. It's quite difficult to consistently make more than that on your investments on an after-tax basis. Yet making less would mean you were continuing to lose ground financially.

Third, you might make a consistent profit exceeding 20% per year. If this happens, you should consider leaving your present employment and moving to Wall Street! There are top professionals there, being paid hundreds of thousands of dollars per year, who aren't as good at investing as you appear to be. As of June 30, 2000, *only one in eight diversified U.S. stock funds* had returns as high as 20% per year for the previous ten-year period (a time when the stock market was booming in an unprecedented way).

The dilemma facing those who would try to invest their way out of debt reminds me of Darrell Royal, who coached several University of Texas Longhorns football teams to national titles. When asked why his teams ran with the football so much, he replied: "Because when you pass, three things can happen and two of them are bad!" Keep this truth in mind: No investment is as secure as a repaid debt. Putting your desire to invest ahead of repaying your debt obligations is usually a sign of immaturity, not financial sophistication. It requires thoughtful self-discipline not to overuse your access to credit.

Here is a tried-and-true five step formula for using your monthly surplus to wipe out your debt in the fastest possible time.

1. Stop adding to your debt. Today. No exceptions, no excuses. Obviously, you can't get *out of* debt if you keep going *into* debt. This is fundamental. The remaining steps will not work if you fail here.

2. List all your debts—credit cards, personal loans, college loans, car loans, home equity loans, and house mortgage—in order according to the amount you owe. Include your minimum monthly payment. I also like to show the interest rate, but that's strictly for informational purposes; it has no bearing on the order in which you will pay off the debts. We target the smallest debt first because it has a motivational benefit. When you see progress being made, you're encouraged to continue being faithful to the program.

(Many people elect not to include their mortgage on the list because they don't feel it's realistic to expect to pay it off early. We'll look at that decision in chapter 4. For now, I want to include so I can show the impact it would have.)

3. Determine the minimum amount you will pay every month until your debt load is erased. One way is to simply add up the current minimum monthly payments you're now making. But if you really want to jump start the process, look for ways to tighten your belt a little more (or bring in some extra income) so you can increase this number. This should be possible because the minimums set by the credit card companies are abnormally low. Most credit cards require just 2%-3% of your total balance as a minimum monthly payment. They don't want you to pay off your balance quickly—the longer it takes, the more they'll make on your interest payments.

4. Target your smallest debt first, applying any extra monthly surplus you come up with toward it. When that debt is paid off, take the money you had been paying on it and add it to the amount you're paying on your second smallest debt. Debt counselor Dave Ramsey calls this technique the "debt snowball," presumably because the continual rolling over of your monthly payments toward each succeeding debt grows in a powerful way.

5. Persist, persist, persist. For motivation, prepare a time line that shows how long it will take you to get debt-free. Reflect on how much money you'll be saving on interest costs by speeding up the process.

To see a debt snowball in action, look at the sidebar on the next page where we will track the experience of Tom and Linda, a young couple with a typical variety of debts. Table A shows their situation when they first begin. They have consumer loans totaling $25,167 plus a remaining balance on their house mortgage of $89,060. Their minimum monthly pay-

One Young Couple's Budgetary Journey
...continued from page 35...

to live by it last year presented challenges of a financial kind.

How did Angie and I do overall? (I thought I'd cut right to the chase since I know some of you can't wait to find out.) Well, not too bad for a first effort. Naturally, we did better than expected in some areas and worse in others. Even those of us who are entrenched in financial teaching can still have difficulty. We spent more than we had planned on clothing, gift-giving, and food (eating out gets us everytime!). It was disappointing that we managed to apply only about $5,600 of our income towards our debt retirement even though we had projected to retire much more of it. Still, that's progress—we're headed in the right direction. We learned that several things need to happen for a budget to work out the way you hope.

• **You need good planning.** There's no doubt we would have done much worse if we weren't operating from a budget. Fortunately, we had carefully crafted a spending plan based on reasonable projections that allowed us to measure our progress as the year unfolded.

• **You need to make the most of your opportunities.** In July, Angie was invited to apply for a job as a sales rep for a condominium and patio home developer. After considerable prayer and discussion, we decided she should go for it. It meant leaving her position as a real estate agent where her income potential was higher (but based solely on commissions) to one that offered a set salary with a bonus based on sales. This has turned out to be a wonderful blessing for us—financially and for her overall peace of mind.

• **You need to make midyear adjustments.** In light of the change in Angie's income, we had to look for ways to save more money. One step we decided on was to sell my car. Last August, I handed over the keys to my personal transportation. It wasn't easy to do. It was the ideal car—low insurance premiums, great gas mileage (45 mpg!), and would last a lifetime (Honda). But we recognized that the hassle of sharing a car for now was worth the savings on loan payments, maintenance, gas, and insurance. Also, when we move to our first home (a condo acquired at great savings thanks to Angie's job perks), Angie will be able to walk to work. So having a second car moved from being a necessity to more of a luxury. And we save about $250 a month before any upkeep costs!

• **You need to say "no" more than you'd like.** Giving up a car sometimes is easier than turning down friends who ask you out to dinner or to denying yourself a sweater at 50% off. This area was a tough one for us, but we're getting better at it. We're increasingly able to view our current life-style sacrifices as necessary steps on the road to achieving important longer-term goals.

• **You need good health.** This sounds like a no-brainer but it is key. You can do everything else right and still come up short due to the dreaded "unforeseen circumstances." Our budgeting efforts were good, but there were a few events along the way that caused a surge in the budgetary ebb and flow. I was out of the office for almost three weeks due to my knee surgery and lost a significant amount of salary income—ouch! A recent trip to the dentist cost us our entire yearly dental budget. These were good reminders of why a savings reserve is so important.

So, there's a little bit of insight into our past financial year. Perhaps you'll learn something from our experience that will make your budget journey less difficult. Looking to the year ahead, we hope to earn more, save more, retire more debt, and give more! Becoming better stewards of God's money and being able to give more generously to His work is our goal—both at home and here at Sound Mind Investing.

TOM AND LINDA'S DEBT SNOWBALL STRATEGY

Table A: At the Outset

Debt Item	Balance Due	Minimum Payment	Interest Rate
Visa	$ 836	$ 125	2.9%
Discover	1,412	42	16.9%
MasterCard	1,786	83	15.9%
Student Loan	8,696	317	7.0%
Car Loan	12,437	395	12.0%
House	89,320	692	8.5%
Total	$114,487	$1,654	

Table B: After 7 Months

Discover	$ 1,219	$ 167	16.9%
MasterCard	1,354	83	15.9%
Student Loan	6,799	317	7.0%
Car Loan	10,485	395	12.0%
House	88,623	692	8.5%
Total	$108,480	$1,654	

Table C: After 15 Months

MasterCard	$ 768	$ 250	15.9%
Student Loan	4,535	317	7.0%
Car Loan	8,081	395	12.0%
House	88,095	692	8.5%
Total	$101,479	$1,654	

Table D: After 19 Months

Student Loan	$ 3,152	$ 567	7.0%
Car Loan	6,805	395	12.0%
House	87,820	692	8.5%
Total	$97,777	$1,654	

Table E: After 25 Months

Car Loan	$ 4,606	$ 962	12.0%
House	87,393	692	8.5%
Total	$91,999	$1,654	

Table F: After 30 Months

House	$ 86,956	$ 1,654	8.5%

ments total $1,554. Since these are already factored into their budget, their monthly surplus isn't needed to make those payments. They decide to use $100 of their monthly surplus for their debt elimination strategy. This brings their total monthly payments to $1,654. This is the amount they will pay each month until their creditors are all paid.

Even though their new Visa card is still offering a sweetheart 2.9% introductory interest rate, Tom and Linda begin their program by targeting the Visa debt first because it's the smallest. They send in $125 each month (even though the minimum payment that appears on their Visa statement requires far less). Table B shows the results after seven months. Most of their debt balances have fallen rather slowly due to their making only the minimum payments required, but the Visa debt has been paid off entirely. Now they have $125 a month available they no longer need to send to Visa. Resisting the urge to spend this new "found" money, they begin paying it toward their Discover card bill, the next debt on their list. They had previously been paying $42 a month; now they can send in $167.

At the 15-month mark, the Discover bill is history, and they move on to the MasterCard debt. Adding the $167 they had been paying to Discover to the $83 going to MasterCard allows them to up their monthly payment to $250. Since the outstanding MasterCard balance at that point is just $768, it doesn't take long to completely eliminate that debt. In the 19th month, they're able to increase the monthly student loan payment to a hefty $567 ($317 previously plus $250 from the retired MasterCard debt), and take just six months to finish it off.

With the student loan being paid off by the 25th month, they take that $567 and add it to the $395 a month going toward the car loan. The new payment of $962 a month makes short work of the remaining balance. In just 30 months, then, Tom and Linda paid off over $25,000 in non-secured debts, and saved themselves over $3,000 in interest charges to boot.

Plus, they now have an extra $962 a month in their monthly surplus. They've had to sacrifice to stay on course (which involved living within their budget and not adding any new debt), and you can't blame them if they want to celebrate a bit by using that $962 for lifestyle treats they've been denying themselves. Or they might take just part of it for enlarging their budget a bit, and put the rest toward a long-term investing strategy.

But, just for the sake of argument, let's say they decide to keep rolling their debt snowball and go after the house mortgage. Originally a 30-year, $90,000 loan, there's still 26 years to go. How long would you guess it would take to retire the remaining $86,956 if they paid an extra $962 a month toward their principal each month? Just 5½ years! Not only would they then own their house free and clear, but they'd *save over $110,000 in interest payments* by paying their mortgage off almost 20 years early! ◆

CHAPTER PREVIEW

Credit Cards: Are You Using Them or Are They Using You?

I. **Statistics show that many consumers are carrying high levels of credit card debt... and paying for it.**

    A. In 1999, 55 million households with revolving credit-card debt paid an average of more than a thousand dollars in interest and fees.

    B. The average credit card balance is $7,000; the average household has 10 credit cards; 1.3 million Americans filed for bankruptcy in 1999.

    C. When paying by credit card, consumers spend 25-30% more than when paying with cash.

II. **Consumers continue to use and abuse credit cards for various reasons.**

    A. Reasons for using: convenience, rewards, emergencies, and necessity.

    B. Abuses: keeping up with the Jones', making only the minimum payments, and lack of knowledge.

III. **Whether or not you pay your full credit card balance each month is the customizing variable for determining which types of credit cards are best for you.**

    A. Full-balance payers should focus on no-fee cards with 25-day grace periods.

    B. Balance carriers should focus on low interest cards and getting free from credit card debt.

IV. **A plan is offered for digging your way out of credit card debt.**

    A. Assess your situation in order to develop a spending strategy. Decide which cards you're going to pay off first.

    B. Steps to take to make sure you're using the lowest rate cards available.

    C. Additional tips include: close your old accounts, make the most of your grace period, make more frequent payments, beware cash advances, stay on top of things, and celebrate as you go.

    D. Check your credit report for accuracy annually.

V. **Honestly assess your credit card motives. Analyze how your credit card usage may be hindering or helping you achieve your financial goals.**

My Thanks to
Cindy Biller
for her willingness to step
into the fray and conduct
the research needed to
complete this chapter.

A Credit Card Vocabulary
Before we go any further,
let's review some basic
credit card lingo.

• Annual Fee
Flat fee some credit cards
charge you each year for
having their credit card.

• Transaction Fees
Fees for cash advances, late
payments, going over your
credit limit, etc. Some credit
cards even charge an inactivity
fee if you don't use your card.

• Finance Charges
Interest costs and all related
transaction costs.

• Annual Percentage Rate
(APR)
Interest rate measuring your
credit cost as a yearly rate.

• Periodic Rate
Interest rate applied to your
outstanding account balance
when calculating your current
finance charge.

• Grace Period
The number of days you're
allowed to pay off your balance
before the credit card company
starts charging you interest.
Once a balance goes unpaid in
any month, the grace period is
lost until the balance is once
again paid down to zero.
Typically this means that new
charges on that card begin
incurring interest costs the day
the purchase is made.

Times have sure changed since Jesus taught using parables from everyday life. Here's one that just wouldn't make much sense to most Americans these days . . .

. . . "Suppose one of you wants to build a tower. Will he not first sit down and estimate the cost to see if he has enough money to complete it? For if he lays the foundation and is not able to finish it, everyone who sees it will ridicule him, saying, 'This fellow began to build and was not able to finish'" (Luke 14:28-30).

A little short on drachmas right now? No problem. Charge the building materials you need to your Visa or MasterCard. Don't worry about paying off the balance at the end of the month. Not everybody does. After all, the average credit card balance is around 30 silver talents... wait... make that $7,000.

Of course, that means you'll have to pay some interest for "borrowing" from the credit card company. Lots of interest. In 1999, 55 million households with revolving credit card debt paid an average of more than a thousand dollars in interest and fees. A thousand dollars! It's painful to think of what these families could be missing. If they *didn't* pay $1,000 in credit card interest and fees each year and instead invested that money in a 11% savings plan, over their spending lifetime (roughly 40 years) they would have accumulated $716,677 in the bank.

The credit card statistics are rather amazing. According to American Debt Management Services, the average household has ten credit cards. Experts believe that when paying by credit card, people spend 25-30% more than when paying with cash. (No wonder so many retailers encourage us to pay with plastic!) It just doesn't feel like real money, and so it's easy to get in over our heads. That's the main reason 1.3 million Americans filed for bankruptcy in 1999.

Most of us are aware of the pitfalls of credit cards, so why do we continue to use them?

• **Convinced by convenience.** Simply put, they're easy. And you can use them almost everywhere. Why mess with carrying cash or writing all of those checks? Just pull out that handy, little card and you're on your way. And how about the luxury of pay-at-the-pump gasoline? Enough said.

• **Just no other way around it.** Some times you can't get what you want any other way. From buying online to reserving a hotel room, credit cards seem to be the new necessity.

• **Seeking rewards.** From frequent-flyer miles to insurance and extended warranties, we love the perks. We figure, we're going to spend the money anyway, so why not get something for it?

• **Keeping up with the Jones'.** That old green giant gets the best of us. We see something we want but don't want to wait until we can pay for it outright. We work hard and feel like "we deserve it."

• **Emerging emergencies.** Like a comforting security blanket, that extra credit card is always there—just in case.

• **Perishing for lack of knowledge.** By focusing on the monthly minimum rather than the total cost, some of us justify credit purchases by rationalizing that we can afford the minimum credit card payment. This leads to our first lesson in negative compounding interest. By then, it's often too late and we're overwhelmed by the deep, dark hole of credit card debt.

Basically, there are two main credit card user types: those who pay their balances off every month and those who carry a balance from month to month. If you pay your full balance every month . . .

. . . you should be looking for a no-fee card with a 25-day grace period. The credit card's interest rate is less important to you, because you don't anticipate paying it. Be aware, however, if you don't pay your balance in full, the *grace period will not apply* to any purchases you make thereafter until the balance has once again been reduced to zero. For this reason, it may be wise to have a spare credit card for use in such a case, even if you don't anticipate ever using it.

You are the type of user that credit card companies don't like because they don't make money off of you (isn't that nice). Therefore, some credit card companies really sock it to you any way they can—for instance, by charging hefty finance charges and fees if your payment is even a day late or charging inactivity fees. Read the fine print before you choose a card (as well as any new information they send you later) and don't be afraid to complain to them if you feel you've been treated unfairly. If they won't resolve your complaint to your satisfaction, you can always cancel the card and take your business elsewhere.

If you're carrying credit card debt from month to month and paying those nasty finance charges. . .

. . . you're probably already looking for a way to dig out of the credit card hole. So, how do you do it?

• **Assess your situation.** It may be painful, but lay it all out on the table. Compile a list of all of your credit cards, debt amounts, interest rates, and monthly payments.

• **Develop and implement a spending plan strategy.** Sit down with your spouse and evaluate your budget (see pages 31-34). Decide where to "tighten your belt." Allocate as much as you can to paying off your credit card balances quickly. You may have to make some tough decisions, like whether or not you can afford your car, house, or life-style. Determine to stop using credit cards entirely until you're out of credit card debt (use cash or debit cards).

Credit Card Deals

Listings of the best credit card deals can be found at www.bankrate.com and www.banx.com.

Also, check out bankrate.com's credit calculator which allows you to compare between two potential credit cards.

Credit Counseling

One of the most well known credit counseling organizations is The National Foundation for Consumer Credit. The Atlanta office of the Consumer Credit Counseling Service is a member. Visit them at www.cccsatl.org.

For Updated Information

The Internet is constantly changing, and the above sites may have moved or ceased operations by the time you read this. For an up-to-date list of the better online resources related to credit cards, visit the SMI website at www.soundmindinvesting.com.

• **Find the lowest rate.** If you're currently in a situation where you're carrying a balance from month to month, you should focus on finding the lowest effective interest rate. Since you don't pay off the full balance each month, grace periods don't affect you, even if the card has one (unless the company uses a balance calculation method that excludes new purchases—see clipboard below).

Be aware that not all interest rates are created equal! Because of differences in calculation methods, total finance charges may vary significantly between cards with identical APR's. So, in order to make an "apples-to-apples" comparison, it's important to understand how they're calculated.

Now you're ready to make some money-saving changes. First, call your existing credit card companies and negotiate for lower rates.

Marc Eisenson calls this "Dialing for Dollars." In his newsletter, *The Pocket Change Investor*, he writes:

"Each of your statements lists a customer service number. Call, and say the appropriate version of 'You're charging me a $20 annual fee, plus 19.8% interest. I'm seeing a lot of cards advertised with much lower rates and no annual fees. Will you waive my fee and lower my interest rate?' If you have at least a one-year history of timely payments (even of only the minimum required), the answer will probably be 'Yes.' You don't have anything to lose, and not asking is an automatic 'No!' Be tough, if necessary. Don't expect an immediate 'delighted to be of service.' You'll likely be put on hold while your record is reviewed. If the verdict isn't to your liking, ask if they would prefer that you trade in their card for a better deal from one of their 6,000 hungry competitors. And always feel free to take it to a higher authority— ask for a supervisor."

METHODS OF CALCULATING FINANCE CHARGES

<u>Average Daily Balance Method</u>. Interest is calculated based on the average amount owed during the previous month. You receive credit for your payment beginning on the day it is received by the credit card company. This is the most common method used.

For example: your balance is $2,000 and you sent in a payment of $1200, which was received on the 15th of the month. Your APR is 18% (1.5% monthly). Under this method, the calculation balance is $1,400 ($2,000 for 15 days and $800 for 15 days). The finance charge will be $21 ($1,400 times .015).

<u>Adjusted Balance Method</u>. Interest is calculated only on the unpaid balance of your account. This method results in the lowest finance charge.

Example: The calculation balance is $800 ($2,000 minus $1,200 for all 30 days). Finance charge equals $12 ($800 times .015).

<u>Previous Balance Method</u>. Interest is charged on the entire balance owed at the end of the previous billing cycle. Of these three common methods, this one results in the highest finance charge.

Example: The calculation balance is $2,000 (entire previous balance for all 30 days). Finance charge equals $30 ($2,000 times .015).

<u>Beware of cards that use "Two Cycle Billing"</u> where interest on the balance is retroactive to when the purchases were actually posted to the account. This method results in the highest finance charges of all. Since your statement probably won't say "Two Cycle Billing" on it, look for any references saying you'll be charged interest on a purchase made during a previous billing cycle. Or, you can always call and question the credit card company directly.

If that doesn't prove fruitful, then it's time to begin playing the "Transfer Game."

You've probably heard about this—transferring an existing balance to a new card in order to get a low, introductory interest rate. Some people shuffle their balances from one card to another when the introductory period expires. By doing this, all of their payment goes toward reducing the debt's principal, rather than paying interest. Since this reduces their profitability, credit card companies are making the process more expensive. Many are now charging "transfer fees" or treating transfers like cash advances (see next page).

To find the best deals, gather all of those junk-mail credit card mailings. Line them up and look for the best offers. *Read the small print* and if anything is unclear, don't hesitate to call the issuer for the answers you need. Other avenues worth exploring are the Internet (check the resources shown on page 41) and your credit union (since they're nonprofit organizations owned by their members, they often have good deals).

Some important questions to ask before transferring your balance include:

- Is there a balance transfer fee?
- How long does the introductory rate last?
- Does the introductory rate apply to both transferred balances and new purchases?
- Will the issuer cancel the introductory rate if your payment is late or if you are late paying other financial obligations?
- What are the terms of the credit card once the introductory rate expires (interest rate, annual fee, "over limit" fees, late fees, etc.)?
- How long will it take to complete the balance transfer process?

You're well on your way to escaping the credit card pit, but a few additional steps remain.

- **Close old accounts.** As you pay off and transfer balances, close unnecessary accounts immediately. Your total available credit line will be analyzed to determine your credit risk to a given credit card company (which in turn affects the interest rate they're willing to give you). There's a possible exception, however. If you've always been prompt in your payments and have a good standing with a credit card you've used for a long time, that can improve your credit score—you may not wish to close such accounts.

• **Pick a payment strategy.** Most folks in debt make it a priority to pay off their highest rate cards first. I tend to favor paying off the lowest balance cards first (see pages 36-38). Higher rate cards generate the heftiest finance charges, but there's a definite psychological boost that comes when completely paying off one credit card after another. Additionally, consider the following ideas:

◆ **Make the most of your grace period.** Some experts suggest having two credit cards on hand: (1) a low-interest card for carrying balances, and (2) a no-fee card with a 25-day grace period to use for charges you will pay off that month. This allows you to utilize the 25-day, interest-free grace period you would otherwise lose by carrying a balance (see sidebar, page 40).

◆ **Make more frequent payments.** Interest accumulates every single day you carry a balance. So, you can reduce the amount of interest you pay simply by sending in payments every two weeks (or twice a month) instead of just once a month. Tell the company in advance that you will be sending biweekly payments, and ask them what you need to do to get them processed quickly. Some credit card companies have specific guidelines to follow, such as writing your account number on every check and sending your payment to the proper address. The Fair Credit Billing Act requires issuers to process payments the day they are received. However, if any of their guidelines are not met, they have up to five days to credit the payment. Each day is money, so it's worth checking.

◆ **Beware cash advances.** If at all possible, do not get cash advances on your credit card. Most cards charge a cash advance fee of 2%-4% of the advance amount. Upon taking the advance, interest begins to accrue immediately at a rate that is typically *higher* than your regular interest rate. Lastly, any payments you make will be *applied to the lower interest balances first*!

• **Stay on top of things.** Credit card companies can change their terms quarterly or by written notice, so pay attention to everything they send you. They may decide to increase your interest rate because they feel your risk has increased. Watch out—increasing your credit limits or making late payments (to them or any other creditor) may qualify you for a rate hike! Make sure to check your credit report annually (see page 45).

• **Celebrate as you go!** You're following a long, hard road, so it's important to celebrate when you've reached certain milestones, like paying off an account or reaching the halfway point. Be creative—get the family together for a bill burning or bake a cake!

Credit Card Calculators
The Tools page at www.soundmindinvesting.com has several helpful credit card calculators. Figure how soon payoff will occur when you alter your payment amount, or plug in the annual fee to see if the corresponding interest rate is justified. Tools to answer these and other questions are provided.

A SOUND MIND BRIEFING

Is It Time for Your Annual Credit Report Checkup?

by Andrew Pryor

While looking to purchase a home recently, I met with my mortgage lender who, as standard procedure, had pulled my credit report. To my dismay, there appeared on the list numerous credit accounts that I had closed years earlier. There were others that I forgot I even had (remember that time you were offered a 20% discount on your Eddie Bauer purchase if you would agree to charge it to your new Eddie Bauer credit card?).

In addition to the active and closed accounts listed, there was a list of everyone who had looked into my credit over the past two years (most of which were credit card companies who later sent me unsolicited "special" offers). The credit agencies had used my credit history to "pre-qualify" me to various companies (such as banks, car dealers, credit card companies, mortgage lenders) who are looking for new customers. But before anyone was prepared to offer me "pre-approved" credit, they had to check me out. So there are all these inquiries on my credit report that make it appear at first glance as if I had been applying for credit with wild abandon! Our credit report showed us in a very positive light. We haven't a mark against us. But there were accounts open that I didn't use, let alone need, and I was energized by the thought that they could, in any way, hinder my ability to close this home purchase on schedule (or get other credit I may need down the road). So now began my mission to tidy up my credit report. I was naive in thinking it would be easy.

My research began with a few questions. First, how did the credit agency get my private information and what does a credit rating ultimately mean? Well, periodically my creditors (banks, credit card company, etc.) provide this information to the leading credit reporting agencies—Equifax (800-997-2493), Trans Union (800-916-8800), and Experian (888-397-3742). Over the years, as I travel the credit highway, taking out and then paying off car loans, student loans, credit cards, etc., my creditors report my activities to these agencies.

The lenders use this information to establish a rating scale. This scale is quite mysterious. They use a "credit scoring" method which gives points based on the weights of various credit experiences such as bill-paying history, late payments, age of accounts, etc. Each lender assigns "points" and "weights" according to its own criteria. You'll never know quite where you stand until the lender has obtained your credit report and gone though this process. This is very unnerving to me.

As I began my effort to remedy all this, I found out it was going to cost me more than my time. Unless you live in a state that requires credit agencies to provide, upon request, a copy of your credit report for free once a year, you have to pay up to $8 for the privilege of learning whether private, potentially damaging information about you, is even accurate.

Anyway, the first thing I needed to decide was which agency to contact for my information (Equifax, Trans Union, or Experian). They all have credit data on me, and presumably, it's similar in each case. My first thought was to see if I could get my reports over the Web. Each of the three credit agencies has a Web site, but alas, all you can do is order your report there. They still use the good old U.S. Post Office to send them to you, presumably for security reasons.

After a week or so, I received a copy of my credit report. My main area of concern had to do with what I found in the "revolving credit" section of my report. I only had one credit card . . . that I was aware of. But my credit report said I had three additional credit cards—two retail store cards and one Visa card. This was leftover debris from my earlier adventures in using credit. I called the two retail companies (using the telephone number provided on the credit report) and had the accounts closed effective that day. I also asked them to send me a confirmation letter as well as send a letter to the credit reporting bureau. Next, I called the Visa company. I thought I had closed this account over two years ago! Indeed, they told me my Visa account was "technically" closed (whatever that means), but promised to send the appropriate documentation to Experian to let them know the account was officially closed in 1997.

It's important to clean up this kind of thing because these accounts are considered to represent available credit. Even if you never use the cards, potential creditors (the ones you need like mortgage lenders or the local bank where you go for a car loan) get the impression that you have a large amount of credit at your disposal. In their eyes, this makes you a higher-risk borrower. I, for one, don't want to be refused a car loan because of the Visa company's bad record keeping.

The reports are pretty easy to understand once you've read the instructions and picked up on what the many abbreviations and codes mean. Along with the credit report, the agencies provide information on how to report mistakes, handle disputes, or report fraudulent activity. As these things go, my experience in cleaning up my credit report was relatively hassle-free. Hopefully, yours will be also.

As appeared in the Sound Mind Investing newsletter. Andrew Pryor is the webmaster for www.soundmindinvesting.com. He sometimes doubles as a contributing author to the SMI newsletter who reports on the never-particularly-pleasant battle of the budget.

**As we wrap up our discussion of credit cards,
take a moment to consider why you use credit cards (pages 40-41).**

Remember, your credit card usage should complement your overall financial strategy. Determine how the use of credit cards affects your ability to stay on your budget, and by extension, your ability to reach your goals. Identifying any unhealthy tendencies is the first step towards overcoming them. Ask the Lord to show you practical ways to improve in your handling of credit.

One alternative to credit cards that sacrifices little of their convenience is using debit cards. These cards are a hybrid of credit cards and checks. You use them like credit cards, but the funds are automatically withdrawn from your checking or savings account, as they would be if you'd written a check. By treating these plastic purchases like a check, you save yourself the end of the month trauma of discovering long-forgotten charges on your credit card statement.

Since debit cards access your money directly (and immediately), you may be in for some headaches if your card number is stolen and you don't realize it quickly. Until the problem is resolved, you may have bounced checks and corresponding fees. However, in the long run, your debit card theft liability is very similar to that of a credit card. ◆

CHAPTER PREVIEW

The Importance of Having Your Home Paid For

I.   **If you can't afford to make extra principal payments on your home mortgage and at the same time put money into a retirement plan, which should have the priority?**

    A.   As we see by following the experiences of Rob and Dan, contributing to the retirement plan is more profitable from an economic viewpoint. Ultimately, it's a decision based on your personal convictions with respect to debt.

    B.   It's generally not advisable to cash in one's retirement plan in order to retire the mortgage.

II. **As a general rule, surplus funds are better used for paying off the mortgage on your home than they are for investing because:**

    A.   You could lose your home if the investments don't work out as planned, possibly leaving you more in debt than ever.

    B.   You could lose your home if your present level of income falls due to being disabled or laid off, general economic recession, or childbearing.

    C.   My recommendation is that you *not* consider other investments (as opposed to paying off your mortgage) unless the three listed conditions are met.

III. **Home equity loans are quite dangerous because you can lose your house for nonpayment. They should have the top priority for repayment, even ahead of other consumer debt.**

IV. **The parable of two families: the LiveHighs and the ThinkSmarts.**

    A.   In identical financial situations, the LiveHighs choose to finance their higher standard of living by taking a thirty-year mortgage when buying their home; the ThinkSmarts elect a fifteen-year mortgage on a less expensive (but functionally similar) home.

    B.   After fifteen years, the ThinkSmarts paid their mortgage in full and began redirecting their monthly mortgage payments into their retirement investment account. You'll likely be greatly surprised at how much more the ThinkSmarts have in their retirement account after thirty years than the LiveHighs have.

"If we can't afford to make extra principal payments on our home mortgage and at the same time put money into our retirement plan, which should have the priority?" . . .

. . . is a question I receive quite often. Unfortunately, there's no one-size-fits-all answer—your age, your tax bracket, what you would do with the tax savings from your mortgage interest, how long you expect to live in your home, and your general attitude toward being debt-free all play significant roles.

Let's say that two readers of this book who have different goals are each wrestling with this question. Rob is leery of Social Security and wants to begin building his retirement funds immediately. Dan thinks being in debt is more of a concern and plans on using any monthly surplus to make additional principal payments on his mortgage.

For comparison purposes, let's make their two situations identical: They both have new $50,000, fifteen-year fixed rate mortgages; both can set aside $600 out of each month's paycheck (their monthly mortgage payment is $507, leaving them each an extra $93 for payment of the principal or investment in a retirement account); both are in the 34% tax bracket (federal plus state), and both have the opportunity to contribute to a retirement plan at work that will earn 9%, the same rate as their mortgages.

When they make their first month's mortgage payment, $375 of it is tax deductible as interest expense. This will lower each of their taxes by $128 a month (34% of $375). What they do with that $128 savings can make a big difference.

Let's assume that both Rob and Dan would like to get their hands on that savings sooner rather than later. They would get it back when they filed their income tax returns anyway, so why wait? So, they both change the withholding instructions they give their employers so that about $128 less is withheld for income taxes each month. By adding that amount to the extra $93 left from their monthly surplus, they each now have an extra $221 to work with. Rob contributes his into his company's 401(k) plan while Dan takes the cash and makes an extra principal payment on his mortgage.

Now here's where it can really get confusing. To construct an accurate picture, we have to recognize that Rob gets a second tax deduction—this time for putting money into the retirement plan. Rob's $221 contribution is worth

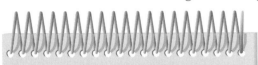

ROB EMPHASIZES SAVING FOR RETIREMENT

At End of Year	Balance Due on Mortgage	Value of 401(k) Account	Tax Savings Mortgage Interest	Tax Savings 401(k) Contributions
1	$48,347	$4,172	$1,507	$1,350
2	46,540	8,651	1,454	1,323
3	44,562	13,458	1,397	1,294
4	42,400	18,617	1,334	1,261
5	40,034	24,149	1,265	1,226
6	37,447	30,081	1,189	1,187
7	34,617	36,438	1,107	1,144
8	31,521	43,247	1,017	1,098
9	28,135	50,539	918	1,047
10	24,431	58,342	810	991
11	20,380	66,690	692	930
12	15,949	75,616	562	864
13	11,102	85,154	421	791
14	5,800	95,341	267	711
15	0	106,215	97	624
Summary	$0	$106,215	$14,037	$15,841

another $75 tax savings, which he could then also put into his 401(k). But then that $75 contribution would save him an additional $25 in taxes, which he could also put into his 401(k). But then that $25 . . . well, you get the idea. If Rob took maximum advantage of this, he could ultimately put $334 into his company retirement plan that first month (the $93 extra plus his tax savings of $128 for mortgage interest plus another $113 in tax savings for contributing to the company 401(k)).

Assume that both men are able to take the maximum advantage of the available tax savings as the years pass. Dan pays down as much extra on his mortgage each month as he can and pays it off completely in nine years. At that point, he shifts all the money he formerly put toward his mortgage each month into his retirement plan. He also adjusts his withholdings to take maximum advantage of the tax savings his contributions create.

At the end of fifteen years, their experiences can be summarized this way. Both men had the same out-of-pocket expenditures—$600 per month over fifteen years, totaling $108,000. In return, they both accomplished paying their $50,000 mortgage loans in full and were able to invest for retirement. It's interesting to note that, although they proceeded according to different time tables, Rob and Dan ultimately saved an equal amount ($29,878) on their taxes. This was due to each of them always taking full advantage of the tax-deductibility of mortgage interest and 401(k) contributions with their surplus dollars.

The important difference in their financial situations after fifteen years is found in the value of their retirement accounts. Rob's 401(k) grew to $106,215 and Dan's to $87,454. Although they had both saved the same amount in taxes which could then be invested for retirement, Rob's savings were "front-loaded." That meant he could put them to work in his 401(k) earlier

DAN EMPHASIZES PAYING OFF HIS MORTGAGE

At End of Year	Balance Due on Mortgage	Value of 401(k) Account	Tax Savings Mortgage Interest	Tax Savings 401(k) Contributions
1	$45,653	$0	$1,470	$0
2	41,040	0	1,333	0
3	36,146	0	1,188	0
4	30,954	0	1,034	0
5	25,444	0	871	0
6	19,598	0	697	0
7	13,395	0	514	0
8	6,813	0	319	0
9	0	258	111	87
10	0	11,737	0	3,709
11	0	24,293	0	3,709
12	0	38,027	0	3,709
13	0	53,050	0	3,709
14	0	69,481	0	3,709
15	0	87,454	0	3,709
Summary	$0	$87,454	$7,537	$22,341

than Dan could. In this way, Rob was able to take greater advantage of the tax-deferred compounding of profits. The difference in his 401(k) would have been even greater if Rob's employer contributed matching funds. Dan's retirement account later came on strong, but Rob's head start was too great.

Should you follow Rob's example? Not necessarily. To make it work, you've got to be able to aggressively use all of the tax savings, and more important, you need fifteen years of relative stability in your job, the economy, and the tax code. That seems to be asking a lot from the next decade.

The advantage of following Dan's approach is: It quickly provides the security of debt-free home ownership, which will better enable you to weather any economic storms; in case of an emergency, the wealth in your home is more accessible than assets tied up in a retirement plan; and while Rob's return in the 401(k) could fall below 9%, Dan's interest savings on his mortgage will not.

It's one thing to temporarily lower or eliminate putting money into a retirement plan in order to work on a debt-reduction plan; it's another altogether to close out your retirement plan.

Questions such as, "Should I cash in my pension plan in order to pay off my mortgage?" or, "Should I close my IRA and take the proceeds to pay off my consumer/car loans?" involve much more serious decisions than the example we just discussed.

The steps, once taken, are irreversible. You can't change your mind later. So it's important to understand and weigh all the factors. Be sure you understand the tax consequences of prematurely withdrawing money from a tax-deferred plan. Let's say you cash in $10,000 before age 59½ (or 55 in some plans). First, the IRS hits you with a 10% penalty. That leaves $9,000. Next there are the ordinary federal income taxes. Assuming you're in the 28% marginal bracket, there goes another $2,800 (the penalty isn't deductible). So you only have $6,200 of your original $10,000 left to apply against your debts. Then there is the opportunity cost of not having the $10,000 compounding tax deferred for years into the future. So, it's a pretty costly decision from a tax standpoint.

To look at it from a strict financial planning point of view, I asked Jim Shoemaker—a certified financial planner (CFP) and the president of his own financial planning firm in Memphis, Tennessee—what advice he would give in such a situation:

> To a large degree, it depends on the person's age and whether they are currently managing their debt successfully. By "managing" I mean they are making consistent progress month by month and can see the day coming when they will be debt-free, even if it's a few years off. The 40-45 year age range is roughly the dividing point—getting one's debt under control before the end of this five year period is critically important.

> If a person is 40 or younger and is currently managing their debt, I would advise they leave their retirement funds alone. However, if they are heavily debt-ridden (for example, $25,000-$35,000 in debt with an income of $35,000-$50,000 and no realistic options of getting the debts paid), I would say to go ahead and get the debt under control even though there is a heavy penalty and tax bite. Now, I'm not talking about home mortgages here, just consumer-type debts and home equity loans. If a person is over 45 and has still not overcome their debt, it becomes very difficult to effectively deal with debt as well as retirement. It's a difficult decision, but I would be hesitant to eliminate one's retirement fund because, at that late date, time is no longer on their side.

Recommended Resource
The Banker's Secret
by Marc Eisenson

If you have a mortgage, this could be one of the most important books you'll ever buy! Eisenson has a simple premise: Prepayments on your loan prove that there is no reason to keep your family enslaved in debt for thirty years while you pay the bank back three to four times the mortgage money you borrowed. "In fact, the only difficult thing about pre-paying is understanding how such a good idea could have been kept a 'banker's secret' for so long." Highly recommended! (See excerpt on page 55.)

Don't be too quick to give up on the idea of making short-term lifestyle adjustments that would result in a greater monthly surplus. Examine all of your budget items closely—are there ways to lower them further? Or, are there assets you could sell (a second car, bicycles, boats, guns, stereos, etc.) and apply toward your debt retirement?

Up to this point, we've been looking at the merits of paying down your mortgage versus investing in or maintaining your retirement plan. Now let's look at a similar question that involves investing outside a tax-deferred account.

Powerful tax incentives at work in the earlier analysis worked in favor of Rob's strategy of investing versus Dan's strategy of paying down his mortgage. And as I pointed out, if Rob's employer was matching his 401(k) contributions, the case would have been even more compelling. However, these advantages are missing when we talk about investing in regular brokerage accounts.

In those situations, I believe most families are better served if any surplus funds are initially used to pay down the house mortgage rather than used for investing. First, as we've already discussed, investments don't always pan out as hoped. You might be left with more debt than ever—and possibly even lose your house! Second, you probably are assuming that your income will continue at its present level or higher. But what if you are disabled, or laid off, or unexpected developments harm your business? Be careful about presuming on the future. And third, your patience will eventually be rewarded. The guaranteed interest savings from a faster pay-down will free up other funds that can be used for future investing (as we saw with Tom and Linda in chapter two).

I would recommend that you *not* consider other investments (as opposed to paying down your house mortgage) unless these conditions are met:

❶ Both spouses are in *complete* agreement that the investment should have the top priority;

❷ The remaining unpaid balance on your mortgage is less than 75% of the current value of your house (for example, your house would sell for around $120,000 and you owe less than $90,000 on your mortgage); and

❸ The investment will provide a return that is virtually certain to be greater than the interest rate on your mortgage (such as when an employer matches your 401(k) contributions).

If these three criteria are present, using your surplus income for investing rather than paying extra on your mortgage could be considered a reasonable and prudent decision. (This assumes you already have an adequate contingency fund in place—see chapter five.) I want to make clear, however, that what we are talking about here applies only to first mortgages.

Do not boast about tomorrow, for <u>you do not know what a day may bring forth</u>.
Proverbs 27:1

A stingy man is <u>eager to get rich and is unaware</u> that poverty awaits him.
Proverbs 28:22

"Home equity loans" are another story altogether. Americans used to take out second mortgages as a last resort. Now . . .

. . . many consider them a sign of savvy tax planning. Why the change in our thinking? Aside from the obvious fact that our entire society has become increasingly addicted to debt, we should understand the major roles played by the federal government and our friendly bankers. First, Congress got the ball rolling when it passed tax legislation that eliminated the income tax deduction for consumer interest payments unless they were made on a home mortgage. Then, lenders made it easy for us by offering low teaser rates and often waiving closing costs and other fees. Toss in the fact that, with interest rates so low, the cost of borrowing is less than it has been for quite a while. Now homeowners are using these loans to pay for everything from vacations to college tuition to new cars. Everybody seems happy, so what's the problem?

I don't like these loans for the same reasons that banks love them. First, these loans greatly increase the amount of money banks can safely lend you (and therefore the amount of interest they receive). One thing most Americans don't need is more credit and more debt. Second, if anything goes wrong with your loan, the bank is protected and can always foreclose on the house. It's one thing when getting laid off or having unexpected medical expenses shoots a hole in your monthly budget and your new car is repossessed. It's quite another when they come for your house!

There are other concerns as well. Some lenders are letting homeowners borrow up to 100% of their equity—where would you ever get the money to pay off such a large loan? Years of building equity through your monthly payments can be completely erased by one problem loan. Especially beware of loans that allow you to pay interest-only during the term of your loan and then call for immediate payment of the full principal. Finally, if the loan has a variable rate, check how high your rate could conceivably get during the life of the loan. Interest rate "caps" vary widely, from as low as 15% to as high as 25%! All in all, they're a threat to your financial safety, and their payment in full should be a priority.

Refinancing your mortgage, in order to take advantage of lower interest rates and/or shorten your payment schedule to a fifteen-year maturity, can result in significant savings on interest expense.

Mortgage Rates
Up to date listings of the best mortgage rates can be found at www.bankrate.com.

Refinancing your mortgage involves paying your existing mortgage off early by taking out a new one at a lower rate. The key statistic in deciding whether to refinance is learning how far down the road you "break even." Here's what you do. First, shop for the best deal and learn (1) what your total closing costs will be (excluding any pre-payments for insurance, taxes, or interest) and (2) what your new monthly payment will be. Next, subtract the amount of your new payment from your old one. This tells you how much you'll save each month. Finally, divide this monthly savings into your closing costs. This tells you how many months before the refinancing pays for itself (tax considerations aside). That's your break-even point; after that, you're saving every month.

Here's an example: If your new monthly payment would be $120 less than your current one, and if your total closing costs (including points) were $2,400, then it would take twenty months' worth of savings to pay your expenses ($2,400 divided by 120). After that, you'd be ahead an extra $120 each month.

It can get confusing trying to compare different proposals, so here's a handy way to convert points into a percentage rate: treat each point as if it added ¼ of 1% to your loan rate. Example: a 7% rate with two points is roughly the same as a 7½% rate with no points.

Once you know the break-even point for each loan you've been quoted, the main consideration is how long you expect to be in your present home. If you don't think you'll be there long enough to reach the break-even point, forget it. If you think you'll be there past break-even and decide to go ahead, you still have to decide whether to take a loan that features a lower rate but more points, or a higher rate with fewer points. The general rule is that the shorter the time past break-even that you expect to live there, the more you should lean toward the lower transaction costs. That means a shorter stay equals fewer points with a higher rate; a longer stay equals more points but a lower rate.

> ### MORTGAGE "POINTS"
>
> A typical mortgage loan, in addition to the interest rate you pay, carries two or three "points." Each point is equal to 1% of the loan amount and is charged by the lender to cover the up-front costs of originating the loan, appraisals, title search, legal fees, and so on. These points are subtracted from your proceeds at the time of your loan closing.
>
> For example: If your new mortgage is for $80,000 and you are charged three points, then you really only receive cash of $77,600 at the loan closing ($80,000 times 3% equals $2,400 in points paid).

To keep things simple, many lenders offer a "no points or closing costs" option where they let you skip the points and closing costs entirely . . .

. . . in exchange for a higher interest rate. Then it becomes simply a matter of comparing the interest rate they quote you with the rate you're paying now. For example, if you're currently paying 7.75% but can get a "no points or closing costs" rate of 7.40%, you're guaranteed to save. In fact, there's no reason you wouldn't want to refinance many times over the years when the advantages are this clear cut. Sure, there's some paperwork involved, but there's probably nothing else you can do that will pay you (in saved interest) such a high hourly rate for your time! I'd check every ninety days, and consider refinancing whenever you can save at least one-quarter of a percent on a "no points or closing costs" basis. Depending on the overall level of rates, you'll save $6,000–$7,000 in interest over thirty years on a $100,000 mortgage for *every* one-quarter percent reduction in your rate. However, the shorter the remaining term of your mortgage, the less you will save. With under ten years remaining on a thirty-year mortgage, it is unlikely that refinancing will result in much savings.

Here are some other shopping tips that can help you save money. First, look into getting a fifteen-year mortgage rather than a thirty-year one. The monthly payment will be higher, but the interest rate is lower. The savings in interest is dramatic! Second, if you refinance and end up with a lower monthly payment than you're now making, the temptation will be to take the savings and spend it elsewhere. Don't do it! Instead, send in the same amount using two checks. One check will be for the new monthly payment; the other can be applied to pre-paying principal and hastening the day when you own your home free and clear. Other points to keep in mind:

- You can refinance with the original lender or go to a new one.

- Find out when the rate on your loan will be "locked in" (permanently set). Is it when you apply? When the loan is closed? Many borrowers have been hurt when interest rates rose after the original proposal was made but before the lender locked in the rate.

- Get a commitment in writing of the exact terms of the mortgage being offered and how long the offer is good for. It should include the circumstances under which the lender would be allowed to back out (for example, in case of a dispute over the appraised value of your home).

- Check with your loan officer or processor to find out when the appraisal and credit agency reports are due back. Call on the expected dates to see if everything checks out.

Before leaving this topic, let us salute the money-saving virtues of 15 year mortgages. Consider the saga of the LiveHighs and the ThinkSmarts.

Two partners named LiveHigh and ThinkSmart had a lot in common. They each owned half their business, paid themselves equal salaries, were both married, and had two kids each. They had both saved $20,000 and were ready when the big moment that they'd worked so hard for finally arrived: the day they went looking for that first new house for their families.

They each were planning to start investing $200 per month into their new retirement accounts, and both had also decided they could afford monthly payments of around $925 on their house mortgages. LiveHigh knew just the house he wanted—it had an extra large corner lot and a spacious deck for cookouts. He figured that with interest rates down now, he could pick up a thirty-year, 7.75% mortgage that, along with his down payment, would enable him to afford the $150,000 price tag.

ThinkSmart liked the house next door. It was just like LiveHigh's except it was on a much smaller lot and lacked the backyard deck. The $120,000 price was appealing because it meant his $925 monthly payment would fit just right with a fifteen-year, 7.5% mortgage. He put down his $20,000 and signed on the dotted line.

A SOUND MIND BRIEFING

Big Savings Through Mortgage Pre-payments

by Marc Eisenson

When you take out a loan, you agree to pay back the amount borrowed plus interest. That's fair. But you've probably never realized just how much interest can be. For example, on a $90,000, 30-year mortgage, written at 7.5% interest, the total payback will be over $226,500. That's more than $136,500 in interest charges on a $90,000 loan. More than one and one-half times what was borrowed! Shocking, isn't it?

Well, take heart. Making small, frequent pre-payments with pocket change—that money most of us would never invest, or miss—will save a substantial portion of the more than $136,500 in interest that this $90,000 loan would normally incur. Pre-payments are not additional costs. They are simply small amounts paid sooner.

Every month, or whenever you are expected to make a payment to your lender (for convenience we'll assume all borrowers are homeowners and all lenders are banks), the bank's computer calculates the amount of interest you owe for having used its money during the previous month, and subtracts that interest from the amount of the check you send in. What's left is credited toward the outstanding balance of your loan.

To make it easy to keep track of how much interest you are being charged and how much of each payment is being credited toward the principal of your loan, it is necessary to use an appropriate pre-payment schedule. These computer printed charts, often referred to as amortization schedules, separate out the interest and principal components of each monthly payment, along with the balance remaining after each payment has been made.

Shown above is a pre-payment schedule showing the payments during various time periods for our sample loan. When each payment is made, the balance of the loan gets reduced by the amount of the principal portion only, not by the amount of the total monthly payment. If the sample loan shown were your mortgage, you would be expected to pay $629.30 every month for thirty years. You could not pay less, or skip any payments without risking a foreclosure. But, you could pay more.

For illustrative purposes, let's assume that you are about to mail

MORTGAGE SCHEDULE

Amortization based on 30 year,
$90,000 loan at 7.5% interest.
Monthly payment of $629.30

Payment Number	Interest Portion	Principal Portion	Balance Remaining
1	$ 562.50	$ 66.80	$ 89,933.20
2	562.08	67.22	89,865.98
3	561.66	67.64	89,798.34
120	489.09	140.21	78,114.25
121	488.21	141.09	77,973.17
122	487.33	141.97	77,831.20

in mortgage payment #1. If you add $67.22 (principal payment #2) to the $629.30 which is due every month, and mail in a single check for $696.52, the bank will properly credit your pre-payment of $67.22 and you won't have to make interest payment #2. You will never pay that $562.08!

Next month, when you mail in your check for $629.30, it will be credited as if it were payment #3, since the principal portion of payment #2 will have already been credited, and the interest payment which the bank's computer will show as due, is the interest amount shown for payment #3. Now for the bonus: Not only will that $67.22 save you $562.08, but it will also reduce the term of your loan by one month. That's pre-paying in a nutshell. The only place where you can earn more just as safely with such tiny investments is by pre-paying on your credit cards.

You can begin pre-paying at any time; however, the sooner you begin, the greater your savings will be. That's because interest payments are higher and principal payments are lowest at the inception of the loan. Later on, the savings will still be substantial, although smaller. Let's look at a portion of the schedule of our sample mortgage ten years down the road. We'll assume that no pre-payments have been made. Assume an additional principal payment of $141.97 is mailed in with payment #121 (for a total of $629.30 + $141.97 = $771.27). You will save $487.33 (interest payment #122) and retire the loan one month earlier. The following month's payment would be #123, not payment #122.

Note that even after 120 monthly payments of $629.30 each have been made, totalling $75,516.00 (120 x $629.30), the balance on this loan has only been reduced by $11,885.75 ($90,000 less $78,114.25). The remaining $63,630.25 ($75,516.00 paid less the $11,885.75) all would have gone toward interest—almost 70% as much as was borrowed in the first place!

If pre-paying seems like a good idea to you, get a pre-payment schedule for your loan and begin! No matter what type of loan you have, whether it's a fixed rate, adjustable, or bi-weekly, the more you pre-pay and the sooner you begin, the more you will save!

Amortization Calculator

If locking in the higher payments of a 15 year loan is too scary, consider prepaying your 30 year loan. The net effect can be the same as a 15 year loan, without the obligation of higher payments.

One of the best ways to prepay (see previous page) involves using a loan amortization schedule. To create one for your loan, see the Tools page at www.soundmindinvesting.com.

But godliness with contentment is great gain. For we brought nothing into the world, and we can take nothing out of it.

1 Timothy 6:6–7

As time passed, the business grew slowly but steadily. We pick up our story fifteen years later as ThinkSmart is writing the check for his final mortgage payment. What a great feeling! He and his wife decide to go out for the evening to celebrate. They talk about how much fun it would be to "trade up" to a nicer home but agree they don't want to get back into mortgage debt again. Instead, they decide to increase the amount they put into their retirement account. Every month they deposit the $925 that formerly went to the mortgage company.

We can fast-forward fifteen more years to the end of our story. Mr. and Mrs. LiveHigh are happy. After thirty years, they have written their final mortgage check. As they think of the future, they agree: "With this taken care of at last, it's time to begin putting more money into our retirement account."

Next door, ThinkSmart and his wife are also thinking of the future. Their quarterly statement came today, and the current balance in their investment account is quite impressive! As they look through some travel brochures, they agree: "With this much in savings, it's time to begin enjoying some of the fruits of our labor."

Assuming that both families earned 9% on their retirement investments over the years, how much more do the ThinkSmarts have than the LiveHighs?

First, let me point out the *reason* the ThinkSmarts have more: they were willing to accept a lifestyle with more modest amenities. Although the houses themselves were quite similar, the ThinkSmarts were willing to do without the backyard deck and more spacious lot size. For most couples who have debt problems, their difficulties began when they obligated themselves to a larger mortgage payment than was reasonable given their income.

This is especially true if they relied on two incomes when computing their ability to comfortably make long-term monthly mortgage payments. In that event, if either income is interrupted for any reason—the economy, corporate strategic planning, technical obsolescence, disability, or childbearing—they automatically have a financial problem on their hands.

Now, here are the numbers reflecting the surprisingly high costs of the LiveHighs' lifestyle. After thirty years of paying on their mortgage and contributing to retirement, the LiveHighs have $368,895 in their retirement account. Meanwhile the ThinkSmarts, after paying off a smaller mortage in only fifteen years, have $721,545 in their retirement account. Thus, they have $352,650 more, almost twice as much. The extra amenities ended up costing the LiveHighs far more than they could have ever imagined! ◆

SECTION 2

Saving for Future Needs

There is precious treasure in the dwelling of the wise,
but a foolish man swallows it up.

Proverbs 21:20

"Naturally, the higher the interest rate,
the greater the penalty for early withdrawal."

CHAPTER PREVIEW

Do You Have Adequate Savings?

I. **Before risking your money in the stock and bond markets, you should have an adequate contingency fund set aside in a separate savings account.**

   A. It serves as a contingency fund for dealing with the unexpected. Financial planners frequently recommend six months' living expenses as an adequate size. You'll want to invest your contingency fund in an account that is immediately accessible and provides complete safety. We'll go shopping for just such investments in chapter six.

   B. Second, your savings reserve can be used as an accumulation fund where you save for major expenditures that are not provided for in your monthly budget. Typically, an accumulation fund allows you to have a longer time frame in mind (say, a year or more before you'll need to withdraw the money). In that event, you can improve your returns by looking at a different set of investment options. We'll do that in chapter seven.

II. **An automated savings program is an effective way of imposing self-discipline and helping you build your contingency fund.**

   A. Offered by most savings institutions and money market mutual funds; the amount you wish to save is automatically deducted from your paycheck and put into your savings.

   B. The amount you save should be based on your age and gross income. Financial planners commonly suggest saving 5%–10% of your income while in your twenties, eventually moving up to 15%–20% prior to retirement.

III. **Money makes money (simple interest), and the money that money makes, makes more money (compound interest).**

   A. "Compound" interest refers to an arrangement where you earn interest on both the initial principal *and* the interest previously earned on that principal.

   B. Our tale of two savers—Jack and Jill—has a surprising winner. The moral is to invest early and often. Small amounts can make a big difference.

The Scriptures encourage us to plan for the unexpected, equating planning with being wise:

"Go to the ant, you sluggard; consider its way and be wise! It has no commander, no overseer or ruler, yet it stores its provisions in summer and gathers its food at harvest."

Proverbs 6:6-8

"In the house of the wise are stores of choice food and oil, but a foolish man devours all he has."

Proverbs 21:20

Even if you have not completely reached your Level One goal of becoming debt-free, it's still a good idea to begin setting aside some money for emergencies or large purchases.

When I created what I call the "Four Levels" sequence in my *Sound Mind Investing* newsletter, the idea was to help my readers set reasonable and prudent priorities. As discussed in Section One, I believe you're best served if you make getting debt-free your first priority (see pages 35-36). In my newsletter, I refer to this as working at Level One. Now we come to the subject of this Section—the importance of building a savings reserve for future needs. This is Level Two.

It is appropriate to work on Level One and Level Two at the same time. Although it is economically sensible to first pay off debts that are carrying high interest charges, I don't feel you should use every spare penny for that purpose. Everyone needs a savings reserve, which can serve two purposes.

First, it is a contingency fund for dealing with the unexpected. Perhaps you will have unanticipated medical or auto repair expenses. Or, it might be a case of a temporary layoff at work or a disabling injury. If you don't have a "cushion" to fall back on, you'll eventually wind up back in debt because of the unhappy financial surprises that come everyone's way occasionally. By having this money set aside and readily available, you can "borrow" from yourself rather than from family members or your bank.

How large should your contingency fund be? Many financial planners recommend having from three to six months' living expenses set aside. In my monthly newsletter, I suggest a fund of $10,000. The amount is up to you, but I would think living expenses for at least three months would be a minimum. You'll want to invest your contingency fund in an account that is immediately accessible and provides complete safety. We'll go shopping for just such investments in the next chapter.

Second, your savings reserve can be used as an accumulation fund where you save for major expenditures that are not provided for in your monthly budget. Such items might include replacing your old car, buying some new furniture as the family grows, or funding that home remodeling project you've been looking forward to. Typically, an accumulation fund allows you to have a longer time frame in mind (say, a year or more before you'll need to withdraw the money) than is the case with your contingency fund. Liquidity is no longer as important. In that event, you can improve your returns by looking at a different set of investment options. We'll do that in chapter 7.

To be sure you save, pay yourself first.

When one of my sons came to me for help in getting his finances organized, the first thing I did was get him set up on a pay-as-you-go basis using the so-called "envelope" system. That's where you cash your paycheck(s) and immediately divide your income into several envelopes, one for each of your major spending areas. When the money in a particular envelope is gone, that means no more spending in that area until the next payday.

Modern technology has enabled us to improve on this approach—now we use the "Ziploc™ bag system" so all the loose change doesn't fall out!—but there's one thing technology can't do, and that's to restrain us from overspending. That part still requires self-discipline, sacrifice, and a long-term perspective. Arriving at financial independence is very satisfying, but the journey can be tough along the way.

Here's the process my son used as he worked on building his Level Two contingency fund. *After* setting aside his tithe and taxes, what was left was his spendable income. This was the "pie" that he proceeded to "cut" several ways. The first piece of 10% went into his Level Two contingency fund account. Then, the remainder of his spendable income went into bags for his current bills, debt repayment, and monthly living expenses.

His contingency fund came in handy twice during his first few months using the system—to pay for emergency brake and transmission repairs. The money in the savings account was used up, and he had to begin building it anew. But having it on hand prevented him from going back into debt to pay for those items. That's why it makes sense to set aside some savings in a contingency fund.

Automation beats procrastination.

When it comes to saving, despite your best intentions, it's easy to rationalize putting it off until the next paycheck. So it often helps to have some of your money put aside automatically before you have the opportunity to spend it. Here are two paths to automated savings:

• Sign up to have part of your paycheck (you decide how much) automatically deposited into your savings account at your credit union or local bank. It's easy, convenient, and offers some useful discipline. Plus, your savings are insured and available for withdrawal without penalty whenever you wish.

• For a higher rate of return, set up automatic transfers from your bank account to a money market mutual fund (which we'll look at in detail in the next chapter). Such funds typically accept transfers of $50 and up on either a weekly, every other week, or monthly basis. Most money market mutual funds offer this service; call them and ask for the forms to get started.

Savings Tools
Want to figure out how long it will take to hit your savings goals? Or how much you'd save by changing a habit or two? Calculators for these tasks, plus other helpful saving tools are available at www.quicken.com/banking_and_credit/saving/.

Consider a strategy of saving 5%–10% of your gross income when you're in your twenties. Initially, this will go toward building your contingency fund. Once that's in place, your savings can be used for a down payment on a house and other large purchases. Then, move up to 10%–15% in your thirties and forties. Usually at this age, the primary use of savings is to invest for retirement. In your fifties, as home buying and child-rearing costs are tapering off, you might be able to boost your savings rate to the 15%–20% area in final preparation for your approaching retirement years.

Sometimes, Level Two folks feel they can't do anything very exciting from an investing point of view.

The folks at Levels Three and Four seem to have all the fun. Meanwhile, you're still trying to save $10,000 for those "contingencies." It can seem like an impossible task. If you feel that way, you're short-changing the impact you can make. The power of compounding works to help you as you save.

For example, let's assume you're starting today with nothing in the bank. If you can save $10 each week and put it in a savings account, it will grow to $10,000 in 12.8 years. Admittedly, that seems pretty far away. How about working harder on your budget and increasing your savings from $10 a week up to $30? That gets you to your $10,000 goal in just 5.4 years. That's much better. And if you start out with $5,000 in the bank rather than from scratch, the time required drops to only 2.5 years.

You can alter the variables to fit your particular situation (see table at left). Just keep in mind that every dollar in additional savings and interest earned contributes to the compounding process and gets you to your destination that much faster. You can achieve your Level Two goal sooner than you think through commitment and careful planning.

YEARS NEEDED TO ACCUMULATE $10,000

If you start with	Assuming you add this much each week:				
	$10	$20	$30	$40	$50
$0	12.8	7.6	5.4	4.2	3.5
$1,000	11.0	6.7	4.8	3.8	3.1
$2,000	9.4	5.8	4.2	3.3	2.7
$3,000	7.9	5.0	3.6	2.8	2.3
$4,000	6.5	4.2	3.1	2.4	2.0
$5,000	5.3	3.4	2.5	2.0	1.7
$6,000	4.1	2.7	2.0	1.6	1.3

This table assumes your money will earn interest at 6% per year. Although rates are lower than that at present, the average money market return over the past decade has been greater than 6%. There has been no adjustment for taxes because they may or may not apply to a given situation.

Many years ago, I came across a book with a rather unforgettable title: *Money Makes Money, and the Money Money Makes Makes More Money.*

As you might expect, it was about the power of compound interest. The word "compound" refers to something composed of two or more parts. Familiar examples include a chemical compound (a substance composed of two or more elements) and a hospital/medical compound (a building where two or more functions, like surgery, doctors' offices, nursing care and laboratory, are combined into one large facility).

In financial terminology, "simple" interest refers to interest being paid on the principal only. Assume you deposited $1,000 in a one-year bank CD that paid simple 7% per year interest. After the first month, you would have "earned" a small amount of interest, around $5.83. But the bank isn't going to pay it to you until the year is up; it is going to hold onto it. And even though it's yours, it is not going to pay you any interest for having it around to use over the coming year. The bank is obligated to pay you interest only on one part of your account—your principal. After the year, you'd have earned $70.00 in simple interest.

Now, let's change the terms of the CD to one of "compound" interest, where interest will be paid on *both the principal and the monthly interest earned* as the year goes along. The first month, the bank pays you only on your principal, just as before, because you haven't earned any interest yet. But after the first month, it credits your account with that $5.83. Now, for the coming month, you're going to earn interest on $1,005.83 instead of your original $1,000.00 of principal.

The second month you earn $5.87 in interest, only 4¢ more. By the end of the year, you've earned total interest of $72.29. That's $2.29 more than simple interest would have paid, and it came your way just by changing one word in the CD agreement and without increasing your risk. Suppose we change the CD to pay weekly compounding. Instead of giving you credit for your earned interest just once a month, the bank will do it once a week. It turns out that at year's end you've earned $72.46 in interest.

Daily (or "continuous") compounding has become the most common offer. If we used daily compounding in our CD example, the total interest earned would have been $72.50. That's the same as a simple interest rate of 7.25%. So, by changing from simple interest to daily compounding, you would have effectively improved your return by ¼% per year.

Does it seem too small an amount to really matter? For just $1,000 and for only one year, perhaps so. But when you consider how much you will have on deposit in a savings account over your lifetime, the difference of ¼% per year in return can amount to tens of thousands of dollars.

The unrelenting power of compound interest is one of your greatest investing weapons.

Consider this updated version of the saga of Jack and Jill. Jack started a paper route when he was eight years old and managed to save $600 per year. He deposited it in an IRA investment account that earned 10% interest. Jack continued this pattern through high school and "retired" from the paper-delivery business at the ripe old age of 18. All told, he saved $6,600 during that time. He left his savings to compound until he reached 65 and never added another dollar during the entire intervening 47 years.

Jill didn't have a paper route, but waited until her post-college days to start her savings. At age 26, she was sufficiently settled to put $2,000 into her IRA retirement fund. This she continued to do each year for 40 years. She also earned a 10% compounded return on her savings. Now, the question is which fund was larger at age 65—Jack's IRA into which he put $6,600 or Jill's into which she put $80,000?

Change A Habit. Boost Your Savings.

I am going to point out something about your spending that you may never have thought of (and may not be able to get out of your mind once I put it there). Have you ever stopped to consider what the "future value" of the money you spent today could have amounted to?

That is, if you'd saved it rather than spent it, what would it be worth as you neared retirement, say in twenty years?

For example, let's say you spend $4 each workday for lunch on the job. What if you decided to fast once a week and save that $4 rather than spend it? You continue to do this once a week for twenty years. Invest it at 7% and it would grow to . . . (drum roll) . . . $9,067!

Surprised? I thought so.

Now, start applying that same logic to other adjustments you can make in your lifestyle. Would you rather have a soft drink once a day, or $7,964 in extra liquidity in twenty years? Or what if you could save $60 a month in gas and parking if you were to carpool or take the bus? You might be more inclined to endure the extra hassle when you realized you were going to have an extra $31,256 waiting for you down the road. And if you buy cigarettes at a pack-a-day rate, that's $23,892 up in smoke. Well, you get the idea. Think about it.

How Much Does Impulse Buying Reduce Your Savings?

You have to begin looking on impulse purchases as one of your most formidable foes in the battle to save more.

Impulse purchases usually violate the following rules for wise shopping: shopping around for the best buys, keeping tight control on the use of your credit card, buying only what you really need, buying what's practical, and checking carefully for quality.

Larry Burkett suggests maintaining an "impulse list" that works like this:

• Never buy anything unless you have budgeted for it. Instead, write it down on your impulse list.

• Get at least three prices for the same item from different sources.

• Wait at least ten days to buy it.

• Never have more than one item on your list.

Larry says, "I use this system, and with rare exceptions, I never buy anything on impulse. Do you know why? Because long before I have found two more prices on the first item, I find two more items I would rather have. A person could easily go broke saving money on good buys.

The only way to conquer the impulse is self-discipline. Without discipline, no budget will help. 'For a man is a slave to whatever has mastered him' (2 Peter 2:19b)."

Surprisingly, Jack is the winner. His IRA has grown to more than $1,078,700, an amount equal to *more than 162 times* what he put in as a child. Jill also did quite well with hers, which grew to $973,700. But Jack's earlier start, even with smaller amounts and deposits for far fewer years, was too much to overcome thanks to the tremendous power of compounding. That's because when Jack was 26, the age at which Jill began her IRA savings, the interest earned in his account was more than the $2,000 Jill was putting in. The moral is: invest early and often—even small amounts can make a big difference!

"Every time we almost reach our contingency fund goal of having $10,000 set aside for future needs, a reason to spend some of it comes along (car dies, hospital bill). Do we have to postpone moving into the stock market until we replenish what was spent . . .

. . . or can we apply our monthly surplus to Level Two and Level Three at the same time?" This question from one of my readers gave voice to the frustration that many investors feel. After building their contingency fund (often from scratch over a period of a few years), they're tired but exhilarated. *At last*, they think, *debt-free, a large contingency fund to serve as a financial safety net, and we're finally ready to begin working on our long-term retirement portfolio.* Then, boom! An unexpected expense comes along and knocks down the balance in their contingency fund. Now they have to return to the drudgery of building it back up again. It seems they'll never get beyond this stage. Is all this caution about having a contingency fund really necessary?

Many of my monthly newsletter readers, having a conscientious desire to do the "right" thing in terms of setting priorities and following the counsel I offer, have tended to look at the Four Levels process as a set of laws rather than guidelines. I often receive questions with the words "do we *have* to?" and "*can* we?" in them. Such questions make me a little nervous because they imply that there are right and wrong answers that are absolute. There aren't. That's why I constantly alert my readers to beware of the self-proclaimed "experts" who have all the answers.

Financial management involves making highly personal decisions, and every counselor should avoid appearing dogmatic unless obedience to a biblical command is at stake. My primary goal is to encourage you to take reasonable and informed steps, which I believe will provide you with emotional comfort in the present and financial security in the future. The point is simple: although I can make recommendations, *you have to live with the consequences.* Therefore, it is my expectation that, ultimately, you will do what you believe is best and take responsibility for the results.

If you want to begin investing in stocks and bonds while still building (or replenishing) your contingency fund, that's a decision you're free to make.

It's not as safe a strategy because you're entering a high-risk undertaking without the solid foundation that is desirable. For example, what if the investments don't pan out, and more unexpected events arise to further deplete your contingency fund? On the other hand, everything could go well and you might even be better off financially a few years down the road.

There is no way of knowing ahead of time which would end up being the more profitable course. But it is obvious which approach is the more prudent—rebuilding the contingency reserve first. The general rule, then, is when you withdraw funds from your contingency account, you should make every effort to rebuild it as quickly as possible.

Making the sacrifices necessary to complete Level One (getting debt-free) and Level Two (saving for future needs) is not a lot of fun. But laying this foundation is vitally important and, if you'll commit yourself, it can be done. So, be diligent and be prayerful.

The passage in John 6 is a familiar one. The people had followed Jesus into the countryside where He was resting with His disciples. When Jesus posed the question of where they might get food to feed the great crowd, the disciples responded in terms of what man could do. "Eight months' wages would not buy enough bread for each one to have a bite!"

Jesus, however, always saw such situations in terms of what God could do. When He took action, He routinely made things happen that not only were humanly impossible, but up until the very moment He did them, were completely unimaginable!

To the disciples, the situation seemed hopeless (*"Here is a boy with five small barley loaves and two small fish, but how far will they go among so many?"*). So I wonder what their reaction was when Jesus, in the face of the impossibility of the situation, said, *"Have the people sit down."* As they moved to carry out His instructions, did they understand the implications?

I'd like to think that at least a few of them got an immediate thrill. Sort of like, "Wow! Did you hear that? The Teacher is up to something. There's no food, nowhere to get any food, and no money to pay for the food even if we knew where to get it! And He just says, 'Have the people sit down.' Man! I don't know what He's got in mind, but I bet it's going to be spectacular!" And it was.

This account reinforces several truths about God's faithfulness that are taught elsewhere in Scripture. God's provisions include our physical needs as well as our spiritual ones. God's provisions are unmerited; we've done nothing to deserve them. God's provisions often come after we wait in expectant obedience. God's provisions are generous and overflowing. And over all of this is Christ's complete sufficiency regardless of the circumstances. Ron Dunn once illustrated the truth of Christ's sufficiency this way:

He said to John on the island of Patmos: "I'm the beginning and the end. I'm the Alpha and the Omega." He was saying: "I'm the A and the Z." He's the whole alphabet. Isn't that amazing? I just bought a set of the Encyclopedia Britannica, and you know, I made a discovery the other day. I think I'm going to read through the whole encyclopedia and see if this is really true, but I believe they wrote that entire encyclopedia with only twenty-six letters. Boy, that's something, isn't it? Now my little nine year old girl has a book "See Dick Run,"and I can imagine that they wrote that with twenty-six letters, but to come to the Encyclopedia Britannica or to any book you want to write, and to say I wrote this with just twenty-six letters, I tell you that's amazing to me. You don't need to go outside the alphabet to write anything! And I'll tell you something else—you never need to go outside of Jesus for anything that you need. He's the Alpha and the Omega. He's all that you need.

I know that sometimes the effort to be a responsible steward can be tiring. Whether it's giving faithfully, getting debt-free, saving for the future, making prudent investing decisions, or planning for retirement, it usually includes a sacrifice of time and material comforts. Let me encourage you to continue trusting Him to provide all that you need to be obedient and victorious in these areas.

While our circumstances differ, we all have areas in our lives and work that desperately need His sufficiency. What we hope to accomplish will never happen apart from His provision. From my own experience, I can say that my monthly newsletter is one of them. Even before the first issue was published, my wife Susie and I began setting aside a regular time to pray for God's blessing in our efforts to minister through it. We've kept a prayer journal throughout, and it's very faith-enriching and humbling to see His answers over the years.

God encourages us in His Word to pray expectantly. *"This is the confidence we have in approaching God: that if we ask anything according to his will, he hears us. And if we know that he hears us—whatever we ask—we know that we have what we asked of him"* (1 John 5:14-15).

We're to do all we can do, and then "sit down" and expect Him to do what only He can do. Are you sitting down?   ◆

CHAPTER PREVIEW

Shopping for Safety in Your Emergency Fund

I. **Your emergency fund is not a part of your long-term investment portfolio and should be handled quite differently.**

   A. You should look for a "parking place" for your money that is absolutely safe. The value of your investment should not fluctuate with the markets.

   B. Your investment should be easily convertible to cash without penalties. The rate of return is a lesser consideration than immediate availability.

II. **We review four safe havens suitable for investing your emergency fund savings.**

   A. Banks offer convenience and federal insurance.

   B. Credit unions often offer better rates and service than banks. They also can offer federal insurance.

   C. Money market mutual funds pay 1%–2% more in annual interest than banks. They are not federally insured but are virtually as safe as FDIC-insured accounts. For most savers, they offer the best combination of safety, returns, and convenience.

   1. There are three basic varieties of money market funds: those that invest in IOUs from big businesses, those that invest in IOUs from the federal government and its agencies, and those that invest in IOUs from local and state governments. The interest from the latter is largely tax-exempt.

   2. Shopping for the best deals and opening your money fund account is a relatively simple process. This chapter offers pointers.

   D. U.S. Treasury bills offer the greatest degree of safety and liquidity, but they are not as convenient as other alternatives and their rates are not as high as those offered by money market funds.

   1. T-bills can be purchased in three, six, nine, and twelve month maturities. They can be sold before maturity (if necessary) without a penalty.

   2. The easiest way to invest in T-bills is either through a money market mutual fund or by buying them at your local bank. The most profitable way, because it avoids operating expenses and bank fees, is to buy them directly from the U.S. Treasury.

Your emergency fund is not a part of your long-term portfolio and should be handled quite differently than your other investments.

You should look for a "parking place" for your money that is absolutely safe and can be easily converted to cash without early withdrawal penalties. The interest rate earned is a lesser consideration than assured immediate availability. In this chapter, we'll look at four safe havens that are suitable for this purpose, starting with your local bank.

There are many different ways you can save at your local bank. They may be convenient, but usually they're not your best choice.

In my financial newsletter, I have consistently recommended money market mutual funds as my preferred way to save. They're safe, convenient, offer check writing, and pay higher interest than bank money market accounts. (We'll get into this shortly.) But for those of you who like keeping some of your savings with your friendly neighborhood banker, here's a guide to the often-confusing variety of accounts being offered.

• **Passbook Savings.** This name is a holdover from the days when most people kept track of their savings through the transactions recorded in their little bank savings book. Banks typically offer the lowest rate but have low minimum requirements. They may pay interest either from the day of deposit or, in some cases, the first of the following month. The only reason to have a passbook account is if you can't meet the minimums required for the better-paying types of accounts.

• **NOW Accounts.** This is an interest-bearing checking account rather than a savings account. It is convenient for earning interest while still having your money available for check writing at the same time. When shopping around, look for the one with the lowest "minimum monthly balance" required. To earn your interest, you cannot let your balance fall below this amount. If you do, not only might you lose interest, you may incur additional charges. The minimum is usually around $1,000.

• **SuperNOW Accounts.** These are glorified NOW accounts that require you to maintain a higher minimum balance and in return pay you slightly higher interest. The minimums are usually set at $2,500. If you have that much cash, you want it in a genuine savings account rather than a low-paying checking account.

• **Bank Money Market Accounts.** Notice I said *accounts*. These should not be confused with money market *funds* offered by the mutual fund industry. Bank MMAs pay you lower returns than the open market rates paid by money market funds. Each bank is free to set its own rates, and they can vary widely. The minimum account is usually $1,000, and there is a service charge ($5 or $10) if the balance falls below it. Check-writing privileges are available, but only for a few—typically three—checks per month. The primary advantage of

---

Things You Should Know About FDIC Insurance

The $100,000 insurance limit applies per person and not per account. This means that all checking accounts, savings accounts, certificates of deposit, and business accounts (if run as sole proprietorships) combined at any one bank or S&L are limited to $100,000 of protection.

The $100,000 limit includes any interest you might have coming. For example, if you had $98,000 in CDs which earned $4,000 in interest before the failure, your total recovery would be limited to $100,000 and you would lose $2,000 of the interest.

Not All Banks and S&Ls Carry FDIC Insurance Protection

Many rely on state-sponsored programs instead. Unfortunately, state deposit insurance has proven unreliable in many instances. Here are two precautions you can take. One, immediately move any deposits you have in an institution that carries only state deposit insurance to one protected by FDIC insurance. And two, never exceed the $100,000 limit at any one institution.

bank MMAs is that they are guaranteed by the FDIC up to $100,000.

• **Certificates of Deposit (CDs).** As with other bank offerings, you are loaning money to your bank for a fixed rate of interest. Unlike the others, however, you agree not to withdraw your money for a set period of time. If you take it out early, you forfeit a large part of the interest you would have earned. We'll discuss bank CDs in more detail in the next chapter.

Credit unions are another option. They're to banks what generic drugs are to name brand prescriptions . . .

. . . excellent substitutes that typically give you good value for your money and are just as safe. These nonprofit consumer organizations were started with the idea of providing higher savings rates and lower loan rates than profit-making institutions like banks and S&Ls. Approximately one in every five Americans has an account at one of these nonprofit cooperatives. Here's a brief rundown of their strengths and weaknesses to help you assess whether they're a good place for you to stash your contingency fund savings.

 **Service.** Much as with banks, the range of services offered by a credit union largely depends on its size. Areas where they might cut corners include the frequency with which statements are issued, the availability of automated teller machines and electronic transfers, and the number of branches. On the plus side, many credit unions offer discounts on automobile and life insurance. A survey reported by *Consumer Reports* indicated that members of credit unions were, on average, twice as likely to voice satisfaction with the service they received as were customers of commercial banks.

Safety. Approximately 90% of credit unions are protected by a federal agency that insures their deposits just like the FDIC does for banks. (Don't settle for state-sponsored or private deposit insurance—many have had problems in the past.) However, the rules governing which kinds of accounts are insured and for how much can be confusing. To be absolutely sure you're fully covered, request the booklet *Your Insured Funds* from your credit union (or you can write for a copy to the National Credit Union Administration, Washington, D.C. 20456). Have an officer go through it with you and explain which sections apply to your account.

Rates. The good news is that surveys have routinely indicated that credit unions pay better savings rates than banks. The bad news is that there are two possibly offsetting drawbacks: (1) The surveys reflect national averages, but the credit union you are eligible to join may be "below average." Make sure yours measures up. (2) Many credit unions do not pay interest based on your *average* monthly balance but on your *lowest* monthly balance. Such a policy dis-

Use Your Savings to Help Others Help Themselves

Over the past two decades, the Self-Help Credit Union in North Carolina has made over $700 million in loans to assist approximately 11,000 low-income families—people who cannot qualify for loans from customary lending sources—to purchase homes and build businesses.

According to Self-Help's website (www.self-help.org), its "development strategy is based on the belief that ownership allows people to improve their economic position."

Despite the relative neediness of Self-Help's target audience, its losses on loans have been less than 1%, similar to the experience of conventional lenders. Your savings can contribute to this worthy mission via a membership in the Self-Help Credit Union.

When you become one of Self-Help's depositors (federally-insured up to $100,000 for each depositor), you help create innovative housing and job opportunities for others while earning competitive market rates on your account. There is a one-time $25 membership fee of which $20 is tax deductible. For information, call 800-966-SELF.

courages you from drawing on your savings; if that's your intention, a money market fund might be preferable.

Eligibility. Most credit unions are sponsored by employers or trade and community associations, and they limit membership to employees or those with geographical proximity. However, there are some that cater to the investing public at large, so it's worth calling the Credit Union National Association (800-358-5710) to see if there is one in your area that you could join.

Now, let's turn to a third safe haven for your emergency savings— money market mutual funds. What is a money market fund, anyway?

When you open a savings account or buy a CD at your bank (that is, lend them your money), your bank turns around and lends your money to others at a higher rate than it's paying to you. Obviously, the less it pays you on your savings, the more profit it makes. The problem with this arrangement is that you and your bank are financial adversaries.

Fortunately, there are other borrowers, the "big time" players, who would like you to loan to them *and will pay you more interest than your bank will*. These organizations include the federal government, big corporations, and even other banks. However, to do business with them readily, you need a go-between. That's where a special type of mutual fund comes in, one that specializes strictly in the short-term lending of money in the financial markets. Hence, its name: money market fund.

Your money market fund is on *your* side; it will try to get you the best rates it can, while still not taking undue risks. You give the fund your money; the fund gives you one of its shares for every $1 you put in. It takes your money and loans it out to the big time players, almost always getting a rate of interest 1% to 1½% higher than your bank will pay you over the same time period. The value of your money market fund shares doesn't fluctuate; they're kept at a constant $1—the same amount you paid for them.

As the fund earns interest from its investments, it "pays" you your portion by crediting you with more shares. You earn interest, that is, receive more shares, every single day. The longer you leave your money in, the more shares you'll have. In this way, you are assured of getting all of your money back, *whenever* you want it, plus all the interest you've earned in the meantime.

Newcomers to money market mutual funds often hesitate to use them because they don't carry FDIC protection. This caution is unnecessary. Thanks to the short-term nature of their portfolios (average maturity of all their holdings cannot exceed 90 days) as well as Securities and Exchange Commission (SEC) regulations governing quality (95% of portfolio must receive one of the two highest ratings for credit-worthiness) and diversification (no more than

Money Market Funds are specialized funds that take your money and make very short-term loans to big businesses, the U.S. Treasury, and state/local governments. They are a way of pooling your money with other small investors and getting a better deal on interest rates. Think of it as a savings account disguised as a mutual fund.

Advantages of Money Market Funds Great for savings or for using as a temporary holding place for money that might be needed in the near future. Virtually as safe as FDIC-insured bank accounts but typically pay 1%–1.5% more.

Disadvantages of Money Market Funds There's no set level of interest that you can count on earning. You receive whatever the short-term rate is, and it changes constantly.

5% of portfolio invested with any one issuer, U.S. government excepted), money market mutual funds are essentially as safe as insured bank accounts.

Opening a money market fund account is like opening a checking account—a few forms to sign and you're on your way (see page 75).

With these advantages, you wonder why anyone would still use the traditional bank savings-type accounts. Yet the data show . . .

. . . that hundreds of billions of savers' dollars continue to reside in savings accounts. It seems to me that many savers simply don't understand the difference between bank money market *accounts* and money market *funds* sponsored by mutual fund organizations. They think it's all the same kind of thing. But there's a big difference! Investors in a money market mutual fund receive all of the fund's investment income after very small operational expenses are paid. Depositors in a bank money market account, on the other hand, are merely creditors of the bank and are paid as little as the market will bear. Because it comes out of their pockets, banks naturally want to pay as little as they can get away with. That explains why banks and S&Ls will always offer interest rates lower than money market mutual funds (unless they're desperate for cash, in which case you don't want to loan them your money, anyway).

There are three different kinds of money market funds.

❶ The most common are the ones that loan money to businesses and banks. I'll refer to these as corporate money market funds because they invest primarily in bank certificates of deposit and commercial paper. This kind pays the highest yield to investors and is the most popular.

BIG BUSINESS

❷ For people who want added safety, there are money market funds that loan money only to the federal government and its agencies. Given the excellent track record of the corporate kind, it's debatable whether the added caution of sticking strictly with Uncle Sam's securities is worth the slight reduction in yield. For the past fifteen years, the value has been more in the peace of mind investors receive rather than in actually providing additional safety.

FEDERAL GOVERNMENT

❸ For people who are in high tax brackets, there are money market funds that invest only in tax-free municipal bonds that are very close to maturity. The income is free from federal income taxes, and if you invest in a single-state tax-free fund for your state of residence, your income is exempt from state income taxes as well.

STATE/LOCAL GOVERNMENTS

Just What Does A Money Market Fund Own?

Money market funds search the world over for above-average yields consistent with high quality. To qualify, a borrower generally must be rated in one of the two highest credit-quality categories for short-term securities by at least two of the nationally-recognized rating services.

The kinds of investments owned by money market mutual funds are quite varied:

• U.S. Treasuries IOUs backed by the "full faith and credit" of the U.S. government. Having no default risk, these are the safest of all securities.

• U.S. Agency debt IOUs issued by agencies of the federal government. It is generally acknowledged that the government has a moral obligation to prevent any of its agencies from defaulting.
(continued on page 73)

There is a fiercely waged competition for money market fund deposits (like yours). And one of the principal weapons is a sales tactic called an "expense waiver."

Money market funds, by definition, invest in short-term money market instruments. This means all of them are pretty much investing in the same securities—bank CDs, commercial paper, and U.S. Treasuries. This being the case, you wouldn't expect a great deal of difference in the yields they earn for their shareholders. But you'd be wrong. The operating expenses they charge for running the fund, which come out of their investors' profits, can vary dramatically. Some funds charge up to four times as much as others that run a tighter ship. Many, in an attempt to attract new business, go so far as to absorb all (or a portion) of the operating expenses themselves. This practice is called "undertaking."

Since these "undertakers" don't pass on their full costs to the shareholders, they can pay them higher returns. The industry average for money fund operating expenses is sixty "basis" points. (A basis point is 1/100 of one percent, so sixty basis points equals .6% per year.) If your money fund earned 4.8% on its investments and charged the industry average for operating the fund, your yield for the year would be just 4.2%. But if the fund manager absorbed all the operating expenses, you'd get the full 4.8%.

In effect, they're discounting their services, and will often continue this practice for a year or more in order to more quickly build their assets under management. Testimony to the intense competition for your savings dollar among money funds is the fact that about half of all money funds have engaged in undertaking to some degree.

Dreyfus used this tactic in launching its Worldwide Dollar Fund in the early 1990s. Initially, the fund engaged in an aggressive undertaking strategy and, as a result, its yield regularly placed number one in the money fund rankings. This enabled the fund to grow very quickly. After it became one of the largest money market funds in the country, Dreyfus decided to start charging the full fare, and then some. By 1996, the yield on Worldwide Dollar was a full 1.25% below the yield offered by the leading

CHARACTERISTICS OF MONEY MARKET FUNDS

1. Safety. Although not insured by the government, money market mutual funds operate under Securities and Exchange Commission guidelines that make them very safe.

2. Liquidity. You can have your money back whenever you want with no withdrawal penalties. This is important to you because you might need your contingency funds on short notice.

3. Higher returns than bank money market accounts. Money market mutual funds have historically paid 1.0%–1.5% more than bank-sponsored money market accounts.

4. More responsive to interest rate trends. When interest rates move, money market funds are quick to reflect the new level—either higher or lower—due to their ultra short maturities.

money funds. Yet thousands of investors maintained their Worldwide Dollar accounts at Dreyfus, either because they did not keep informed and did not understand that their formerly top-ranked fund was performing poorly or they simply were not willing to expend the effort to change. Such a casual approach will cost them a lot of money over a lifetime of investing.

Is there anything "bad" about investing with funds that engage in undertaking? No, as long as you understand that they can decide to stop being so generous at any time. If you ask them, they will generally tell you how long they plan to continue their undertaking strategy. Once their growth targets are met, they will understandably want to charge the going rate for their services and begin to profit from their success. Naturally, they're hoping you'll remain a shareholder. But why should you? Don't be like the indifferent or uninformed shareholders of Dreyfus Worldwide Dollar. You shop the sales at your local mall, don't you? You should shop money funds the same way.

The leading money market mutual fund year after year has been one that is waiving its expenses. The leaders in the years to come are likely to do the same. That's why your attitude toward money market funds should be, "What have you done for me lately?" Call your fund periodically and ask for the most recent seven day compounded yield. You should be willing to change money funds annually if need be, always moving to the fund that is "having a sale," that is, virtually giving away its fund management services and passing the savings on to its shareholders.

To intelligently shop for a good money market fund, you need to understand the way yields are listed in the paper.

Barron's is an inexpensive source of data for savers. If you've spent much time looking through monthly financial magazines, names like *Money*, *Kiplinger's*, *SmartMoney*, and *Worth* are probably familiar to you. What you may not know, however, is that a lot of up-to-the-minute data and other helpful information is available in *Barron's*, the Dow Jones company's weekly newspaper. Published every Saturday, it contains investing data and articles on various markets. It is current up through the previous day.

Each issue of *Barron's* is divided into three sections. The first section contains articles that deal with the economy, stock and bond markets, the international scene, and real estate. There are also interviews with money managers who discuss their investing styles and their opinions on the markets. There is often some very interesting reading here, but this is not the main reason I'm suggesting you familiarize yourself with *Barron's*. It's in the "Mutual Funds" section where you'll find the current data on money market funds.

The listings are updated weekly, and provide current yield and average maturity information on many hundreds of money market funds, of both the

---

• Commercial paper
Short-term IOUs of very large companies. Because these IOUs are not backed by collateral, money funds typically invest only in commercial paper of the highest quality.

• Certificates of deposit
IOUs issued by banks. Money market funds buy CDs with high face values ("jumbo CDs") which are not government insured due to the $100,000 ceiling.

• Yankee CDs
IOUs issued in the U.S. by foreign banks with branches here.

• Eurodollar CDs
IOUs issued by foreign banks or by the foreign branches of U.S. banks.

• Repurchase agreements
Short-term loans with a very high quality asset (such as a U.S. government security) serving as collateral. "Repos" have very short life spans, generally coming due in one to seven days from the date issued.

• Bankers acceptances
Short-term loans with the guarantee of a bank serving as collateral. Most frequently, these arise in international commerce transactions.

• Municipal bonds
Short-term IOUs of states and city municipalities. The interest paid on these securities is exempt from the federal income tax. These IOUs would typically be owned only by money funds that specialized in this area. The listings for tax-exempt money funds are generally separate, following the listings for taxable funds. For more on tax-frees, see page 159.

taxable and tax-free variety. Many are designed for large institutions and require exceedingly large minimums (you can tell because the word "institution" or "institutional" is usually part of their names), but the majority are available to the average investor. Plus, they indicate which funds are temporarily absorbing part or all of their operating expenses and passing the savings on to shareholders.

In the "Market Week" section, there's a "money fund report" that shows industry-wide data, including what the average money fund is paying. Then you'll know whether your fund is above or below average in its performance.

Since most of the major money market mutual funds offer similar services and portfolio risk, the decision as to which to buy usually rests on where the best returns are to be found. In researching this information in the newspaper, it is common to find two different yields listed for each fund.

MONEY MARKET MUTUAL FUNDS

A listing of hundreds of taxable and tax-free money market funds appears in most newspapers at least once a week. You can also find one in Barron's and the Thursday edition of The Wall Street Journal.

The Average Maturity indicates the number of days before the average CD or corporate commercial paper is due to be repaid to the fund. The money will then be re-loaned at the current rate. The lower the average maturity, the more quickly the fund will reflect changes in interest rates.

The Seven Day Compounded Yield is the number you're interested in. Remember though, when interest rates start moving, these yields will change quickly to reflect the new realities.

Most mutual fund organizations offer several kinds of money funds.

A large majority of money funds invest primarily in bank CDs and corporate IOUs. They have names like MM, Cash, or Prime.

Fund	Avg Mat	7Day Yield	7Day Comp	Assets
Value Line Cash Fund	43	5.84	6.01	366
Van Kampen Reserve Class A	48	5.72	5.88	440
Van Kampen Reserve Class B	48	4.98	5.10	172
Van Kampen Reserve Class C	48	4.97	5.09	36
Vanguard Admiral Treasury	60	6.02	6.20	5901
Vanguard Federal MMF	62	6.28	6.48	5448
Vanguard Prime MMF/Instl	56	6.53	6.74	2172
Vanguard Prime MMF/Retail	56	6.35	6.55	44237
Vanguard Treasury MMF	62	5.84	6.01	4094
Victory Federal MMF (k)	49	6.23	6.42	853
Victory Prime Oblig Fund	54	5.93	6.11	2512
Victory US Govt Oblig Fund	33	5.68	5.84	1799

The money funds that limit their investments to the U.S. government use names like Treasury, Federal, or simply Govt.

Funds that are currently waiving part or all of their management fees (see page 72) are indicated by a "k" symbol.

This fund's portfolio is $853 million in size. Economies of scale can benefit investors once a fund surpasses about $5 billion. Note the Vanguard Prime Retail fund has over $44 billion.

The first percentage listed is usually called the "Seven Day Average (or Current) Yield." This reflects the annualized equivalent of what the fund earned for its shareholders over the past week. The limitation of this measure is that it ignores the long-term benefits of daily compounding. So, to more accurately reflect the actual results from investing in a money fund over time, another yield is shown. This percentage is called the "Seven Day Compounded (or Effective) Yield." This is what an investor would actually earn over a one-year period at last week's rate.

The rate of interest you earn changes a little bit every day because the funds have such short average portfolio maturities. This simply means that their "loans" are ultra short-term—almost every day, at least one of these loans is repaid to the fund. The fund must then take this money and loan it out all over again at a new rate. This constant process of re-lending the money in the pool causes money market fund yields to change rather quickly. That means the numbers published are slightly dated, but are sufficiently accurate for comparison purposes.

The general rule is that you want a long average maturity when rates are falling (so the fund can enjoy the old, higher rates for as long as possible), and you want a short average maturity when rates are rising (so the fund can get its money back quickly and reinvest it in the newer, higher-paying securities). And the stars of the show will be those that know how to keep their expenses down—or waive them altogether—and thereby pass the greatest returns through to their shareholders.

Moving your savings to a money fund really isn't a difficult process. These pointers should help make the transition an easy one.

First, call the funds in which you're interested and ask a few questions (see next page). After learning which offer the most attractive combination of yield and features, ask them to send their information package. Don't worry, this doesn't obligate you to do business with them.

The material you receive will include an application form and prospectus. The application form may look intimidating, but is actually quite simple and will take only a few minutes to complete. If you have any questions, you can call the fund's toll-free number and get all the help you need. Some of the questions request that you make choices (which can be changed at any time) among different convenience options. Most fund companies offer an option where you can automatically have your savings invested with them. Check the appropriate box if this is what you desire. To take advantage of check-writing privileges (which I recommend), simply check this option and provide the appropriate authorized signature(s). One disadvantage is that some funds do not return your canceled checks; however, they will send a copy of any check you may need if you request it.

WOULD TAX-FREE MONEY MARKET FUNDS GIVE YOU A BETTER RETURN?

Tax-free money funds invest solely in the IOUs of state and local governments which will mature sometime within the next year. These bonds were originally issued in order to raise money for the construction of public projects like roads, schools, and hospitals, and now the time is close at hand when they will be repaid in full. They are called municipal bonds (or "munis") because of the governmental units which issue them.

By law, the interest earned on such bonds is exempt from federal income taxes. Because of the value of these tax benefits to investors, issuers of tax-free bonds can borrow money at lower interest rates than those paid by other borrowers. Even though their yields are lower, you might be better off investing in tax-free money funds. Here's how to find out—use the formula explained in the example below to convert the yield of any tax-free fund to its *equivalent before-tax yield*. Then you can compare apples with apples. All you need to know is your "marginal" tax rate. At present, the federal tax law provides for five basic tax rates (which start at 15% and can rise as high as 39.6%). How high up the tax ladder does your income take you? That's your marginal rate.

If the Zurich taxable MMF is yielding 5.28% and Strong's tax-free fund is yielding 3.54%, who would benefit from using the tax-free fund?

For a 31% Marginal Tax Bracket Investor
1 minus .31 = .69
3.54% divided by .69 = equivalent to a 5.13% pre-tax rate

For a 36% Marginal Tax Bracket Investor
1 minus .36 = .64
3.54% divided by .64 = equivalent to a 5.53% pre-tax rate

The tax-free fund would be the better deal for savers in the 36% tax-bracket (or higher) but not those in the 31% bracket (or lower). This will not always be the case. Money fund yields can change quickly, so it pays to run the numbers regularly.

Tax-free money funds offer the same liquidity and other advantages as their taxable counterparts, but there are a few additional considerations that make their risk slightly higher. For one, there is a default risk on muni securities where there is virtually no such risk for other money market securities like Treasuries and bank CDs. Another is that, due to the limited number of muni securities available at any one time, tax-free money funds have occasionally had to extend their average maturities or lower their quality standards in order to acquire the dollar amounts needed.

Having said this, however, the increased level of risk is relatively small due to the diversification you get when buying shares in a large money fund portfolio.

Finally, fill in the amount that you will be depositing into your new money market mutual fund account and attach your check. Getting started in saving with money funds is as easy as 1-2-3.

Money market mutual funds offer check-writing privileges that make them a much better deal than a similar account at your local bank.

One of the most popular accounts offered by banks and S&Ls is the NOW account, which is basically an interest-bearing checking account. Such accounts typically require minimum balances of $1,000 and pay interest of about 1% less than the leading money funds. Many savers are not aware that a money market mutual fund set up with check-writing privileges is a better alternative. While most money funds request that checks not be written for small amounts (say less than $250), they often place no limit on the number of checks written, nor do they charge for the service. Depending on your needs, it might be better to go with a money fund with a slightly lower yield in return for more check-writing flexibility.

This presents individual savers with the opportunity to safely and quickly improve their rate of return by a full 1% and more. And for businesses, which by law are not currently permitted to earn interest on their checking account balances, money market mutual funds represent the difference between earning interest or not earning interest. That doesn't seem too difficult a choice.

Here's how to use your money fund as a checking account.

First, order a full supply of checks. Usually you'll get no more than a handful unless you make a specific request. Also, you'll want to give written authorization to your fund to make *wire transfers* to your bank (and possibly your brokerage firm) in response to your telephone request.

Second, use your local bank checking account for all salary and investment income deposits. Once a week, transfer the bulk of your account balance to your money fund. In order to get it to your money market fund even faster, you can ask your bank to "wire it" through the Federal Reserve. Banks charge extra for this service, so you would only want to transfer money this way if the interest you would earn by getting it there a few days faster would exceed the bank wire charge. Many money funds let you do this all online which, if you're wired to the Internet, is very convenient.

QUESTIONS TO ASK WHEN SHOPPING FOR A MONEY MARKET FUND

• What is your recent 7-day compounded yield?
• What is the minimum needed to open an account?
• How many checks am I allowed to write each month?
• What is the minimum amount I can write a check for?

SOME LEADING MONEY MARKET FUNDS FOR YOUR CONSIDERATION

In mid-2000, these funds were being recommended to readers of the Sound Mind Investing newsletter. Yields, and therefore the recommendations made in SMI, change regularly. Before investing, check Barron's or SMI for current yield information as described in this chapter.

Regular	Minimum	Telephone
TIAA-CREF Money Market	$ 250	(800) 223-1200
Vanguard Prime Portfolio	3,000	(800) 662-7447
Zurich Money Market Fund	1,000	(888) 987-4241

Government-Only	Minimum	Telephone
Fidelity U.S. Govt Reserves	$ 2,500	(800) 544-8888
Vanguard Federal Money Mkt	3,000	(800) 662-7447
Zurich Govt MMF	1,000	(888) 987-4241

Tax-Free	Minimum	Telephone
Strong Municipal Money Mkt	$ 2,500	(800) 368-1030
Vanguard Tax-Exempt Money Mkt	3,000	(800) 662-7447
Zurich Tax-Free MMF	2,000	(888) 987-4241

Third, pay all bills of $250 and up with a money fund check. This can include your rent or mortgage payments, credit card and auto loan payments, major repairs, insurance, and schooling, among others. And last, be sure to let your fund know that you want your canceled checks back. Some funds hold them in their files unless you request them, and this complicates reconciling your monthly statement.

With this arrangement, not only do you earn a market rate of interest on your idle checking balances, but interest is earned until the checks you write clear your money fund (which can take a week or more). Interest earned on routine checking account balances can be significant for an individual and dramatic for a business.

We can't leave this subject of "parking places" for your emergency fund without looking at our fourth safe haven—U.S. Treasury bills.

When the government issues bonds that have very short maturities, they are called Treasury "bills" (or "T-bills" for short). T-bills are initially sold to investors in three-month, six-month, nine-month, and one-year maturities. The minimum denomination is $1,000. You can buy them when they are newly issued, either directly from the Federal Reserve or through your bank or broker. You can also buy them after they've been issued (in what's called the "secondary" market to distinguish it from newly issued securities that are being purchased directly from the issuer). When you buy your T-bills in the secondary market, you are buying them from another investor who wishes to sell. Your broker serves as the intermediary. Regardless of how you buy them, you can always sell them before maturity through your bank or broker without an interest-rate penalty (although there is a transaction cost).

The greatest advantage of T-bills is their safety and liquidity. Also, the interest earned on T-bills, as with all Treasuries, is exempt from state and local—but

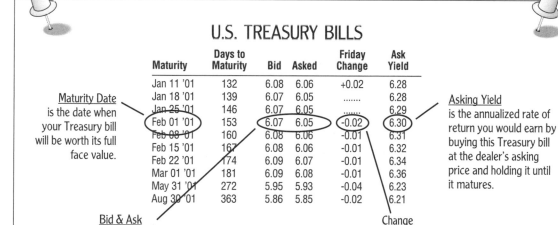

U.S. TREASURY BILLS

Maturity	Days to Maturity	Bid	Asked	Friday Change	Ask Yield
Jan 11 '01	132	6.08	6.06	+0.02	6.28
Jan 18 '01	139	6.07	6.05	....	6.28
Jan 25 '01	146	6.07	6.05	....	6.29
Feb 01 '01	153	6.07	6.05	-0.02	6.30
Feb 08 '01	160	6.08	6.06	-0.01	6.31
Feb 15 '01	167	6.08	6.06	-0.01	6.32
Feb 22 '01	174	6.09	6.07	-0.01	6.34
Mar 01 '01	181	6.09	6.08	-0.01	6.36
May 31 '01	272	5.95	5.93	-0.04	6.23
Aug 30 '01	363	5.86	5.85	-0.02	6.21

<u>Maturity Date</u> is the date when your Treasury bill will be worth its full face value.

<u>Asking Yield</u> is the annualized rate of return you would earn by buying this Treasury bill at the dealer's asking price and holding it until it matures.

<u>Bid & Ask</u> are the prices at which dealers are willing to buy and sell Treasury bills expressed in terms of the bill's yield. Ignore these numbers and focus on the column on the far right.

<u>Change</u> shows how much the yield to investors changed during the previous day of buying and selling. A negative change means that your cost of buying Treasury bills actually rose, leaving you with a lower yield. A positive change means that your cost of buying Treasury bills fell, thereby offering you a better yield.

Investing via "TreasuryDirect"

TreasuryDirect accounts are popular with investors. Here are the steps involved in buying a 13-week T-bill.

• Obtaining the forms. Call the Federal Reserve branch nearest you and request the *Treasury Direct Investor Kit.* As you'll learn, T-bills are sold through an "auction" process. The minimum order is $1,000. They are issued in "book entry form" similar to a savings account.

• Opening your Account. After reviewing the *Investor Kit,* turn to page 10 for detailed instructions on completing the application form.

• Ordering your T-bill. Complete the form, being sure to check the "noncompetitive" box. This means you are willing to accept, sight unseen, the yield that results from the auction process. In other words, you'll accept "the going rate." This assures your order will be filled. If you are unclear on any of the information required, call for clarification. If you want the proceeds from your investment automatically reinvested after thirteen weeks, you can indicate that on the form. You can pay for your T-bill with a certified personal check or cashier's check, or by authorizing the Treasury to debit your bank account. When mailing, "Tender for Treasury Bill" should be printed at the bottom of the envelope.

• Collecting your interest. Unlike bank CDs, T-bills are sold at a discount from their face value (also called par value). For example, it might cost you $986. After thirteen weeks, it would be worth $1,000. The increase of $14 is your interest. At the end of the investment period, the Treasury will direct-deposit your money into your bank account (or reinvest it at the next auction if you prefer).

• Selling before maturity. If you need to sell your securities before they mature, you can mail a form to the Chicago Federal Reserve Bank. They will get three price quotes and accept the highest bid. The cost for this is $34 for each Treasury security sold.

For more information, contact the Federal Reserve Branch nearest you, or visit the TreasuryDirect web site at www.treasurydirect.gov.

not federal—income taxes. The disadvantage is that you can't lock in long-term yields due to their short-term nature.

There is one aspect to T-bills that often confuses the new investor: they are sold in "discount" form. That simply means you buy them at less than their face value, and when they mature you get the full face value. The difference between what you pay and what you get back at maturity is your "interest."

For example, assume you bought a one-year $10,000 T-bill at a 6.00% discount. That means you paid $9,400 ($10,000 face value less the 6% discount of $600). You hold it for one year, during which time you receive no interest. After the year is up, you receive the full $10,000 face value. This means you earned interest of $600. Now, here's the tricky part. Even though your discount was only 6.00%, your actual rate of return was 6.38% (the $600 return you received divided by the $9,400 you actually invested).

Should you buy T-bills directly from the U.S. Treasury or invest in them via a Treasury-only money fund?

Do you want the highest possible yields, or are you willing to sacrifice a little interest in return for convenience? The *easiest way* to buy T-bills is through a money market fund that specializes in investing only in very short-term securities of the U.S. government. T-bills can also be purchased at your broker or local bank for a fee (usually one-half to one percent). However, this convenience comes at a cost—the fund operating expenses and bank fees reduce your net return.

You can *avoid fees and realize better returns* by skipping the middleman and dealing directly with the government. This can be done by opening your own "Treasury Direct" account (see sidebar).

We've reviewed four safe havens—banks, credit unions, money market funds, and T-bills—for the storage of your emergency fund.

For most investors, the best combination of safety, returns and convenience will be found in the top-yielding money market funds.

Now, it's time to go shopping for the best places to invest your accumulation fund, that part of your savings reserve where you're saving for major expenditures that are not provided for in your monthly budget. An accumulation fund allows you to have a longer time frame in mind (say, a year or more before you'll need to withdraw the money). In that event, you can improve your returns by looking at a different set of investment options as we'll do in chapter seven. ◆

CHAPTER PREVIEW

Shopping for Higher Returns in Your Accumulation Fund

I. **As a Level 2 saver, your goal is to steadily build savings reserves that can serve two functions.**

A. As an emergency fund to draw from when unexpected expenses hit (as we discussed in the last chapter).

B. As an accumulation fund for making a large purchase (which is our topic in this chapter).

II. **An accumulation fund allows you to have a longer time frame in mind, anywhere from one to five years before you'll need to withdraw the money. Liquidity is no longer as important, and you can likely improve your returns by looking beyond the options we considered in chapter six.**

III. **In this chapter, we look at four ways to invest your accumulation fund.**

A. Certificates of deposit offer safety and reasonable returns but lack some flexibility due to the early withdrawal penalties. You should be willing to shop nationwide if you want the best rates. Building a "savings ladder" is one way to diversify the interest-rate risk while maintaining a degree of flexibility.

B. If you won't need to cash in for six to twelve months, consider *ultra* short-term bond funds. These funds typically have such low volatility that many consider them reasonable substitutes for money market funds for certain situations. Strong Advantage has been the star of the ultra short-bond group.

C. If you won't need to cash in for two to three years, short-term bond funds offer the potential for better returns at a slight increase in volatility. Data from the past decade indicates that the leading short-term bond funds have a slight performance edge, both in the magnitude of their returns as well as the consistency in which they outperformed Strong Advantage.

D. If you won't need to cash in for four or more years, consider a mortgage-backed bond fund. Ginnie Maes offer attractive yields and pay monthly dividends which you would reinvest in more shares. For periods of four years or more, Vanguard's Ginnie Mae fund outperformed the above options during the 1990s.

Strange as it might seem, as a Level 2 saver you're not *primarily* interested in maximizing your interest income. Rather, your goal is . . .

. . . to steadily build savings reserves that can serve two functions: as an emergency fund to draw from when unexpected expenses hit (as we discussed in the last chapter) and as an accumulation fund for making a large purchase (which is our topic in this chapter).

One of the characteristics of an emergency fund investment is liquidity—the ability to easily and quickly convert it to cash. That's why money market mutual funds are good places to store your emergency fund savings.

An accumulation fund, on the other hand, allows you to have a longer time frame in mind (anywhere from one to five years before you'll need to withdraw the money). Liquidity is no longer as important, and you can likely improve your returns by looking beyond the options we considered in chapter six.

We're going to look at four different ways you can invest your accumulation fund, beginning with an investment . . .

. . . that you're probably already familiar with—certificates of deposit (CDs) at your local bank or credit union. As with other bank offerings, you are lending money to your bank for a fixed rate of interest. Unlike the others, however, you agree not to withdraw your money for a set period of time (the "term" of the CD) anywhere from one month to as long as five years. The longer you commit to leaving your money, the higher interest rate the bank will usually pay you. If you take it out early, however, you forfeit a large part of the interest you would have earned.

When investing in a certificate of deposit, your decision is guided by your interest rate expectations. For example, you would not want to invest in a two-year CD now (that is, tie your money up for two years) if you knew that rates would be rising through the coming year. In that event, you'd invest instead in a three-month CD. When it matured in ninety days, you could then reinvest the proceeds in another three-month CD at the new, higher rate. This is called keeping your maturities "short." Conversely, if you had a reasonable certainty that rates would fall over the next twelve months, you would feel free to lock-in today's higher rates by investing in a two-year CD. This is called "extending" your maturities.

SHOPPING FOR CDS LONG DISTANCE

As you phone around or surf the Web for the best deals in bank CDs, here are some questions to ask.

❑ Are my deposits here insured by the FDIC?

❑ What is the stated rate of interest (the rate before compounding)?

❑ What is the "annual effective yield" (the return after compounding)?

❑ If I don't keep a certain minimum amount on deposit, or if I close my account within a certain period of time, will I be charged a fee?

❑ Will I earn interest from the day of deposit without a hold being placed on my check?

❑ What penalty do you charge for early withdrawal on CDs?

❑ When my CD matures, how much time do I have before you automatically roll it over into a new CD?

❑ Will you notify me first?

The difficulty, of course, lies in knowing what rates will do over the coming year. This dilemma is known as the "interest rate" risk. As I'll explain in chapter 14 ("The Basics of Bonds"), even investing professionals who specialize in studying the economy have poor records of predicting the direction of interest rates. So, should you prepare for rising rates, falling rates, or both?

What you should do depends on your personal goals and needs. If your accumulation fund needs can be met by locking in for a longer term and earning the higher return, then that's probably the thing to do. You trade off the possible opportunity of making a little more in return for the knowledge that the present deal will *assure* that you reach your goal (which is, after all, the primary objective).

Another way to decide is to ask yourself: Which scenario would frustrate me the most—missing the opportunity to lock in a satisfactory rate, or missing the opportunity to make a little more?

If you still can't decide, I would suggest taking the short-term CD. This will give you another chance to make the decision in a few months when either (1) your own circumstances are more clear, or (2) the trend in interest rates seems more settled.

One popular strategy for dealing with interest-rate risk is to build a "savings ladder."

Assuming you find current interest rates generally satisfactory, you might desire to lock them in for the next few years. That's where a strategy of building a "ladder" of staggered maturities can help boost your returns while surrendering only a portion of your liquidity.

Say you have $5,000 to invest. Tell your bank that you want to divide it evenly among CDs with the following maturities (yields shown were available in mid-2000): 6 months (7.15%), 1 year (7.35%), 18 months (7.4%), 2 years (7.5%), and 30 months (7.6%). Each six months when your $1,000 CD comes due, reinvest the proceeds in a new 30-month CD. Eventually, you'll have all your savings earning interest at the higher-paying 30-month CD rate, yet one-fifth of your savings will reach maturity (and be available to you) every six months. You'll still have some flexibility.

Many investors buy CDs from their local bank without shopping around. This can be a costly mistake. Why limit yourself to your local market if the banks there are not offering CDs that are competitive with insured CDs available outside your area? Every month in my *Sound Mind Investing* newsletter, I list some of the top-yielding insured bank CDs around the country. As mentioned in the last chapter, *Barron's* is also a good source for this kind of information. On the front of the "Market Week" section, you'll find a table of contents that will

Best CD Yields
To find the top CD yields online, point your browser to www.bankrate.com, or check the Level 2 page at www.soundmindinvesting.com.

Wire Transfers
are a very quick way to move your money between banks. Your funds travel through the Federal Reserve bank wire system (It generally takes a few hours) and, if done early enough in the day, the receiving bank will give you credit for your money the same day you send it. Check with your bank to find out how early in the day they need to receive your instructions and what they charge for this service.

A SAVINGS LADDER OF CDs

Until Maturity	Interest Rate	6Mos Interest On $1,000	Total Interest
6 Months	7.15%	$35.75	$35.75
12 Months	7.35%	$36.75	$72.50
18 Months	7.40%	$37.00	$109.50
24 Months	7.50%	$37.50	$147.00
30 Months	7.60%	$38.00	$185.00

Average 7.4% Return During First 6 Months

point you to "savings deposit yields." The rates shown are the highest yields reported for various savings-type investments offered by federally insured banks across the country. The categories include money market accounts and CDs of six, twelve, thirty, and sixty months duration. The minimum amount required for each and 800 numbers to call are shown.

When shopping for CDs long distance, be sure to verify that you will earn interest from the day of deposit without a "hold" being placed on your check (see the sidebar on page 80 for a list of other questions you might want to ask). Obtain a pre-assigned account number, and write it on your check along with the inscription "For Deposit Only." Send a cover letter with instructions as well as your daytime phone number.

The remaining investment options we'll look at in this chapter have something in common—they're all bond-oriented mutual funds.

Before going further, however, I need to make sure you understand a little about bonds and how they work in relation to changes in interest rates. We'll get into this in more detail later, so if you find this primer too brief just move on over to chapter 14 ("The Basics of Bonds") for a fuller explanation.

Bonds are like IOUs. They are a promise to repay the amount borrowed at a specified time in the future (called the "maturity date"). Bond funds diversify among a great many individual bond issues, each of which has its own maturity date. Learning the "average" maturity for all the bonds in a portfolio tells you a lot about the risk of investing in that fund.

Now, for purposes of this chapter, here are the most important things you need to know about bond funds: (1) The value of a bond fund moves up or down a little each day the markets are open, depending on changes in the level of expectations for interest rates. (2) When interest rates go *up*, bond values go *down*. (3) When interest rates go *down*, bond values go *up*.

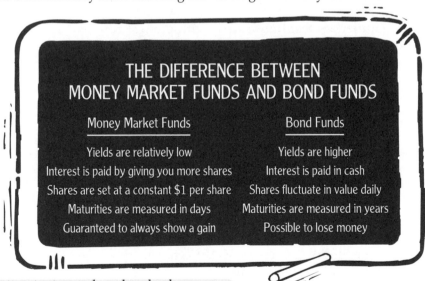

THE DIFFERENCE BETWEEN
MONEY MARKET FUNDS AND BOND FUNDS

Money Market Funds	Bond Funds
Yields are relatively low	Yields are higher
Interest is paid by giving you more shares	Interest is paid in cash
Shares are set at a constant $1 per share	Shares fluctuate in value daily
Maturities are measured in days	Maturities are measured in years
Guaranteed to always show a gain	Possible to lose money

(4) The *longer the average maturity* of the bonds in the portfolio, *the more it will go up or down* in value.
(5) The *shorter the average maturity* of the bonds in the portfolio, *the less it will go up or down* in value.

If you knew that interest rates were going down over the coming six months, you'd want to own a long-term bond portfolio because it will increase in value the most. Conversely, if you knew that interest rates were going up over the coming six months, you'd want to own an ultra short-term bond portfolio because it will decrease in value the least (or not at all).

To better control your risk, you'll want to match your expected holding period (how long you will stay invested in a bond fund before selling your shares) with bond funds of particular maturities. That is the process we'll be looking at during the rest of this chapter.

If you won't need to cash in for six to twelve months, consider *ultra* short-term bond funds.

Bond funds in the ultra short-term category typically have such low volatility that many consider them reasonable substitutes for money market funds for certain situations. The portfolios of these funds cover a wide range of bonds, including Treasuries, mortgage-backed, and various grades of corporates. The theory is that, under most market conditions, the diversification combined with very short maturities will more than compensate for any quality concessions. If all goes well, shareholders will receive returns that are superior to money funds while taking little additional risk.

For example, look at the returns of the Strong Advantage fund (table at right), one of the stars of the ultra short-bond group. It is the largest fund in the group, and ranked number one for the five years ending on 12/31/99. The fund normally invests at least 75% of assets in investment-grade (very high quality) debt securities. However, the key to its performance has been its managers' ability to successfully navigate the lower quality high-yield segment of the bond market where it's allowed to invest up to 25% of assets. Management usually pushes this allocation to the limit, taking on more credit risk than any other fund in this category. The managers have also invested in mild forms of derivatives from time to time.

Strong claims they have adequate safeguards in place, however, and the fund's record to date is testimony to the success of their strategy. The table compares the returns generated by Advantage since its inception with those from Vanguard Prime, one of the consistent performance leaders among money funds. Strong has been the winner in eight of the eleven years. The first exception was 1990, when the high-yield market was hurt by the economic recession. This reflects the fund's vulnerability when the economy slows. The other exceptions were 1994 and 1998, both years when rising interest rates hurt most bond funds badly. Still, it should be noted that Advantage has yet to have a losing year.

The bottom half of the table shows the annualized results for the average 12-, 6-, and 3-month holding periods. Note that even for holding periods as brief as three months, Advantage was generally the better choice. There were only two occasions when shareholders lost money, and the losses were insignificant. Furthermore, by extending the holding period to six months, there were no losing periods. While Strong Advantage does not offer the absolute day-to-day safety of a money market portfolio, it has rewarded investors willing to accept a degree of extra risk.

ANNUAL COMPARISONS STRONG ADVANTAGE VS. VANGUARD PRIME

Year	Strong Advantage Bond Fund	Vanguard Prime Money Market
1989	9.5%	9.4%
1990	6.6%	8.3%
1991	10.6%	6.1%
1992	8.4%	3.7%
1993	8.1%	3.0%
1994	3.6%	4.1%
1995	7.5%	5.8%
1996	6.7%	5.3%
1997	6.5%	5.4%
1998	4.8%	5.4%
1999	5.3%	5.0%
Avg 12 Months	6.9%	5.4%
Best 12 Months	11.5%	9.4%
Worst 12 Months	3.3%	3.0%
Avg 6 Months	7.0%	5.5%
Best 6 Months	12.7%	9.9%
Worst 6 Months	2.2%	2.9%
Avg 3 Months	7.0%	5.6%
Best 3 Months	13.8%	10.1%
Worst 3 Months	-0.8%	2.9%

If you won't need to cash in for two to three years, short-term bond funds are (pardon the pun) a strong alternative to Strong Advantage.

The first table below shows the annualized performance of Strong Advantage over various two-year periods since its inception. For comparison, I also show the results of four leading short-term bond funds. (Don't be thrown off by the misnamed Fidelity fund—its holdings consistently place it in the short-term bond group.) If you study the numbers, you'll find that the short-term bond funds have a slight performance edge, both in the magnitude of their returns as well as the consistency in which they outperformed Strong Advantage.

At the bottom of the table, I've listed the average result, the best result, and the worst result of 109 two-year holding periods between 1989 and 1999. For greater accuracy, these numbers were calculated using "rolling" periods. Market results are usually stated in terms of calendar years. For instance, you might look at the performance numbers for the Strong Short-Term Bond fund and conclude that the worst two-year results during the past 11 years occurred during 1993-94 when the annualized return was 3.6%. But investors don't buy bond funds only at the beginning of the year, so that number is somewhat misleading as to the potential risk. That's where the use of "rolling" periods can be helpful. Here's how I ran the calculations.

After looking at the results from buying on January 1, 1989, and holding for 24 months, I then "rolled" to the next month to see what happened if the fund had been purchased on February 1, 1989 and held for 24 months. Then I moved to March 1 and did the same thing. And so on. Continuing in this way, I computed the results for a total of 109 different 24-month holding periods. This is in contrast to just ten such periods when only calendar years are considered. Using this more exhaustive process provides a somewhat better picture of the degree of volatility and level of returns that can be expected from an investment. In the example above, I found that the worst-case two-year performance for the Strong fund was actually 2.9% (April 1, 1993–March 31, 1995). You'll find that number at the bottom of the table.

Okay, so much for the methodology. What did we learn? We learned that over two-year holding periods,

TWO-YEAR COMPARISONS STRONG ADVANTAGE VS. SHORT-TERM BOND FUNDS

	Strong Advantage Fund	Dreyfus S-T Income	Fidelity Intermediate Bond	Strong S-T Bond	Vanguard S-T Corporate
1989-90	8.1%	new	9.7%	6.7%	10.3%
1990-91	8.6%	new	11.0%	9.8%	11.1%
1991-92	9.5%	new	10.2%	10.6%	10.1%
1992-93	8.3%	new	9.0%	8.0%	7.1%
1993-94	5.8%	4.5%	4.7%	3.6%	3.4%
1994-95	5.5%	5.5%	5.1%	4.9%	6.1%
1995-96	7.1%	8.6%	8.1%	9.3%	8.7%
1996-97	6.6%	7.2%	5.6%	6.9%	5.9%
1997-98	5.6%	6.2%	7.4%	5.9%	6.8%
1998-99	5.0%	5.2%	4.1%	4.6%	4.9%
Avg 24 Mos	7.0%	N/A	7.7%	7.3%	7.5%
Best 24 Mos	9.7%	N/A	12.5%	12.2%	11.9%
Worst 24 Mos	4.9%	N/A	3.5%	2.9%	3.3%

THREE-YEAR COMPARISONS STRONG ADVANTAGE VS. SHORT-TERM BOND FUNDS

	Strong Advantage Fund	Dreyfus S-T Income	Fidelity Intermediate Bond	Strong S-T Bond	Vanguard S-T Corporate
1989-91	8.9%	new	11.3%	9.3%	11.2%
1990-92	8.5%	new	9.3%	8.8%	9.8%
1991-93	9.0%	new	10.8%	10.2%	9.1%
1992-94	6.7%	new	5.2%	4.6%	4.7%
1993-95	6.4%	6.7%	7.4%	6.3%	6.4%
1994-96	5.9%	5.7%	4.6%	5.5%	5.7%
1995-97	6.9%	8.5%	8.0%	8.6%	8.1%
1996-98	6.0%	6.2%	6.2%	6.2%	6.1%
1997-99	5.5%	6.2%	5.2%	5.4%	5.6%
Avg 36 Mos	7.1%	N/A	7.6%	7.3%	7.4%
Best 36 Mos	9.1%	N/A	12.2%	10.7%	11.2%
Worst 36 Mos	5.5%	N/A	3.6%	4.6%	4.7%

odds favor getting a better result from a top-performing short-term bond fund than from Strong Advantage. The average result and best-case results were superior; only the worst case scenario favored Strong. Even then, it was a question of earning a lower return rather than actually losing money. The data from the study of three-year holding periods (bottom table) shows the same pattern.

Why are the short-term funds better for longer holding periods? Reason number one: Bonds with longer maturities (quality considerations being equal) typically pay higher yields. Then why not always buy bonds with longer maturities? Because of reason number two: When interest rates go *up*, bond values go *down*, and the *longer the average maturity* of the bonds in the portfolio, *the more it will go down* in value. So when you extend your maturities, you should expect some occasional setbacks as interest rates fluctuate. Over the course of several months or even a year, you can lose money in a short-term bond fund. But if you hold on for two years, you make back the first year's losses and then some (at least this has been the experience of bond funds since the late 1970s).

To be sure, the data is not conclusive. Many times you would have been better off with Strong Advantage. The historical pattern shows you what the tendencies are, but that's no guarantee they'll hold up during the specific period you invest. In sum, if you want to take the more conservative route, go with Strong Advantage. If you're willing to take a little extra risk in search for a better return *and are committed to at least a two-year holding period*, the short-term bond funds are certainly worth a look.

If you won't need to cash in for four or more years, consider a mortgage-backed bond fund.

You may think your local lender keeps your mortgage payment, but guess again. Most likely the ultimate recipients are shareholders in a special kind of bond fund. Because they invest in fixed-rate mortgages which meet the standards of the Government National Mortgage Association (GNMA), such funds are often called Ginnie Mae funds. Here's how a typical mortgage investing cycle affects the Ginnie Mae investor.

• Let's say your neighbor Jim takes out an FHA or VA insured mortgage. The local bank or savings and loan that made the loan doesn't keep it on its books. Instead, it's combined with others that have similar terms (say thirty-year loans with an 8% rate). When the bank has at least $1 million of these loans, it sells them as a package to big institutional investors. In this way, it makes a quick, small profit and has its money back to go out and make more loans.

• The buyers take the package to the Government National Mortgage Association to be sure it meets certain standards. Then, it is assigned a pool number to show that the timely payment of the interest and principal on every mortgage in the package is guaranteed by the "full faith and credit" of the U.S. government.

The Family Tree of Mortgage-Backed Investments

Fixed-Rate Mortgages are the typical home mortgage, with a set rate for a fifteen or thirty year period. Their most serious drawback is that you never know when they'll mature because homeowners have the right to prepay their mortgages whenever they can find a better deal. Funds that specialize in these have long track records for you to consider.

Collateralized Mortgage Obligations are an attempt to eliminate some of the uncertainty caused by the prepayment risk. They do this by "putting you in line" as to when you receive principal back from mortgage prepayments rather than distributing the prepaid principal proportionately to all the shareholders at once. Don't invest in these unless you thoroughly understand what happens to the CMO's payback rate and yield if rates change by two or three points. And plan to hold them until maturity—they're not designed for easy resale.

Adjustable-Rate Mortgages are the kind where the interest rate is moved up or down periodically to more closely match the rates that are prevailing at that time. Funds that specialize in these are fairly new; it's too soon to see how they'll fare during a period of rising interest rates. I would suggest waiting and watching.

• A mortgage-oriented bond fund, like Vanguard's GNMA fund, buys the pool of mortgages and is thereafter entitled to have the monthly mortgage payments, minus a small servicing and insurance charge, "passed through" to it from the original lenders (the local banks and mortgage companies) who are receiving the homeowners' monthly checks. And what does Vanguard do with the money when they get it? They pay the interest portion out to their shareholders every month and reinvest the principal portion in more pool certificates. If you're a shareholder in the Vanguard fund, you'd end up with a portion of Jim's monthly mortgage payment (which would be taxed to you as ordinary income).

The reward from investing in Ginnie Maes is they offer higher yields than are usually available with money market and short-term bond funds (see table below). For example, since 1985 the average annual return from Vanguard's Ginnie Mae fund was about 9% compared to 6% for the Vanguard Prime Money Market fund. Their biggest drawback is that if interest rates *fall*, the homeowners in the pool will take out new lower-rate mortgages and pay off their old high-rate mortgages. Then, instead of receiving interest from a pool of higher-yielding mortgages for years to come, the Vanguard fund gets its money back all at once and must reinvest it. Of course, by this time rates have fallen and yields are much less attractive. Bummer. This dilemma is called the "prepayment risk." On the other hand, if rates *rise*, the fund is left with a pool of mortgages that pay a below-market rate, and fund shares will fall in value to compensate (just like other bond funds do). Holding the fund for at least four years goes a long way to offsetting this risk.

This is illustrated in the table. I've taken three funds from Vanguard—their Prime Money Market fund, Short-Term Corporate Bond fund, and GNMA fund—and compared their performance over various holding periods during the past 15 years. You can see that, on average, the GNMA fund is the consistent winner. However, because safety is vital for the money in your accumulation fund, you have to look at worst-case scenarios. Study the bottom row of data. If you don't want to commit to holding your investment longer than one year, then the Prime Money Market Fund is the best choice. The worst return for any twelve month period between 1985-1999 for the money fund was 3.0%. Due to short-term volatility, the other two funds had occasions where they lost money over one-year holding periods.

When you stretch your time horizon out to two or three years, you see that the short-term bond fund offers the better combination of risk and reward. But for investors willing to stay the course for four or five years, the Ginnie Mae fund looks to be the best—even at its worst, it still outperformed the other two options. For Level 2 savers who won't be needing their accumulation fund for several years and are comfortable with a degree of volatility, Ginnie Maes are worth considering. ◆

GNMA BONDS BECOME THE WORST-CASE WINNERS AFTER FOUR YEARS

Data Based On Rolling Periods 1985-1999	1 Year Prime MMF	1 Year ShrtTrm Bond	1 Year GNMA Bond	2 Years Prime MMF	2 Years ShrtTrm Bond	2 Years GNMA Bond	3 Years Prime MMF	3 Years ShrtTrm Bond	3 Years GNMA Bond	4 Years Prime MMF	4 Years ShrtTrm Bond	4 Years GNMA Bond	5 Years Prime MMF	5 Years ShrtTrm Bond	5 Years GNMA Bond
Avg Return	6.0%	7.9%	9.0%	6.0%	7.8%	8.9%	6.0%	7.8%	8.9%	5.9%	7.8%	8.9%	5.9%	7.9%	9.0%
Best Return	9.4%	17.3%	23.8%	8.9%	13.6%	17.5%	8.4%	11.2%	13.9%	8.1%	10.7%	13.0%	7.7%	10.3%	12.7%
Worst Return	3.0%	-0.1%	(-1.5%)	3.2%	3.3%	(2.4%)	3.6%	4.7%	(3.9%)	4.1%	5.4%	(5.6%)	4.4%	5.8%	(6.7%)

CHAPTER PREVIEW

Preparing for College

I.   **Planning for college is a subject of almost universal concern, but won't be overwhelming if you start early enough as well as let your children know that paying for college is their responsibility as well as yours.**

II. **When investing your college fund, you have two key decisions to make.**

   A.   The first one is what kind of account do you want to set up? The type of account you select primarily determines two things—who owns the account, and what the tax liability will be for any profits. Popular options include:

      1.   A Uniform Gifts to Minors Act (UGMA) account.

      2.   An Education IRA account.

      3.   State-Sponsored Prepaid Tuition Plans.

      4.   State-Sponsored College Savings Plans.

   B.   The second key decision is how you should invest the money you put into that account. Investments often recommended when planning for college:

      1.   Insurance policies and annuities. Insurance policies and annuities traditionally have been sold as education funding vehicles.

      2.   Fixed income investments. Often utilized for college planning are certificates of deposit, Series EE bonds, and zero coupon bonds.

      3.   No-load stock mutual funds. They're simple to invest in and the return, historically, has exceeded the rate of inflation and the rate of rising college tuition costs.

III. **State-sponsored college savings plans are quickly becoming the savings vehicle of choice for many parents and grandparents. In them, your money is invested in a diversified portfolio of stocks and fixed income securities.**

   A.   Shop around. The key factors are the quality of the investment managers, number of asset allocation choices, and the level of management fees.

   B.   Look closely at your asset allocation options. Portfolios start out being pretty aggressive when the child is a toddler but are automatically changed in the direction of less risk as the years pass. Make sure the allocation options fit with your desires as to how aggressive you wish to be.

   C.   Consider the fees. They can vary by more than 1% annually, and make a big difference over many years.

Thanks to Scott Houser, my long-time friend and a partner with Ronald Blue & Co. for his contributions to this chapter.

Investing for a college education may be one of the most written about subjects on the planet.

Generally speaking, married couples have kids. And all parents, almost from day one, worry about paying for their child's college education. The Gallup organization has reported that 86% of Americans believe that a college education will be beyond the reach of most families in the future. It's a subject of almost universal concern.

Since 1980, as measured by the consumer price index, college costs have grown 2-2½ times faster than inflation. Estimates of $150,000-$200,000 are tossed out as the total cost package for getting one child through a good school. Some people may pay that amount, but most can't and you don't have to, either. What follows are some practical tips on tackling what can easily be the single largest expense item of your life.

COLLEGE COST CALCULATOR

Years Until College	Monthly Investment Per $1,000	Expected 4 Year Cost After Aid	Monthly Investment Needed
3	$24.90	$36,379	$906
4	18.01	37,834	681
5	13.89	39,348	547
6	11.15	40,922	456
7	9.21	42,559	392
8	7.76	44,261	343
9	6.64	46,031	306
10	5.75	47,873	276
11	5.02	49,788	250
12	4.43	51,779	229
13	3.93	53,850	212
14	3.50	56,004	196
15	3.14	58,244	183
16	2.82	60,574	171
17	2.55	62,997	161
18	2.31	65,517	151

Footnotes: The second column shows the amount of investment needed each month in order to accumulate $1,000 over the period of time shown assuming an annual return of 7% net after taxes. Example: A monthly investment of $13.89 will grow to $1,000 over five years. The source for expected four-year college costs (tuition, fees, books, room and board, transportation, and other) is The College Board's estimate of the national average cost for living on campus at a four-year public school. The third column shows the four-year net cost assuming total costs increase at the rate of 4% per year and that financial aid will cover 30% of the total cost. The final column shows the amount needed to fund that portion of the expected four-year cost which is not covered by financial aid. Example: For a child who will be entering college in ten years, a regular monthly investment of $276 would grow to approximately $47,873 during that time. Private colleges (not shown) cost more than twice as much as public ones.

Get started now.

On the investing side, you want to start early because the amount of time you have available to let the principle of compound interest work for you makes a huge difference in your eventual investment results.

The "College Cost Calculator" dramatically illustrates the importance of getting an early start. For example, if you have 14 years before your youngster goes off to college, you only need to set aside $196 per month in order to build a college fund of about $56,000. This assumes a 7% net return (as explained in the footnotes). That $56,000 is expected to represent about 70% of the amount that will be needed to pay for four years of college at a public school; it's assumed your child will be responsible for the other 30% (see next page).

On the other hand, if you get off to a late start the situation changes on two fronts. The good news is that inflation will not have as much time to increase the cost of education, so you won't need to raise as much money. The bad news is that your opportunity for compounding is also diminished. Say you have just six years remaining until college days arrive for your youngster. You'll need to invest $456 every month in order to accumulate the almost $41,000 you'll need for the parents' 70% share.

Of course, as with any set of projections, there are several general assumptions built into the data that will ultimately miss the mark. But they are useful for their shock value and getting your attention.

The earlier you begin, the more risk you can take. This means selecting an aggressive portfolio that is 100% stocks and adding short-term bonds or money markets as you get closer to the time when you'll need the money. The state-sponsored savings plans we'll be talking about later automate this process for you.

Let your kids know that paying for college is their responsibility as well as yours.

It's no longer assumed that parents pay the full costs of their children's college education. According to the American Council on Education, parents and students now combine to pay a little under 60% of college costs; student aid, either from the school itself or from the taxpayers, pays the remaining 40%. The "College Cost Calculator" assumes a more conservative 30% level of assistance. For this reason, it's imperative that parents and students understand the ins and outs of financial aid (see page 95).

Spending for college is no different than any other purchasing decision. Some of us cannot afford the most expensive car in the showroom and some of us cannot afford to foot the bill for an expensive college education. Let your children know how much you will try to contribute toward their college education. If they can find a school for that amount of money, great. If not, it's up to their savings, summer jobs, scholarships, financial aid, and student loans to make up the difference.

To get them started thinking along these lines, it helps to open a college savings account when they're very young. Some families are able to begin when the child is born with cash gifts received from grandparents. It doesn't have to be a large amount, but opening the account early makes a statement that this is an important expense that must be planned for. Over the years, the account can be added to with checks received for birthdays, earnings from yard work, baby-sitting, etc.

Compounding is a wonderful tool. If you invest just $1,000 in an growth-oriented mutual fund earning 10% annually, that sum will grow to $5,560 in eighteen years—more than five times your money. Not bad. Not many of us can save the entire amount of our children's college education, but all of us can save more than we think we can if we start early and add periodically. Even having $5,560 in your pocket builds confidence when staring at the college-costs mountain.

When it comes to investing your college fund, you have two key decisions to make. The first one is what kind of account . . .

. . . do you want to set up? This is a separate issue from how you should invest the money you put into the account (which we'll get to shortly). The investment account is set up to serve as a repository for the securities you invest in. The type of account you select primarily determines two things—who owns the account, and what the tax liability will be for any profits.

The natural inclination of most parents is to retain ownership of the savings

Websites to Help with Your College Planning
www.savingforcollege.com
www.collegesavings.org
www.smartmoney.com/ac/collegeplanning/
www.kiplinger.com/managing/college

For Updated Information
The Internet is constantly changing, and the above sites may have moved or ceased operations by the time you read this. For an up-to-date list of the better online resources related to college planning, visit the SMI website at www.soundmindinvesting.com .

being set aside. Not only are many parents reluctant to simply turn property over to an immature or spendthrift child, there's also the desire to have the flexibility to use it for something else if an unexpected need arises. A drawback, however, is that the college funds are vulnerable to creditors. If the investments are owned in your name and you are successfully sued for any reason, the courts can reach the assets to satisfy any claims against you. This is of more practical importance to professionals such as doctors and accountants.

Unless your annual taxable income (for those married, filing jointly) exceeds $40,100, there's no tax reason to give up ownership—you're paying the lowest rate of 15% on investment income already. However, between $40,100 and $96,900 your marginal rate rises to 28%. When you're in this bracket it can pay to look for ways to move the tax rate on the kids' investments back down to the 15% level. There are several ways to do this, each offering its own collections of advantages and trade-offs—generally in the area of either taxability or investment flexibility.

• **A Uniform Gifts to Minors Act (UGMA) account.** This kind of account, called a Uniform Transfers to Minors Act (UTMA) account in some states, essentially gives the money to the child outright. The parent, however, does retain control of the assets until the child reaches the age of majority (18 or 21, depending on the state). All that needs to be done for paperwork purposes is to have the investment registered as: "Mr. John Doe as

WHICH KIND OF ACCOUNT IS BEST FOR YOUR FAMILY?

	UGMA/UTMA Custodian Account	Tax-deductible Education IRA	State-sponsored Prepaid Tuition Plan	State-sponsored Investing Plan
Who will own the assets in this kind of account?	The child, although parent controls until child reaches legal age.	The parent or legal guardian.	The donor who sets up the account.	The donor who sets up the account.
Who can set up such an account?	Anyone.	Single tax filers with Adjusted Gross Income $95K-$110K. Joint filers $150K-$160K.	Anyone.	Anyone.
How much can you put in each year?	As much as you want. Children can receive up to $10K per year from each person free of Federal gift taxes.	$500 limit per child under 18 years old.	Varies by state. $50,000 maximum may apply.	As much as you want up to a maximum $50,000 lump sum per donor per child per year.
How are the earnings taxed?	• For children under 14, the first $700 is tax-free; the next $700 is taxed at 15%. Gains above $1400 are taxed at the parents' rate. • For children 14 and older, gains are taxed at the child's rate, usually 15%. For investments held 5 years, maximum tax is 8%.	Earnings grow and distributions are made free of federal income taxes provided that the assets are eventually used for qualified college-related expenses. State income tax treatment varies.	With respect to federal taxes, the difference between the amount contributed and the benefit eventually received is taxed to the student as ordinary income in the year the benefit is received. State income tax treatment varies.	With respect to federal taxes, earnings grow tax-deferred until used for qualified college-related expenses. They are then taxed to the student as ordinary income in the year the distribution is made. State income tax treatment varies.
How must the money be spent?	No restrictions on how the money can be spent as long as for the benefit of the student.	Must be used for specified college-related expenses before the student reaches 30.	Must be used for specified college-related expenses at participating institutions within the state.	Must be used for specified college-related expenses at participating institutions anywhere in the U.S.
What is the penalty for not following through and using the funds as you originally planned?	None.	If funds are not used as required, income taxes are generally due on the total assets as well as a 10% penalty on the earnings.	Varies by state. Typically receive original principal plus small return on which tax is due. Penalties may apply.	If funds are not used as required, income taxes plus a 10% penalty are due on the earnings (unless student receives scholarship, dies, or becomes disabled).

custodian under the Uniform Gifts to Minors Act." (If you have a number of children to whom you wish to give money, you will need to have a separate account for each child.) It's so commonplace that virtually all banks and mutual funds should be able to help you set one up. Once money is put into this account, the parent has *permanently* given up ownership.

Gains in an UGMA account are taxed at the parent's tax rate for children under 14. For children 14 and over, they are taxed at the child's rate. Practically speaking, for most middle income savers, the actual tax paid is minimal for UGMA investments. UGMA accounts have fallen a bit out of favor, but many financial planners still like them because of their flexibility. The eventual use of the funds in the account is not restricted to paying for a college education, and can be used to pay a wide variety of child-related expenses (for example, summer camp). One drawback for those who expect to apply for financial aid: Money held in your child's name counts more heavily than money held in the parent's name. The result could be less financial aid.

• **An Education IRA account.** In 1997, Congress created a new tax favored vehicle, the Education IRA (EdIRA). Parents who qualify (e.g., those filing jointly who have an adjusted gross income below $150,000) may contribute up to $500 per child, per year, to an EdIRA. The contribution is not deductible, but all earnings in the EdIRA grow tax-deferred. $500 per year may not seem like much, but it adds up if you start early. Contributing $500 per year into an EdIRA for 18 years with an earnings rate of 10% would accumulate to almost $23,000. Earnings on this contribution will be distributed tax free provided that the distributions are used to pay the beneficiary's college education expenses.

As with any IRA account, the use of these funds is restricted for certain purposes. For example, no contribution to an EdIRA can be made during any tax year in which contributions are made to a qualified state tuition program on behalf of the same beneficiary. I could go on with other restrictions, but if a $500 per year investment sounds like it would fit with the other financial needs of your family, learn more about EdIRAs.

• **State-Sponsored Prepaid Tuition Plans.** In general, prepaid state tuition plans promise that your investment in the plan will cover tuition at any school in the state no matter what the cost at the time your child enrolls. Consider this recent example from Florida's College Prepaid Program: For the enrollment period that just ended, a lump sum payment for a child in the fourth grade of $8,226 would cover all of the child's future tuition and fees for four years at a state university—guaranteed. The price is locked in regardless of future increases in state tuition.

I can remember several years ago when these plans were introduced, the jury was still out on whether they were a good deal or not. In general, time has proven these investments to be sound for those parents who wanted a no-risk alternative to pay for a college education. These plans actually have more flexibility than is readily apparent. If Junior decides to break a five generation tradition and forsake Home State U. (gasp!) in favor of its arch rival in the state next door, generally the amount contributed to the plan and all or some of the earnings will be refunded to the parents.

• **State-Sponsored College Savings Plans.** These plans are quickly becoming the savings vehicle of choice for many parents and grandparents. Here is an

Investing in A UGMA Account

The leading no-load fund companies offer college investing programs that are easy to establish and monitor, including UGMA accounts.

Most offer step-by-step worksheets that will help you estimate educational expenses and establish a strategy for meeting those needs. They'll waive their usual minimums if an automatic monthly investment of $50-$100 is chosen (electing this option is a great way to exercise self-discipline).

This strategy of investing the same dollar amount every month, regardless of market conditions, is called dollar-cost-averaging (DCA). It's a very popular way to invest in no-load growth mutual funds.

DCA mechanically guides your investing so you acquire more shares when they are more attractively priced. You don't have to worry about timing. (I'll discuss DCA in detail in chapter 19.) Plus, it allows you to begin with small amounts. This helps you to begin sooner rather than later so you can take greater advantage of the principle of compound interest.

introductory primer prepared for my *Sound Mind Investing* newsletter by William B. Ertel, CPA, CMFC, and a financial planner in the Charlotte, North Carolina office of Ronald Blue & Co.

What is a QSTP? A QSTP is a tax-advantaged way to save for college, graduate school, or other forms of higher education. QSTPs are established by individual states to conform to code section 529 but no two plans are identical. The most attractive plans are open to any U.S. resident (rather than just residents of their state) and offer a diversified investment strategy.

Which state plan is best? The best plan for you depends on your individual circumstances. Contact states individually or ask your financial advisor for assistance. Investment options and application information can be researched at www.collegesavings.org, the website of the College Savings Plan Network. Because of the possible state tax benefits, research your home state's plan first.

Who can participate? Any U.S. citizen may participate. There are no annual income limitations for this plan. An adult, usually a parent or grandparent, establishes a QSTP account for a child. There are no age limitations for the child beneficiary. The child must have a Social Security number. Accounts can be opened with an initial deposit or by establishing an automatic draft from a checking account.

Investment options? Code section 529 prohibits the parent from actually controlling the investments. Several state plans are managed by mutual fund companies (see page 96) and offer varying investment mixes based on the child's age. Some states offer only very conservative investment options.

Does the child have to attend a state school? No. The student can use the assets for any accredited post-secondary institution in the U.S. If a child earns a scholarship, the parent can receive distributions, to the extent of the scholarship, without a penalty. If the child does not attend a qualifying school, the parent can transfer the account to another child or withdraw the assets and pay taxes and a 10% withdrawal penalty. Many transfers can occur without any tax consequences.

What are the federal tax advantages? There are two main advantages. First, assets grow free of federal income taxes. Secondly, money distributed from the QSTP is taxed to the student as ordinary income *at the student's tax rate* in the year of distribution. Naturally, not all of the distribution is taxable—some of the distribution will be return of the original principal with the balance as investment earnings. A parent in a high tax bracket can allow investment savings for a student to be taxed deferred and eventually taxed in the student's lower bracket.

What about state tax savings? Many state plans offer generous state tax deductions for contributions made by residents in their own state.

What are contribution limits? Many plans allow annual contributions per child up to $10,000. However, a special tax provision allows nontaxable contributions of $50,000 to be treated as five consecutive annual contributions. A parent or grandparent can make this contribution, but many plans permit only one

---

Series EE Savings Bonds

These bonds are sold through most banks and come in many denominations. The purchase price is one-half of the face amount, so a $50 bond can be purchased for $25 and, if held long enough, will grow to be worth its face value of $50. This doubling in value is, in effect, your interest. The length of time it will take to double depends on how interest rates behave during the life of the bond.

Some of the advantages of Series EE bonds include:

• Safety
They're backed by the full faith and credit of the U.S. government.

• Tax advantages
The interest is exempt from state and local taxes, and the federal taxes aren't payable until you cash them in.

• Saving for college
If you buy them and later cash them in to pay for college tuition, you may owe no taxes on the interest you earned. They carry a federal tax exclusion which, for families meeting certain income limits and other conditions, makes the interest tax-free.

• Discipline
They are most commonly purchased through payroll deduction savings plans, so you can impose discipline on yourself by automating your savings.

(continued >)

contributor per child. Contributions, however, cannot be made to an Education IRA *and* a QSTP on behalf of the same child in the same year, regardless of who makes the contribution. Accordingly, a QSTP should be considered by parents or grandparents who are ineligible for Education IRAs due to income limitations or who have the ability to contribute more than the current Education IRA limitations.

Why is this so attractive? A major drawback of Education trusts and custodial accounts is that overfunding these vehicles could result in a child controlling a substantial amount of money at a young age. A QSTP allows the contributor, not the student, to retain the assets if they go unspent for qualifying educational costs. While taxes and a 10% penalty would result from an unqualified distribution, the risk of the child receiving too much money too quickly is eliminated. Any balance left over after education can provide a young adult or college graduate some financial assistance to get started with a career or family and can be a great way for parents to continue to teach and instruct their children on the proper uses of money.

The QSTP may not only be a valuable vehicle to help you provide for the costs of a college education but also to protect your children from receiving too much money before they are spiritually and socially equipped to responsibly manage it.

Now for the second key decision. After selecting the kind of account you want to set up, it's time to decide how you should invest the money you put into that account.

Let's look at the various types of investments often recommended as good ways to invest the money set aside when planning for college.

• **Insurance policies and annuities.** Insurance policies and annuities traditionally have been sold as education funding vehicles. However, with the advent of the many tax-advantaged accounts discussed in this article, life insurance and annuities are not, in my view, an efficient education funding solution.

• **Fixed income investments.** Generally, fixed income investments take a principal sum that is on deposit, pay a fixed rate of interest, and if held to maturity, avoid any risk of loss of principal. Fixed income investments often utilized for college planning include certificates of deposit, Series EE bonds, zero coupon bonds, and two relatively new types of bonds—I Bonds and Treasury Inflation Protected Securities (see sidebar on page 162). Their primary advantage is the safety of principal they offer, but their obvious drawback is they limit your upside growth. Generally, fixed income investments should be used only if you (1) cannot stand any stock market risk, or (2) have a child who is almost college age and you wish to guarantee the safety of your principal for the next year or two until it will be needed for college expenses.

(continued from page 92)

On the other hand, Series EE bonds have these drawbacks

• Relatively low return
The return on Series EE bonds rise and fall along with the yields on five-year Treasuries. Since U.S. government securities are considered to be among the safest of investments, the returns they offer are among the lowest.

• Limitations on tax exclusion
The tax exclusion starts to phase out when the family's adjusted gross income, modified to include Social Security and other retirement income, exceeds $81,100 or $54,100 for single filers (indexed for inflation). The income test is applied when you cash them in, not when you buy them. If your income outpaces inflation over years of saving and investing, you could end up going over the income limit and facing an unexpected tax bill.

• Limitations on college expenditures
To be tax-free, the interest proceeds can only be used for tuition and related expenses (e.g., books and lab fees). This excludes using them for room and board, two of the major cost components. As a result, scholarships and grants that lower these expenses can reduce or eliminate the tax-free nature of your bonds' interest. Also, should your child decide to skip college, the interest is fully subject to federal taxes.

If you're thinking of using Series EE savings bonds for college, or even if you're considering cashing in bonds bought previously, be sure to pick up the buyer's guide available at most banks. It will explain in detail the strict rules that apply.

• **No-load stock mutual funds**. My favorite investment vehicle for the average family. Why? Because, they're simple to invest in and the return on no-load stock funds historically has exceeded the rate of inflation and the rate of rising college tuition costs. You do not have to be an investment expert to know that those who have invested in the stock market have received historically high returns during the '80s and '90s. Investing $100 per month in a stock fund for 18 years at an annual rate of return of 12% would yield a college savings fund of $76,543. That same $100 per month invested in a fixed income investment yielding 6% would equal $38,929. (Both examples assume taxes are deferred.) Over the long haul, it pays to take a little risk.

This brings us back to the state-sponsored savings plans (pages 91-93). In them, your money is invested . . .

. . . in a diversified portfolio of stocks and fixed income securities. To familiarize you with how they work, let's look for a moment at the plans offered by New Hampshire and Iowa. For their investment managers, they use the services of Fidelity and Vanguard respectively, two of the country's leading mutual fund organizations.

It's the nature of these plans that, even though it's your money going into the plan, you forfeit any right to make investment decisions. This is part of the federal law that gives these plans their tax-advantages. Typically, you can expect the state to set up guidelines so that the investment mix is automatically changed in the direction of less risk as you move toward your child's college years (Utah being an exception).

LOWERING YOUR RISK
AS YOUR CHILD ADVANCES
TOWARD COLLEGE AGE

	New Hampshire (Fidelity)		Iowa (Vanguard)	
Age	Stocks	Fixed	Stocks	Fixed
0	88%	12%	80%	20%
1	88%	12%	80%	20%
2	88%	12%	80%	20%
3	88%	12%	80%	20%
4	85%	15%	80%	20%
5	85%	15%	80%	20%
6	85%	15%	60%	40%
7	73%	27%	60%	40%
8	73%	27%	60%	40%
9	73%	27%	60%	40%
10	63%	33%	60%	40%
11	63%	33%	40%	60%
12	63%	33%	40%	60%
13	50%	50%	40%	60%
14	50%	50%	40%	60%
15	50%	50%	40%	60%
16	25%	75%	20%	80%
17	25%	75%	20%	80%
18	20%	80%	20%	80%

• **New Hampshire/Fidelity.** To manage risk, the Fidelity plan is composed of seven portfolios made up of Fidelity stock, bond and money market funds. Each portfolio is designed for a specific age, ranging from an 88% commitment to stocks for children three years and younger to just 20% in stocks for those in college (see table at left). Upon enrollment in the plan, your child is automatically assigned to one of the seven portfolios based on date of birth. As your child ages, Fidelity automatically exchanges your units in one portfolio for units of equal value in the next age-appropriate portfolio. Investors who sign up to make automatic payments directly from their bank accounts can open an account with a minimum initial investment of $50 a month or $150 per quarter. Otherwise, there is an initial minimum investment requirement of $1000. There are no sales loads imposed on your purchases.

• **Iowa/Vanguard.** The Vanguard plan is similar in its investment features, but uses fewer portfolios —the four Vanguard LifeStrategy funds (see page 205). As the table shows, the Vanguard plan is somewhat more conservative in its allocations, automatically moving to lower stock allocations at earlier ages. Whether this is good or bad depends on your view of the markets and risk-taking. Accounts can be opened with a minimum initial investment of $50 a month. As with the Fidelity plan, this is a no-load product.

Congress put the states in charge, and each one is doing its own thing—creating different rules for who can participate, how much can be put in, how the money will be invested, and so on. Eventually there will be 50 different plans, creating a lot of confusion for parents as to where they should

A SOUND MIND BRIEFING

Plan Now: College with Little or No Debt Is Possible

by Robert Frank

Approximately 60% of all students from four-year colleges graduate with significant debt. Depending upon the college or university, the average debt for those students currently ranges from $10,000 to $22,463, according to a 1999 study published in the *U.S. News & World Report*. Overall, the average debt nationwide was about $15,000.

Imagine starting your career or marriage $15,000 in the hole ($30,000 if both of you were recent graduates), not including credit card debt. Minimizing college debt requires planning, work and, hopefully, a number of grants and scholarships.

About 74% of all financial aid available in the United States comes from federal or state grants and loans. The vast majority of that money is awarded based on "financial need" and is doled out in many cases on a first-come first-served basis. The primary tool nearly all colleges and universities use to measure a student's financial need is the Free Application for Federal Student Aid (FAFSA). Don't let the name throw you, this form is used by both private and public institutions.

1. January is the best time to apply for college grants/scholarships. FAFSA forms are accepted beginning January 2 for the following fall quarter. Virtually all financial aid officers will advise you to get your FAFSA form in as close to New Year's Day as possible. Even if you don't expect to qualify for a government grant, you should submit a FAFSA form as early in the year as possible. There are three major reasons why:

• Most colleges have private scholarships, grants and work-study awards available, but they want to stretch that money as far as they can. Consequently, they often won't consider you for financial aid until they know you have already tried to land a government grant and how much you will receive. Scholarship recipients are usually selected early in the year. So in order to have a clean shot at that money, you must submit your FAFSA early.

• The lion's share of financial aid money for the following academic year is committed during the "first round" of applications. The deadline for first round applications varies from college to college, but usually falls somewhere between March 15–April 30. If you miss that deadline, the reality is you miss your chance at nabbing a nice catch from the largest pool of money available for that year. From there on, you're trolling for leftovers.

• If you submit your application early and there is an error of some kind in it, your application is sent back and you are temporarily kicked out of the process. If you apply early as I'm suggesting, chances are you'll have time to make any needed corrections, resubmit the application and still qualify for the first round of money.

2. Know the game rules. Before you fill out your FAFSA, you need to understand how the game is played. The basic primer is a free, 54-page government pamphlet called The Student Guide. You can get a copy through most college financial aid offices, or by calling 800-433-3243.

Two highly rated books providing strategies for obtaining funding are Don't Miss Out: The Ambitious Student's Guide to Financial Aid, by Robert and Anna Leider, and Financing College, by Kristin Davis. Read these and you'll know more about financial aid than 90% of the public. If you plan to mine the Internet, save yourself days of fruitless surfing with College.edu. This book is an inexpensive road map to scores of valuable sites.

3. Need doesn't mean needy. Government grants are based primarily on financial need, as opposed to merit. However, don't confuse the term "need" with "needy." The amount of money a person can receive is determined by the income and assets of the student (and his or her family, if the student is a dependent). Other items taken into account include the number of family members, how many dependents are attending college, and how much tuition and fees are. Generally speaking, the lower your assets and income, the more financial aid you may receive.

Even if your family income exceeds $50,000 per year, don't give up, especially if you are applying to a private college. Most private colleges have substantial scholarship funds available, and they are using them more and more to discount their higher tuition sticker price and attract middle- and upper-middle-income families. For example, 93% of this year's freshmen at DePauw University in Indiana, received merit scholarships averaging $7,965.

4. Where your assets are invested can affect your results. Where you have your money invested can make a major difference in your EFC— the amount colleges expect the family to pay based on your FAFSA. The FAFSA form considers income and assets in the form of cash, dividends, savings, checking, certificates of deposit (CDs), stocks, real estate investments (excluding your house) and other forms of taxable and nontaxable income. The form does not consider home equity or money already invested in Keogh, IRA, 401(k) and 403(b) plans. Here's one idea that will potentially enhance your results. If you need to buy a computer or car or other necessary item before your student begins college, it may be best to buy them before January 1 of the year you file your FAFSA. By lowering your reportable assets, the proportion of college costs expected to be paid by the family (your EFC level) will also be reduced.

So, advance planning can make a big difference in the amount of assets you must claim and how much funding you can receive. In fact, it is best to begin this planning at least one or two years early.

As you consider financial strategies, the question of ethics often arises. Government rules are relatively clear and there are many things you can do "legally." The more important question is what would the Lord have you do? (Proverbs 3:5-6 and 16:2). Obviously, it is more important to maintain your integrity and provide a godly witness than to save a few dollars.

set up their program. Here are my suggestions as to which factors are most important.

• **Shop around.** Look beyond your state's borders. Most state plans offer state tax deductions for contributions made by their residents, and this often convinces parents to look no further. But other factors, such as the quality of the investment managers, number of asset allocation choices, and the level of management fees, can quickly outweigh the value of a state tax deduction. The table below shows 12 of the 21 states (as of October 2000) which have no residency requirements—they've opened the door to all comers. Others will be joining the list as time goes on, but there's no need to wait. Use this list as your starting point, or check www.savingforcollege.com for the current list.

• **Look closely at your asset allocation options.** Most plans have been designed to run on autopilot with portfolios that start out being pretty aggressive when the child is a toddler but are automatically changed in the direction of less risk as the years pass. This helps assure the needed cash will be available as your student enters college. Make sure the allocation options fit with your desires as to how aggressive you wish to be.

COLLEGE SAVINGS PLANS OPEN TO INVESTORS NATIONWIDE
SOURCE: WWW.SAVINGFORCOLLEGE.COM

State	Investment Manager	Portfolio Options	Minimum Contribution	Phone	www.
Arkansas	Merrill Lynch	9	$50/month	877-442-6553	thegiftplan.com
California	TIAA-CREF	10	$25/month	877-728-4338	scholarshare.com
Colorado	SalomonSmithBarney	7	$50/month	888-572-4652	scholars-choice.com
Connecticut	TIAA-CREF	10	$25/month	888-799-2438	aboutchet.com
Delaware	Fidelity	7	$50/month	800-544-1655	fidelity.com/delaware
Iowa	Vanguard	4	$25/month	888-446-6696	collegesavingsiowa.com
Maine	Merrill Lynch	9	$50/month	877-463-9843	nextgenplan.com
Massachusetts	Fidelity	7	$50/month	800-544-2776	mefa.org
Missouri	TIAA-CREF	10	$25/month	888-414-6678	missourimost.org
New Hampshire	Fidelity	7	$50/month	800-544-1722	fidelity.com/unique
New York	TIAA-CREF	10	$25/month	877-697-2837	nysaves.com
Virginia	State of Virginia	7	$25/month	888-567-0540	vpep.state.va.us

• **Consider the fees.** Just as with a mutual fund, there are ongoing operating expenses charged to your account. These fees can vary by more than 1% annually, and make a big difference over many years.

All things considered, I'd begin my search by checking out the websites of the TIAA-CREF and Fidelity plans. These firms offer proven investment managers, an adequate number of portfolio options, and reasonable fees.

We've covered a lot of ground in this chapter . . .

. . . and much of it is technical and may be new to you. The decisions you make—what kind of account to open and which investments to put into that account—involve trade-offs between control, flexibility, and tax advantages. Only you can decide which features are of greatest importance to your family.

Don't spend so much of your time trying to figure out the *very* best option that you postpone making a decision. Get informed (I've given you a start), pray for wisdom and discernment (and continue doing so until you have a peace about your decision), and get started! Then, keep your eyes and ears open—Congress is expected to continue "fine-tuning" the rules so that more families are encouraged to save and invest for their childrens' college education. ◆

SECTION

3

THE THIRD LEVEL OF FINANCIAL FITNESS

Investing Your Surplus

Jesus went on to tell them a parable, because...the people thought that the kingdom of God was going to appear at once. He said: "A man of noble birth went to a distant country to have himself appointed king and then to return. So he called ten of his servants... 'Put this money to work,' he said, 'until I come back.' "

Luke 19:11-13

"Hey, isn't that the guy the boss hired
to manage our new high-tech stock fund?"

What Investing Is and Why It's Actually Quite Simple

I. Investing occurs when you put your money to work in a commercial undertaking subject to modest levels of risk. You expect a reasonable return over time.

    A. It is not the same as speculation, which also puts your money to work in a commercial undertaking but involves a very high level of risk. Speculation offers the possibility of a very large return in a relatively brief period of time.

    B. It is not the same as gambling, which subjects your money to a very high level of risk in an attempt to profit from the outcome of a contest or game of chance. With gambling, there's a possibility of an unusually large return in an exceptionally brief period of time.

II. Investing is simple because you have only two basic choices.

    A. There are investments where you become a lender.

        1. These are generally the lower-risk kind. The primary risk to watch out for is that you might get locked in to a poor rate of return for many years, so the financial strength of the borrower is of great importance.

        2. The most common borrowers include (1) banks and savings and loans, (2) local, state, and federal governments, (3) large corporations, and (4) insurance companies.

    B. There are investments where you become an owner.

        1. These are generally the higher-risk kind. The primary risk here is that the value of what you own could fall, so the economic outlook and its effect on your holdings is of great importance.

        2. The most common investments where you become an owner include common stocks, real estate, precious metals, and collectibles.

    C. How you divide your money between these two basic choices has a greater impact on your eventual investment results than any other single factor.

III. The one fundamental rule of investing you should never, ever, *ever* forget is:

    A. The greater the return being offered, the greater the risk you're taking.

    B. This is always the case—whether those making the offer tell you or not, whether it's obvious or not, and whether you know it or not.

**I've been an investment adviser for over twenty years.
During that time, I've had the courage of my convictions
(some might say audacity!) to go to people and say . . .**

. . . "You can trust me with your hard-earned money. I'll protect it while I make it grow." There have been good years, accompanied by rankings in the top 5% of money managers nationwide. It seemed as if everyone was my friend, and I loved coming to work in the morning. I thought, *What a great business to be in!*

There have also been years when I was too conservative. My clients' profits were not as high as they might have been. I made money, but not as much as some of my competitors made that year. Asking, "What have you done for me lately?" many of my clients left in search of greener pastures. After several months of this, I dreaded coming to work in the morning. I thought, *What a terrible business to be in!*

Most people seem to have the impression there's something special about being an investment adviser. I've been at social gatherings where people who throughout the evening had hardly noticed me suddenly came alive when they learned that I manage investments for a living. Judging by their new interest in me, I have been instantly transformed from my usual normal self into someone of great charisma and charm. What accounts for this?

**I've come to believe it's because people secretly think
of investing as being like magic.**

It's the kind of "wow" reaction a magician receives when, after placing a little kitten into a cage and covering it, he removes the cover to reveal a growling, full-grown tiger. "Amazing—did you see *that*? How'd he do *that*?!" Where did the kitten go? Where did the tiger come from? What happens under that cover, anyway? It's amazing and mysterious!

Isn't this similar to the kind of reactions we have when we read of the futures trader who made millions in a single week? Or the real-estate tycoon who always seems to know where to buy next? Or the college student who started out buying penny stocks in meager amounts and a few years later is worth more than $20 million? It all seems so impossible. How do they ever do it?

Our imaginations and curiosities are kindled. Unlike the kitten, which doesn't actually turn into a tiger, the modest sums of these gifted individuals actually do turn into fortunes. But—and here's where the misconception comes in—it's a mistake to call what they do "investing." It's "speculating."

• Investing occurs when you put your money to work in a commercial undertaking, subject to modest levels of risk, and expect a reasonable return over a long period of time. What's reasonable? About 3%–5% more than the rate of inflation.

• Speculating also involves putting your money to work in a commercial undertaking, but it involves a level of risk so great that it's theoretically possible to lose most or all of your capital (the actual amount you invested). In return for this high risk, the speculator has the possibility of making an unusually large return (perhaps doubling or even tripling his/her money) in a relatively brief period of time—usually a couple years at most. This is also frequently accompanied by borrowing additional sums for the undertaking and accepting personal responsibility for repaying those sums regardless of the outcome of the venture. Financial options, commodity futures trading, and leveraged real estate projects are common forms of speculation.

• Gambling subjects your money to an *exceedingly* high level of risk in an attempt to profit from the outcome of a contest or game of chance. There is the possibility of an unusually large return in an exceptionally brief period of time—perhaps measured in minutes or hours. A sure sign that an activity falls under the "gambling" heading is when *the activity exists solely for the sake of creating wagering opportunities*. For example, apart from wagering, there would be no reason for casinos, horse racing, or lotteries to exist.

Gambling should be avoided by all. Speculating should be avoided by all except those with a professional interest and degree of expertise. But investing is an activity that all of us, as stewards of God's resources, are unavoidably called to. Once you understand that investing involves taking only prudent risks and seeking reasonable returns, it takes a lot of the magic and mystery out of it.

Do not wear yourself out to get rich; have the wisdom to show restraint. Cast but a glance at riches, and they are gone, for they will surely sprout wings and fly off to the sky like an eagle.
Proverbs 23:4–5

People who want to get rich fall into temptation and a trap and into many foolish and harmful desires that plunge men into ruin and destruction. For the love of money is a root of all kinds of evil. Some people, eager for money, have wandered from the faith and pierced themselves with many griefs.
1 Timothy 6:9–10

Like it or not, as a steward of God-given time, talents, and resources, you're an investor.

Investing is simply giving up something now in order to have more of something later. When you put your money into a savings account, you are making an investment decision (less spendable money now in order to have more spendable money later). When you volunteer your professional services or personal talents now in order to serve in a ministry, you're making an investment decision (less free time or current income now in order to have a greater sense of fulfillment and eternal gains later). When you take a day off without pay in order to spend time with your family, you're making an investment decision (less income now in order to have stronger family ties and happy memories later).

Your goals seem reasonable: Make as much as you can but don't lose any of your savings. You're eager for good advice but wonder whom you can trust. You would like to feel confident but usually feel a little confused. You are caught in the constant tension between risk and reward. If you feel this way, I've got good news!

Investing is actually quite simple . . .

. . . because you only have two basic choices: investments where you become *a lender to someone* and investments where you become *an owner of something*.

Investments where you *lend* your money are generally the lower-risk kind. Assuming you do a good job of checking out the financial strength of the borrower, the primary risk is that you might get locked in to a poor rate of return for many years. We'll cover investing-by-lending in detail in chapter 14.

Investments where you *own* something are generally the higher-risk kind. The primary risk here is that the value of what you own could fall, so the economic outlook and its effect on your holdings is of great importance. We'll be looking at investing-by-owning as it pertains to the stock market in chapter 15.

**What I'm about to tell you is very important,
so please pay close attention: The way in which . . .**

. . . you divide your investment capital between these two basic choices of "loaning" or "owning" *has a greater impact on your eventual investment returns than any other single factor.*

INVESTING BY LENDING

| **Banks, S&Ls, and Credit Unions** (which you loan to when you open savings accounts and buy their certificates of deposit) | **Large Corporations** (which you loan to when you give your money in return for corporate IOUs—commercial paper and bonds) | **The National Government** (which you loan to when you give your money in return for Treasury IOUs—bills, notes, and bonds) | **Local and State Governments** (which you loan to when you give your money in return for their IOUs—that is, bonds—which pay tax-free interest) | **Insurance Companies** (which you loan to when you give your money in return for insurance company IOUs—cash value life insurance and fixed annuities) |

Think of your investments as being like a garden. Some people like to grow flowers and others prefer to grow vegetables. Some enjoy doing both. The one decision that has the greatest influence over what your garden looks like and the kind of harvest you'll ultimately have is this: How much of your garden should you devote to flowers and how much to vegetables? Once you decide that, you know a lot about what to expect in terms of the risks involved and the potential results *even if you haven't yet decided which kinds* of flowers or vegetables you're going to plant. Once you decided how you were going to allocate your space, the kind of harvest you were going to have was, to a great extent, already predetermined.

Now, let me shift your thinking to the investment arena. Studies have shown that 80% or more of your investment return is determined by how much of your portfolio is invested in stocks (flowers) versus bonds (vegetables), and only about 20% is determined by how good a job you did at making the individual selections. This surprises most people, because the investment industry gives far more attention to telling you about hot stocks and mutual fund performance rankings than to explaining the critical importance of asset allocation (that is, how much space you make in your investment garden for stocks versus how much room

INVESTING BY OWNING

Stocks	**Real Estate**	**Oil & Gas Syndications**	**Precious Metals**	**Farmland**
(where you become part owner of a business—"preferred" stock shares give you first claim on dividends)	(where you become an owner of land and/or buildings purchased primarily for their income-generating potential)	(where you pool your money with other investors and head for the great outdoors in search of undiscovered sources of energy)	(where you become an owner of actual gold, silver, or platinum—some investors prefer to hold gold/silver in the form of coins)	(where you become an owner of land used for growing crops—typically held for future price appreciation rather than income)

THE RISKS AND RETURNS
OF OWNING VS. LOANING
OVER VARIOUS 5-YEAR
HOLDING PERIODS

5 Year Period	"Own" (Stocks)	"Loan" (Bonds)	50% Each
1941–1945	17.0%	3.4%	10.5%
1942–1946	17.9%	3.2%	10.7%
1943–1947	14.9%	2.2%	8.7%
1944–1948	10.9%	2.4%	6.9%
1945–1949	10.7%	2.2%	6.6%
1946–1950	9.9%	1.8%	6.0%
1947–1951	16.7%	0.9%	8.9%
1948–1952	19.4%	2.0%	10.8%
1949–1953	17.9%	1.9%	10.0%
1950–1954	23.9%	2.3%	13.4%
1951–1955	23.9%	2.0%	13.2%
1952–1956	20.2%	1.1%	10.9%
1953–1957	13.6%	2.1%	8.4%
1954–1958	22.3%	1.0%	12.3%
1955–1959	15.0%	−0.3%	7.8%
1956–1960	8.9%	1.4%	5.7%
1957–1961	12.8%	3.8%	8.8%
1958–1962	13.3%	3.6%	9.0%
1959–1963	9.9%	4.5%	7.5%
1960–1964	10.7%	5.7%	8.5%
1961–1965	13.2%	3.8%	8.8%
1962–1966	5.7%	2.9%	4.6%
1963–1967	12.4%	0.3%	6.6%
1964–1968	10.2%	0.4%	5.5%
1965–1969	5.0%	−2.2%	1.6%
1966–1970	3.3%	1.2%	2.5%
1967–1971	8.4%	3.3%	6.1%
1968–1972	7.5%	5.8%	6.8%
1969–1973	2.0%	5.6%	3.9%
1970–1974	−2.4%	6.7%	2.4%
1971–1975	3.2%	6.0%	5.0%
1972–1976	4.9%	7.4%	6.5%
1973–1977	−0.2%	6.3%	3.4%
1974–1978	4.3%	6.0%	5.5%
1975–1979	14.8%	5.8%	10.4%
1976–1980	13.9%	2.4%	8.4%
1977–1981	8.1%	−1.3%	3.7%
1978–1982	14.0%	5.6%	10.2%
1979–1983	17.3%	6.9%	12.5%
1980–1984	14.8%	11.2%	13.4%
1981–1985	14.7%	17.9%	16.4%
1982–1986	19.9%	22.5%	21.4%
1983–1987	16.5%	14.1%	15.4%
1984–1988	15.4%	15.0%	15.2%
1985–1989	20.4%	14.9%	17.7%
1986–1990	13.1%	10.4%	11.9%
1987–1991	15.4%	10.4%	13.0%
1988–1992	15.9%	12.5%	14.3%
1989–1993	14.5%	13.0%	13.8%
1990–1994	8.7%	8.4%	8.6%
1991–1995	16.6%	12.2%	14.4%
1992–1996	15.2%	8.5%	12.0%
1993–1997	20.2%	9.2%	14.8%
1994–1998	24.1%	8.7%	16.4%
1995–1999	28.6%	8.4%	18.5%

you allocate to bonds). We'll look at this in great detail in chapter 16 where I'll teach you a very simple strategy which puts your focus on "how much you put where" rather than "which ones."

For now, I just want you to recognize that the economic forces that influence the two basic choices are different. It's possible for you to invest-by-lending your money to a financially strong company like General Motors in return for one of its bonds and, even in the midst of a deep recession, earn a nice return. On the other hand, it's also probable that if you chose to invest-by-owning stock of the same corporation and thereby become one of its part owners, the same recession would have caused serious harm—hopefully temporary—to the company's earnings and dividend payments. As a part owner of the business, you would have likely watched your investment in the company lose value even while its creditors (like the investors who bought GM's bonds) were happily collecting their interest payments.

Of course, that's just looking at the risk part of the equation. The other side of that coin is that the owners of a company can enjoy great prosperity during those times in the business cycle when the economy is healthy and growing. The creditors, meanwhile, continue receiving only the interest payments to which they are due.

The reference table of annualized returns (at left) illustrates this risk/reward relationship. Consider the five-year period from 1987 to 1991 near the bottom. The table indicates that investors who allocated 100% of their capital to being owners (by investing in the shares of stocks in those blue-chip companies that are part of the Standard & Poor's 500 Stock Index) would have received a total return of 15.4% *per year* during that time. This is despite the fact that the crash of 1987 occurred early in the period. By comparing the "own" column with the "loan" column, you can also readily see that with rare exceptions since World War II, stockholders who held for at least a five-year period did far better than bondholders during the same period.

Investors who decided to allocate 100% of their money to becoming lenders would have earned 10.4% per year during the 1987–1991 period. (This assumes their returns were similar to the bonds included in the Salomon Brothers Long-Term High-Grade Corporate Bond Index, which is an average of more than 1,000 publicly issued corporate debt securities.) They would have made less money and taken less risk. The final column on the right shows the experience of investors who don't want to cast their lot entirely with either camp, but choose to split their capital equally between the two basic choices—50% in stocks and 50% in bonds. (The reason the 50/50 column is not simply the average of the other two columns is due to the effects of reallocating the portfolio back to one-half of each kind of investment at the beginning of each new year. This annual process is often referred to as "rebalancing.") You'll note that this middle-of-the-road course has consistently been profitable.

All investing eventually finds its way into the American economy. It provides the essential money needed for businesses to be formed and grow—for engineering, manufacturing, construction, and a million and one other services to be offered and jobs to be created. You can either be a part owner in all this, tying yourself to the fortunes of American business and sharing in the certain risks and possible rewards that being an owner involves. Or, you can play the role of lender, giving your money to others in order to let *them* take the risks and knowing you are settling for a lesser, but more secure, return on your money.

How to divide your funds between these two kinds of endeavors is your first and most important investing decision. Everything else is fine-tuning.

Of course, no discussion of investing is complete without including the potential risks involved . . .

. . . in making an investment. There is one fundamental rule that you should never, ever, *ever*, forget—the greater the potential reward being offered, the greater the risk involved in making that investment. Let me say that again. The greater the potential reward being offered, the greater the risk involved in making that investment. Or, in everyday plain English, *There's no free lunch.*

Countless people have learned this simple lesson only after losing thousands (and often hundreds of thousands) of dollars in an investment that was "just as safe" as a money market account but offered a higher return. The truth is that the link between risk and reward is as certain as the link between

THE POTENTIAL FOR HIGHER RETURNS
ALWAYS CARRIES A PRICE TAG

You reap what you sow.

There's no free lunch!

The greater the reward, the greater the risk.

A simple man believes anything, but <u>a prudent man gives thought to his steps</u>.
Proverbs 14:15

The simple inherit folly, but the <u>prudent are crowned with knowledge</u>.
Proverbs 14:18

Plans fail for lack of counsel, but <u>with many advisers they succeed</u>.
Proverbs 15:22

sowing and reaping. It's inescapable. Anyone who tells you differently is either self-deceived or is trying to deceive you.

Think about it for a second. The world's safest and most liquid investment is a 90-day U.S. Treasury bill. Investors in T-bills are loaning money to the U.S. government (which represents the world's largest economy and has never defaulted on its debts). They'll get it back in just three months, not a very long period of time. It's the closest thing to a "sure thing" that the world of finance has to offer. Let's say the U.S. government will pay you a 5% annualized return. Anyone else competing with the U.S. government for your investment dollar will have to offer you more than 5%; otherwise, you have no incentive to do business with them. Why not? Because by definition they are not as creditworthy and represent a greater risk. Anyone else who wants your money *will have to* offer you a better return just to get your attention.

Every investment involves your parting with your money and handing it over to others who are going to use it for their own purposes. In return, it will cost them something. Naturally, they want their costs to be kept as low as possible. That is, they don't want to give you a dollar more than is absolutely necessary. But, as we've just seen, it *is* absolutely necessary to offer you more than you can get by investing in risk-free U.S. T-bills. In fact, it's necessary to offer you more than you can get from *any* lower-risk alternative. Otherwise, you'll always select the lower-risk alternative.

If they promise you 10%, it's only because *they have to*. They're not just being nice. There's something about the investment—credit risk, market risk, interest rate risk, something—that makes their investment less attractive than other investments you could make which would pay you, say, 9½% with less uncertainty.

This relationship between risk and reward is one of the fundamental truths you must accept in order to succeed in investing.

As we go along, I'll be giving you some basic rules of thumb concerning this and various other investing truisms. My goal will not be just to help you understand them—I want you to "own" them. I want you to develop convictions concerning them. It will be the strength of these convictions that, in future years, will continue to provide you with a reliable compass for navigating the often turbulent waters of economic life. ◆

CHAPTER PREVIEW

What Mutual Funds Are and Their Advantages to Investors

I. **For most investors, mutual funds represent the best way to assemble a well-balanced, diversified portfolio of securities.**

   A. A mutual fund is simply a big pool of money formed when thousands of small investors team up in order to gain advantages that are normally available only to wealthy investors.

   B. The money in the pool is managed by a hired professional who is paid based upon the size of the pool and, in some cases, on his/her performance results.

   C. The money in the pool can only be invested according to the "ground rules" that were drawn up when the pool was first formed. Most mutual funds limit their investments to a particular kind of stock or bond that is the specialty of the professional managing the pool.

II. **Mutual funds can make your investing easier and safer. Twenty advantages of mutual fund ownership are listed and explained. Among them are:**

   A. They reduce risk by providing extensive diversification. This means their price movements are less volatile and more predictable than individual stocks.

   B. They keep commission costs low while managing the pool.

   C. They provide experienced, full-time professional management that gives your holdings individual attention on a daily basis.

   D. Their past performance is a matter of public record.

   E. They allow you to efficiently reinvest your dividends.

   F. They offer many convenient services, such as automatic investing and withdrawal plans, check-writing privileges, handling all the paperwork, creating reports for tax purposes, and providing safekeeping of your money.

   G. They can be used for your IRA and other retirement plans.

   H. They allow you to sell your shares and leave the pool at any time.

Investment Company
is the technical name
for a mutual fund.

Mutual Fund
is a company that combines the
funds of many investors into
one larger pool of money, and
invests the pool in stocks,
bonds, and other securities
consistent with its area of
specialization. For this service,
the company typically charges
an annualized management fee
that approximates 1.5% of the
value of the investment.

Portfolio
is a collection of securities
held for investment.

Net Asset Value
is the market value of a single
mutual fund share.

Security
is a financial instrument that is
bought and sold by the
investing public. The majority
are stocks, bonds, mutual
funds, options, and ownership
participations in limited
partnerships. All publicly traded
securities are subject to the
regulation of the Securities and
Exchange Commission.

**Securities and Exchange
Commission (SEC)**
is an agency in Washington that
regulates the securities
industry. SEC rules govern the
way investments are sold, the
brokerage firms that sell them,
what can be charged for selling
them, what information must be
disclosed to investors before
they invest, and much more.
The SEC is charged with
looking after the general
welfare of the investing public.
All mutual funds come under
SEC supervision.

Abraham Lincoln received an invitation to deliver a college commencement address. The exact date had not yet been set . . .

. . . and he was asked how much advance notice he would need. He said that depended on how long they wished him to speak: "If you want me to speak for just fifteen minutes, I'll need three weeks' notice. If it's for an hour, I'll only need three days' notice. And if you'll let me speak all day, I can start right now!"

The point behind his humorous answer is that it takes a great deal of preparation time to be economical in one's presentation while still covering all the essentials. I thought of Lincoln as I was reviewing all the books in my investment library that were written solely on the subject of mutual funds. I've collected fourteen different ones over the years; they average more than 264 pages each! Can I hope to teach you more about mutual funds than is already covered in those fourteen books? Probably not, especially when you consider that they run collectively to over 3,700 pages!

I'm going to do something that may be even more valuable to you—teach you a lot *less*. I'm going to mercifully leave out . . .

. . . a lot of material that is best reserved for a more in-depth study, and focus on only those things you need to know about mutual funds in order to benefit from them. And put that way, there really isn't all that much for you to learn. This section of the book will serve as a primer, and a primer teaches only the basics.

One last word before we begin. The fund industry has experienced explosive growth over the past decade. The sheer number (more than 11,000 at last count!) and types of different funds is overwhelming. As a result, I find that many people feel a little confused, if not intimidated, by the whole topic. Of course, it can be scary tackling a brand new subject, especially one that can so dramatically affect one's financial future. If you feel the same way, take heart! I've written this book especially for you. Ready? Let's get started!

The easiest way to understand a mutual fund is to think of it as a big pool of money.

The *Barron's Dictionary of Finance and Investment Terms* defines a mutual fund as a "fund operated by an investment company that raises money from shareholders and invests it in a variety of securities." My plain-English definition is that it's (1) a big pool of money (2) collected from lots of individual investors (3) that is managed by a full-time professional investment manager (4) who invests it according to specific guidelines. When you put money in a mutual fund, you are pooling your money with other investors in order to gain advantages that are normally available only to the wealthiest investors. You are transformed from a small investor into part owner of a multimillion dollar portfolio!

What do you get in return for your investment dollars? You receive shares that represent your ownership in part of the pool. The value of the shares is calculated anew at the end of every day the financial markets are open. Here's how it's done. First, you take the day's closing market value of all the investments in the fund's pool. To that number, you add the amount of cash on hand that isn't invested for the time being (most funds keep 3%–5% of their holdings in cash for day-to-day transactions). That gives you the up-to-the-minute value of all the pool's holdings. Next, you need to subtract any amounts the pool owes (such as management fees that are due to the portfolio manager but haven't yet been paid). This gives the net value of the assets in the pool. Finally, you divide the net value by the total shares in the pool to determine what each individual share is worth. This is called the net asset value per share and is the price at which all shares in the fund will be bought or sold for that day. It is also the number that is reported in the financial section of the newspaper the next morning.

What kinds of securities do mutual funds invest in? That depends on the ground rules . . .

. . . set up when the pool was first formed. Every mutual fund is free to make its own ground rules. The rules are explained in a booklet called the prospectus that every mutual fund must provide to investors—that is where you learn what types of securities the fund is allowed to invest in.

As we learn about mutual funds, I'll be using examples that might give you the mistaken impression that they invest only in stocks. This is most assuredly not the case. Mutual funds invest in just about every type of security around, including corporate, government, and tax-free bonds, federally-backed mortgages, and, as we saw in chapter 6, money market instruments like bank CDs, commercial paper, and U.S. Treasury bills. For the average person, mutual funds are the very best way to assemble a well-balanced, diversified portfolio containing many different kinds of securities. But in order to simplify things, I'll primarily use mutual funds that are stock-oriented when I'm explaining how funds work.

HOW THE XYZ MUTUAL FUND CALCULATES ITS DAILY CLOSING PRICE

List of Investments	Closing Price	Shares Owned	Market Value
Alcoa	$ 65.500	6,400	$ 419,200
Allied-Signal	58.000	8,900	516,200
American Express	46.750	9,700	453,475
A T & T	62.375	7,500	467,813
Bethlehem Steel	13.125	12,000	157,500
Boeing	82.375	3,000	247,125
Caterpillar	68.750	7,200	495,000
Chevron	58.500	4,400	257,400
Coca-Cola	45.500	3,800	172,900
Disney	60.750	2,200	133,650
DuPont	80.000	3,500	280,000
Eastman Kodak	76.500	9,100	696,150
Exxon	83.875	6,000	503,250
General Electric	79.875	4,600	367,425
General Motors	55.500	6,600	366,000
Goodyear	52.250	8,400	438,900
IBM	108.625	3,300	358,463
International Paper	41.250	2,900	119,625
McDonald's	47.750	9,500	453,625
Merck	62.125	4,000	248,500
Minnesota Mining	67.375	3,500	235,813
J. P. Morgan	86.375	7,700	665,088
Philip Morris	91.500	2,300	210,450
Proctor & Gamble	87.75	3,100	272,025
Sears	50.25	5,000	251,250
Texaco	82.125	8,600	706,275
Union Carbide	43.375	9,200	399,050
United Technology	109.875	6,800	747,150
Westinghouse	18.250	7,000	127,750
Woolworth	20.500	9,500	194,750

Market Value of Investments	$ 10,961,802
Plus: Cash on Hand	+ 265,619
Less: Expenses Payable	– 6,744
= Net Value of Pool Assets	$ 11,220,677
Divide By: Number of Shares	524,388
= Net Asset Value Per Share	$ 21.40

A mutual fund will usually limit its investments to a particular kind of security. For example, assume you want to invest only in quality blue-chip stocks that pay good dividends. As it turns out, there are a large number of mutual funds whose rules permit them to invest only in such stocks. No small company stocks, stock options, long- or short-term bonds, precious metals, or anything else. By limiting their permissible investments, mutual funds allow you to pool your money together with that of thousands of other investors who wish to invest in similar securities.

Mutual funds are almost certain to play an important role in your financial future because they offer many benefits which will make your investing program easier and safer. Here are twenty of their major advantages.

Advantage #1: Mutual funds can reduce the anxiety of investing.

Most investors constantly live with a certain amount of anxiety and fear about their investments. This is usually because they feel they lack one or more of the following essentials: (1) market knowledge, (2) investing experience, (3) self-discipline, (4) a proven game plan, or (5) time. As a result, they often invest on impulse or emotion. The advantages offered by mutual funds can go a long way toward relieving the burdens associated with investing.

Advantage #2: Mutual fund shares can be purchased in such small amounts that it makes it easy to get started.

If you have been putting off starting your investing program because you don't know which stocks to invest in and you can't afford your own personal investment consultant to tell you, mutual funds will get you on your way. It doesn't require large sums of money to invest in mutual funds. Most fund organizations have minimum amounts needed in order to initially open your account, which usually run from $1,000 to $3,000. And if that's too much, most funds have dramatically lower minimums for IRAs and "automatic deposit accounts" where you agree to make regular monthly deposits to build your account.

MINIMUMS NEEDED TO OPEN SYSTEMATIC INVESTMENT ACCOUNTS
(AS OF SEPTEMBER 2000)

Fund Organization	Normal Minimum For Opening A Regular Account	Normal Minimum For Opening An IRA Account	Minimum When Opening Automatic Deposit Account	Automatic Monthly Deposit	For More iInformation
American Century	$2,500	$1,000	$2,500	$50	(800) 345-2021
Dreyfus	$2,500	$750	$100	$100	(800) 645-6561
Fidelity	$2,500	$500	$2,500	$100	(800) 544-9697
Invesco	$1,000	$250	$50	$50	(800) 525-8085
Janus	$2,500	$500	$500	$100	(800) 525-8983
Neuberger Berman	$1,000	$250	$100	$100	(800) 877-9700
Scudder	$2,500	$1,000	$1,000	$100	(800) 225-2470
Stein Roe	$2,500	$500	$1,000	$50	(800) 338-2550
Strong	$2,500	$250	$50	$50	(800) 368-1030
T. Rowe Price	$2,500	$1,000	$50	$50	(800) 638-5660
TIAA-CREF	$250	$250	$250	$25	(800) 223-1200
USAA	$3,000	$250	$50	$50	(800) 382-8722
Vanguard	$3,000	$1,000	$3,000	$50	(800) 662-7447

Advantage #3: Mutual fund accounts can also be added to whenever you want—often or seldom—in small amounts.

After meeting the initial minimum (if any) to open your account, you can add just about any amount you want. To make your purchase work out evenly, they'll sell you fractional shares. For example, if you invest $100 in a fund selling at $7.42 a share, the fund organization will credit your account with 13.477 shares ($100.00 divided by $7.42 = 13.477).

Advantage #4: Mutual funds reduce risk through diversification.

Stock funds typically hold from 50 to 500 stocks in their portfolios; the average is around 100. They do this so that any loss caused by the unexpected collapse of any one stock will have only a minimal effect on the pool as a whole. Without the availability of mutual funds, the investor with just $2,000 to invest would likely put it all in just one or two stocks (a very risky way to go). But by using a mutual fund, that same $2,000 can make the investor a part owner in a very large, professionally researched and managed portfolio of stocks.

Advantage #5: Mutual funds' price movements are far more predictable than those of individual stocks.

Their extensive diversification, coupled with outstanding stock selection, makes it highly unlikely that the overall market will move up without carrying almost all stock mutual funds up with it. For example, on August 14, 2000, when the Dow jumped 148 points, more than 98% of stock mutual funds were up for the day. Yet, of the more than 3,300 stocks that traded on the New York Stock Exchange, only about half ended the day with a gain. The rest ended the day unchanged (15%) or actually fell in price (33%).

Advantage #6: Mutual funds' past performance is a matter of public record.

Advisory services, financial planners, and stockbrokers have records of past performance, but how public are they? And how were they computed? Did they include every recommendation made for every account? Mutual funds have fully disclosed performance histories, which are computed according to set standards. With a little research, you can learn exactly how the various mutual funds fared in relation to inflation or other investment alternatives.

"DIVERSIFICATION"

The spreading of investment risk by putting one's assets into many different kinds of investments.

Mutual funds are usually regarded as relatively low in risk because they are so widely diversified. While some of their holdings are moving up in value, others are standing still or moving down. So, the price changes somewhat cancel each other out. The effect of this is to increase the price stability of the overall portfolio. Thus, while an investor is unlikely to score a huge gain in any one year holding mutual funds, he is also unlikely to incur a huge loss. For the average investor, this relative price stability is one of the primary advantages of investing through mutual funds.

Open-End Funds
sell as many shares as necessary to satisfy investor interest. You can buy and sell shares directly through the fund organization. They are the most common kind.

Closed-End Funds
have only a limited number of shares available. To buy and sell, you go through a stockbroker and transact with other investors just as you do when dealing in stocks.

Blue Chip Stocks

are shares of large, well-known companies that have long records of profit growth, dividend payments, and reputations for quality products or services.

Dividends

are payments to shareholders as their share of the profits. They are usually made quarterly and are taxable in the year they are received.

Bull Market

is a market with rising prices of sufficient duration to indicate an upward trend.

Bear Market

is a market with falling prices of sufficient duration to indicate a downward trend.

Advantage #7: Mutual funds provide full-time professional management.

Highly trained investment specialists are hired to make the decisions as to which stocks to buy. The person with the ultimate decision-making authority is called the portfolio manager. The manager possesses expertise in many financial areas, and hopefully has learned—through experience—to avoid the common mistakes of the amateur investor. Most important, the manager is expected to have the self-discipline necessary to doggedly stick with the mutual fund's strategy even when events move against him for a time.

Advantage #8: Mutual funds allow you to efficiently reinvest your dividends.

If you were to spread $5,000 among five different stocks, your quarterly dividend checks might amount to $10 from each one. It's not possible to use such a small amount to buy more shares without paying very high relative commissions. Your mutual fund, however, will gladly reinvest any size dividends for you *automatically*. This can add significantly to your profits over several years.

Advantage #9: Mutual funds offer you automatic withdrawal plans.

Most funds let you sell your shares automatically in an amount and frequency of your choosing. This pre-planned selling enables the fund to mail you a check for a specified amount monthly or quarterly. This allows investors in stock funds that pay little or no dividends to receive periodic cash flow.

Advantage #10: Mutual funds provide you with individual attention.

It has been estimated that the average broker needs 400 accounts to make a living. How does he spread his time among those accounts? The common-sense way would be to start with the largest accounts and work his way down. Where would that leave your $2,000 account? But in a mutual fund, the smallest member of the pool gets exactly the same attention as the largest because everybody is in it together.

Advantage #11: Mutual funds can be used for your IRA and other retirement plans.

Mutual funds offer accounts that can be used for IRAs, Keoghs, and 401(k) plans. They're especially useful for rollovers (which is when you take a lump sum payment from an employer's pension plan because of your retirement or termination of employment and must deposit it into an IRA investment plan account within sixty days). The new IRA rollover account can be opened at a bank, S&L, mutual fund or brokerage house and the money then invested in stocks, bonds, or money market securities. These rollover accounts make it possible for you to transfer your pension benefits to an account under your control while protecting their tax-deferred status. They are also useful for combining several small IRAs into one large one.

Advantage #12: Mutual funds allow you to sell part or all of your shares at any time and get your money quickly.

By regulation, all open-end mutual funds must redeem (buy back) their shares at their net asset value whenever you wish. It's usually as simple as a toll-free phone call. Of course, the amount you get back will be more or less than you initially put in, depending on how well the stocks in the portfolio have done during the time you were a part owner of the pool.

Advantage #13: Mutual funds enable you to instantly reduce the risk in your portfolio with just a phone call.

Most large fund organizations (usually referred to as "families") allow investors to switch from one of their funds to another via a phone call and at no cost. One extremely popular use of this feature is to switch back and forth between a growth-oriented stock fund (during bull markets) and a more conservative income or money market fund (when the stock market weakens and a bear market threatens). This exchange feature enables you to act quickly on the basis of your stock market expectations.

Advantage #14: Mutual funds pay minimum commissions when buying and selling for the pool.

They buy stocks in such large quantities that they always qualify for the lowest brokerage commissions available. An average purchase of $2,000 of stock will cost the small investor $60 to buy and sell. That's a 3% commission charge. On the other hand, the cost is a mere fraction of 1% on a large purchase like $100,000. Many investors would show gains rather than losses if

Prospectus
is a formal written offer to sell a security. Mutual funds provide them free to investors. They explain the fund's investment objectives, its performance history, the fees they will charge, the special services they offer, and a financial statement. Basically, a prospectus explains the ground rules under which a mutual fund operates.

A GLIMPSE INTO A MUTUAL FUND PORTFOLIO

Most mutual funds report to their shareholders each quarter, providing market commentary, performance data, and a list of the fund's current holdings.

Note that this growth fund is reporting that only 85% of its portfolio is invested in stocks. Most funds, even those dedicated to investing in stocks, will keep a small percentage of their holdings in CDs and Treasury bills to use for future purchases as well as to pay shareholders who wish to sell their fund shares on any given day.

COMMON STOCKS (85.3%)

	Number of shares	
Retail and Distribution (15.9%)		
Dayton-Hudson Corp.	205,000	$ 11,634
Gap, Inc.	48,000	2,568
Liz Claiborne, Inc.	58,000	1,552
Toys "R" Us, Inc.	568,000	14,413
Wal Mart Stores, Inc.	548,000	15,618
Walgreen Co.	180,000	8,212
Group Total		$ 53,997
Consumer (13.2%)		
American Brands, Inc.	51,000	$ 3,417
Walt Disney Co.	16,000	1,638
McDonald's Corp.	132,000	3,679
PepsiCo. Inc.	197,000	14,775
Philip Morris Co., Inc.	358,000	16,155
Rubbermaid, Inc.	135,000	4,995
Group Total		$ 44,659
Technology (6.4%)		
Automatic Data Processing, Inc.	247,000	$ 12,443
Computer Sciences Corp.	20,000	782
Cisco Systems	251,000	8,503

Current market value (in millions of dollars)

Percent of the total portfolio that's invested in a particular industry or sector of the economy.

Risk
is usually defined in terms of the potential an investment has for wild swings up and down in its market value. The term "volatility" refers to the extent of these price swings. An investment with high volatility (meaning very wide, often abrupt, swings in its market value) is defined as high risk. An investment with low volatility (meaning narrow, usually gradual swings in its market value) is thought of as having low risk.

Capital Gains
are the profits you make when you sell your investment for more than you paid for it.

Closing Price
is the price at which a security last traded before the close of business on a given day.

Volatility
refers to the tendency of securities to rise or fall sharply in price within a relatively short period of time.

This website created by the no-load fund industry offers articles and resources to help you understand mutual funds and the benefits of long-term investing. Check it out at www.mfea.com.

they could save almost 3% on every trade! The mutual-fund pool enjoys the savings from these massive volume discounts, enhancing the profitability of the pool. Eventually, then, part of that savings is yours. These commission savings, however, should not be confused with the annual operating expenses which every shareholder pays (see pages 121-122).

Advantage #15: Mutual funds provide a safe place for your investment money.

Mutual funds are required to hire an independent bank or trust company to hold and account for all the cash and securities in the pool. This custodian has a legally binding responsibility to protect the interests of every shareholder. No mutual fund shareholder has ever lost money due to a mutual fund bankruptcy.

Advantage #16: Mutual funds handle your paperwork for you.

Capital gains and losses from the sale of stocks, as well as dividend and interest income earnings, are summarized into a report for each shareholder at the end of the year for tax purposes. Funds also manage the day-to-day chores such as dealing with transfer agents, handling stock certificates, reviewing brokerage confirmations, and more.

Advantage #17: Mutual funds can be borrowed against in case of an emergency.

Although you hope it will never be necessary, you can use the value of your mutual fund holdings as collateral for a loan. If the need is short-term and you would rather not sell your funds because of tax or investment reasons, you can borrow against them rather than sell them.

Advantage #18: Mutual funds involve no personal liability beyond the investment risk in the portfolio.

Many investments, primarily partnerships and futures, require investors to sign papers wherein they agree to accept personal responsibility for certain liabilities generated by the undertaking. Thus, it is possible for investors to actually lose more money than they invest. This arrangement is generally indicative of speculative endeavors; I encourage you to avoid such arrangements. In contrast, mutual funds incur no personal risk.

Advantage #19: Mutual fund advisory services are available that can greatly ease the research burden.

Due to the tremendous growth in the popularity of mutual fund investing, there has been a big jump in the number of investment newsletters that specialize in researching and writing about mutual funds. Some promote timing strategies that tell you when to buy and sell, others focus on just the funds at one of the giant organizations such as Fidelity and Vanguard, and others recommend balanced, diversified portfolios of mutual funds geared to your risk tolerance and stage of life. They usually publish once a month, and average $152 per year (although the majority range from $89 to $149) in cost. To get information on my *Sound Mind Investing* newsletter, which focuses in part on mutual fund selection and includes updated fund recommendations each month, use the post card tucked into this book, or visit our website at www.soundmindinvesting.com.

Advantage #20: Mutual funds are heavily regulated by the SEC and have operated largely scandal-free for decades.

The fund industry is regulated by the Securities and Exchange Commission and is subject to the provisions of the Investment Company Act of 1940. The act requires that all mutual funds register with the SEC and that investors be given a prospectus, which must contain full information concerning the fund's history, operating policies, cost structure, and so on. Additionally, all funds use a bank that serves as the custodian of all the pool assets. This safeguard means the securities in the fund are protected from theft, fraud, and even the bankruptcy of the fund management organization itself. Of course, money can still be lost if poor investment decisions cause the value of the pool's investments to fall in value.

Think of mutual funds as offering the convenience of something you're pretty familiar with: eating out! Someone else has done all the work of . . .

. . . developing the recipes, shopping for quality at the best prices, and cooking and assembling the dinners so that foods that go well together are served in the right proportions. For mutual funds, that's the job of the professional portfolio manager—he develops his strategy, shops for the right securities at the best prices, and then assembles the portfolio with an appropriate amount of diversification. And the analogy doesn't stop there. Just as there are many different dinner entrees to choose from at most nice restaurants (such as steak, seafood, chicken, pasta, and so on), there are also many kinds of mutual funds to choose from at most fund organizations. Each kind has its own "flavor."

The graphic on the next page is a partial listing of the daily mutual fund section that appears in the newspaper. Vanguard is

IN A NUTSHELL

With mutual funds . . .	With individual stocks . . .
1. The fund portfolio manager decides what stocks to buy and sell and when's the best time.	1. You decide what stocks to buy and sell and when's the best time.
2. You get the added safety that comes from diversifying among lots of different stocks.	2. You get the high-risk, high-reward potential that comes from concentrating on just a handful of stocks.
3. You can invest any amount you want (above the minimum) and receive fractional shares.	3. Stock prices affect how much you can invest because you have to buy whole shares.
4. You can easily and efficiently reinvest all of your dividends.	4. It's difficult to reinvest all your dividends because the amounts are usually so small.
5. You can transfer your money between funds the same day.	5. It usually takes five business days to get your money when you sell.
6. You pay no sales charges when buying or selling no-load funds.	6. Discount brokers' commissions can cost 1% each time you trade.

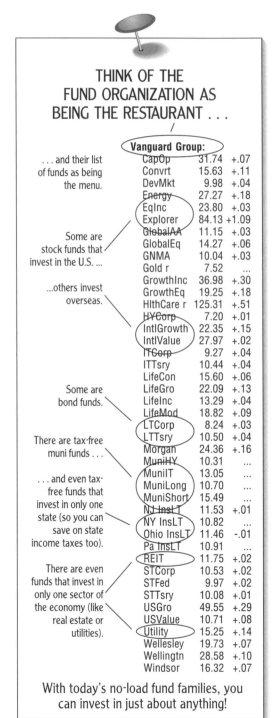

THINK OF THE
FUND ORGANIZATION AS
BEING THE RESTAURANT . . .

Vanguard Group:

. . . and their list of funds as being the menu.	CapOp	31.74	+.07
	Convrt	15.63	+.11
	DevMkt	9.98	+.04
	Energy	27.27	+.18
	EqInc	23.80	+.03
	Explorer	84.13	+1.09
Some are stock funds that invest in the U.S. ...	GlobalAA	11.15	+.03
	GlobalEq	14.27	+.06
	GNMA	10.04	+.03
	Gold r	7.52	...
...others invest overseas.	GrowthInc	36.98	+.30
	GrowthEq	19.25	+.18
	HlthCare r	125.31	+.51
	HYCorp	7.20	+.01
	IntlGrowth	22.35	+.15
	IntlValue	27.97	+.02
	ITCorp	9.27	+.04
	ITTsry	10.44	+.04
	LifeCon	15.60	+.06
Some are bond funds.	LifeGro	22.09	+.13
	LifeInc	13.29	+.04
	LifeMod	18.82	+.09
	LTCorp	8.24	+.03
	LTTsry	10.50	+.04
There are tax-free muni funds . . .	Morgan	24.36	+.16
	MuniHY	10.31	...
	MuniIT	13.05	...
. . . and even tax-free funds that invest in only one state (so you can save on state income taxes too).	MuniLong	10.70	...
	MuniShort	15.49	...
	NJ InsLT	11.53	+.01
	NY InsLT	10.82	...
	Ohio InsLT	11.46	-.01
	Pa InsLT	10.91	...
There are even funds that invest in only one sector of the economy (like real estate or utilities).	REIT	11.75	+.02
	STCorp	10.53	+.02
	STFed	9.97	+.02
	STTsry	10.08	+.01
	USGro	49.55	+.29
	USValue	10.71	+.08
	Utility	15.25	+.14
	Wellesley	19.73	+.07
	Wellingtn	28.58	+.10
	Windsor	16.32	+.07

With today's no-load fund families, you
can invest in just about anything!

one of the giants in the no-load fund industry, and it offers quite a "menu" for its investors. The point here is to show you *how many different funds you can find at a single fund organization*. Want a conservative blue-chip stock fund? Try Windsor. Perhaps something a little more aggressive? Check out Explorer or U.S. Growth. Prefer bonds instead? Vanguard has funds that specialize in corporates, governments, and tax-frees. Want short-term bonds instead of long-term? No problem—it offers funds that have different portfolio maturities for all three bond categories. The trend among fund organizations is to offer investors a choice in just about every investing specialty and risk group imaginable.

There are three primary ways you can profit from investing in mutual funds.

When you make your mutual fund investment, you will receive shares to show how much (that is, what portion) of the pool you own. The value of those shares fluctuates daily according to how well the investments in the pool are doing. If the overall value of the stocks held in the pool goes up today, the value of the fund's shares will go up today, and vice versa. The greater the volatility, the greater the risk. The price you pay for your shares is based on the worth of the securities in the pool on the day you buy in. Typically, the closing price is used for establishing their market value. For this reason, mutual funds are usually bought or sold only at the day's closing prices. This means that it doesn't matter what time of day the fund receives your order—early or late—you'll still get that day's closing price.

You can profit from your shares in three primary ways. First, the dividends paid by the stocks in the portfolio will be paid out to you periodically, usually quarterly. Second, if the portfolio manager sells a stock for more than he paid for it originally, a capital gain results. These gains will also be paid out periodically, usually annually. And third, when you're ready to sell your shares in the pool, you might receive back more than you paid for them. ◆

11

How Mutual Funds Are Sold and the Best Way to Buy Them

I. **There are two primary ways to go about investing in mutual funds.**

   A. "Load" fund organizations sell their shares to investors through a sales network of brokers, insurance professionals, and financial planners. A percentage of every dollar you invest (which can run as high as 8½%) goes to the salesperson with whom you do business.

   B. "No-load" fund organizations sell their shares to investors directly. They don't have a sales force to represent them, and so there need not be a "load" charged to the investor; 100% of every dollar invested goes to work on the investor's behalf.

II. **There are ongoing costs associated with owning mutual fund shares.**

   A. All mutual funds charge an on-going fee for the costs associated with the services of the portfolio manager. This is the way they make their money.

   B. All mutual funds charge an on-going fee for operating expenses such as: office, staff, equipment, bank custodial services, reporting to shareholders, and legal and auditing services.

   C. About 70% of stock funds charge an on-going fee for marketing expenses.

   D. Collectively, the on-going expenses cost shareholders in the average stock fund around $16 annually for every $1,000 of account value. The way this is commonly stated is that the average fund's "expense ratio" is 1.6%.

III. **You should select a fund organization based on the amount of money you have available to start with and the kinds of investments you wish to focus on.**

   A. If you have $2,500 or less to begin with, you must initially look for fund organizations with low account minimums.

   B. As your portfolio grows in value, you may eventually want to open accounts with more than one fund organization in order to have a greater selection of funds to choose from.

   C. For accounts of $25,000 and more, the services offered by "mutual fund supermarkets" such as Schwab and Fidelity offer maximum convenience, flexibility, and selection at a reasonable price.

What does it cost to buy mutual funds?
That depends on how you buy them . . .

. . . whether you go to them or they come to you. Mutual funds earn their profits by the management fees they charge, which are based on the amount of money they are responsible for investing. The more investors' money they manage, the more they make. Naturally, they want to attract as many customers as possible.

So-called "load" funds get new customers by having a sales force of stockbrokers, financial planners, and insurance professionals sell their funds for them. These funds charge a sales fee, which is added on top of the fund's net asset value. This markup cost can run as high as 8½% on every dollar you invest. The load applies to all purchases you make in the fund, not just the first time; some load funds even charge to reinvest your dividends for you (which I think is going a bit far). In return, the salesperson comes up with recommendations as to which funds might be best suited for your goals and completes all the paperwork to get your account opened. The load is the way the salesperson is rewarded for opening and servicing new accounts. If you would never get around to doing the research needed to select funds that are right for you, the salesperson provides an important service by doing this work for you and motivating you to action.

"No-load" funds, on the other hand, have chosen to deal directly with investors. They don't have a sales force to represent them—they believe plenty of investors are willing to do their own research and paperwork in order to save on the sales load. *They don't come to you; you go to them.* Of course, they make it as easy as possible through their advertising, 800 numbers, and customer service departments. Since they don't have salespeople to pay, they don't charge the load (thus the name "no-load"). By showing some initiative, you can save the 5%–8½% load that is commonly charged. That means *all the money* you put into your fund account goes to work for *you.* I recommend you limit your investment shopping to no-load funds. You'll learn all you need to know in this book to select the funds that are right for you, and you'll save thousands of dollars in loads over the years.

But (I can hear many of you asking) what about investment performance? Is it true that load funds get better results than no-load funds?

Sometimes they do, and sometimes they don't. Let me explain it to you this way. One of the major college basketball rivalries is the one between the University of Louisville and the University of Kentucky. People around here are fiercely devoted to their favorite teams. The question of who's best is settled once a year—but only briefly. Bragging rights only last until the next time they play. Since the team lineups are constantly changing, the question

---

No-Load Fund
is a mutual fund that is sold without a sales commission, either when you buy or sell your shares. This is usually done by the mutual fund organization not using a sales network and selling directly to the investor.

Load Fund
is a mutual fund that is sold to investors through a sales network, typically by stock brokers, financial planners, and insurance agents, and for which the investor pays a markup or sales charge.

Front-Loaded Fund
is a kind of load fund where the sales commission is paid in advance at the time the shares are purchased. The shares you get when you buy front-loaded funds are typically called "Class A" shares (see page 120).

Back-Loaded Fund
is a kind of load fund where a sales commission may be owed at the time the shares are sold. This kind of commission is also sometimes called a deferred sales charge. These are most commonly assessed by funds affiliated with major brokerage firms. This approach allows the firms that use them to sell shares through their commissioned brokers without charging front-loads. The firm is able to pay the brokers from these back-end loads and from the hidden 12b-1 charges. Typically, if you sell during the first year, you are charged a back-end commission ranging from 4% to 6% of the amount originally invested. The percentage drops each year, gradually declining to zero after four or five years. They are deducted from your proceeds when you pull your money out (see page 120).

of superiority is fought anew each season. If you look at the two programs over time, they're pretty evenly matched.

That's also the way it is in the great "load fund" versus "no-load fund" debate. Which kind has the better performance? The truth is they're pretty evenly matched. Neither group is inherently better than the other, just as none of the top college programs is inherently superior to the others. One year college A is best, the next year college B, and so on (although a John Wooden or a Dean Smith can come along and dominate every now and then, but that's to their credit, not the institution's).

In the same way, one year several of the no-load categories will outperform their load counterparts. The next year it could well be the other way around. Each group will have their share of winning results, and the "margin of victory" is usually quite small. They're so close that it's anyone's guess who will lead in performance in the coming year. Both load and no-load fund organizations hire top professionals in an attempt to bolster their performance results, which are, after all, what they are selling. So why should you expect either type to be inherently superior to the other? You shouldn't.

However, that doesn't mean they're equally attractive. The load that investors pay comes out up-front, which means they're "in the hole" the day their account is opened. Load funds *must* be consistently superior over time in order to be a better investment than a comparable no-load fund. This places the burden of proof on the load funds.

More on Load vs. No-Load Performance

"As far back as 1962, a special study was performed by the Wharton School of Finance for the Securities and Exchange Commission. It found 'no evidence that higher sales charges go hand-in-hand with better investment performance. Instead, the study showed that fund shareholders who paid higher sales charges had a less favorable investment experience than those paying less.'. . .One of the best studies was an exhaustive comparison of loads versus no-loads covering income, growth, and stability. Conducted in 1971 by Fundscope, it concluded: 'Because so many no-load and so many load funds perform both above-average as well as below-average, you must reach the conclusion there is just no relationship, no correlation, between load and results.'. . ."

From <u>The Handbook for No-Load Fund Investors</u>

COSTS OF INVESTING IN MUTUAL FUNDS

Type of Fee:	Applies To:	You Pay:
Front Loads	Load funds only	When you buy
Operating Expenses	All mutual funds	A little each day
12b-1 Fees	About 70% of all funds	A little each day
Deferred Sales Charges	Load funds only	If you sell within 4–6 years
Exit Fees	A few no-load funds	If you sell within 30–180 days

Don't let class confusion fool you.

To keep track of the mountain of data generated by the mutual fund industry, I subscribe to a pretty neat service offered by Morningstar, the leader among organizations that monitor the investment performance of mutual funds. For a mere $895 a year, I receive a computer CD each month that is packed with the equivalent of several thousand pages of data. The current one has information on 11,460 mutual funds. A few years ago, there were half that many.

Much of this dramatic growth is attributable to a feeding frenzy on the part of investors. The public's appetite for stock investing has been huge, and fund organizations have responded in fine capitalistic fashion by meeting the demands of the marketplace. A considerable number of the new funds, however, aren't really "new" at all. They're old load funds trying to look more like no-loads by creating new "classes" of shares. If you study the offerings of load fund organizations these days, you'll often find they offer three ways of investing in the same fund.

● **Class "A" shares.** This is the traditional load fund arrangement where you pay a sales charge to the broker or financial planner who introduced you to the fund, and this charge is deducted from your investment at the time you make it. Whereas this used to run 8.50%, competitive pressures from the no-loads have taken their toll. The most common front-end load is now 5.75%, and some are as low as 3.00%. In addition to this one-time sales charge, you also pay the on-going annual operating expenses which are common to all mutual funds.

● **Class "B" shares.** These shares move the load from the front-end to the back-end, where it gradually diminishes the longer you hold your shares. A typical arrangement might call for you to pay a 5% load if you sell your shares during the first year, a 4% load if you sell during the second year, and so on until you pay no load at all if you hold on for more than five years. Your broker still receives a sales commission, but it comes from the fund organization rather than immediately from your account.

How does the fund recoup this money? By adding it to the fund's annual expenses, which makes them higher than they otherwise would be. So (surprise!) you're the one who ultimately pays; you just do it a little every day rather than all at once up front. After six to eight years, some fund organizations will automatically convert your Class "B" shares to Class "A" shares (which pay lower—that is, normal—annual expenses) on the basis that by then you'll have "paid your dues." Other organizations aren't so fair-minded and continue to gouge you indefinitely.

● **Class "C" shares.** At first glance, these seem the most like no-load funds. They have no front-end loads, and the deferred load, a relatively small 1%, usually applies only to redemptions made during the first year you own your shares. The broker gets no up-front commissions for selling Class "C" fund shares. Instead, he receives a "level load" which is built into the annual expense charge and continues for as long as you own your shares.

Exit Fees are charged by a relatively few funds. They are intended to discourage you from making frequent trades. Such fees can range from a flat $5.00 per withdrawal to as much as $1.00 for every $100 withdrawn. Like back-end loads, they are deducted from the check sent you at the time you sell your shares. Frequently with these arrangements, the exit fees paid by departing shareholders go into the fund assets so as to benefit the remaining shareholders. In that event, exit fees are actually a good thing for long-term investors in the fund.

HOW VARIOUS LOAD AND EXPENSE ARRANGEMENTS ERODE A 10% ANNUAL RETURN

	Pure No-Loads	12b–1 No-Loads	Class A Loads	Class B Loads	Class C Loads
Front Loads	None	None	5.75%	None	None
Deferred Loads	None	None	None	5.00%	1.00%
Expense Ratio	1.15%	1.60%	1.30%	2.05%	2.15%
Sell After Year 1	$10,885	$10,840	$10,245	$10,363	➔$10,785
Sell After Year 2	$11,848	$11,751	$11,136	$11,304	➔$11,632
Sell After Year 3	$12,897	$12,738	$12,105	$12,328	➔$12,545
Sell After Year 4	$14,038	$13,808	$13,158	$13,444	➔$13,529
Sell After Year 5	$15,281	$14,967	$14,303	➔$14,659	$14,592
Sell After Year 6	$16,633	$16,225	$15,547	➔$15,825	$15,737
Sell After Year 7	$18,105	$17,588	$16,900	➔ $17,083	$16,972
Sell After Year 8	$19,707	$19,065	$18,370	➔$18,441	$18,305
Sell After Year 9	$21,451	$20,666	➔$19,969	$19,907	$19,742
Sell After Year 10	$23,350	$22,402	➔ $21,706	$21,490	$21,291

The table on page 120 shows the effects of these various load arrangements over time on a $10,000 investment assuming a 10% average annual return. The annual expenses column is an approximate average for each group as of July 2000.

Two kinds of no-load funds are also included for comparison purposes. One group charges 12b-1 fees (see "marketing expenses" below). The other group, for competitive reasons, elects not to charge 12b-1 fees. As the table makes clear, no-load fund investors enjoy the best of both worlds—no sales charges going in or coming out, and low annual expenses for as long as you stay.

Among the load funds, the advantage initially goes to Class "C" shares, but if you hold them long enough (9-10 years), Class "A" shares win out due to their lower annual expenses. The "arrow" symbol indicates the best deal for each holding period.

What on-going costs are involved in owning mutual funds?

In addition to the sales commissions involved when investing in load funds, there are also the ongoing operating expenses that are charged by *all* mutual funds, whether load or no-load. These are the costs of owning mutual funds over the long haul.

• **Operating expenses.** First, there are the costs associated with making the investing decisions. This means paying for an experienced portfolio manager as well as a staff of financial analysts to help with all the research, and is by far the largest of the operating expenses. Second, there's a lot of administrative overhead involved in having a large office, staff, and equipment. Third, there's the cost of having a bank

ARE LOAD FUNDS WORTH THE EXTRA COSTS?

They're worth it for <u>some</u> people. My thoughts on this are summarized in an exchange of letters I had with a financial planner who sold load funds.

Dear Austin:

I have been in the financial services business for five years. God has blessed my business, and I am very proud of the fact that my clients place a lot of confidence in me in giving them sound, unbiased and godly financial advice. I serve most of my clients as a financial planner in the type of work I do, but I have never charged fees for this. . . . I've seen how you recommend that people should primarily consider no-load funds. The problem I have is that no-load funds don't put bread on my family's table. I do think there are many good funds to choose from that are loaded. I tend to sell funds that are 2%–4% and not ones that are more expensive. I sell mostly larger, reputable funds with long successful track records. Yet, in all this I certainly don't feel I've done my clients a disservice, since they have not had to pay me a fee for the financial planning. I guess what I would like you to do is simply comment on how you feel about this kind of service and how I might better communicate to my clients the reasons I use load funds. —Sincerely, Alan

Dear Alan:

I understand your desire to render an honest service for a fair wage. And I know there are millions of people who are not willing to invest the time to learn the basics and become self-reliant in the area of finances and investing—they need the help of a trustworthy counselor.

A pastor once completed one of my survey forms with the comment: "I do not have the time or inclination to study financial matters, yet I know it is important." He is the kind of person who could benefit from your knowledge and objectivity. In helping him formulate a long-term plan and selecting good mutual funds (obviously, there are excellent funds to choose from in both the load and no-load camps) suited to his personal situation, you are rendering a valuable service. It is only right that you be fairly paid, and load funds make this possible.

Unfortunately, there have been so many well-publicized episodes of blatantly deceptive and self-serving brokers and planners taking advantage of trusting investors that the public is becoming cynical and wary. The primary culprit is a system that rewards stockbrokers based on their sales success (commissions earned) rather than their investment success (customers' profits). It does take a good bit of time to persuade potential clients that you are a person of integrity.

To assure that the welfare of your clients remains uppermost in your mind, I would suggest these guidelines: [1] go the extra mile to make sure the portfolio you are recommending is truly fitted to your clients' needs; [2] make sure they understand the risks and the possible worst case scenarios if they were to withdraw their money earlier than expected; [3] put them in fund families with a wide variety of offerings to accommodate possible future changes; and [4] always remember that we live our lives moment by moment in the sight of God. "To do what is right and just is more acceptable to the Lord than sacrifice" (Proverbs 21:3). —Sincerely, Austin

If you are someone who has neither the time nor inclination to select your own mutual fund investments, then your task is to locate someone like Alan who is informed, experienced, and objective.

maintain the shareholder accounts and safeguard all the money and securities which are constantly coming and going. Fourth, there are the costs of presenting regular reports to shareholders, as well as for legal and auditing services.

• **Marketing expenses.** In addition to all the operating expenses, over 70% of all stock funds also charge some of their marketing expenses to shareholders. These expenses are referred to as "12b-1" fees because of the SEC ruling that permits them, and the money from them can only be used to advertise and sell the fund to prospective investors.

Collectively, operating and marketing expenses cost shareholders in the average stock fund around . . .

. . . $16 annually for every $1,000 of account value. The way this is commonly stated is that the average fund's "expense ratio" is 1.6%. These operating and marketing expenses are not taken out of your account all at once. Rather, in a manner that is invisible to the shareholder, they are charged daily against the fund's net asset value. The price you see in the newspaper has already had that day's share of the costs deducted.

ARE LOWER FUND EXPENSES PREDICTIVE OF HIGHER RETURNS?

3 Year Returns / Ending 7/31/2000

Table A

	(A) Less Than 1.00%	(B) 1.01% to 1.25%	(C) 1.26% to 1.50%	(D) 1.51% to 1.75%	(E) More Than 1.75%
Foreign Stock Funds	11.9%	11.1%	11.5%	9.3%	12.5%
Small Company / Growth Funds	13.1%	10.1%	13.5%	15.9%	19.1%
Small Company / Value Funds	3.4%	2.1%	5.3%	-1.1%	0.7%
Large Company / Growth Funds	19.2%	18.1%	20.6%	21.1%	22.4%
Large Company / Value Funds	6.6%	7.4%	5.3%	8.1%	4.8%

Table B

	(A) Top 25%	(B) Next 25%	(C) Next 25%	(D) Bottom 25%
Foreign Stock Funds	1.53%	1.45%	1.43%	1.74%
Small Company / Growth Funds	1.58%	1.40%	1.35%	1.38%
Small Company / Value Funds	1.41%	1.16%	1.39%	1.48%
Large Company / Growth Funds	1.29%	1.13%	1.17%	1.21%
Large Company / Value Funds	1.15%	1.11%	1.11%	1.22%

When you see fund rankings in financial newspapers and magazines, these expenses have already been deducted; that is, the effects of each fund's annual expenses have been taken into account. That is not usually the case, however, with respect to any sales commissions a fund might charge. Unless the article specifically states to the contrary, sales loads are typically not taken into account when fund performance rankings are compiled. Therefore, the return you would actually receive would need to be adjusted downward by the amount of the sales load.

Investors are frequently told that they can enhance their returns by purchasing stock funds with below average expenses.

While this idea passes the common sense test—"If the fund takes less for overhead and marketing, that leaves more for me"—the surprising fact is that there doesn't seem to be a reliable correlation between the level of expenses a stock fund charges and the returns it earns for its shareholders. One study, by investment adviser

Burton Berry, examined over 400 stock funds and found that less than 2% of the variability of returns was due to differences in the expenses they charged. (Expenses are a more significant factor in fixed income funds. For example, 86% of the variation in money funds returns were found to be a function of expense ratios.)

Table A in the graphic on the far left shows the results of a study where I divided five primary kinds of stock funds into groups based on their expense ratios. Column A, for example, includes the lowest cost funds—those with annual expenses of 1% or less. If low expenses lead to better performance, we would expect the average annual returns of these funds to be the best in each group. Surprisingly, not once was that the case. Instead, we often find the opposite. In three of the groups, the top performance in recent years was turned in by the funds with the *highest* expenses (in circles).

Table B looks at the same data from a different direction. It ranks the funds in each group by performance, separates them into quartiles, and then calculates the average expense ratio for each quartile. Do the funds in the top-performing group (Column A) have the lowest expenses? Not once. In fact, twice they had the highest expenses (circles). On the other hand, we see that high expenses were characteristic of the worst performers in the other three instances.

We shouldn't read too much into the results from a single three-year period. To be sure, the advantages of low costs would be expected to play out over longer time periods. (Had the data been available, a similar study conducted over a period of ten years or longer might well have shown this.) Still, it seems evident that buying a fund *because* it has low annual expenses won't guarantee you better performance. Avoiding funds with high annual expenses gets mixed results—sometimes it has paid off (as with value funds) and sometimes it hasn't (as with growth funds). Perhaps the best use of expense ratios might be as a "tiebreaker" when trying to choose between two funds that both meet all of your other criteria.

If you're interested in doing your own fund "shopping" and saving the costs associated with load funds, which fund organization is best?

Well, best for what purpose? How long do you expect to hold your fund investments? What kinds of funds are you interested in? Are you willing to monitor your funds' progress, or do you want to just buy a few and forget them for the next few years? There is no "best" in an absolute sense; the selection must take place within the context of your personal goals and risk tolerance. A greater number of choices, it seems, creates greater anxiety about making the right decision. Here are some things to keep in mind as you contemplate selecting a no-load fund organization.

1. Each fund organization has its own areas of excellence. For example,

The General Accounting Office of the federal government conducted its own investigation. Its staffers posed as customers and visited eighty-nine banks across the country. In its report, the GAO faulted banks for:

• Not disclosing fund-related costs. The sales brochures given to customers failed to adequately explain the fees which they would pay.

• Inappropriate sales locations. The GAO report indicated that 34% of the banks visited did not clearly separate their mutual fund sales areas from their deposit-taking activities.

• Allowing customers to assume that mutual funds offer the safety of savings accounts. Only about one-third of the banks surveyed included all four of these risk disclosures in their sales presentations. funds aren't federally insured, funds aren't guaranteed by the bank, funds are not the same as savings deposits, and funds go up and down in value.

• Inadequate disclosure of interest rate risk. Investors accustomed to traditional savings accounts usually regard rising interest rates as a good thing—they'll get a better return on their investments. However, when interest rates go up, bond values go down. In 30% of the banks surveyed, this risk was not mentioned to customers who, seeking to improve on low yields, moved their savings into bond funds.

It's obvious, but bears repeating: Make sure you understand the potential risks, transaction fees, and tax consequences associated with an investment before making a final decision.

Opening A No-Load Fund Account

No-load funds attract investors through direct advertising in financial publications (like <u>The Wall Street Journal</u>, <u>Barron's</u>, <u>Forbes</u>, and <u>Money</u>) rather than via a sales network of brokers, insurance agents, and financial planners. They typically call attention to their performance histories or variety of fund offerings in an attempt to motivate you to call for more information. A toll-free number is provided. There is no charge for the material they send you, and they usually do not bother you with personal follow-up calls. An account application form is included with the information package you receive. By contacting their toll-free number, you'll get all the help you need in completing the form.

if you're primarily going to be investing in bond and money market funds, Vanguard is hard to beat. If you're interested in having access to stock funds across the entire risk spectrum, Price and Fidelity have good selections. Or if a large selection isn't important, Janus and American Century's stock funds are usually super during periods of rising stock prices (but beware of them in a bear market!).

2. Consider opening more than one account. If you don't mind the paperwork and can manage the initial minimums, open accounts at two (or more) of the no-load organizations. For example, having an account at Vanguard so you can invest in their fixed income funds, and one at Janus to have access to their stock funds, would be one possible combination. Or, if you're moving two IRAs, put them at different organizations and enjoy a greater selection. The additional annual charges are insignificant.

3. Performance leadership is always changing. Organization A could be doing great now, but its funds could all become sell candidates a year from now. No problem. With no-load funds, you can move your money easily and at no cost. The SMI philosophy involves diversifying across several risk categories. While it's important that you discipline yourself to have a long-term commitment *to the diversification strategy*, you need only make short-term commitments to individual funds and organizations.

When you are ready to begin building your mutual fund portfolio, your "starting place" will primarily depend . . .

. . . on how much money you initially have available. The no-load investment companies listed below are all reputable organizations that offer a variety of funds from which you can choose. They also allow you to move your money from one of their funds into another simply by making a toll-free phone call. As with all true no-load funds, there are no commissions charged to you, either when you invest or when you take your money out. These organizations provide you with a very cost-effective way to proceed with your program.

As your portfolio grows, you will want to diversify further. Although each of the fund organizations shown offers a variety of stock funds, you could run into either of two "problems." One, they might not offer a fund in the exact risk category or area of specialty you are seeking. Or, even if they do offer one, you might find that it

LEADING NO-LOAD FUND ORGANIZATIONS
(DATA CURRENT AS OF SEPTEMBER 2000)

Fund Organization	Normal Minimum For Opening A Regular Account	Number of U.S. Stock Funds	Number of International Stock Funds	For More Information
American Century	$2,500	20	4	(800) 345-2021
Dreyfus	$2,500	17	5	(800) 645-6561
Fidelity	$2,500	35	9	(800) 544-9697
Invesco	$1,000	16	4	(800) 525-8085
Janus	$2,500	12	2	(800) 525-8983
Scudder	$2,500	12	8	(800) 225-2470
Strong	$2,500	21	4	(800) 368-1030
T. Rowe Price	$2,500	26	10	(800) 638-5660
Vanguard	$3,000	30	9	(800) 662-7447

is a relatively poor performer. At this point, it might be time to open a second mutual fund account at a different organization with strengths that complement those of your first organization and match up well with your current needs.

However, along with having such a variety of choice comes housekeeping chores that can be inconvenient and occasionally confusing. You've got multiple sets of 800 numbers, application forms, investment account numbers, organizational policies, and monthly statements to contend with. When you want to sell shares at one organization and buy them at another, you've got to wait for a check from the first fund before sending your check off to the next one (see sidebar at right). And then there's all the tax information to keep track of.

An alternative to multiple fund accounts is to open a single investment account at a "mutual fund supermarket."

Charles Schwab pioneered its Mutual Fund Marketplace in 1992. For a small service fee, Schwab offered access to hundreds of no-load funds through one investment account. It wasn't long before Fidelity, the giant mutual fund organization, came along to one-up Schwab by offering the same service with even more funds to choose from.

Schwab struck back with its OneSource service which eliminated the service fees completely for certain fund families (the so-called "no transaction fee" funds, or NTF for short). Of course, you still had to pay a load if the fund itself charged a load, and not all no-load funds were included in the NTF offer (for those left out, Schwab continued to assess a charge for processing the transaction). In 1993, Fidelity responded by introducing a similar no-transaction-fee service of its own. The battle was on! In the ensuing years, many imitators have arisen. There are now more than 20 fund supermarket services. They differ in some important ways: which fund groups they offer, how many funds are available on an NTF basis, how many funds are available on a transaction basis, the amount of the transaction fee they charge, and the level of customer service.

I should point out that fund supermarkets have some drawbacks. The most significant is that the funds they offer on an NTF basis typically carry higher annual expenses than other funds. Supermarkets may not charge you for buying and selling funds in their NTF lineups, but they do charge the fund organizations. Usually the charge is about $3.00-$3.50 for every $1,000 transacted. The funds turnaround and recapture this cost by passing it through to the fund shareholders as a 12b-1 marketing expense (see page 122). Vanguard, a fund family notoriously committed to keeping costs low for its shareholders, refuses to do this—that's why you don't find any

Changing Fund Organizations?

Why go through a mutual fund supermarket and pay them to do what you can do for yourself? The answer is simple: convenience when moving your investment dollars from one mutual fund organization to a new one where you don't already have an account.

For example, let's pretend that you want to sell your shares at Organization A and invest the money in one of the funds at Organization B. If you weren't using a fund supermarket, here's what you'd need to do:

❏ Mail written instructions to Organization A (with your signature guaranteed by your local bank or broker) to sell your shares.

❏ Wait seven to ten days for your proceeds check to arrive from Organization A.

❏ While you're waiting, contact Organization B and ask them to send you the new account application forms.

❏ When they arrive, complete the forms.

❏ Mail them to Organization B with your check to pay for the new fund shares you want to purchase.

❏ Finally, wait two to three days before you know your order has been processed. (What's been happening in the stock market while you're doing all this waiting is anyone's guess!)

As you can see, moving your money from one fund group to another, although not a particularly difficult task, is time consuming. Fund supermarkets give you access to a broad range of funds from different organizations, and your holdings all appear on the same monthly statement. It's a great service, but comes at a cost.

Websites to Help with Your Mutual Fund Research
www.morningstar.com
www.personalwealth.com
www.smartmoney.com/funds
www.moneycentral.com/investor

For Updated Information
The Internet is constantly changing, and the above sites may have moved or ceased operations by the time you read this. For an up-to-date list of the better online resources related to mutual funds, visit the SMI website at www.soundmindinvesting.com.

Vanguard funds available through NTF programs. According to Morningstar, the fund rating company, funds that do not participate in NTF supermarket programs charge, on average, about .25% less in annual fees than those that do. Other drawbacks to fund supermarkets, depending on the organization, might include:

- May not offer all the funds or fund families that interest you.
- Difficulty in getting transactions made due to the fact that many supermarkets are operated by brokers who cater to stock day traders.
- Additional fees that can apply if your fund balance drops below a stated minimum or if your account is inactive for a period of time.
- Getting charged for selling an "no transaction fee" fund if you own it for less than 180 days.
- Paying above-average management costs for their money market and index funds.

Why expose yourself to potentially higher costs when you can go directly to a no-load organization and buy its fund shares for free? Greater convenience and greater selection. Because the fund supermarkets offer hundreds of different funds to choose from, many of them will be superior performers to those of the one or two no-load organizations where you might have accounts (especially in the stock fund categories). With one toll-free call to phone lines that are answered twenty-four hours a day, or via the Web if you prefer, you can make changes in your portfolio. You'll get one monthly statement that includes your transaction history, dividends, and the current market values for all your holdings.

To me, these advantages outweigh the drawbacks. I personally have three investment accounts; two of them are at fund supermarkets and the third is at Vanguard. For my newsletter readers, I continue to recommend Schwab (800-435-4000) and Fidelity (800-544-9697). They aren't the lowest in cost, but they have a wide variety of funds in their lineups and they typically offer a high level of customer service. The commissions these firms charge are worth it unless your account is a smaller one, say under $25,000. In that case, the fees are too high in proportion to the amounts invested and you're probably better served by dealing directly with a no-load organization (especially if you're using a monthly dollar-cost-averaging approach—see chapter 19). ◆

CHAPTER PREVIEW

Necessary Cautions

I. **The rapid growth of the mutual fund industry in recent years has created an exceptionally crowded and competitive playing field.**

    A. This has led many funds to take added investment risks as they seek to gain a performance edge over their rivals.

    B. The fund industry's system for classifying risk is subjective and open to misinterpretation and abuse.

II. **As a result of the exceptional growth and the ways in which many funds have responded to it, red flags have been raised that are a legitimate cause for concern to mutual fund investors.**

    A. Red Flag #1: You can't necessarily accept a fund's "investment objective" at face value. The investing boundaries that guide a portfolio manager have become blurred in recent years as funds have changed their by-laws in order to broaden their investing horizons.

    B. Red Flag #2: You can't necessarily accept a fund's diversification claims at face value. Many funds, in the pursuit of higher performance numbers, sacrifice diversification by concentrating their investments in just a few sectors of the economy.

    C. Red Flag #3: You can't necessarily accept a fund's implied performance excellence at face value. The job of any fund's marketing department is to take that fund's performance history and make it look as good as possible. We look at three of the ways that mutual funds will present their performance histories in the manner most likely to attract investors.

    D. Red Flag #4: You can't necessarily accept a fund's rankings at face value. Funds are "graded on the curve" based on the peer group they're placed in. If the risk category definitions are inconsistent in assuring that apples are compared to apples, then the performance rankings based on them are potentially misleading.

III. **Mutual fund investors must accept the responsibility for learning how to shop intelligently. One source of information often bypassed by investors is the fund prospectus. Pointers are offered on how to read it for the essentials.**

When I began my career as an investment adviser in the late 1970s . . .

. . . I chose to specialize in the study of mutual funds. They offered my clients quick and easy diversification within specified boundaries, as well as seasoned professional management. Plus, since there were only about 800 to choose from at the time (compared to thousands of common stocks), the selection process was greatly simplified.

How times have changed! The number of funds has multiplied at a phenomenal rate over the past few years. Morningstar, one of the country's three leading mutual fund reporting services, now carries data on almost 11,500 mutual funds in its database. These days the selection process is no longer a simple one. The sheer number and variety of funds has caused investors to be confused about what is available, let alone what is appropriate.

The fund industry's explosive growth has increased the complexity of monitoring mutual fund performance.

Arriving at a decision is more difficult than it used to be, not merely because you have more choices now, but, regrettably, because it can no longer be safely assumed that fund managers are investing your money prudently.

In recent years, too many fund executives have made poor decisions as they attempted to gain an edge in the face of the enormous competitive pressures that now characterize the fund industry. To better understand the dynamics at work, let's use an analogy based on a business we're all familiar with—the neighborhood supermarket.

Assume that in the "old days" you had three grocery stores in your small town. There was friendly competition but enough business to go around. Then, in a period of fifteen years, the size of your town tripled. With a larger population to feed, the local grocers responded by opening additional stores. The town's growth did not go unnoticed by the grocery chains that had not previously operated in your community, and they came in with new stores as well. Now there are two dozen supermarkets—it seems like there's one on every corner.

The population tripled, but the number of grocery stores grew eightfold. The grocers know that the town can't support all of them and that a shakeout is inevitable. They also know that low prices are the key to attracting shoppers because they see their sales go up and down in direct proportion to how their prices compare to their competitors' prices. So, there is a great deal of pressure on each grocer to have his prices appear as attractive as possible. Each is determined to do what he must in order to be among the survivors, even if it means cutting a few corners here and there.

In the same way, the number of new mutual funds has far surpassed the number of new investors. Mutual fund organizations have hundreds of mil-

---

Morningstar, Lipper Analytical, and Value Line

are large companies that are in the business of collecting, analyzing, and distributing information about mutual funds. They sell their data to financial institutions, publishers, and investors. When you read about mutual fund performance in The Wall Street Journal, Barron's, Business Week, Money, Forbes, or other leading financial publications, the data shown came from one of these three organizations. Because their dominance of the industry is so total, the way they categorize funds for risk and performance is extraordinarily influential in the decision-making of millions of mutual fund investors.

Risk Category

is a way of classifying mutual funds that groups together those with similar investment strategies and similar possibilities of profit and loss. The idea is that they be useful in helping investors compare "apples with apples" when measuring mutual fund performance.

Unfortunately, there is no "official" list of categories used consistently throughout the industry. Morningstar, Lipper, and Value Line each have their own different (albeit similar) ways to classify funds. Because of the great diversity of funds, their systems have grown to include almost 50 different risk categories.

In this book, I have created a simplified system that involves just five basic categories for stock funds and four for bond funds. These will be explained in detail in Section 4.

lions of dollars in fees riding on their ability to attract and keep customers, and the key for them isn't low prices—it's investment performance. *Fortune* summed up the situation this way:

> *In a recent Smith Barney survey of investors, when asked the single most important reason for selecting a fund, 51% looked to past performance over one to five years, not the composition of the fund portfolio or the fund's management philosophy. . . . That emphasis has sent a message to fund companies: short-term performance is paramount. . . . The trouble with this seemingly harmless focus is that fund managers can be pressured to throw caution to the wind as they try to jockey into the winner's circle for one-year performance. The swelling number of mutual fund rankings in almost every business publication has reinforced the short-term bias, moving one-year performance into an elite class. . . . Such measurements have become the standard for investors and the fund managers who serve them.*

In this chapter, we're going to look at some of the "red flags" that are a legitimate cause for concern to mutual fund investors. They all stem, ultimately, from the way the fund industry has taken advantage of the difficulty inherent in categorizing funds by risk. This is important because it allows investors to "compare apples to apples." Let's begin by laying some important groundwork.

In order to analyze their performance, mutual funds are placed into groupings called risk categories.

Morningstar and the other firms place every mutual fund into one of three major camps: equity (stock) funds, fixed-income (bond) funds, and hybrid (a mix of both stock and bonds) funds. This is the easy part.

Within each of the three camps, however, there are sub-categories of risk based on a fund's "investment objective." A problem arises at this point because there are no official categories that all analysts can apply uniformly when assigning funds to a given category. For example, the table on the next page shows four major risk categories for stocks. For each one, you'll find the definitions used by the Investment Company Institute—the mutual fund trade organization—and Morningstar. Notice that they are different.

These definitions are little more than the most commonly stated portfolio objectives as found in fund prospectuses, which describe a fund's theoretical goals and strategies. A fund's actual portfolio has tremendous room for variance while still staying within the broad, subjective guidelines given in the prospectus.

The very fact that there are no official categories that everyone can agree to proves how subjective the risk-assessment process is. After reading a fund's prospectus, the Morningstar (or Lipper or Value Line) analyst assigns the fund to the risk category that seems right to him. In other words, it's merely *each analyst's opinion* based on what the fund says it *intends* to do. Risk, like beauty, is in the eye of the beholder.

Equity Funds
are mutual funds that primarily invest in stocks.

Fixed Income Funds
are mutual funds that primarily invest in bonds.

Hybrid Funds
are mutual funds that have characteristics of both equity and fixed-income funds.

Sector funds
specialize in just one industry (or sector) of our economy, such as banking and financial services, health care, high-tech, or precious metals. They often attract attention because they can turn in excellent performance if their sector of the economy is growing rapidly. The trade-off, however, is a much higher degree of risk due to their lack of industry diversification.

On Fund Names
Under the rules set by the Securities and Exchange Commission, a fund can name itself after a particular kind of security as long as it invests at least 65% of its portfolio in that type of security. For example, in an effort to gain a performance edge, a bond fund could invest up to 35% of its portfolio in higher-yielding, lower-quality corporate bonds and still represent itself as a super-safe "government securities" fund.

What you're looking for in a fund's stated investment objective is an indication of the road the fund is traveling in terms of risk and possible reward. If you saw your neighbor loading up the car for a trip and asked him where he was going, you wouldn't learn very much if all he said was "somewhere warm." That would eliminate a lot of places he *wouldn't* be going, but it really wouldn't pinpoint where he *was* going. That's also true of the way many mutual funds state their objectives. They tell you in very general terms what they are allowed to do, but beyond that the door is left open for a lot of "creativity" on the part of the manager. It's the irresponsible use of this creative freedom on the part of some fund managers that is a growing cause for concern, as we shall now see.

Red Flag #1: You can't necessarily accept a fund's "investment objective" at face value.

The investing boundaries that guide a portfolio manager ("it's OK for our fund to invest in this area but not in that area, to take these risks but not those") have become even more blurred as funds have changed their by-laws in order to broaden their investing horizons. Funds are being more aggressive in seeking a performance advantage. I have read of instances where:

• A growth-and-income stock fund held large positions in high-yield bonds and dropped 20% in value in six months when the junk bond market fell.

THE FOUR MAJOR INVESTMENT OBJECTIVES OF STOCK FUNDS

	Annualized Return July1995-June2000	Standard Deviation July1995-June2000	Definitions Used by the Investment Company Institute	Definitions Used by Morningstar Mutual Funds
Aggressive Growth	22.9%	32.3	Seek maximum capital appreciation (a rise in share price); current income is not a significant factor. Some may invest in out-of-the-mainstream stocks . . . and may also use specialized investing techniques such as option writing or short-term trading.	Seek rapid growth of capital and use investment techniques involving greater-than-average risk, such as short-selling, leveraging, and frequent trading.
Growth	21.5%	22.7	Invest in the common stock of companies that offer potentially rising share prices. These funds primarily aim to provide capital appreciation (a rise in share price) rather than steady income.	Seek capital appreciation by investing primarily in equity securities of companies with earnings that are expected to grow at an above-average rate. Current income, if considered at all, is a secondary objective.
Growth & Income	18.4%	17.8	Invest mainly in the common stock of companies that offer potentially increasing value as well as consistent dividend payments. Such funds attempt to provide investors with long-term capital growth and a steady stream of income.	Seek growth of capital and current income as near-equal objectives, primarily through equity securities.
Equity Income	14.8%	15.3	Seek a high level of income by investing primarily in stocks of companies with a consistent history of dividend payments.	Seek current income by investing at least 50% of their assets in equity securities with above-average yields.

Standard deviation is a measure of volatility usually equated with risk. The highest risk funds are at the top and the lowest risk funds at the bottom. Because there is a direct correlation between risk and reward, it's not surprising that they both decline as you move down the list.

•Two-thirds of equity income funds, which purportedly specialize in high-dividend-paying stocks, yielded less than 2% during 1999 because they went for growth instead.

• A leading bond fund in the "high quality corporate" category owes its superior record compared to its peers to the fact that it routinely invests about one-third of its portfolio in lesser quality bonds rated BBB or lower.

• A supposedly stable short-term government bond fund dropped 22% in one year because the manager had made a big bet on the direction of interest rates by investing heavily in "derivatives" (complicated securities—which I don't begin to understand—whose value is derived from some other underlying asset or index).

Consider the table at right. As with the table on page 130, the highest risk category is at the top, lowest risk group at the bottom. Look first at the high/low range of performance for the funds in each category over the twelve-month period. I can understand a very wide range of results in the top two groups because those funds are taking large risks and can make or lose money more quickly. Investors who buy these funds understand the high risk/reward potential (or they should!). But look at the growth-and-income group, where the worst performing fund *lost* 26.1%. During the same period, the Standard & Poor's 500 stock index

THE INADEQUACY OF USING A FUND'S STATED INVESTMENT OBJECTIVE AS A GUIDE TO RISK
SOURCE: MORNINGSTAR   FOR THE 12 MONTHS ENDING 6/30/2000

Investment Objective	12 Month: Best	Worst	Yield: High	Low	HighTech As High As	Foreign As High As
Aggressive Growth	161.0%	2.1%	5.6%	0.0%	95%	45%
Growth	257.3%	−24.7%	6.5%	0.0%	98%	54%
Growth & Income	65.1%	−26.1%	8.7%	0.0%	93%	34%
Equity Income	39.5%	−32.0%	9.7%	0.0%	45%	25%

(a mix of growth and income stocks) *gained* about 7%. If the categories were useful guides to risk, how could any fund in that category lose money, let alone such a huge amount?

Next, look at the yield columns, which are a measure of the dividends paid to shareholders. The table shows the best and worst yielding funds in each category. You would normally expect *no* dividends from funds in the aggressive growth group and *significant* dividends from those in the equity-income group. Yet there was a fund in the aggressive growth category that yielded 5.6%, and more surprisingly, 82 funds in the growth-and-income category that yielded 0.0% (paid no dividends at all). If they're not going to generate current income, why are they in this group? Furthermore, although not shown in the table, seven out of ten of the growth-and-income funds yielded less than 1%.

Another area where category labels can be misleading has to do with the degree to which U.S. stock funds hold shares in companies overseas. You might think that if you wanted to invest internationally you would need to choose a "global" fund (which can invest anywhere) or a "foreign" fund (which can invest anywhere except in the U.S.). Not so. As the table shows, there are funds in three of the four categories that have more than one-third of their entire portfolios invested outside the U.S.

Not only does this kind of behavior mean investors are taking risks of which they are unaware, but it also makes it more difficult to evaluate the quality of the job being done by the portfolio manager. For example, if Fund A moves significantly ahead of Fund B in its performance, is it because the manager has done a better job of selecting securities, or because he took a big risk, loaded up on options, and made a speculative killing? In their attempts to achieve top-performing results, many funds have resorted to high-risk strategies that are not readily apparent on the surface. Raw performance rankings, which previously implied excellence, may now merely represent temporary speculative success.

Red Flag #2: You can't necessarily accept a fund's diversification claims at face value.

One of the big selling points of mutual funds is that they offer lower risk due to the diversification in the portfolio. Many funds, however, in the pursuit of higher performance numbers, are turning that concept on its head by concentrating their investments in just a few sectors of the economy.

In a meeting with my staff in late 1995, I illustrated this by pointing to Robertson Stephens Value + Growth, one of the leading funds in the performance rankings at that time. Whereas most funds in its peer group showed gains over the previous twelve months of 16%–28%, the Robertson Stephens fund was up a stunning 70%! It was a case where the fund's performance was *too* good. I indicated there was no way the fund could have achieved such returns without making a huge speculative bet on the high-tech sector. I hadn't looked this up; it was self-evident that the shareholders of that fund were being exposed to a high degree of risk. The Morningstar data confirmed that the fund entered that year with an 80% stake in high-tech. I wondered if the shareholders knew this. After all, the fund was categorized as a medium-risk growth fund (not a sector fund or even an aggressive growth fund). It also contains the word "value" in its name, which implies a lesser degree of risk.

This tendency has only increased in the intervening years. At the end of 1995, fewer than forty equity funds had committed 50% or more of their portfolios to technology stocks. By mid-2000, 290 equity funds were invested that way. Now, there's nothing wrong with investing in technology. It's an exciting area. I'm merely saying that funds that have such heavy concentration in a single area of the economy should be clearly labeled as such lest investors assume they are as diversified as their name would imply.

Another way that funds shoot for higher performance is to concentrate their holdings in a smaller number of stocks. The Fidelity Magellan fund, managed by the renowned Peter Lynch during its rise to prominence, was $10 billion in size and invested in approximately 1,000 different stocks at the time Lynch stepped down in 1990. By 2000, its size had grown to over $100 billion, but it held only about 375 stocks under its current manager. Ten times as much money was invested in less than one-half as many stocks. That is a significant reduction in diversification with a corresponding increase in risk. This could present an especially difficult situation if the manager is forced to sell some of his holdings quickly due to shareholder redemptions.

Red Flag #3: You can't necessarily accept a fund's implied performance excellence at face value.

Mutual funds are promoted on the basis of how much money they've made for their shareholders. That's why their ads are usually filled with claims of "great" performance. The job of any fund's marketing department is to take that fund's performance history and make it look as good as possible. Fortunately for them, rare is the fund that hasn't hit a hot streak somewhere along the way. Using the results of the three hypothetical funds shown below, let's look at some of the ways that mutual funds will present their performance histories in the manner most likely to attract investors.

• **Picking the best time period.** The Standard & Poor's 500 stock index serves as the benchmark to beat for most stock market professionals. If they have significantly outperformed the S&P 500 over the long haul, they will certainly trumpet that in their ads. If not, one trick is to find a shorter time period in which they had relatively good performance. Take the Allen Fund, for example. It didn't compare too well over the past decade—the S&P grew at an average compounded rate of return of 11.0% versus just 10.1% for Allen. Shortening the time period to five years doesn't help, either, because Allen still trailed the S&P. But the final three-year period looks pretty good, thanks to a strong 1997. In their ads, the managers of the Allen Fund play up the market conditions of recent years and proudly show off their superior performance.

• **Using average returns rather than compounded returns.** Unfortunately for the Brown Fund, it's difficult to select *any* time frame that makes it look like a particularly promising performer, so the managers adopt a different strategy in their advertising. Rather than deal in *compounded* returns as is customary, they present their gains in *average* terms. A $1,000 initial investment in Brown over the past ten years would have grown to $2,600, a total gain of 160%. Divide that by ten years and you get an average return of 16.0% per year. However, achieving 160% over ten years requires a *compounded* return of just 10.0% (which was inferior to the 11.0% compounded growth turned in by the S&P). But to the casual reader of the ad, an average return of 16.0% per year sounds pretty impressive.

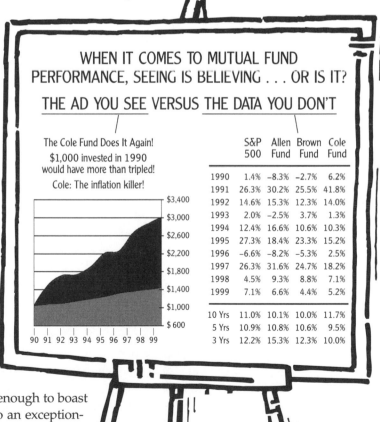

WHEN IT COMES TO MUTUAL FUND PERFORMANCE, SEEING IS BELIEVING . . . OR IS IT?
THE AD YOU SEE VERSUS THE DATA YOU DON'T

The Cole Fund Does It Again!
$1,000 invested in 1990 would have more than tripled!
Cole: The inflation killer!

	S&P 500	Allen Fund	Brown Fund	Cole Fund
1990	1.4%	−8.3%	−2.7%	6.2%
1991	26.3%	30.2%	25.5%	41.8%
1992	14.6%	15.3%	12.3%	14.0%
1993	2.0%	−2.5%	3.7%	1.3%
1994	12.4%	16.6%	10.6%	10.3%
1995	27.3%	18.4%	23.3%	15.2%
1996	−6.6%	−8.2%	−5.3%	2.5%
1997	26.3%	31.6%	24.7%	18.2%
1998	4.5%	9.3%	8.8%	7.1%
1999	7.1%	6.6%	4.4%	5.2%
10 Yrs	11.0%	10.1%	10.0%	11.7%
5 Yrs	10.9%	10.8%	10.6%	9.5%
3 Yrs	12.2%	15.3%	12.3%	10.0%

$3,400
$3,000
$2,600
$2,200
$1,800
$1,400
$1,000
$600

90 91 92 93 94 95 96 97 98 99

• **Emphasizing dollars earned rather than percentage returns.** The Cole Fund has a ten-year record that is slightly better than the S&P, but not enough to boast about. Besides, most of that was due to an exceptionally good year way back in 1991. More recently, the fund has done relatively poorly, although it has man-

aged to eke out some gains each year. So the managers of Cole decide to advertise their performance in dollar terms rather than in percentage terms. A shareholder who held through
the entire ten-year period would have seen his initial investment triple in value, and the
graph in the ad (far left) illustrates the steady growth. To make the fund's performance appear even more powerful, the results are shown in contrast to inflation rather than the S&P
500 benchmark, which it barely surpassed. An investor coming across the Cole Fund ad would
likely have reacted favorably to its performance claims. So, be alert. There's often much more
than meets the eye in mutual fund performance claims.

Red Flag #4: You can't necessarily accept a fund's rankings at face value.

This problem flows logically from Red Flag #1, not being able to accept a fund's "investment objective" at face value. If you can't count on the risk categories to be consistent
in comparing apples to apples, then the performance rankings based on them are potentially misleading. Assume that the ABC Fund is classified as a "large-cap blend" fund by
Morningstar (meaning it invests in large size companies using a combination of growth
and value strategies) while the Lipper analyst, due to using slightly different criteria, puts
it in the "large-cap growth" category. In that event, which is the "correct" classification to
use when evaluating the excellence of the fund's performance? For example, if ABC averaged 24.0% per year over the past five years, was that good? It depends who you ask.

Lipper would rank ABC's performance against the other funds it placed in the large-
cap growth fund group. Since pure growth strategies were the big winners in the second
half of the 1990s, let's say the average fund in that group returned 25.3% per year. Compared to that, ABC's returns were below average. Consequently, its standing in the Lipper
rankings would not be very impressive. Turning to Morningstar, let's assume the average
fund in its large-cap blend group returned 20.6% during the same period. ABC's average
annual return of 24.0% was terrific as far as Morningstar was concerned—good enough to
rank in the top 20% of its peer group—and Morningstar's rankings would reflect that. When
you're being "graded on the curve," it's good to be in a class of underachievers.

This is a mighty important matter to the folks at the ABC Fund. It determines whether
they can advertise their fund as an excellent performer or an also-ran. Which measurement
service's rankings do you believe ABC will refer to in its full-page ads? Morningstar's, of
course. In this example, the fund has done nothing wrong. It is merely taking advantage of
a difference of opinion between Morningstar and Lipper. There have been instances, however, where funds have been suspected of "gaming" the fund rankings, that is, attempting
to have their fund placed in a risk category where its performance would earn it a high rank-
ing relative to the other funds in that group. *Worth* magazine explained it this way:

> *Fund managers can accomplish this sleight of hand in part because fund categories are so
> loosely defined, and because funds are commonly listed under the heading suggested by the vaguely
> worded investment objectives found in their prospectuses. This allows managers, in effect, to choose
> the heading under which their funds will be ranked, a cozy arrangement from the not-too-distant
> time when the whole industry was small and stodgy rather than the cutthroat world of 11,500 or*

more funds it has become. . . . Wall Street professionals have suspected for years that gaming was widespread. Until recently, they haven't had much evidence to back them up, but two independent studies now appear to confirm that gaming not only exists, but may be more widespread than anyone imagined. Both research efforts concluded that more than half of all mutual funds are misclassified in performance rankings. And more than one out of ten is listed inaccurately enough that investors could be misled about their true nature, according to one study.

In spite of these concerns, let's not throw the baby out with the bath water.

As we saw in chapter 10, mutual funds offer many advantages to the average investor. The answer is not to avoid mutual funds entirely, but rather to learn how to shop for them intelligently. This means you must accept responsibility for getting the information you need and reading it sufficiently well so that you understand the risks as well as the rewards. The place to start, even though it has its limitations, is with the fund's prospectus.

Mutual fund prospectuses are usually boring, filled with unfamiliar terms, and set in small print. Although investors are continually admonished to "read the fund prospectus carefully before you invest or send money," I doubt that many do so. If you're among the legions who routinely toss fund prospectuses onto your read-it-when-I-find-the-time stack, you're missing out on some important information the government wants you to have.

Basically, putting your money in a mutual fund is like taking an investment journey, and the prospectus outlines the details of the trip—where it wishes to go in terms of its goal, the strategy it will use to get there, how much risk it will take on the way, and what it will charge you to ride along. Here are some things you should know about prospectuses.

❶ **A prospectus is for marking in.** Don't hesitate to make notes in the margins or mark in some way the items that you don't understand. Then use that as a checklist when taking your questions back to the fund or your broker. Don't leave a concern unaddressed or a doubt unresolved.

❷ **A prospectus is a legal document.** That's why it tends to read poorly. The fund's attorneys have made sure that it contains only those promises that the fund is fully confident it can keep. As a result, it contains no performance guarantees.

❸ **A prospectus has a limited shelf life, usually a little over a year.** Aside from the historical data that needs to be updated, there are other items that can change as well: the amount of sales loads (if any); the level of management fees and operating expenses; policies that govern buying (e.g., the minimum required to open an account) and selling your shares (e.g., how frequently you can exchange them for shares in other funds within the same organization and if there's a charge).

❹ **A prospectus has five sections of particular interest.** Get your yellow highlighter out—here's how you can find the essentials in ten minutes flat.

• **Investment Goals and Strategies.** This section tells you what the fund hopes to accomplish (regardless of what the name of the fund implies). The objective is usually stated in terms of growth (buying securities that go up in value) and income (making regular dividend or interest payments to you). Here you'll also find the strategy the fund will use as it attempts to achieve its objectives. Does it have a value or growth orientation, or prefer small companies over large ones? You'll learn if the fund is *committed* to buying certain kinds of securities ("80% of the fund's assets will be invested in investment grade bonds rated AA or higher"), or merely *permitted* to buy them ("manager may engage in trading exchange-traded covered options").

• **Risks.** This is where they tell you that you can lose money owning shares in the fund. The boilerplate warnings here shouldn't come as a surprise, but read them anyway and make sure you know what they mean. Ask enough questions so that you have a good idea of what the worst-case-scenario is likely to be.

• **Past Performance.** This includes the fund's annual returns to shareholders over several years, usually in comparison to a benchmark like the S&P 500 or Russell 2000 index. Look to see if there is a great deal of year-to-year variability (big gains, small gains, and some losses all seemingly mixed together) versus consistent performance in the areas where the fund is supposed to be strong (stability, growth, or income). Does the fund have a strong record because of just one or two good years? Caution: even a good long-term record can be misleading if the manager who achieved it is no longer running the fund. Don't assume there's any correlation between the fund's past and your future.

• **Fees and Expenses.** Here's where you'll find a breakdown of the maximum sales loads (if any). Are the sales fees up front, or contingent on how long you own your shares? Do they apply to reinvested dividends as well as your initial deposit? Are there redemption fees to pay? There is also data on the annual operating expenses of the fund. These are the invisible costs that you never see on your monthly statement. Performance numbers, such as those published in financial magazines, already take operating expenses (but not sales fees) into account.

• **Buying/Selling Shares.** This lays out how you buy/sell shares in the fund as well as services offered like reinvestment options, wire transfers, check-writing privileges, etc. The important thing here is to be clear on what you have to do to sell your shares. Can you do it over the phone? How long before you'll get your money? Make sure you understand this thoroughly and have any necessary forms on file with the fund.

The most important paragraph in any prospectus is found on page one. It says something like this: "The Securities and Exchange Commission has not . . . determined whether this prospectus is accurate or complete." It's up to you to ask the right questions.

If this chapter has been discouraging, take heart! Later in this book, I'm going to show you how to assure that the funds you buy are suited to your personal needs.

First, in chapter 16 I'm going to introduce you to a special breed of mutual funds called "index" funds that, by their very nature, avoid the red flag traps we've just discussed. In chapter 17, I'll then show you how to assemble them into a portfolio that reflects your current age, goals, and tolerance for risk. And in chapter 18, we'll go out into the marketplace and look at some funds that are suitable for those who are just getting started. You need go no further than this to have a winning long-term strategy. ◆

Income Taxes and Your Mutual Fund Investments

I. **Mutual funds are simply conduits through which you invest. The capital gains/losses and dividend/interest income they receive are treated as if they were yours personally.**

   A. Investment companies periodically pay to their shareholders the interest and dividends the funds receive on their investments.

   B. Investment companies periodically pay to their shareholders the capital gains the funds make when selling their investments.

   C. The date that these distributions are set aside from the fund's assets for payment to shareholders is called the "ex-dividend" date. This is the significant date as far as income taxes are concerned, not the later date on which you receive the distribution check in the mail.

II. **The tax accounting for mutual funds can be confusing, even to veteran investors.**

   A. Buying just prior to a fund distribution does not result in an actual gain, but merely results in incurring an immediate tax liability.

   B. Distributions are taxable in the year they are declared, not in the year they are received by the investor.

   C. There are two kinds of capital gains to keep in mind—those the funds can earn by buying and selling within the fund portfolios, and those investors can earn by selling their fund shares for more than they paid for them.

   D. The IRS recognizes three different methods for computing capital gains on fund shares. If you sell part (rather than all) of your shares in a fund, you can select the one that results in the lowest tax liability.

III. **Timing your selling so as to minimize or postpone your tax liability is a natural inclination; however, it should not supersede the normal common sense disciplines built into your long-term strategy.**

If you're tempted to skip this chapter until next year at tax time, don't do it! The sooner you understand what will be needed to complete next year's 1040 form . . .

. . . the sooner you can begin organizing your thinking and record keeping to make things much easier on yourself. Also, you can avoid making a costly year-end investment that will unnecessarily raise your taxes (see common misconceptions one and two on pages 139-140). I promise to do my best at making this as clear as possible—but nobody can keep it from being boring! So go for a cup of coffee if need be, and get ready to make some good notes in the margins.

Mutual funds are among the most flexible of all investments from a tax standpoint. That's the good news. Calculating your taxable income, however, is made more complicated by a maze of rules and exceptions to the rules at both the federal and state levels. That's the bad news. Because tax laws vary so widely from state to state, I can't proceed very far into planning tax strategies; there are just too many possible scenarios. What I will do is give you a basic foundation so that you can read and plan intelligently in relation to your particular tax bracket and state of residence.

The first major point I want to emphasize is that mutual funds are simply conduits through which individuals invest in securities.

In the process of investing, mutual funds incur capital gains and losses and receive dividend and interest income on their investments. From a tax point of view, all of this is done in behalf of their shareholders. *It's as if you owned all the investments outright, and the gains and losses that result are all your personal gains and losses.* There are three ways mutual funds can generate profits in your behalf:

❶ They invest in stocks that pay dividends. Mutual funds collect the dividends and pay them out to you periodically.

❷ They invest in bonds or short-term debt securities that pay interest. They collect the interest and pay it out to you periodically.

❸ They sell one of their investments for more than they paid for it, thereby making a capital gain. They keep track of these gains (and offset them against any capital losses) and pay them out to you periodically, usually annually. If they end up with more capital losses than gains, they carry the losses over to the next year; you would receive no payment for the year just ending.

All of these payments to you, regardless of the source—whether dividends, interest, or capital gains—are called "distributions." The fund decides whether to make these periodic distribution payments monthly, quarterly, semi-annually, or annually.

A fund goes through a two-step process in making distributions. First, it "declares" the amount of the distribution . . .

. . . it intends to make, and sets aside the appropriate amount of cash that will be needed to write you a check. Let's say your fund declares a 25¢ per share distribution, and that there are one million shares owned by investors. This means the fund will be paying out a total of $250,000 to its shareholders at this time. Once the money is earmarked for distribution in this way, the fund no longer counts the $250,000 when it does its daily bookkeeping (see page 109). This has the effect of suddenly lowering the net asset value of the fund—one day the money was being counted as part of the fund, and the next day, the day of the declaration, it wasn't. To indicate to investors that the net asset value is lower than it otherwise would be because of the distribution, an "x" appears next to the name of the fund in the daily newspaper listings. The date this happens is called the "ex-dividend" date, *and it is the significant date as far as your taxes are concerned.*

The second step of the distribution process is when the fund actually mails your check to you. It can be anywhere from a few days to a month later. This is called the "payment date" and is important only to you (and the other shareholders) because that's when you finally receive the cash that has been promised. The payment date has no significance when computing your taxable income.

Let's look at some of the common misconceptions that investors have about fund taxation.

Misconception #1: "It's a good idea to invest in a mutual fund just before one of its periodic distributions."

Actually, it's a bad idea because it will create an immediate tax liability for you. There is no actual profit in owning a fund on the day it goes ex-dividend because the amount the shareholders are to receive is deducted from the value of the fund that same day. If an investor buys a fund today and the fund declares a distribution tomorrow, *the investor owes tax on the amount of the distribution.* This may seem unfair, as the profits were earned by the fund long before the new investor made his purchase. Still, someone has to pay the tax on those profits, and it falls to the "shareholders of record" *at the time of the distribution* to do so.

When a fund makes a distribution, the price of its shares falls by the exact amount of the distribution. This has the effect of reducing the investor's capital gains tax

> **HOW DISTRIBUTIONS ARE REPORTED IN THE NEWSPAPER**
>
> Monday's closing price for the XYZ Fund was $6.00 per share, up 4¢ from Friday's closing price. On Tuesday, the net asset value fell 10¢ a share due to a slight drop in the stock market that day. The fund also declared a 60¢ per share distribution on Tuesday. The listing for XYZ in the newspaper for those two days would look like this:
>
> | Monday | XYZ Fund | 6.00 | + .04 |
> |--------|----------|------|-------|
> | Tuesday | XYZ Fund | x5.30 | − .70 |

liability in the future. Most funds make distributions at roughly the same time each year, and most funds announce distributions in advance. This presents an opportunity for savings. Just before purchasing shares of any mutual fund, call the fund and ask if a distribution will be made soon. If a distribution is scheduled within a few days, you might want to wait and purchase your shares the day after the distribution to avoid its tax impact.

Misconception #2: "If I don't receive my distribution check until after the end of the year, I don't have to pay taxes on it this year."

From a tax standpoint, distributions fall into two classifications: (1) "capital gain" as described above, and (2) "income," a mutual fund's dividend and interest earnings, less its management fees and other operating expenses. Short-term capital gain, interest, and dividend income distributions are all currently being taxed at identical rates.

Your tax liability is based on the ex-dividend date, not the payment date. If the ex-dividend date is in the current year, your tax liability is also. The fund is required to prepare IRS Form 1099-DIV for everyone who was a shareholder on any day a distribution was declared. You will receive a copy (and so will the government), which lists the various distributions you will be taxed on, and where to report them on your form 1040 return.

Misconception #3: "As long as I don't sell any of my mutual fund shares, I can't have any capital gains."

This seems logical. Assume you buy fund shares at $10 and still own them at the end of the year. Since it is too soon to know whether you will receive more or less than $10 per share when you sell them, it would seem to follow that it is also too soon to know whether you'll have a capital gain to pay taxes on. What this overlooks is that the mutual fund *itself*, within its portfolio, is continually buying and selling securities. Each time it sells one, it has another capital gain or loss. Since the tax law considers all of this as being done on your behalf, you participate in your fair share of that gain or loss *whenever a fund declares a capital gain distribution.*

When you eventually do redeem (sell) your fund shares, any capital gain or loss from the original purchase must be reported on Schedule D of your form 1040 tax return just like any other investment. One easy way to put off paying this kind of capital gains tax is simply to avoid selling mutual funds for gain just before the end of the year. If you sell in December, then taxes will have to be paid by April 15, just three and a half months later. Instead, you might wait to sell out of a profitable position until the first week of January. The tax on such gains would then not be owed until April of the following year. This postpones paying your tax liability more than fifteen months. By the same token, a good time to sell a fund if you have a loss is in December, as the loss will be deductible on the tax return filed only a few months later.

Misconception #4: "To calculate my capital gain from selling my fund shares, I subtract the amount I paid for them from the proceeds I received when selling them."

This is only true in the simplest instance—where you bought all your shares at the same time, received no distributions while you owned them, and sold them all at the same time. In that case, it's pretty straightforward as described. However, if you either receive distributions, acquire your shares over time (for example, through dollar-cost-averaging or reinvesting your dividends), or sell only part of your holdings, there is more work to be done. Let's look at the most common situations.

• **When you receive a distribution.** Keep in mind: *you aren't really gaining anything when you receive a distribution because the amount of the distribution is deducted from the value of your shares.* For example, assume you buy 100 fund shares at $8.00 each. Your total cost is $800. The value grows to $12.00 per share, and your investment becomes worth $1,200 (100 shares multiplied by $12.00 each). If a $1.00 per share dividend distribution is declared, you will receive a check for $100 (100 shares multiplied by $1.00). However, on the ex-dividend date, the value of your shares immediately drops to $11.00 each because $1.00 per share has been taken out of the fund's asset pool to be mailed to shareholders. You haven't gained; you still have $1,200 in value—$1,100 in fund shares (100 shares multiplied by $11.00) and $100 cash. The fund has merely "robbed Peter to pay Paul."

The tax consequences work like this. If you had sold your shares *before* the ex-dividend date, you would have a $400 capital gain ($1,200 proceeds minus $800 cost). If you sell your shares *after* the ex-dividend date, you would have a $300 capital gain ($1,100 proceeds minus $800 cost) *plus* $100 in dividend income; thus, you still have total taxable income of $400. The ex-dividend date didn't change the amount of your profit; it only changed the tax nature of your profit.

• **When you reinvest your dividends.** If you routinely have your fund distributions reinvested in more shares, you must be careful to avoid double taxation. When calculating your tax liability, you must add the cost of the additional shares purchased with your dividends to the amount originally invested in the fund. This will raise your tax "basis" in the fund shares you've acquired. In this way, you'll avoid being taxed twice—initially on the dividends and again later as a capital gain when the fund shares are sold.

For example, let's take our previous example and make a change: Instead of receiving the $100 distribution in cash, you instruct your fund to reinvest it in more shares. On the ex-dividend date, the value of the fund dropped to $11.00 per share. At that price, the $100 would purchase an additional 9.09 shares, bringing your total shares to 109.09. The $100 distribution must be reported on that year's federal 1040, and taxes must be paid.

Later, you sell all of your shares for $11.00 each, which brings in proceeds of $1,200 (109.09 shares multiplied by $11.00 per share). Will you be taxed on your $400 gain? No. The total cost of the shares (for capital gains purposes) is the initial $800 *plus the $100 on which tax has already been paid*, making a total of $900. Thus, the taxable capital gain from the $1,200 proceeds received the following year is only $300 rather than $400.

• **When you dollar-cost-average.** If you routinely add to your fund holdings through frequent new purchases, you should be especially careful to keep careful records of the dates, amounts invested, and number of shares purchased. That's because you will later need detailed and accurate information concerning your many different purchases in order to compute any capital gains that might result when your shares are eventually sold. This is all the more true if you later sell part (rather than all) of your shares. See the chart at left for an explanation of the options you have under the tax laws. After you choose one of these methods for a particular fund, you must use it every time you sell shares from that fund.

HOW TO COMPUTE YOUR TAXABLE GAINS AND LOSSES

	Using the First-In, First-Out Method	Using the Average Cost Method	Using the Specific Cost Method
How to Do It	Unless you say otherwise, the IRS assumes that you sell your shares in the same order as you bought them.	You calculate the average price paid for all the shares in the fund that you own. Divide the total dollars invested (including any distributions reinvested) by the number of shares you own.	Send the fund written instructions saying that you are selling the shares purchased on such-and-such a day at such-and-such a price.
Advantages and Disadvantages	If your early purchases were at higher levels, this method will give you tax losses; if your early purchases were at lower levels, this method will create taxable gains.	Could either raise or lower your taxes depending on how the other alternatives work out.	A little more trouble, but gives you the most flexibility for managing your tax liability from year to year.

Under the general heading of "other assorted things you should know" are the following items.

• The IRS is available year-round to answer your tax questions—call (800) 829-1040. It also offers free materials on various topics—call (800) 829-3676 to request IRS forms and publications. You can begin with publication 910, which is an explanation of all the *other* publications that are available.

• The best tax advantage available for mutual fund investing is to carry out as much of your long-term program as possible within an IRA or other tax-deferred type of account.

• Whenever you "switch" between funds at the same mutual fund organization, it's the same as selling your shares in the fund you are leaving. Calling it a switch doesn't change the fact that you are selling one fund and buying another. Unless you are moving out of a money market fund, every switch has tax consequences.

• Using the special checks your bond fund might supply also has tax consequences. That's because the fund sells some of your shares in order to honor your check. As a result, you'll have a taxable gain or loss on the shares sold. This is not the case with money market funds because they always maintain a level $1.00 per share value.

• Investors in tax-free funds don't completely avoid dealing with tax considerations. For example, capital gains distributions from the funds and capital gains you might make on the sale of your shares are taxable just like with any other security. Tax-free income is generally free from federal tax, but not all the dividends you receive will necessarily be exempt from state tax; check with your fund if in need of clarification. Also, special rules apply under a variety of situations (for example, investors who receive tax-exempt income from shares in a municipal bond fund that was held for six months or less and sold for a loss). Request IRS Publication 564 for more information on the taxation of mutual funds.

• If you invest in international stock and bond funds, mutual funds are to notify you if you are entitled to claim a tax deduction for taxes that the fund paid to a foreign country. For more information, request IRS Publication 514.

• The tax documentation you will receive from your mutual fund each year includes: confirmation statements telling you the date, price, and number of shares transacted when buying and selling fund shares; form 1099-B reports the proceeds from selling shares during the year (it can be used to help you compute your capital gains or losses); and form 1099-DIV reports the details of dividend and capital gain distributions for which you owe taxes.

For More Help
Vanguard has helpful educational material available regarding Mutual Funds and Taxes. Visit them at www.vanguard.com/educ/lib/plain/taxes.html

IRS Website for Individuals
www.irs.treas.gov/ind_info/index.html

To View IRS Forms or Publications
www.irs.treas.gov/forms_pubs/index.html

I felt it was important to equip you with some basic tax-planning knowledge. My recommendation, however, is that you not buy or sell primarily for tax reasons.

Although I acknowledge that it is legitimate to minimize one's tax liability by using any of the applicable strategies mentioned here, a preoccupation with taxes can be counterproductive. Sometimes a few days in the market can make a big difference as to the price you pay or receive for your shares. Don't let tax considerations sidetrack you from following the disciplines you will be building into your long-term strategy. ◆

SECTION

4

THE FOURTH LEVEL OF FINANCIAL FITNESS

Diversifying for Safety

Divide your portion to seven, or even to eight, for you
do not know what misfortune may occur on the earth.

Ecclesiastes 11:2

"I'm relaxing in the jacuzzi watching t.v. when one of those financial interview
shows comes on. They're talking about how easy it is to make a killing in high-
tech stocks. By that time I've already sold my company and am pretty well set
financially, ya know, but of course, who can't always use a little more? So..."

CHAPTER PREVIEW

The Basics of Bonds

I. **Bonds are merely long-term IOUs.**

    A. They are a promise to repay the amount borrowed at a specific time in the future. They pay a fixed rate of interest that doesn't vary over the life of the bond. They carry higher risks than money market funds due to their longer average maturities.

    B. There are two major risks associated with investing in bonds, both of which can be neutralized.

        1. The first risk is that you might lend to someone who is not credit-worthy. This risk is neutralized by loaning only to the federal government and financially strong corporations. Investing in a bond mutual fund adds safety through diversification.

        2. The second risk is that you could get locked into a below-market rate of return. This risk can be neutralized by loaning only for the short term. The advantage of longer maturities is that you receive a higher yield. The disadvantages of longer maturities are that the value of your bonds can go down due to either their quality rating being lowered or rising interest rates.

II. **By using the two main influences on risk, we can create a "risk profile" for categorizing bond funds that will greatly simplify the process of selecting the bond funds that are best for you.**

    A. This results in four distinct categories (or "peer groups"), each having its own risk characteristics in terms of quality and average maturities.

    B. The risk profile enables us to build a "risk ladder." I provide ten-year performance histories based on an average of all the funds in each of the four risk categories. I also point out risk characteristics you should understand.

III. **Tax-free bonds are issued by state and local governments. The interest received from tax-free bonds is exempt from federal income tax and also exempt from state income tax in the state where the bond is originally issued.**

IV. **Although they have advantages, investing in bond funds has two drawbacks that don't apply to investing in individual bonds: they never reach maturity, and, under certain conditions, they may have tax disadvantages.**

Bonds
are IOUs in the form of investment certificates.

Issuer
is the business or government that is borrowing the money.

Maturity Date
is the time at which the borrower is due to pay the bond in full.

Coupon Rate
is the percent of interest stated on the bond that the borrower agrees to pay to investors. It stays fixed throughout the life of the bond.

Par
is the face value on the bond, usually $1,000. This is what investors are to receive when the bond matures.

Deep Discount Bonds
are those that can be purchased far below their par value. This means investors receive, in addition to the regular interest payments, the added benefit of getting back much more at maturity than they paid for the bond originally. This extra enticement is needed either because the coupon rate being paid is below the current levels available to investors or because the issuer's credit rating has slipped and full payment at maturity is in doubt.

Average Maturity
is the average number of years it will take for all the bonds in a bond fund portfolio to mature. As a general rule, the longer the average maturity, the greater the risk in the portfolio.

Greater self-confidence—the kind needed to take charge of your financial future—comes with knowledge and experience.

In this book, I'm working on adding to the first, *but you're the only one who can add to the second.*

Let me encourage you to keep at it. It's worth the effort because nobody will take as much of a genuine interest in your finances as you will. And, when you think about it, you know yourself better than anyone else does. You know how much money you have to work with and whether you're really willing to risk losing any of it. You know how much you'd reasonably like to make, how much time you have before you need it, and how much patience you bring to the task. Most people know, perhaps even subconsciously, what's best for them.

I've seen this demonstrated time and again in the counseling sessions I have with my readers. After listening to them explain the various alternatives they have, I usually ask, "What would you *like* to do?" The responses are almost always reasonable and carefully thought out. They knew the answers; they just wanted me to confirm them. In the same way that most of us know which foods we *should* be eating and how much exercise we *should* be getting, we also generally know how much risk we should be taking.

You'll find that all of this isn't as complicated as it might sound, especially when you follow the proven investing strategy I'm going to lay out for you in this section. I call the strategy Just-the-Basics because I devised it for people who are relatively new to investing and find themselves a bit overwhelmed by the idea of diversifying across the full risk spectrum. To make matters easier for them, I created a simplified diversification strategy that uses just four no-load mutual funds. It's the epitome of simplicity and low maintenance. I'll explain it in detail in chapter 16, but first I need to lay a little more foundation so you'll be able to clearly understand what I'll be telling you. That requires two brief primers, one on bonds and bond funds (that's this chapter) and one on stocks and stock funds (coming in the next chapter). So, let's get started!

America's largest banks and corporations (not to mention our local, state, and federal governments) need your help . . .

. . . they'd like to borrow some money from you. For a few months or, if you're willing, for several decades. To make sure you get the message, their ads are everywhere. The government promotes safety of principal and has created certain kinds of bonds with special tax advantages. Banks and S&Ls want your deposits and want you to know your money is safe with them because it's "insured." Bond funds tantalize you with suggestions of still higher yields, although in their small print they remind you that "the value of your shares will fluctuate." And of course, insurance companies promote the tax-deferred advantages of their annuities. You're in the driver's seat. To all these institutions, you're a Very Important Person.

Does the thought of "renting" out your money seem strange? Chances are, you do it all the time. You probably think of it as buying a certificate of deposit (or Treasury bill, bond, or fixed annuity), but actually, you're making a loan. The "rent" you're being paid is called interest. In the financial markets, investors with extra money (lenders) rent it out to others who are in need of money (borrowers). The borrowers give their IOUs to the lenders.

Bonds are basically IOUs.

They are a promise to repay the amount borrowed at a specified time in the future. The date on which the bonds will be paid off is called the maturity date and may be set at a few years out or as many as (believe it or not) one hundred years away. At that time, the holder of the bond gets back its full face value (called par value). In order to make bonds affordable to a larger investing public, they are usually issued in $1,000 denominations.

Bonds promise to pay a fixed rate of interest (called the coupon rate) until they mature (are paid off). *This rate doesn't vary over the life of the bond.* Remember that. Once the rate is set, it's permanent. That's why bonds are referred to as "fixed income" investments. As we'll soon see, it's the unchanging nature of the interest rate that causes bonds to go up and down in value.

Why buy bonds?

If you want to protect your principal and set up a steady stream of income, then bonds, rather than stocks, are the answer. Current income is traditionally the most important reason people invest in bonds, which usually generate greater current returns than CDs, money market funds, or stocks.

They also can offer greater security than most common stocks since an issuer of a bond will do everything possible to meet its bond obligations. (Even Donald Trump accepted a humbling at the hands of his banks in order to gain the money necessary to meet his bonds' interest payments.)

The interest owed on a corporate bond must be paid to bondholders before any dividends can be paid to the stockholders of the company. And it's payable before federal, state, and city taxes. Being first in line helps make the investment safer.

Bond funds carry higher risks than money market funds (see pages 82-83). The primary difference has to do with . . .

. . . the *average maturity* of the portfolio. Bond funds diversify among a great many individual bond issues, each of which has its own maturity date. By adding up the length of time until each issue matures and then dividing by the total number of bonds owned, you learn the average amount of time needed for the entire portfolio to be paid off.

While time is passing, many things can happen to interest rates or to the bond issuer (whoever borrowed the money from investors in the first place) to affect the value of the bonds. The more distant the maturity date, the more time for things to potentially go wrong. That's why bond funds with longer maturities carry more risk than ones with shorter maturities.

WHAT BOND RATINGS MEAN

Standard & Poor's and Moody's are the two leading credit rating agencies. They use slightly different rating terminology. S&P is shown on the left (AAA) and Moody's on the right (Aaa). Credit ratings attempt to alert bondholders to the risks of not being paid the interest when due or the principal upon maturity. The lower the rating, the higher the risk *and* the higher the interest rate the borrower will have to pay to attract investors.

AAA / Aaa
Highest rating; extremely strong capacity to pay interest and repay principal; smallest degree of investment risk.

AA / Aa
High quality; very strong capacity to pay interest and repay principal; safety margins are strong, but not quite as exemplary as the AAA level.

A / A
Upper-medium grade; strong capacity to pay interest and repay principal; good debt-service coverage, although vulnerable to cyclical trends.

BBB / Baa
Medium grade; adequate capacity to pay interest and repay principal; however, no room for error. Any further deterioration and these will no longer be considered investment grade bonds.

BB / Ba
Speculative grade; only moderately secure.

B / B
Low grade; lacking characteristics of a desirable investment.

CCC / Caa
Very speculative, with significant risk. May be in danger of default.

CC / Ca
Highly speculative, often in default or otherwise flawed; major risk.

C / C
No interest is being paid, or in default with poor prospects of improvement.

Any drop in the value of the bonds is offset against the fund's interest income. If these losses are greater than the interest received by the fund, the price of the bond fund drops that day. *That's why it's possible for investors in a bond fund to get back less than they put in!*

Let's learn how bond values fluctuate by working through an example. Assume XYZ Inc. wants to borrow $200 million for advanced research . . .

. . . and doesn't want to have to pay the loan back for 30 years. Banks generally don't like to loan their money out for such long periods of time, so the company decides to issue some bonds.

Let's say that XYZ agrees to pay a coupon rate of 9% annual interest. Bond traders would call these bonds the "XYZ nines of 2031." (XYZ will pay 9% interest and repay the loan in 2031.) No matter what happens to interest rates over the next thirty years, XYZ is obligated to pay investors 9% per year on these bonds. No more. No less. If you purchase one of these new XYZ bonds, you will receive $90 per year from XYZ on your $1,000 investment (9% times $1,000). Since bond interest is usually paid twice a year, you would receive two checks for $45 spread six months apart.

The simplest transaction would work this way. Assume that when XYZ first sells its bonds (through selected stock brokerage firms), you buy one of these brand-new bonds at par value. In effect, you lend XYZ $1,000. You collect $90 interest every year for thirty years. It doesn't matter how high or how low interest rates might move during this period, you're still going to get $90 a year because that was the deal that you and XYZ agreed to. Finally, in 2031, XYZ pays back your $1,000. You made no gain on the value of the bond itself; your profit came solely from the steady stream of fixed income you received over the thirty years.

There are two major risks to watch out for in the world of bonds. The first is that you might not get all your money back.

The pros call it the "credit risk" because you're depending on the creditworthiness of the borrower. You're taking the risk that the issuer of the bond might go into default. This means the borrower is not able to keep up its interest payments or even pay off the bonds when they mature. This is the worst-case scenario that faces all bond investors.

To help evaluate this risk, ratings are available that help determine how safe the bonds are as an investment. Standard & Poor's and Moody's are the two companies best known for this. There are nine possible ratings a bond can receive (see sidebar notes, page 150). Most bond investors limit their selections to bonds given one of the top four ratings. As you might expect, the lower the quality, the higher rate of interest investors demand in order to reward them for accepting the increased risk of default.

By definition, all other borrowers are less creditworthy than the U.S. government. Therefore, borrowers who are in competition with the federal government for your money *must* pay you more in order to give you an incentive to lend to them instead of Uncle Sam. That's why U.S. Treasury bills establish the floor for interest rates. Other rates are higher than the T-bill rate depending on how creditworthy the borrower is.

If XYZ gets into trouble due to poor management and earnings, its ability to pay off its bond debts . . .

. . . may come into question. Assume its quality rating is lowered from AAA to A, and that shortly thereafter you need to sell your XYZ bond to meet an unexpected expense. A buyer of your bond will now want a greater potential profit to reward him for the possibly greater risk of default. As a practical matter, it may seem to be a very minor increase in risk, but the buyer will want compensation nevertheless.

But remember, the interest that XYZ pays on these bonds is fixed at $90 per year and can't be changed. The only way anyone buying your bond can improve his profit potential is *if you will lower the price of your bond*. Then, in addition to the interest received from XYZ, the buyer will also reap a profit when he ultimately collects $1,000 (if all goes well) for a bond he bought from you for only, say, $900.

Thus, as the quality rating of a bond falls, sellers must lower their asking prices in order to make the bond attractive to potential buyers. Always remember that a bond can become completely worthless if the issuer gets into financial difficulty and defaults.

How can you minimize the credit risk? One way to eliminate it altogether is to stick solely with U.S. Treasuries. The drawback, however, is that because U.S. government bonds are widely regarded as the world's safest fixed income investments, the interest rates they pay investors are lower than those of corporate bonds. The most common way to minimize the credit risk is to add safety through diversification. Spread your holdings out among many different bond issues. That's where bond funds (which we'll discuss shortly) can play a helpful role.

How "Yield" Is Different from "Gain" and "Total Return"

In the late 1980s, as interest rates fell on bank CDs and money market funds, savers went in search of higher returns. They saw that some highly publicized bond funds were "yielding" 12% and more, so off they went. When the junk bond market crashed, investors found they could be receiving a great yield and still lose money! The average high-yield bond fund fell about 10% in value in 1990. A few dropped more than 20%. Focusing on yield alone can be dangerous because the highest yielding funds are the ones with the lower quality ratings or the longest average maturities.

When evaluating whether an investment has been successful, there are two questions to be addressed. First, how much income from your investment did you receive? And second, did you get back more than you put in, less than you put in, or the same as you put in?

The income you received while your money was tied up is called the yield and is always expressed in annualized terms. If you invest $1,000 in an XYZ bond and it pays $90 every year in interest, it is yielding you 9.0% ($90/$1,000). Now, when you eventually sell your investment, if you receive back more than you paid for it, you have a capital gain. Let's say your $1,000 investment is sold after three years for $1,300, giving you a $300 gain.

Both the yield and the gain represent partial returns; only when you combine them do you get the total picture, hence the name total return. The total return is usually expressed in annual compounded terms. In our example, you invested $1,000 and received back a total of $1,570 over three years ($270 in dividends plus the $300 gain).

To learn what your total return was in annual terms, you ask, "What rate of growth is needed to turn $1,000 into $1,570 in three years?" By using a financial calculator that can perform time-value-of-money computations, you learn that it takes about a 16.3% per year rate of growth to do that. In other words, if you could invest $1,000 at 16.3% for three years, you'd have approximately $1,570 at the end of that time. In the example, you know that part of the growth came from that 9% annual yield. But how did you get from 9% to that 16.3% total return? By selling for a gain and picking up that extra $300. The 9% yield that you received as you went along, plus the $300 gain at the end, made it possible for you to achieve a very nice 16.3% annualized total return.

But what if the bond had gone down $300 instead of up $300. That makes the result look quite different. You invested $1,000, and after three years have just $970 ($270 in dividends minus a $300 loss) to show for your efforts. Your total return is now negative; while you were collecting your 9% yield with the thought that you were making money, you were actually losing, on average, about 1% per year!

The second major risk facing bondholders, and the one that is the greater of the two, is that you could get locked into a below-market rate of return.

The pros call this the "interest-rate risk." It's the same dilemma you face when trying to decide how long you should tie up your money in a bank CD, but it has even greater significance when investing in bonds. If you invest in a two-year CD when it turns out that a six-month one would have been better, you're only missing out on better rates for eighteen months. Try making that eighteen *years*, and you get an idea of how painful it can be when holding long-term bonds during a period of rising interest rates.

A fear of inflation leads to rising long-term interest rates. Just for the moment, assume that you're back in 1980 and inflation is running at 12% per year. Now ask yourself this question: Would you be willing to pay full price for a thirty-year, $1,000 bond with an 9% coupon rate? Not likely. The bond would only be paying you $90 in interest per year at a time when you need $120 just to keep up with inflation. You'd be agreeing to a deal that would guarantee you a loss of purchasing power of $30 each year. Eventually, you'd get your $1,000 back, but it wouldn't buy nearly as much then as it does now.

But what if the seller would lower the price of the bond so you could buy that bond at a big discount? If you only had to pay $750 for a $1,000 bond, it might make economic sense. The $90 interest per year—remember, the coupon rate stays fixed throughout the life of the bond—would represent a 12% return ($90 received in interest divided by the $750 invested). Now, at least you're even with inflation. Plus, when the bond matures thirty years down the road, you get a full $1,000 back for your $750. That's 33% more than you paid for it.

So you can see that high inflation (or even the fear of high inflation) causes bond buyers to demand a higher return on their money in order to protect their purchasing power. And in order to create that higher return, bond sellers must lower their asking prices. That's why the bond market usually goes down when any news comes out that could reasonably be interpreted as leading to higher consumer prices.

Here's how this affects your XYZ bond. Although you originally intended . . .

. . . to hold onto your XYZ bond for the full thirty years, real life is rarely quite that simple. Very few investors hold onto their bonds for so long a period of time. Let's say that you decide to sell your XYZ bond and use the money for a really worthwhile purpose—like buying tickets to the Final Four basketball championship. You want your money back *now*, not in 2031.

Where do you sell it? In the bond market where older bonds (as opposed to new ones just being issued) are traded. Your stockbroker can handle it for you. Assuming that XYZ is still in tip-top financial condition with a AAA credit rating, you might expect to get all of your $1,000 back. Well, maybe you will, and maybe you won't. The big question is: *what is the rate of interest being paid by companies that are now issuing new bonds?*

If the rate of interest being paid on new bonds is higher than what your bond pays, you've got a problem. Assume that interest rates have gone up since you bought your

XYZ bond, and that new bonds of comparable quality are now paying 11%. Why would any investor want to buy your old XYZ bond that will pay him just $90 per year in interest when he can buy a new one that will pay $110? Obviously, if both bonds cost him the same price, he wouldn't. So, to sell your bond you will have to reduce your asking price below $1,000 to be competitive and attract buyers.

On the other hand, if interest rates have *fallen*, to let's say 8%, then the shoe is on the other foot. Your old bond that pays $90 per year looks pretty attractive compared to new ones that pay only $80. This means you can sell it for a "premium," meaning more than the $1,000 par value you paid.

Here's the lesson: anytime you sell a bond before its maturity date, it will either be worth less than you paid for it (because interest rates have gone up since you bought it) or worth more than you paid for it (because interest rates have gone down since you bought it).

NEW YORK EXCHANGE BONDS

Surprise! Did you know you can buy bonds on the New York and American Stock Exchanges? These are bonds that were issued in the past and are now being bought and sold in what's called the "secondary" market (the primary market is when new bonds are sold to investors when they are first issued). The secondary market is where you go to sell a bond you bought when it first came out, but then changed your mind and decided you didn't want to hold onto for twenty years after all. Your broker, who is a member of the Exchange, can sell it for you there just like stocks.

Name
is the company that borrowed the money initially and is (1) responsible for paying the interest regularly and (2) paying the amount owed on the bond when it matures.

Maturity Date
is the year when the bond matures. Only the last two digits are shown. This Borden bond issue would be known as the "eight and three-eighths of sixteen" and would mature in 2016.

Coupon Rate
is the interest the borrower pays to the bondholder. It stays constant throughout the life of the bond. Since bonds usually come in $1,000 denominations, this DuPont bond pays $84.50 per year interest (8.45% x $1,000).

Bonds		Cur Yld	Vol	Close	Net Chg	
AldSig 9 7/8	97	9.2	21	107 3/4	−	3/8
ATT 5 5/8	95	5.7	145	99 1/2	+	1/8
Amoco 7 7/8	96	7.6	15	103 1/8	−	3/4
Banka 8 7/8	05	8.7	55	102 1/4	+	1/4
BellPa 7 1/8	12	7.7	43	92 1/2	+	1/8
BethSt 8.45s	05	9.3	73	90 3/8	+	3/8
Bordn 8 3/8	16	8.4	33	100	−	1 1/2
Chiquta 11 7/8	03	11.3	98	105 3/8	−	1/2
ChryF 9.30s	94	9.2	175	100 5/8	+	1/8
Chrysir 8s	98	8.4	9	94 7/8	+	3/4
Citicp 8.45s	07	8.6	29	98 1/4	+	1/4
CmwE 7 5/8	03F	7.8	4	98	+	7/8
DetEd 9.15s	00	9.0	6	101 1/2	−	1 1/2
DuPont 8.45s	04	8.3	29	102	+	1/8
Exxon 6s	97	6.2	20	97 1/2	+	3/8
GMA 7.85s	98	7.8	40	101 0/0	−	3/4

Current Yield
is the number you're interested in as a buyer. It tells what your return would be if you bought the bond at yesterday's closing price of $1,020 for a $1,000 bond. It's computed by dividing your annual interest by the amount you invest ($84.50 divided by $1,020 = 8.28%).

Net Change
is almost always the result of movements in interest rates. As we'll soon see, bond prices and interest rates move in opposite directions. Since most of these changes indicate that bond prices rose, it's reasonable to assume that interest rates fell the previous day.

Volume
is the dollar value (expressed in thousands) of all the bonds of this issue traded yesterday. $145,000 of this AT&T bond traded. The bigger the better, because it means you have lots of trading activity—which is what you want because it will help the market be more efficient and you'll get a better price when buying or selling.

That's why it's possible to lose money even with investments like U.S. Treasury bonds. For example, 30-year Treasuries suffered losses exceeding 14% in value in just five months during 1993-94 when the interest rate pendulum began to swing in the direction of higher rates. They're safe from default, but nobody can protect you against rising interest rates.

Of course, if you hold onto your XYZ bond until it matures in 2031, it will be worth $1,000. At that time, XYZ will repay the par value to whoever owns its bonds. The closer you get to a bond's maturity date, the more the bond's price reflects its full face value. That's why interest rates eventually lose their power to affect the market value of a bond.

The longer you have to wait until maturity, the longer you are vulnerable. How can you shorten the wait (and therefore reduce the risk)? Buy old bonds that were issued many years back and are now only a few years from their maturity. The shorter the maturity, the less volatile a bond's price will be.

Short-term bonds, then, represent a middle ground between the money market and the long-term bond market. They have much less interest-rate risk than long-term bonds and still pay higher yields than money market funds.

How do you distinguish among the large number of bond mutual funds and select the ones most appropriate for you?

There are many varieties of bond funds. They differ in whether they're committed to investing in high quality bonds or will specialize in higher-risk, higher-yielding ones of lower quality. They differ in the maturities of their portfolios—some seek to keep their average weighted maturities at four years or less, others want to keep theirs at no less than twenty years. Some generate taxable dividends, others tax-free dividends. Some limit themselves to the U.S. market, whereas others are permitted to invest overseas. Now imagine that you started mixing and matching all these possibilities to see how many different combinations are possible. The answer? A lot! More than you want to read about—one writer on the bond market published a book spanning 1,426 pages!

To bring some kind of order out of this chaos, I've grouped bond funds in a way that should be most helpful for beginners. These aren't the "official" groupings used for comparing risk and performance among mutual funds. In fact, there's no such thing. The Investment Company Institute, which is the trade association for the mutual fund

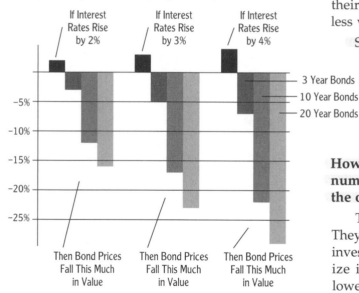

BOND PRICES FALL
WHEN INTEREST RATES RISE

This graph shows the various effects on short-term, medium-term, and long-term bond portfolios when interest rates go up. The point is not only that interest rates and bond prices move *opposite* to each other, but also that the longer term the bond, the greater the price movement.

If Interest Rates Rise by 2%

If Interest Rates Rise by 3%

If Interest Rates Rise by 4%

3 Year Bonds
10 Year Bonds
20 Year Bonds

−5%
−10%
−15%
−20%
−25%

Then Bond Prices Fall This Much in Value

Then Bond Prices Fall This Much in Value

Then Bond Prices Fall This Much in Value

industry, has its way of grouping fixed income funds. Morningstar and Lipper, the two major mutual fund reporting services, have their own ways—and each is different from the other. Their classification systems are rather complicated; I wouldn't even consider trying to explain them to you or using them in this book. Instead, I have created my own way of classifying bond funds that I believe you will find relatively easy to understand and use. Here's how it works.

First, I divide all U.S. bond funds into two groups. One group is composed of those funds that invest in a diversified portfolio of bonds that are taxable and have no unusual features. These are the funds I regard as primary when assembling a bond portfolio. The other group includes what I call "special purpose" bond funds because they invest in bonds with distinctive features. This group includes mortgage-backed bonds (pages 85-86), zero-coupon bonds (see sidebar at right) , tax-exempt bonds (pages 159-160), convertible bonds, and international bonds.

I'll illustrate bond fund risk by using a graphic device that I call a "risk profile."

As we've discussed, there are two major threats facing lenders. The first is the risk that the bonds will go into default. The extensive diversification you achieve in a bond mutual fund virtually eliminates this risk as a meaningful threat.

Bonds are issued by borrowers from all across the "credit-worthiness" spectrum. The U.S. government is regarded as the borrower highest on the quality scale. Even there, many experts make a distinction between direct obligations of the U.S. Treasury versus those of government agencies, the latter being considered as ever so slightly lower in quality.

Then come corporate bonds issued by financially strong companies that receive "investment grade" ratings (AAA, AA, A, and BBB—see page 150 for definitions of bond ratings). The subtle

WHEN IT COMES TO BONDS THAT CARRY A HIGH INTEREST-RATE RISK, ZERO-COUPON BONDS ARE THE ULTIMATE!

Would you be interested in buying bonds that pay "zero" interest? That's right, no interest at all. Doesn't sound very appealing, does it? But what if I was willing to sell you a three-year $1,000 zero-coupon bond for $760? Invest $760 for three years and get $1,000 back. If you said yes, good move! Although you would be receiving no interest for three years, when you finally got your $1,000 it would represent an effective yield of +9.58% per year before taxes.

Zeros are a special breed of bond that pay no current interest. They retain the interest you earn and automatically reinvest it. When the bond matures, you receive all the interest and principal at one time.

Zeros were created in the early 1980s by the brokerage community for large pension investors who needed to know exactly how much they would be getting back at specific times. Zeros make this possible by hedging what is called the "reinvestment risk." With normal bonds, when you receive your semi-annual interest payments, you are faced with the task of reinvesting. If interest rates have fallen, you won't get as attractive a rate on your reinvested amounts as you did on the original bond. That's the reinvestment risk. Zeros eliminate this concern because the issuer, in effect, makes you this offer: "I promise to let you reinvest at the initial rate throughout the life of the bond. But to keep things simple, rather than mail you a check and have you mail it back, I'll just keep the interest money here."

Zeros are especially suited for those investors who plan on holding their bonds to maturity. Because you know up front the rate at which your money will be reinvested over the life of the bond, you can calculate a predictable rate of return for the entire period. This makes planning easier and explains why many individuals buy zeros for their children's education.

Zeros have two unpleasant drawbacks. First, the IRS taxes you on the interest you earn from your zeros each year even though you won't actually receive it until they mature. That makes them better choices for tax-sheltered accounts like IRAs and 401(k)s. Second, zeros are very sensitive to changes in interest rates. In fact, they are the ultimate in high "interest-rate risk" bonds. Their market prices rise and fall much more dramatically than regular bonds as rates fluctuate. If all goes well with the issuer, the bonds will be worth their full face value when they mature, but if you need to sell them prior to maturity in a climate of rising interest rates, you might be shocked at how much they have dropped in value.

I'm not that excited about zeros. But if you truly desire to buy some, here are my suggestions: (1) wait until you have reason to believe that interest rates are at or near a peak; (2) buy only the U.S. Treasury kind; (3) buy only as many as you are fairly certain you can afford to hold until they mature; and (4) buy them only in your IRA or other tax-deferred accounts in order to escape the income taxes.

credit distinctions among investment grade bonds may be of interest if you're buying only a few issues, but they are less important when buying into a mutual fund portfolio. Defaults are rare events at this level of quality, and even if one should come along, the investor is well protected by the diversification.

For purposes of assessing the credit risk, I don't make a distinction between funds investing only in U.S. government-backed bonds versus those that also invest in high-quality corporate bonds. Taken individually, of course, the government bonds are of higher quality. But, as a practical matter, in a diversified portfolio that includes a sampling of BBB-rated bonds, the differences in risk are insignificant. Even the so-called "general corporate" bond funds will invest to some extent in Treasury securities (in order to balance out some of their risk as well as put idle cash to good use in case they can't find enough of the lesser grade bonds they like). Since they obviously can own large amounts of governments, we shouldn't think of them as buying only bonds issued by businesses. Therefore, I'm treating funds that invest in any of the above kinds of bonds the same. Their overall credit quality will range from AAA to BBB, and they will be placed in one of the three lower diamonds in our risk profile (see step one in sidebar at left).

BUILDING A RISK PROFILE FOR BOND FUNDS: STEP #1

Separate funds according to the credit-worthiness of their portfolios

Mixed Quality ❹
High Quality ❸
High Quality ❷
High Quality ❶

BUILDING A RISK PROFILE FOR BOND FUNDS: STEP #2

Separate funds according to the average maturities of their portfolios

Various Maturities ❹
Long Term ❸
Medium Term ❷
Short Term ❶

BUILDING A RISK PROFILE FOR BOND FUNDS: STEP #3

Combine criteria to create four distinct risk categories based on overall credit quality and average portfolio maturities

Mixed Quality Various Maturities ❹
High Quality Long Term ❸
High Quality Medium Term ❷
High Quality Short Term ❶

That leaves the bonds of weaker companies, the so-called "junk" bonds, that must pay higher yields to attract investors.

Junk bonds are corporate bonds that have been given low ratings by independent grading firms such as Moody's and Standard & Poor's. The ratings are intended to evaluate a company's financial strength and, accordingly, its ability to pay both the principal and interest on its debts as they come due. Generally, bonds rated in the top four categories are considered "investment grade" quality. Only several hundred of the strongest companies qualify for these high ratings.

That leaves several thousand companies stuck with the "junk" label, although naturally there are differences in financial strength even here. There are distinctions between those companies that just barely failed to qualify for an investment grade rating and those that have problems so severe that they have already filed for bankruptcy protection. If you want the higher yields that these companies offer (in order to entice investors to buy their bonds), the trick is to sort through these lower-rated offerings and pick the strongest of the weak. That's the task of the fund manager.

Junk bond investors are realistic enough to expect some of their holdings to eventually default. Studies have shown that it's normal for 1.5% to 2.5% of junk bonds to default in any given year. That's why the diversification provided by the fund is so essential—it spreads out this risk over a sufficiently large number of bonds to reasonably assure that its default experience will be in this range. The higher yields paid by junk bonds compensate investors for this expected small loss of capital.

Here's how it might work. Say the average yield in the fund portfolio is 12% on junk bond holdings of $1 million. That means the fund would receive $120,000 in interest payments throughout the year. Assume that the fund experiences a 2.5% default rate ($25,000 of their bond holdings). Even in a default, bonds don't typically become worthless; bondholders usually recoup 40%–50% of the principal value of the bonds. If the fund recouped 40% of its investment in the bad bonds, it would get $10,000 of its capital back. That means the fund lost $15,000 on the defaulting bonds, which would be offset against the interest income. After all is said and done, the fund would still come out $105,000 ahead for the year.

A healthy economy is very important to buyers of junk bonds because it helps maintain a positive cash flow that enables even weaker companies to keep up with their interest payments. While a recession spells trouble for everybody, it can be especially devastating for companies with high debt loads. It's the same problem faced by families with high credit card and other consumer debt.

With this dynamic in mind, it's easy to see why junk bond funds often respond to economic events more like stock funds do. For instance, *high-quality* bond funds returned about 15% in 1991. But stock and *junk* bond funds, even though the economy was in a recession, returned a surprisingly strong 33% and 37%, respectively. Why? Because, like the stock market, junk bonds are valued based on *anticipated events* in the economy six to nine months away. Investors began expecting the recovery to kick in and greatly improve the cash flow of the companies that had issued the bonds. (Junk bonds flourished during the strong economies of 1986 and 1988.) This appeared to lower the risk, and the high yields looked great in comparison to other savings-type investments, which had fallen to extremely low levels.

Due to their high risk, funds that invest in junk bonds will be placed in category four, the uppermost of the four diamonds in the risk profile. Step one (upper left) summarizes the placement of funds based on the risk of default.

The second major threat facing bond owners is that of rising interest rates— as rates go up, bond prices go down.

A bond fund's average portfolio maturity tells us more about the risk of that fund than just about any other factor. As you move toward longer maturities, the risk of being hurt by rising interest rates increases. The sooner the bonds in your portfolio mature, the sooner your fund manager can go out and buy bonds paying the new higher rates. It follows, therefore, that the shorter the average portfolio maturity of a bond fund, the less its price volatility.

We reflect this in the second step of building our risk profile. Because the short-term portfolios pose the least risk, we assign them to the lowest diamond; the medium-term funds go into category two; and the long-term portfolios, which have the highest risk among high quality bond funds, are placed in category three.

Now to put all this together. As you can see in step three, the two fundamental risk considerations combine to create four distinctive risk categories. The diamond that is positioned lowest in the profile (category one) is also the category with the lowest risk because it combines the safety of high quality bonds with shorter maturities. The category that is positioned highest in the profile (category four) is the category with the highest risk because it features bonds of mixed quality that also have medium-to-long-term maturities. The two diamonds in the center are for bond funds with risk in between the two extremes. Once you know which of these four risk categories a bond fund falls in, you know a lot about that fund's likely volatility as well as its potential for gain or loss.

Let's apply the lessons you've learned about bonds as we study the "risk ladder" for bond funds below.

It's called a risk ladder because it's safest at the bottom, and each step up to the next rung increases your risk. The statistics were compiled from the Morningstar database for the period ending August 2000.

• Notice that the actual risk scores (standard deviation) and ten-year annualized returns for each group show the kind of pattern we'd expect—bond funds in category four have the highest numbers, and they gradually decrease as you move down the

RISK LADDER FOR BOND FUNDS
SOURCE: MORNINGSTAR PRINCIPIA 8/31/2000

Risk Category	Standard Deviation	10 Year Avg	2000 8 Mos	1999 Return	1998 Return	1997 Return	1996 Return	1995 Return	1994 Return	1993 Return	1992 Return	1991 Return
4 Invest by Lending: Bond Risk Category 4 Bond funds that invest in high-yield junk bonds, typically of medium-term maturities	7.2	10.0%	−0.7%	4.3%	0.1%	13.5%	14.2%	17.1%	−3.3%	18.8%	17.2%	36.7%
3 Invest by Lending: Bond Risk Category 3 Bond portfolios of generally high quality with long-term average maturities (over 10 years)	5.8	8.0%	6.6%	−4.2%	8.0%	11.0%	2.7%	21.5%	−5.7%	12.7%	7.7%	17.0%
2 Invest by Lending: Bond Risk Category 2 Bond portfolios of generally high quality with medium-term average maturities (4–10 years)	4.3	7.3%	5.3%	−1.2%	7.6%	8.7%	3.1%	16.5%	−3.9%	9.6%	6.7%	15.2%
1 Invest by Lending: Bond Risk Category 1 Bond portfolios of generally high quality with short-term average maturities (4 years or less)	2.3	6.3%	4.2%	2.2%	6.2%	6.6%	4.3%	10.4%	−0.7%	6.1%	5.5%	12.1%

ladder. The ladder was devised based on theory as to how risk and return relate to each other in bond investing, and the experience of the different risk categories during the 1991-2000 period demonstrates that the theory holds up in actual practice.

• Notice that the short-term category-one funds did better (as expected) in years like 1994 and 1999 when rising interest rates hurt bond prices. Conversely, the more volatile long-term funds were the performance winners during years like 1995 when rates were falling.

• Notice that the high-yield category-four funds march to a different drummer. There is a relatively consistent pattern that shows up when comparing the year-by-year results of the funds in categories one through three; however, the performance of the category four funds seems almost random. That's because, as I pointed out earlier in this chapter, junk bonds often behave more like stocks due to their sensitivity to the strength in the economy.

Tax-free bonds: they're not for everybody . . .

. . . but if I'm going to talk about them in this book, it's now or never—after all, this is the bond chapter.

Here's the deal. You work hard, live frugally, save your money, and invest it carefully. Then, when the fruit of your labor and sacrifice—your interest check—arrives, state and federal tax agents show up and demand their cut. Their combined share (for most families) starts at about one-third and can climb to almost one-half of your investment earnings. Obviously, any investment that can avoid such a heavy penalty is worth knowing about.

Tax-free bonds (also called "municipal" bonds) are debt securities issued by state and local governments. By law, the interest earned on such bonds is exempt from federal taxes. If the issuer is a city in your state, or the state itself, the interest is also exempt from the state income tax. Because of the value of these tax benefits, issuers of tax-free bonds can borrow money at interest rates lower than those paid by other borrowers. That means they won't pay as much in interest, but what tax-free funds do pay, you can keep entirely!

Would you benefit from investing in tax-free bonds? That depends on your "marginal" tax bracket. At present, the federal tax law provides for several tax brackets—15%, 28%, 31%, 36%, and 39.6%—to be applied against your taxable income. Different rates apply for singles and married persons. See the table above for the tax brackets as they were in 2000. The brackets are adjusted annually for inflation. How high up the tax ladder does your income take you? The highest rate you pay is called your marginal rate.

UNDERSTANDING TAX BRACKETS

Taxable income is what is left after reportable income is offset by your exemptions, deductions, and other permitted subtractions.

2000 Tax Brackets	For Single Taxpayers	Married, Filing Jointly
15.0%	Up to $26,250	Up to $43,850
28.0%	$26,250–$63,550	$43,850–$105,950
31.0%	$63,550–$132,600	$105,950–$161,450
36.0%	$132,600–$288,350	$161,450–$288,350
39.6%	Above $288,350	Above $288,350

There's an easy calculation you can make to see if you're better off receiving a higher rate of interest that is taxable or a lower return that is tax-free (see page 75). Due to a provision in the tax code that affects the deductibility of itemized deductions, tax-frees are even more attractive than the formula would imply if your adjusted gross income rises above the $100,000 area.

If you believe you would benefit from investing in tax-frees, I strongly encourage you to diversify widely to minimize the risk of defaults. This can easily be accomplished by investing in three no-load muni funds rather than putting all your money into just one. I suggest staying with top-quality bonds rated A or better all the way (see sidebar, page 150). When you call a fund that you're considering, ask for a breakdown of the quality ratings of their holdings. This is often called a credit analysis, and it will tell you what percent the fund has in AAA-rated bonds, AA-rated bonds, and so on.

There is even more incentive to switch to tax-frees if you live in a high-tax state. There are so-called "single state" tax-exempt funds . . .

. . . that invest solely in tax-free securities issued from within that one state. This means the interest income is *double tax-free:* from state income taxes as well as federal ones. This brings us to another factor that complicates the computation. New Yorkers, for example, could have combined federal, state, and local taxes totaling as high as 48%. For such a taxpayer, investing in a New York-only tax-free fund yielding 3.8% would generate an equivalent before-tax return of 7.31%. Since this is significantly higher than the hypothetical 5.5% bank CD, such a bond fund makes sense from a tax point of view for some investors.

TAX-EXEMPT BONDS

Issue	Coupon	Maturity	Price	YTM
Allegheny Co Hospital Dv Pa	5.375	12-01-25	90	6.10
Chicago Board of Education	6.000	12-01-26	98	6.15
Dade Co Fla Ser	5.750	10-01-26	95	6.12
Dade Co Fla School Board	5.500	05-01-25	92 3/8	6.06
Dade Co Fla Water & Sewer	5.500	10-01-25	93	6.01
Delaware River Pa Revenue	5.500	01-01-26	92 7/8	6.02
Denver Colo Airport Sys	5.600	11-15-25	91 3/4	6.21
Houston Tx Water & Sewer	5.250	12-01-25	89	6.05
Mass Bay Transit	5.625	03-01-26	93 5/8	6.09
Murray City Utah Hosp	4.750	05-15-20	81 1/2	6.23
NC Muni Power Agency	5.375	05-15-20	91 1/2	6.05
New Orleans La Exhibit Hall	5.600	07-15-25	93 1/8	6.11

Issuer is the city, state, or government agency that borrowed the money initially.

Coupon Rate is the rate of interest paid by the issuer. The owner of this bond will receive $5.50 per year for each $100 of face value of bonds owned.

Maturity Date is the date when the bond's issuer is scheduled to pay investors the full face value of the bond.

Current Market Value is the last price at which the bond was traded for the day. This bond is valued at $92.875 for each $100 of face value.

Yield to Maturity This is the return an investor would earn by buying this bond at the quoted price and holding it until it matures in 2026.

Be aware, however, that a huge amount of diversification protection is lost with this approach. It seems to me this is a significant drawback—you'll have all your muni investments riding on the financial condition of only your state and its financial strength. For example, the state of Massachusetts's well-publicized financial difficulty in 1990 led to a lowering of its credit rating. Bond buyers would no longer pay the same price for Massachusetts tax-free bonds—they demanded additional discounts, and bond values plunged. With concerns mounting about the financial health of several of our major cities and states, many analysts question the wisdom of placing much of one's savings at higher risk merely to save a percent or so on taxes.

In concluding this chapter on bond market basics, let's look at how investing in a bond fund differs from investing in a portfolio of individual bonds that you put together yourself.

Investing in a pre-assembled portfolio via a bond fund offers convenience and professional management, but there are some drawbacks.

1. Bond funds never reach maturity. The job of the bond fund manager is to maintain the fund's average maturity at the level stated in its prospectus. For example, the Vanguard Long-Term Corporate Bond Fund is committed to keeping the average weighted maturity of its portfolio between fifteen and twenty-five years. As time goes by and maturities shorten, the manager will need to replace some of the shorter-term bonds with longer-term ones in order to stay within the stated range. Although time is passing, the fund never gets close to the day when the entire portfolio matures and every shareholder will cash out whole.

This is different from what takes place if you buy an individual bond. Assume you invest in one which has a fifteen-year maturity. Each year, it moves closer to the date when it will be paid off. That means the tendency of your bond to experience wide price swings in its market value is reduced year by year. Eventually, there will come a time when you will receive all your money back. This is not an assurance that investors in bond funds have (zero coupon bond funds are an exception to this).

2. Bond funds may rob Peter to pay Paul. Typically, bond fund investors are seeking regular income. This leads most bond funds to distribute income to their shareholders on a monthly basis. Because their portfolios are constantly undergoing change, bond funds don't receive the same amount of interest income on their holdings every month. That means the amount of income they distribute varies slightly from month to month. Or at least it should. But shareholders prefer that the amount of the monthly check they receive be predictable and consistent. Some bond funds have responded to this by paying out a set amount. The problem arises when the set amount turns out to be more than the fund actually earned. Assume the portfolio manager finds it reasonable to believe that the fund's earnings will be approximately $1.20 a share over the coming year. Accordingly, he sets a monthly payout of 10¢ per share.

Now, suppose his estimate is off. Perhaps interest rates have fallen, and the new money coming into the fund can't be invested at the formerly high rate. At this point, the fund manager has two options. One, he can invest the new money at the lower rates. If he does this, the fund's income per share will come in below expectations. Ultimately, the monthly payout will have to be reduced (because the earnings won't be there to support it) and shareholders will be disappointed.

Alternately, he can invest the new money in "premium" bonds. These are bonds which were issued a year or two earlier when interest rates were still high, and because they carry such attractive coupon rates, they sell in the marketplace at a premium over par value (say $1,150 for a $1,000 bond). The trade-off is obvious—in order to have more income now (i.e., maintain the high payout rate), the manager will have to settle for less

**Websites to Help with
Your Bond Research**
www.investinginbonds.com
www.pimco.com/
bonds_resources_frms.asp
www.bondmarkets.com/
pages/investor.shtml

**To Check Out Bonds with
Built-In Inflation Protection**
www.publicdebt.treas.gov/
sav/sbiinvst.htm
www.publicdebt.treas.gov/
sec/seciis.htm

For Updated Information
The Internet is constantly
changing, and the above sites
may have moved or ceased
operations by the time you
read this. For an up-to-date
list of the better online
resources related to bonds,
visit our website at
www.soundmindinvesting.com.

later (because he is guaranteed to lose $150 in value per bond between now and the maturity date). If he chooses this course, the losses in the premium bonds will gradually eat away at the price per share of the fund and shareholders will be disappointed.

Individual bonds, on the other hand, don't require any special action in order to assure that the interest income received is predictable and consistent. They're that way by design. Most bonds make regular interest payments at six month intervals, and the amount of the payment is always the same. A thirty-year $1,000 bond with an 8% coupon rate will make payments of $40 every six months for the next thirty years.

Buying premium bonds is not a "bad" strategy per se. After all, you have a higher level of income to offset the losses in market value. The significance has more to do with the taxes paid by investors. Buying premium bonds has the effect of adding to current income and taking away from capital gains. As long as income is taxed at higher rates than capital gains, this works to the detriment of the shareholder. This problem is neutralized if the shares are held in a tax-sheltered account like an IRA, 401(k), or 403(b) plan.

What kinds of bonds should you buy, since you don't know (and neither does anyone else!) where interest rates are headed?

I suggest that you make your mistakes on the side of caution. To minimize risk, don't go further out than about ten years — the reward just isn't worth the risk. According to the respected Ibbotson Associates research firm, since the late 1920s, ten-year Treasuries have averaged 5.1% per year (with just six losing years) versus 4.8% for the higher risk thirty-year bonds (which had eighteen losing years). Another study indicated that nine out of ten years, the yield on a ten-year Treasury is equal to 85%-95% that of a thirty-year bond but with just 60% of the risk.

In our Just-the-Basics strategy, we'll use a middle-of-the-road approach by investing in a bond fund that typically has an average maturity of 9-10 years. On the risk ladder (see page 158), it falls into category two. For the ten years ending August 2000, it generated an average annual return of 7.9%, which compares nicely with the 7.3% turned in by the average category-two bond fund. Furthermore, it did so with less volatility (a standard deviation of 4.0 compared to 4.3 for the average fund). Higher return at less risk—such a deal!

We'll talk more about this fund in chapter 16. For now, it's time to turn our attention to the stock market. ◆

$$\diamondsuit\ 15$$

CHAPTER PREVIEW

Stock Market Basics

I. **Stock shares represent part ownership in a business.**

    A. As an owner, you have the right to participate in the future growth of the company. You will receive dividends if the company decides to distribute money to shareholders rather than retain it for future growth needs.

    B. The stock market is where the buying and selling of part ownerships in businesses takes place. Stock market prices rise and fall for the same reasons other prices do: from supply and demand forces that reflect economic conditions.

II. **There are two major risks to your capital when you invest in stock shares and become a part owner in a company.**

    A. The first is that the company might fail and your investment be totally lost. This risk can be controlled through prudent selection and diversification.

    B. The second is that the entire market for stocks can be adversely affected by economic conditions that might have nothing to do with your company. This risk can't be avoided but is minimized by holding your shares through a complete economic cycle.

III. **When assessing risk, knowing the average size of the companies in which a fund invests as well as the investing "style" used by the manager provides helpful guidance.**

    A. *Large* companies are generally safer to invest in than *small* companies, although they typically don't have the capital gain potential.

    B. Two of the major styles of investing are *value* and *growth*. The value approach is the more conservative because of its emphasis on getting your money's worth.

    C. The funds with the lowest risk/reward characteristics will be those that follow a large company/value strategy. The highest risk/reward potential is found among funds that employ a small company/growth strategy.

IV. **Major market uptrends are called "bull markets" and downtrends are called "bear markets." In an attempt to avoid losses during bear markets, many investors practice market timing, a strategy not recommended for the average investor.**

Common Stock

is the term used to describe the units of ownership in a corporation.

Initial Public Offering (IPO)

is when a corporation offers to sell its stock to investors for the first time. The proceeds, less what the company owes for the broker's services, go to the company.

Secondary Offering

is when a corporation offers to sell previously issued stock which is held by founders and other insiders. The proceeds, less what is owed for the broker's services, go to the individuals who are selling, not to the company.

Limited Liability

is one of the attractions of stock ownership. It means that shareholders have no financial obligation to assist the company should it be unable to pay its liabilities.

Preferred Stock

is a special class of stock that pays dividends at a promised rate. Holders of preferred stock must receive their dividends before any may be paid to common shareholders. They also take preference over common shareholders in receiving back the par value of the stock in the event the company is liquidated. Preferred stock typically does not carry voting rights.

Par Value

is the face value printed on a security. In the event of a corporate liquidation, preferred shareholders receive preference over common shareholders to the extent of receiving back the par value of their preferred shares.

What we call "stocks" are actually pieces of paper that represent ownership in a company.

When corporations desire to raise money from investors for long-term working capital, they have two choices. One, they can borrow it by selling bonds. This approach means that the company will have to make regular interest payments to the bondholders, as well as pay all the money back some day. The investors play the role of lenders.

Or two, the company can sell part ownerships in the company by offering *stock*. In that case, the investors play the role of owners. They are usually entitled to voting rights (which allow them to participate in electing the board of directors who oversee the running of the company, to vote on whether to merge with or sell to another company and under what terms, etc.), and they share in any dividends the board of directors may decide to pay out. However, they will not receive any interest payments on their investments (because they are owners, not lenders) and cannot necessarily count on ever getting their investment money back. Their fortunes are tied in with the future success or failure of the company.

When you decide to invest in shares of stock you've actually made a decision to "go into business." Just as with any business owner . . .

. . . you're last in line when it comes to dividing up the money that's (hopefully) pouring in from happy customers. Your company has to pay the suppliers that provide a variety of needed goods and supporting services. It has to buy equipment and then keep it well maintained. It has employees' salaries, related payroll taxes, health insurance, and retirement benefits to support. It needs to carry property, liability, and workman's compensation insurance. It regularly needs financial and legal services and must continually deal with government reporting requirements and other red tape.

Depending on the business, it might also need to invest large sums in product research and development, or massive sums for sales and marketing. And if it has borrowed any money for expansion or seasonal cash flow needs, it must pay the interest in full. Finally, if your company manages to pay all these bills and still has any money left over at year's end, governments at the local, state, and federal level all show up demanding a share of the profits.

All of this happens before you, the owner, receive a penny. Nobody said it would be easy. Whatever money is remaining at the very end, if any, is called the net profit. What you are hoping for is that there will be some net profits every year, and the net profits this year will be greater than the net profits last year. If these two things happen consistently—and despite the odds, they occasionally do—then you have a good chance of prospering along with the company.

Investors buy stock with the hope of either (1) sharing in the company's profits while they own the stock, or by . . .

. . . (2) eventually selling their shares for more than they paid. For example, you might receive cash payments from the company as it distributes some of its accumulated profits to the owners—that's called dividend income. Or the board of directors might decide it's better to pay little or no dividends for the time being, preferring instead to keep the money to use for the additional expansion of the company. As the company's sales and profits grow over time, the price of its shares will hopefully gain in value as well—that's called capital growth. Dividend income and capital growth are the two primary rewards investors hope to receive in return for the risks they assume when they become shareholders in companies.

Newcomers to stock investing are often confused as to what it is that makes the price of shares go up or down each day.

Perhaps you've seen scenes of the stock trading activity at the New York Stock Exchange (NYSE) on the news and wondered what's going on down there. Well, "what's going on" is that thousands of investors worldwide have sent buy and sell orders through their brokers for stocks listed on the NYSE, and they all collide on the floor in a kind of controlled chaos.

Come along, and I'll take you through a typical trade. Let's start by assuming that you own 100 shares of stock in Ford. As a shareholder, you are one of the owners of Ford Motor Company. Perhaps not a major owner, but an owner nevertheless. As a part owner, you share in Ford's profits, if any. When Ford pays its shareholders a dividend, all the owners receive some money in proportion to how much of Ford they own.

As it so happens, there are new people every day who decide they, too, want to own stock in Ford. Perhaps they are portfolio managers who have extra money from investors to put to work and believe that Ford is the best value in the auto industry. Or, perhaps they are people who like the fact that Ford pays an annual dividend of $1.14 per share. If they buy shares for $24 each, that $1.14 represents a yield of 4.75% on their money. For whatever reason, they want to buy shares in Ford.

It is also apparent each day that some of the current part owners of Ford decide they don't want to be part owners anymore. Let's say you're one of them. Perhaps you've decided that foreign imports are going to devastate American car makers, and you don't want to be in the automobile manufacturing business anymore. Or maybe you still like Ford's competitive position in the industry but fear the economy is heading into a recession that will hurt Ford's profits and possibly cause Ford to reduce its $1.14 dividend. Or maybe it has nothing to do with Ford or the economy; you just need the money for a down payment on a house, or for college tuition, or something else.

Leverage

means owning a larger amount of securities than you can pay for in cash by borrowing the rest. It can greatly magnify gains and losses, and is considered a high-risk strategy.

Short-Selling

is the practice of borrowing shares (from a broker) in a company and selling them at the current price. This is done in the hope the price will fall, allowing you to repay the borrowed shares at a later date with ones repurchased at a lower price.

Stock Exchange

is an organized marketplace where the shares of companies that meet certain criteria with respect to size and shares outstanding are traded among its members. Such shares are said to be "listed" on the exchange.

Over-the-Counter

is a market where securities are traded between brokers over the phone or through a computer network rather than on the floor of an organized exchange.

Secondary Market

involves the trading of securities on stock exchanges and over-the-counter which takes place after the securities are originally issued. The proceeds from such transactions go to the investors who are selling, not to the companies that originally issued the securities. For example, when Ford stock is traded daily on the New York Stock Exchange, the money paid by buyers goes to the investors who are selling, not to Ford, which received its money when the shares were initially sold in the "primary" market.

Dow Jones Industrial Average

(DJIA) is the oldest and most widely quoted of all market indicators. It is an average of the stock prices of 30 of the nation's strongest blue-chip companies. Unfortunately, the DJIA was originally conceived as a "price-weighted" index. This means higher priced stocks have more influence than lower priced ones. For this reason—and the fact that only 30 stocks are included— some analysts consider the Dow the least representative of daily market action. This is ironic in light of the stature it enjoys.

Standard & Poor's 500 Index

(S&P 500) is a market-weighted index published by Standard & Poor's, another giant financial news and information company. It represents about 80% of the market value of all NYSE-traded stocks. Composed of 500 large companies from all the major sectors of the economy, it is more representative than the DJIA as to what the overall market did on a certain day. As such, it has long been used by investing professionals as the benchmark against which they measure their own investment performance results. Further testimony to its perceived accuracy, the U.S. Commerce Department selected this index to represent the stock market in its Index of Leading Economic Indicators.

Russell 2000 Index

measures the performance of 2,000 smaller-size companies. This index, not widely followed by the general public, is the benchmark against which the performance of small-company oriented mutual funds is compared. It is to small-stock money managers what the S&P 500 is to large-stock managers.

The point is you want to sell your shares in Ford. Now, where do you find all those new buyers I said were out there? For the most part . . .

. . . on the trading floor of the NYSE where people stand around all day buying and selling part ownerships in companies. That's where your stock-broker comes in. All the major brokerage firms are members of the NYSE, and they have employees there whose job it is to carry out your orders.

So, you call your broker and tell him to sell your 100 shares immediately at the best price he can get. The order is sent to a floor worker, and when the market opens at 9:30 EST, he goes to the place on the floor where Ford stock is traded. When he arrives, he encounters workers from other firms who are also carrying customer instructions to sell or buy Ford shares. On this particular morning, let's assume there are many more shares of Ford ready to be sold than there are to be purchased. In other words, the current supply of Ford stock for sale is greater than the demand for Ford stock at the current price. Although Ford last traded the day before at $24, it seems the most any buyer will offer this morning is $23. Since that's the best price available, your representative sells your shares at that price. Soon, "F 23" flashes across stock quotation machines all over the country, recording the fact that 100 shares of Ford (so well-known it is noted by the single-letter symbol F) just changed hands at $23 a share.

Who decided the price of Ford should drop that morning? The free market did—that is, the collective decisions of buyers and sellers (like you) from all over the world acting in their own self-interest made it happen. At the old price of $24, there were more shares of Ford to be sold than there were buyers for them; to attract more buyers, a lower price was necessary.

Throughout the day, every time Ford shares change hands, the number of shares and price will appear on the ticker tape. The price of the very last transaction of the day will appear in the next morning's paper as the "closing price." If that closing price is less than the previous day's closing price, then Ford will be said to have gone down that day.

What does it mean when we say that "the market was up" today?

Ford Motor is just one of more than 5,000 stocks for which daily price quotes are available. In order for the stock market to "go up," do all of them have to go up, or just a majority, or just a few of the important ones?

In a sense, there's no such thing as "the stock market." The term is so broad that it's misleading. It sounds so singular, as if all stocks were moving as one. In fact, they rarely do. Some stocks go soaring to the heights while others are disappearing into bankruptcy. Some represent companies that are larger and more powerful than many countries, whereas others are little more than wishful thinking disguised as businesses.

Asking what the stock market did yesterday is akin to asking what the weather was like yesterday. In some places it was unseasonably warm and others below zero; some places it was wet and others dry. To make sense of the question—and get a meaningful answer—you have to be much more precise: "What was the weather like *in Atlanta* yesterday?"

To help investors speak about the stock market with greater precision, market "averages" (or "indexes") were devised.

Stock indexes attempt to measure changes in value, over time, of a specific group of stocks. Some are very broad-based (Wilshire 5000), which means they communicate information in only the most general of terms. Others are more narrow in their focus (Dow Jones Utilities), which makes them more useful for understanding how stocks with specific characteristics are performing.

Indexes serve as benchmarks against which you can evaluate the investment performance of the stocks or mutual funds you own, but it's important to use one that is similar in content to your portfolio in order to be sure you're comparing "apples to apples." There are dozens of stock market indexes, but there are only four you need to become familiar with initially (see sidebars).

There are two major risks of owning a business. In our imaginary sale of Ford stock, we saw both of them come into play.

First, there's the risk that *the company you own* will fall on hard times. This is called the "business risk." In the example, this was manifested by concerns of sellers about the effects that foreign manufacturers are having on Ford's sales and profits. It could be due to poor management, technological obsolescence, overwhelming competition, a shift in cultural behavior patterns, changing government policies, or any number of things. Considering all the things that can go wrong, it's a wonder that there are a large number of successful businesses. Separating the future winners from future losers requires knowledge, experience, wisdom, and a fair amount of good fortune. It is very difficult to do well on a consistent basis. If it were not, we'd all be making easy money in the stock market.

The second major risk of owning stocks is called the "market risk." This refers to those times when the stock market *as a whole* is being adversely affected by economic events. This takes place during the periodic recessions that the American economy goes through. In our example, it could be that Ford as a company is doing great, but lots of people still want to sell their

Wilshire 5000 Index is the broadest of all the market indexes. If you had to pick one index that most closely represents the behavior of the entire U.S. market, this would be the one. It represents the value, in billions of dollars, of all the New York Stock Exchange (NYSE), American Stock Exchange (AMEX), and over-the-counter (Nasdaq) stocks for which quotes are available. The name is outdated because the index, which covered about 5,000 issues when it was first published in 1981, now includes 7,000+ stocks. It represents approximately 99% of the total investable U.S. market. The Wilshire 5000, like most stock indexes, is "market-value weighted."

MARKET-WEIGHTED INDEXES

A stock's total market value—also referred to as its market capitalization—is what it would cost you to buy all the shares outstanding at yesterday's closing price. In an unweighted index, each stock has an equal weight. However, in a market-value weighted index, which most of the leading indexes are, each stock influences the index <u>in proportion to its total market value</u>. In the example below, AT&T alone accounts for 75% of the movement in the index.

Company	Unweighted Index	Share Price	Total Shares Outstanding	Total Market Value	Market Value Weighted Index
American Telephone	33.3%	$37	1,336 million	$49.43 billion	75.0%
Compaq Computer	33.3%	$42	78 million	$3.28 billion	5.0%
Texaco	33.3%	$51	259 million	$13.21 billion	20.0%
	100.0%			$65.92 billion	100.0%

Ford shares because they (1) fear a recession is coming and don't want to own any stocks, (2) have already been hurt by a recession and need to sell some of their stock to raise cash for living expenses, (3) have seen the recession drive down home prices and interest rates and are going to sell their stock in Ford to come up with the down payment money for a new house, and so on and so on.

As you can see, people often sell stock shares for reasons that have nothing directly to do with the prospects of the company. Many times, the sale of stock reflects the unfolding realities in the American and world economies and the level of interest rates. At other times selling takes place for purely emotional reasons. It has been said that "fear" and "greed" are the two primary forces that continually drive market activity. It's important to understand that ultimately your shares are worth what the market says they're worth, regardless of how seemingly well or poorly the company itself may be doing.

There's a tendency to view the stock market as moving in lockstep, but behind the scenes . . .

. . . there are performance differences among various groups (as can be seen in the results of leading stock indexes—see bottom of page). The rally in the stock market in 1995 was led by strength in the shares of large companies. What is a "large" company? Is size measured by the number of employees? The most sales? Or profits? Or perhaps the largest amount of assets? All of these are meaningful indications, but the measure most commonly used by investing professionals is "market capitalization" (or "market cap" for short). This merely refers to the current market value of all a company's outstanding stock. In other words, how valuable is the company? If you could buy every one of its shares at today's closing price, how much would it cost you? By this criteria, America's largest company is General Electric, which had a recent market capitalization of more than $500 billion.

Larger companies, like those in the Dow Jones Industrial Average and the S&P 500

DIFFERENT INDEXES FOLLOW DIFFERENT GROUPS OF STOCKS

Index	Characteristics	1999	1998	1997	1996	1995	1994	1993	1992
Wilshire 5000	Very broad-based; includes almost entire stock market	22.0%	21.7%	29.2%	18.8%	33.4%	−2.5%	8.6%	6.2%
Russell 3000	Very broad-based; includes almost entire stock market	19.4%	22.3%	29.5%	19.2%	33.6%	−2.5%	8.1%	6.6%
Russell 1000	Reflects the price movements of 1,000 large companies	19.5%	25.1%	30.5%	19.7%	34.4%	−2.4%	7.3%	5.9%
Standard & Poor's 500	Reflects the price movements of 500 large companies	19.5%	26.7%	31.0%	20.3%	34.1%	−1.5%	7.1%	7.6%
Dow Jones Industrials	Reflects the price movements of 30 large companies	25.2%	16.1%	22.6%	26.0%	33.5%	2.1%	13.7%	7.3%
Nasdaq Composite	Almost all of the smallest companies, tech heavy	85.6%	39.6%	21.6%	22.7%	39.9%	−3.2%	14.8%	15.5%
Russell 2000	Most of the smallest companies	19.6%	−3.4%	20.5%	14.8%	26.2%	−3.2%	17.0%	16.4%

This table illustrates how indexes can be useful in understanding where the strength is in the market. Consider 1992-1993 when the smaller companies in the Russell 2000 turned in far better performance numbers than the larger companies in the S&P 500 and Russell 1000. From 1995-1998, the opposite happened. Some years there is not a material difference between the various indexes—in 1999, for example, the performance of large and small company stocks was similar. In recent years, the Nasdaq Composite, heavily weighted with high-tech and Internet stocks, has marched to its own drummer.

index, are usually stronger in terms of market penetration and financial muscle. Their earnings might be temporarily affected by competitive pressures, technological developments, or a recession, but they are expected to survive and prosper. They have limited potential to grow quickly in size, however; their glory "growth" days are largely behind them.

Smaller companies (sometimes called "small caps") carry higher risk because they are more easily devastated by economic setbacks. On the other hand, they have the potential to grow to ten, twenty, or fifty times their present size. The time to "get in on the ground floor" is when they're still small. Of course, the worst-case loss scenarios from investing in smaller companies is greater, especially for one-year holding periods.

One group is not "better" than another. They offer different strengths which are suitable for different investing needs. Large companies typically offer higher dividends and greater price stability; smaller companies offer higher long-term growth potential. Economic factors influence whether large companies or smaller companies are popular with investors at a given time.

• **Interest rates.** In order to grow, small companies need (1) money and (2) a healthy economy. Larger companies are financially stronger. Smaller companies are more easily devastated by high interest rates or a recession; they need a healthy economy and affordable interest rates to prosper.

• **The strength of the U.S. dollar.** In 1994-1995, a weak dollar helped the large multinational companies that have business abroad (often 20%–40% of total sales). A rebounding dollar cuts the other way. Lower profits for large companies make small companies look relatively more attractive. According to an analyst quoted in *The Wall Street Journal*, there have been three periods over the past decade when the dollar rallied 10% or more. Each time, the Russell 2000, a small company index, significantly outperformed the S&P 500.

HISTORICAL RETURNS FROM MUTUAL FUNDS INVESTING IN LARGE vs SMALL COMPANIES

Source: Morningstar

Year	Large	Small
1986	16.2%	9.4%
1987	2.9%	–4.1%
1988	13.9%	20.0%
1989	25.8%	22.4%
1990	–4.1%	–11.4%
1991	33.6%	46.0%
1992	7.3%	14.2%
1993	10.8%	17.0%
1994	–1.3%	–1.0%
1995	31.7%	27.2%
1996	20.4%	21.2%
1997	27.0%	24.0%
1998	21.2%	–1.8%
1999	19.1%	27.8%
5Yr Avg	19.8%	16.2%
10Yr Avg	17.3%	17.0%
15Yr Avg	15.7%	13.9%

Let's begin building a risk profile for stock funds.

As we did with bonds (pages 155-156), we'll divide a large diamond into four smaller compartments. The idea is to place all stock funds into one of the four compartments using criteria that we feel have the greatest bearing on risk. In this way, we can get a quick insight into the general riskiness of a fund just by seeing in which of the four compartments it is placed. In step one, we'll take the size of the companies in the portfolio into consideration.

It's now common in the industry to use as many as *five* size categories—micro-cap (companies whose stock is worth under $250 million in market value), small-cap ($250 million to $1 billion), mid-cap ($1 to $5 billion), large-cap ($5 to $ 50 billion), and giant (over $50 billion). Even Morningstar, the industry leader in measuring and reporting on mutual fund performance, doesn't go that far. They have three categories: small (which combines micro and small), mid, and large (which combines large and giant). To decide which funds go into which category, Morningstar first looks at all the stocks in a fund's portfolio and calculates the average (or "median") size of those companies. Then, to determine their cutoff points, their analysts employ a somewhat sophisticated methodology that adjusts to an ever-changing market. Typically, their upper limit for defining small companies hovers around $1.5 billion.

Rather than confront you with as many as five stock risk categories based on size, let me explain the process I use for my newsletter readers. For them, I assign stock funds to either a "small" or "large" category. To do this, I consider any fund with a median market capitalization below Morningstar's fluctuating cutoff point as a small company ("small cap") fund. This means I combine the micro- and small-cap groups. All other funds are assigned to a large company ("large cap") category. As a result, I have funds that own medium sized ("mid-cap") company stocks in the same group with funds owning giant-sized companies. I'm cheating a bit here, because the differences in performance between these two groups is occasionally significant. But what we lose in precision, we gain in simplicity. This is a tradeoff I have found most SMI readers are quite happy to make.

For the most part, investing strategies (or "styles") used by portfolio managers of stock funds can be grouped into two major camps—value investing and growth investing.

The "value" camp emphasizes how much you're getting for your investment dollar. This kind of manager primarily considers the present state of a company's assets, earnings, and dividends in arriving at an assessment of its stock's intrinsic value. They prefer to bargain-hunt, and often end up buying unglamorous, unappreciated companies (because that's where the bargains are). Value managers are serious about getting their money's worth. If a bear market comes along, they shouldn't get hurt too badly because many of the stocks they buy have already been beaten down in price (which is when *they* bought them) and hopefully won't fall much further. The drawback is that the reason a stock is bargain priced in the first place is that it either has operating problems or is simply out of favor with investors. It often takes *years* for such stock purchases to bear fruit. This approach is the more conservative, but requires great p-a-t-i-e-n-c-e.

The other style of stock investing is the *growth* camp. The managers with this strategy act on future expectations. They would say, "Look at all the great things the company has going for it! It has a tremendous future ahead." A great deal of their success hinges on the ability to accurately predict corporate earnings a few years into the future. When measured in terms of the company's current earnings and dividends, the stock may appear expensive at present, but if the company can achieve its potential, today's share price will look like a bargain a few years from now. When they're right in their projections and they've got a good economy to work with, they can hit home runs. These are the funds that can gain 50% to 100% in a single good year. But this approach carries more risk because growth stocks typically *are already priced* on the assumption that all the future good news will come to pass. If there are disappointments along the way, the share prices of growth stocks have a lot of room to fall.

HISTORICAL RETURNS FROM MUTUAL FUNDS INVESTING IN VALUE vs GROWTH STRATEGIES

Source: Morningstar

Year	Value	Growth
1986	15.1%	13.9%
1987	−0.1%	1.9%
1988	18.1%	14.7%
1989	21.8%	30.3%
1990	−8.5%	−4.9%
1991	31.1%	51.3%
1992	12.9%	75%
1993	15.4%	12.8%
1994	−1.1%	−1.6%
1995	28.3%	35.0%
1996	21.0%	18.7%
1997	27.3%	20.1%
1998	11.6%	18.7%
1999	14.9%	57.2%
5Yr Avg	17.3%	23.8%
10Yr Avg	16.0%	20.4%
15Yr Avg	14.3%	17.4%

**How are you to know which style of
investing a particular fund is following?**

I begin with the Morningstar calculations which use the average price/earnings and price/book ratios of the fund's current stock holdings portfolio as a guide. Morningstar used these ratios to assign every fund to one of three different style categories: value, growth, and "blend" which is a combination of value and growth. In order to adapt this concept to our easy-to-understand risk profile approach, we do not follow Morningstar's use of a "blend" category. We assign such funds to the growth category. This is done to help assure that those readers who are looking for lower-risk funds—which typically fall into the value category—don't get more volatility than they bargained for. Again, this makes the guidelines somewhat less precise but gains in simplicity and ease of use. In general, value-oriented funds are those which own stocks with *decidedly* below-average prices in relation to earnings and book value. Funds which own stocks with average or above-average prices in relation to earnings and book value are regarded as more growth-oriented.

Historically, both value and growth philosophies have made money, but no investment style results in top performance year after year. As we go through the recurring growth-recession cycle, economic events favor different styles at different times (see performance data, far left). So, the point is not necessarily to try to pick one style over the other—both will have their "day in the sun" at various times. In fact, structuring your portfolio so as to include stock funds using each philosophy is a sensible diversification move.

**When we put it all together as shown on the
right, we have four distinct types of fund
portfolios from which we can choose . . .**

. . . with some degree of confidence that we understand the investment strategy and risk of loss associated with each. The risk is lowest at the bottom of the profile (funds that invest in large companies and use a value strategy) and greatest at the top (funds that invest in small companies and use a growth strategy). Bear in mind that funds are assigned to one of the four groups based on the most current information available. Mutual fund portfolios change on a daily basis, so it's possible for a fund to move to a different risk category periodically as its portfolio holdings change.

BUILDING A RISK PROFILE
FOR STOCK FUNDS:
STEP #1

Separate funds according to
the average size of the companies
in which they invest

BUILDING A RISK PROFILE
FOR STOCK FUNDS:
STEP #2

Separate funds according
to whether they use a
value- or growth-oriented
philosophy of investing

BUILDING A RISK PROFILE
FOR STOCK FUNDS:
STEP #3

Combine criteria to create
four distinct risk categories based
on the size of companies in the
portfolio and the investing style

The risk ladder below shows the risks and rewards in recent years from investing in mutual funds assigned to each category. The numbers reflect the average of all the funds in each group; individual funds will vary. That's the trick, of course—picking the funds in advance that will be above average in their respective risk categories. It's a very tough thing to "beat the market" on a consistent basis as we'll discuss in the next chapter.

If you're beginning to think that the risks of owning stocks are considerable, that's good. You must . . .

. . . have a realistic view of this! The past 18 years provided such a positive economic environment for stocks that many people have lost sight of the fact that stocks can lose value as well as gain it. Let's take a look at the historical record to put things into perspective. "Major Price Trends" (page 174) shows stock price movements over the past 40 years. I've simplified the picture by drawing in only the major price moves of 20% or more. The accompanying tables explain the letter codes on the graph, showing the amount of each move and how long it lasted. For example, the bull market indicated by the letters *A-B* gained 80% (as measured by the S&P 500 stock index) over a forty-four-month period.

Notice two key elements in the graph. First, the overall trend is up. Even the long sideways movement of the 1960s and 1970s had an upward bias. This upward trend reflects the underlying strength of American free-enterprise capitalism. As long as the economy is healthy and the population expanding, businesses have a favorable environment in which they can prosper and grow. That means more profits. And more profits means more dividends being paid to the owners. Stock prices, ultimately, must reflect the earnings and dividends of the underlying companies.

RISK LADDER FOR STOCK FUNDS

SOURCE: MORNINGSTAR PRINCIPIA 8/31/2000

Risk Category	Standard Deviation	10 Year Avg	2000 8 Mos	1999 Return	1998 Return	1997 Return	1996 Return	1995 Return	1994 Return	1993 Return	1992 Return	1991 Return
Invest By Owning: Stock Risk Category 4 Stock funds that invest in smaller companies and employ a growth-oriented strategy	24.9	18.1%	15.9%	43.4%	2.7%	19.9%	18.5%	35.4%	even	16.7%	9.6%	59.1%
Invest By Owning: Stock Risk Category 3 Stock funds that invest in smaller companies and employ a value-oriented strategy	15.7	13.7%	12.6%	5.8%	−5.7%	28.8%	24.6%	22.5%	−0.4%	17.4%	18.4%	36.5%
Invest By Owning: Stock Risk Category 2 Stock funds that invest in large companies and employ a growth-oriented strategy	20.2	19.1%	11.0%	39.1%	23.4%	23.9%	19.4%	33.0%	−1.7%	7.2%	4.5%	45.7%
Invest By Owning: Stock Risk Category 1 Stock funds that invest in large companies and employ a value-oriented strategy	14.9	14.9%	6.4%	7.9%	10.9%	27.3%	21.2%	31.4%	−1.6%	14.4%	9.4%	29.9%

Second, the last two bear markets were abrupt and relatively brief. With instantaneous communication of financial news, everyone trying to act on the same news at the same time creates a traffic jam. Because markets aren't always capable of absorbing a high volume of sell orders quickly, large price markdowns are often needed in order to entice a sufficient number of potential buyers off the sidelines. After the sellers have been satisfied, the way is clear for a new bull market to begin.

To deal with these occasional bear markets, many investors are attracted to a strategy known as "market timing" where they attempt to move out of stocks . . .

. . . near market highs and buy back in near market lows. Market timing is a strategy where, in its purest form, the idea is to be invested in stock, bond, or gold mutual funds *only* during favorable market periods when prices are rising, and then moving all your capital to a haven of safety like a money market fund when prices are falling.

Because "buying low and selling high" is every investor's dream, market timing can sound an alluring call. But is it just another investing fantasy? Superstar investors like John Templeton and Warren Buffett don't even attempt it. The *Harvard Business Review* called it "folly," and *Money* magazine frequently ridicules it. Why are these knowledgeable observers lined up against it? They say it's too difficult to be done *on a consistently* profitable basis, and that newsletter writers have grossly exaggerated its value in order to sell more newsletters. While it sounds good in theory, they submit it doesn't deliver as advertised.

Enter Mark Hulbert, publisher of *The Hulbert Financial Digest*. For more than 20 years, Hulbert's work has served as a kind of *Consumer Reports* of the investment newsletter field. Over time, his research, performance statistics, and writing has gained a wide following. What has Mark Hulbert's years of tracking newsletter recommendations taught him about market timing? In his words:

> *It is an undeniable fact that some newsletters have beaten a buy-and-hold approach with their timing. . . . The proportion of timing newsletters which have beaten the market is significant and can't be explained away as just luck. . . . One goal is to beat the market—to do better than simply buying and holding. But the other goal, which is far less widely recognized, is to reduce risk. Whatever else one might say about the market timing newsletters, this is a goal on which they can, and have, delivered. . . . More than half of the market timing newsletters beat the market on a risk-adjusted basis in each of the three time periods measured. This is a very impressive achievement.*

Hulbert's findings are in line with my own experience—that market timing can indeed reduce risk while improving returns; however, it's not as easy as some would have you believe and it's often mentally and emotionally exhausting. I gained this insight the old-fashioned way—I earned it.

In 1978, a close friend and I decided to launch an investment advisory service based solely on market timing. We were one of the early entries in what eventually became a crowded field. During periods of market weakness, we performed exceedingly well for our clients due to our ability to sell out and move quickly into money market funds. When the eventual rallies occurred, we were nimble enough to get back in and enjoy most (but not all) of the ride up. Our strategy generated returns which saw our average managed account more than triple in value during our first five years of operations.

Our "glory days" faded during the bull market of the mid-1980s. Market timing doesn't work well in bull markets because the occasional moves out of the market eventually prove unnecessary, and you often find yourself buying back in at higher prices. Investors become impatient with these miscues; during bull markets they forget the need to be ready with a defensive game plan. The summer of 1987 still stands out in my memory as one of the worst periods of my professional life. I'll share the grim details with you in chapter 30.

For now, just accept my word for it that successful market timing demands enormous self-control, more than most people are conditioned to give. I'm not a proponent of average investors attempting a market timing strategy on their own. It's just too challenging emotionally. First, there's our natural greed. Peering blind-eyed into an impenetrable future, we hope for the best and talk ourselves into expecting the best. So if our trade turns into a loss and our timing system says to sell, we think, *Surely the market won't go straight down from here. There's bound to be at least a little bounce and I can get out*

MAJOR PRICE TRENDS IN THE STOCK MARKET

The graph omits the smaller up and down cycles, and shows only those price moves of 20% or more as measured by the daily closing price of the S&P 500 Stock Index from 1961–2000. Over the past sixty years, through recessions, wars, inflationary spirals, rocketing interest rates, investment scandals, and economic crises too numerous to mention, American stocks have nevertheless generated an average annual return of over 10% a year to investors. Still, that doesn't mean the occasional setbacks aren't nerve-wracking—especially if one comes along just before you need to sell your shares for college, retirement, or emergency needs.

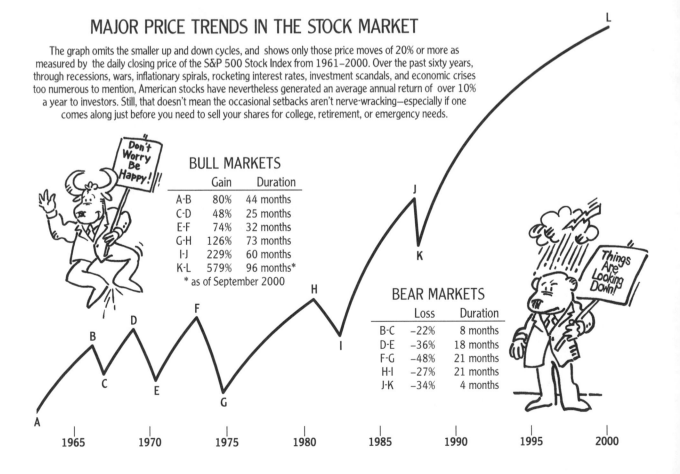

BULL MARKETS

	Gain	Duration
A-B	80%	44 months
C-D	48%	25 months
E-F	74%	32 months
G-H	126%	73 months
I-J	229%	60 months
K-L	579%	96 months*

* as of September 2000

BEAR MARKETS

	Loss	Duration
B-C	−22%	8 months
D-E	−36%	18 months
F-G	−48%	21 months
H-I	−27%	21 months
J-K	−34%	4 months

1965   1970   1975   1980   1985   1990   1995   2000

without a loss. How many times have you decided to sell an investment "just as soon as the price gets back up to what I paid for it?"

Second, there's simple fear. Your system says "buy," but you're convinced by what you've been reading and hearing to expect further weakness instead. This causes you to lack confidence in your system's signal. You decide that if the market can prove itself by rising to Point X, *then* you'll buy. When Point X is reached, you feel better about the market's prospects, but don't want to pay the higher price. Your plan becomes, "I'll buy on a pullback to Point Y." Assume you are given this second chance and Point Y is reached. Perversely, the very weakness that you were hoping for now causes you to doubt the authenticity of the rally. You again hesitate. While you're racked with indecision, the market roars off without looking back. When last seen, you were still trying to muster the courage to get invested.

Against all reasonable expectations, millions of investors expect to astutely select the cream of the investment crop, ride their holdings to the crest of a glorious bull market, and then wisely take their profits. They'll move to the sidelines and let other (presumably less savvy) investors suffer the frustrations of the inevitable correction that follows. Unfortunately, they're living, like children, in a fantasy world.

Many would object at this point and say, "I know that's unrealistic. I don't try to do that." But what then is the motivation, conscious or subconscious, behind the most common questions investors ask, such as: *When* will the rise in interest rates stop? Where is the market headed *next*? Should I buy tech stocks *now*? These are the questions the financial media constantly raise, appealing to our natural desire to make profitable decisions. Yet, they are largely irrelevant to the investor with his eyes fixed on the distant horizon. The long-term investor is asking a different set of questions: Is it even appropriate for me to take on the risks of investing in securities that fluctuate in value? If so, how should I divide my capital between the different kinds of investments (stocks, bonds, real estate, etc.)? What are the growth prospects for the next five years, both in America and various overseas economies? Am I getting good value for my money?

We need to say, along with the apostle Paul, "When I was a child, I talked like a child, I thought like a child, I reasoned like a child. When I became a man, I put childish ways behind me" (1 Corinthians 13:11). To be profitable, we need to put away childish things—such as demanding immediate gratification—and invest by using our reason rather than our emotions.

Every successful investing strategy requires self-discipline.

Self-discipline is the ability to do the right thing at the right time every time. By the "right" thing, I don't mean always making the most profitable decision. That's impossible. Rather, I mean the right thing is to ignore the distractions

Price/Earnings Ratio

The price-to-earning ratio (P/E) is a popular value benchmark used by investors to assess whether a stock is reasonably priced. It's calculated by dividing the price of a stock by its reported earnings for the past four quarters. If your favorite stock, Can't Miss, Inc., is selling for $32 a share and has reported earnings for the past twelve months of $2 per share, it is said to have a P/E of 16 ($32/$2). Historically, a P/E ratio between 10 and 20 has been considered "normal." The P/Es of growth stocks tend to be considerably above-average while those of value stocks are below-average.

When evaluating a stock, it's helpful to determine the current P/E in relation to its historical range. For example, if a stock's P/E over the past 15 years has ranged between 15 and 30 and it's currently at 28, you know the stock is relatively expensive at present.

A problem with using earnings as a guide to stock valuation is that they are very susceptible to manipulation by the company. Accounting principles and IRS rules offer a variety of ways to deal with depreciation, research and development expenses, marketing expenses, inventory costs, and so on. Another problem with using earnings is that optimistic investors often tend to justify higher stock prices by using projected future earnings rather than current earnings when computing the P/E.

of news events and well-intentioned advice and stay with your plan. This is more difficult than it sounds because the markets don't always offer positive reinforcement. In the short run, you can lose money following your plan or you can make money deviating from it. When that happens, "good" behavior is penalized and "bad" behavior is rewarded. It weakens your commitment to following your strategy. If this continues, it isn't long before you're back where you started—making every decision on a what-seems-best-at-the-moment basis. Unless you have a rare and natural gift for investing, that's the last place you want to be.

In the next chapter, I'm going to offer you a strategy that has been designed to minimize the wear and tear on your emotions by making it easier for you to exercise self-discipline and do "the right thing." It's been my experience that:

• **Doing the right thing is easier when the strategy is simple.** Our Just-the-Basics portfolios use relatively few ingredients, and I use plain-English explanations to tell you what to do and why we're doing it. The simplicity lets you see how everything fits together, so you can feel more comfortable making decisions.

• **Doing the right thing is easier when the rules are clear-cut.** Just-the-Basics offers specific guidelines that determine your mix of stocks and bonds and fund selections. You can have more confidence when you know you're making buy/sell decisions that fit into a coherent plan.

• **Doing the right thing is easier when it's not time consuming.** You don't need to read *The Wall Street Journal*, monitor the mutual fund rankings, keep daily charts, calculate moving averages, or anything else. Just-the-Basics requires only an hour or two once a year, usually in January, to perform a little routine maintenance.

• **Doing the right thing is easier when you know that your losses won't kill you.** No strategy is perfect, so you know ahead of time you will have some losses. But when you're well diversified, they won't be devastating. The Just-the-Basics track record in this regard is reassuring.

• **Doing the right thing is easier when you know you're in for the long haul.** You needn't be overly concerned about the quarterly performance in your Just-the-Basics portfolio. There will be occasional setbacks. But we're realistic and understand that's going to happen from time to time. Investing often involves taking two steps forward and one step back. But that needn't alarm us because we've got time on our side.

This book, as well as my monthly newsletter, gets its name from 2 Timothy 1:7. In the King James Version, it reads: *"For God hath not given us the spirit of fear; but of power, and of love, and of a sound mind."* It's interesting that the New International Version translates "sound mind" as "self-discipline." We can look forward to maturing in our faith beyond childish things because *"His divine power has given us everything we need for life and godliness through our knowledge of him who called us by his own glory and goodness. . . . For this very reason, make every effort to add to your faith . . . self-control"* (2 Peter 1:3, 5-6). ◆

Websites to Help with Your Stock Research
www.smartmoney.com
finance.yahoo.com
www.fool.com
www.morningstar.com
moneycentral.msn.com/investor
www.quicken.com/investments/

For Updated Information
The Internet is constantly changing, and the above sites may have moved or ceased operations by the time you read this. For an up-to-date list of the better online resources related to stocks and stock funds, visit the SMI website at www.soundmindinvesting.com.

CHAPTER PREVIEW

A Just-the-Basics Strategy Built Around Six Model Portfolios

I. **Historical data shows that, over time, 80% of professional money managers fail to "beat the market."**

    A. A "loser's game" is that kind of competition where the winner is determined primarily by the mistakes of the loser rather than the skill of the winner. Investing has become a loser's game.

    B. The path to success when playing a loser's game is to play a passive, patient game where the emphasis is on minimizing one's mistakes.

II. **The mutual fund world offers a product that is perfectly suited to playing a loser's game. It's called an "index" fund.**

    A. An index fund doesn't try to beat the market. Its goal is to equal the market by replicating the performance of a major market index like the S&P 500.

    B. The growth in index funds has been explosive in recent years as pension funds, insurance companies, and other large institutional investors, recognizing how extremely difficult it is to regularly outperform the market, have placed huge sums in them.

III. **Our Just-the-Basics strategy uses no-load stock and bond index funds in various combinations to create six portfolios with varying degrees of risk.**

    A. Your most important investing decision is how you divide your money between stocks, bonds, and cash reserves. This "allocation" decision has far and away more influence on your final investment results than any other single factor.

    B. An advantage of Just-the-Basics is that its primary focus is on this all-important asset allocation decision rather than on which mutual funds to purchase. Other advantages of this strategy include guarding against sub-par investment returns, lower expenses, fewer taxable distributions, and easy accessibility.

IV. **Just-the-Basics includes a provision for investing outside the U.S. We discuss the pros and cons of adding an international fund to your portfolio.**

**Traditional money management is founded on
the questionable assumption that . . .**

. . . professional managers can consistently beat the market through research, intelligent risk-taking, and exploiting the mistakes of others. But what if this assumption is largely false?

In this chapter, we'll look at historical data that shows the vast majority of mutual funds underperformed the market over the past decade. It turns out that the secret to winning the money game may be to not try winning at all.

We'll begin our study with an analogy from the world of tennis. I have spent many a Thursday afternoon risking bodily injury and public humiliation on the tennis courts. As a beginner, I concentrated my efforts on trying to learn how to hit the ball correctly. My pregame strategy had little to do with specific plans for hitting the ball to my opponent's forehand or backhand or placing it shallow or deep. My primary concern was pretty simple: Try to keep the ball in bounds! I lost many more points due to the mistakes *I* made than as a result of the actions of my opponents.

In his book on tennis strategy, *Extraordinary Tennis for the Ordinary Player*, Dr. Simon Ramo describes the kind of amateur tennis I play as a "loser's game." By that he means it is the kind of competition *where the winner is determined by the behavior of the loser*. The amateur doesn't win by defeating his opponent; he wins by letting his opponent defeat himself.

Ramo contrasted this with the "winner's game" played at the professional tennis level. In those matches, we are accustomed to seeing consistently precise serves, stunning recoveries, and long, dramatic rallies. Eventually, one player takes a calculated risk and attempts to put his opponent away with an exceptionally powerful or well-placed shot. At the expert level, it is the winning of points that drives the action and determines the outcome.

In short, Ramo observed, amateurs *lose* points and professionals *win* points. To test his hypothesis, he compiled an extensive database of points scored in actual tournaments at both levels. He found a surprisingly consistent and symmetrical tendency. In professional tennis, about 80% of the points are won due to superb offensive execution—a winner's game. On the other hand, in amateur tennis about 80% of the points are lost due to unforced errors—a loser's game.

OK, so what does this have to do with selecting a mutual fund portfolio? In his highly acclaimed book *Investment Policy*, money manager Charles D. Ellis applied Ramo's work to the investing arena. When Ellis studied the investment markets, he saw that it was not uncommon for 80% of the managers of stock and bond mutual funds to underperform their respective markets (see graphs on next page). In their efforts to "score" for their shareholders, they were hitting the ball into the net or out of bounds far too often. It appeared that investing had become a loser's game. It hadn't always been this way:

> *Winner's games can and do sometimes become loser's games. That is what has happened to the "money game" we call investment management. A basic change has occurred in the investment environment; the market came to be dominated in the 1970s by the very institutions that were striving to win by outperforming the market. And that shift made all the difference. No longer was the active investment manager competing with cautious custodians or amateurs who were out of*

touch with the market. Now he was competing with other experts. . . . So many professional investment managers are so good, they make it nearly impossible for any one to outperform the market they now dominate.

The key question under the new rules of the game is this: How much better must the active manager be to at least recover the costs of active management? Recovering these costs is surprisingly difficult. Such superior performance can be done and is done every year by some, but it has not been done consistently over a long period of time by many. . . .

Believing that investment management had evolved into a loser's game, Ellis drew this conclusion: Just as the path to victory in amateur tennis is to play a passive, patient game while letting your opponent take the risks, so the logical strategy for the amateur investor should be the same.

There are advantages to playing a loser's game.

Most investors, consciously or subconsciously, are caught up in playing a winner's game. They're trying to "beat the market." They buy financial magazines and investment newsletters that offer a dizzying array of stock recommendations and mutual fund rankings, and they feel they must respond to fast-breaking news events and trade with a short-term perspective. Theirs is an active strategy where they work harder and take extra risks in what is usually a futile attempt to "win."

Survivorship Bias is the term given to describe the distortion that creeps into mutual fund performance data due to funds passing out of existence each year. For example, in the graphic below, there would have been many more than 294 stock funds which underperformed the index, but they have been liquidated or merged into other funds. Thus, they're no longer in the database to drive the average performance down. As a result of survivorship bias, the number of funds which outperformed the index was actually lower than the 20% shown.

IT'S TOUGH TO BEAT THE MARKET!
For 15-year period ending 8/31/2000. Source: Morningstar

STOCKS

This is a picture of the annualized returns for the 15-year period ending in mid-2000 for the 323 diversified U.S. stock funds that have track records going back to 1985. It shows that fifteen funds had returns of less than 10.5% per year, twenty-one returned more than 10.5% but less than 12.0%, and so on. During this period, the S&P 500 stock index returned 18.0% per year (dotted line). Only about 20% of the funds (top four bars) did better during this particular 15-year period.

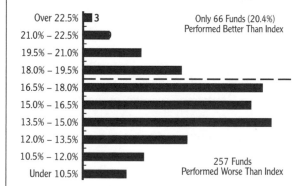

Over 22.5% ▮3   Only 66 Funds (20.4%) Performed Better Than Index
21.0% – 22.5%
19.5% – 21.0%
18.0% – 19.5%
16.5% – 18.0%
15.0% – 16.5%
13.5% – 15.0%
12.0% – 13.5%
10.5% – 12.0%   257 Funds Performed Worse Than Index
Under 10.5%

BONDS

Similarly, this graph depicts the annualized returns for the same 15-year period for 70 high-quality general purpose U.S. bond funds with intermediate- and long-term maturities that have track records going back to 1985. During this period, the Lehman Brothers Aggregate Bond Index (dotted line) returned 8.8% per year. Again, around 20% of the funds (top four bars) did better. Expenses are a bigger factor for bond funds.

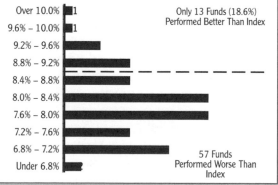

Over 10.0% ▮1   Only 13 Funds (18.6%) Performed Better Than Index
9.6% – 10.0% ▮1
9.2% – 9.6%
8.8% – 9.2%
8.4% – 8.8%
8.0% – 8.4%
7.6% – 8.0%
7.2% – 7.6%
6.8% – 7.2%   57 Funds Performed Worse Than Index
Under 6.8%

One investor/writer expressed his frustration over the investing rat race this way:

> *I could keep my money in stocks, either in many companies or in just a few good ones; I could invest abroad or bring my money home; I could buy and hold or entrust portfolio choices to hot mutual funds; I could shift to bonds; I could prepay my mortgage; or, last—and in the view of Wall Street wisdom, unutterably stupid—I could simply sit on my cash. Like other investors, I balance my fears against my greed, my distrust in easy money against my belief in the eternal upward movement of the market. Like others, I tramp from sage to wizard to priest, gathering portents and signs, each more bewildering than the last, always believing that ahead lies a successful end. In other words, I am a fool.* (Ted C. Fishman, "The Bull Market in Fear," *Harper's* magazine, October 1995.)

In a loser's game, the strategy is more passive (and relaxing!). The path to victory lies in minimizing one's mistakes and being patient. This describes our Just-the-Basics portfolios where we refuse to play the performance game. Instead, we simply invest in selected "index" funds, which, by definition, are going to give us returns similar to the market as a whole.

An index fund is a special kind of mutual fund that has only one objective: to mirror the performance of a market index . . .

. . . such as Standard & Poor's 500 stock index. The portfolio manager invests in the same securities that are used in calculating the index. The fund will make or lose money to the same extent the index after which it is patterned shows gains or losses. For example, if the S&P 500 gains 15% in a given year, then any S&P 500 index fund should also gain about 15% that year. From an investing point of view, what could be simpler?

The growth in the number and size of index funds has been explosive in recent years, thanks to the interest shown by pension funds, insurance companies, and other big institutional investors. More than $400 billion has been invested in index funds, and the overwhelming majority of that is invested in S&P 500-type index funds because it is still the benchmark most investors compare themselves against. All of this "smart" money going into index funds shows how difficult it can be to outperform the market. If it were a simple matter to invest in the right stocks (or bonds) at the right time, everyone would be wealthy.

An investment in an index fund is another way of saying, "It is so hard to consistently do better than the market averages! I'll give up the potential to make *more* than the overall market in return for knowing that I won't make *less*." Once you create your Just-the-Basics portfolios, there's nothing further to do (other than a few hours of annual paperwork) throughout the year except sit back, relax, and hopefully enjoy the ride. By using index funds, we keep pace with the markets virtually without effort. And, as seen in the graphs on page 179, by getting the same returns as the overall market (represented by the dotted line), we'll outperform the vast majority of professional investors. Ironically, we win by *not trying* to win.

Let's now take a look at the funds we'll be using to implement our Just-the-Basics strategy.

Many fund organizations offer index funds, but the ones from the no-load Vanguard Group are especially well suited to this approach. I'll explain the Just-the-Basics concept using the Vanguard funds, starting with the Vanguard 500 Index Fund. This fund attempts to duplicate the performance of Standard & Poor's 500 stock index. It invests in all 500 companies in the same proportion as the weight they carry in the index. It has been around since 1976 and has done an excellent job over the years of fulfilling its mandate. For the ten years ending 12/31/1999, the fund gained 18.1% per year versus 18.3% per year for the S&P 500 index. The small difference is attributable to the costs of operating the fund.

Another Vanguard stock fund will also play an important role: Vanguard Extended Market Index Fund. This fund attempts to provide investment results that correspond to the price and yield performance of 6,500 smaller-to-medium-sized U.S. companies. Naturally, it can't invest in all 6,500, but by using some fancy computer-driven statistical techniques, it buys about 3,000 stocks that, when taken together in the right proportions, act pretty much the same as if all 6,500 were present and accounted for.

Now, here's the neat thing about these two funds: *none of their holdings overlap!* This means that if you invest in both of them, you are essentially investing in 7,000 different stocks ranging from the very small to the very large. *The end result is that you've pretty much invested in the entire American stock market.*

To gain a global flavor, we'll use a third Vanguard stock fund—its International Growth fund. This fund is authorized to invest in stocks anywhere in the world outside the U.S. It's the one fund in our portfolio that is not an index fund (more on this shortly). Finally, we need to add the Vanguard Total Bond Market Index Fund to our arsenal. This fund does in the world of bonds what the first two stock funds do in the world of stocks: acts as if it owns them all. It's designed to track the Lehman Brothers Aggregate Bond Index of more than 6,000 high quality corporate, government, and mortgage-backed bonds of varying maturities. The fund has an average bond quality rating of AA and weighted maturity of around nine years.

HISTORY OF THE FOUR
JUST-THE-BASICS FUNDS

	Intl Growth	Extend Market	500 Index	Total Bond
1985	57.0%	32.0%	31.2%	22.3%
1986	56.7%	11.8%	18.1%	15.5%
1987	12.5%	−3.5%	4.7%	1.5%
1988	11.6%	19.8%	16.2%	7.3%
1989	24.8%	24.0%	31.4%	13.7%
1990	−12.0%	−14.0%	−3.3%	8.7%
1991	4.7%	41.9%	30.2%	15.3%
1992	−5.8%	12.5%	7.4%	7.1%
1993	44.7%	14.5%	9.9%	9.7%
1994	0.8%	−1.8%	1.2%	−2.7%
1995	14.9%	33.8%	37.4%	18.2%
1996	14.7%	17.7%	22.9%	3.6%
1997	4.1%	26.7%	33.2%	9.4%
1998	16.9%	8.4%	28.6%	8.6%
1999	26.3%	36.2%	21.1%	−0.8%
15 Yrs	16.5%	16.3%	18.7%	9.0%
10 Yrs	9.9%	16.3%	18.1%	7.5%
5 Yrs	15.2%	24.1%	28.5%	7.6%

The 15/10/5 year annualized returns are for the periods ending December 31, 1999.

We'll put together these funds in different combinations . . .

. . . so as to produce six portfolios of varying degrees of risk. The portfolio at the low end of the risk scale is invested 100% in the bond fund. This one is designed to incur minimum risk in an attempt to preserve capital while generating current income. As we've discussed, investing by lending is the lowest risk kind of investing.

By increasing the stock allocation in incremental steps of 20%, we begin moving up the risk scale until we reach the high end—a portfolio invested 100% in the stock funds. I suggest that the stock portion of the portfolio be invested one-fifth in International, two-fifths in the Extended Market, and two-fifths in the S&P 500. The table on the next page shows the six Just-the-Basics portfolios and their performance characteristics over the past fifteen years.

When you combine the four Vanguard funds in these various ways, you get the potential rewards of stock ownership along with a reduction in risk due to the less volatile bond portion. Sometimes the funds will move together, but it will often be the case that the bond fund will move opposite the stock funds, and the international stock fund will behave differently from the two U.S. stock funds. When that happens, the price changes somewhat cancel each other out. The effect of this is to increase the price stability of the overall portfolio. Thus, although you are less likely to score a huge gain in any one year when holding a combination of the four funds, you are also unlikely to incur a huge loss. This improved price stability (which equates to lower risk) is one of the primary advantages for the average investor of diversifying through mutual funds.

The portfolio that is best for your situation depends on two factors—your emotional tolerance for risk and the season of life you are now in. In the next chapter, I'll give you some guidelines you can use to select which of the six portfolios is best for you.

The use of index funds as your core holdings merits your serious consideration. Here are several of the advantages they offer:

• **A correct emphasis.** Your most far-reaching investing decision involves how you allocate your money between stocks, bonds, and cash reserves. In *Bogle on Mutual Funds*, Vanguard founder John Bogle quotes a well-known study in claiming that the allocation decision "has accounted for an astonishing 94% of the differences in total returns achieved by institutionally managed pension funds . . . . The 94% figure suggests that long-term fund investors might profit by concentrating more on the allocation of their investments between stock and bond funds and less on the question of *which particular* stock or bond funds to hold" (emphasis added). Other research has indicated that the 94% number is too high—perhaps 60%-70% is closer to the truth. Whatever the actual number may be, virtually everyone agrees that the allocation decision is the most influential one. An indexing strategy forces the investor to focus on the most relevant issue.

• **To guard against sub-par investment returns.** Index funds help assure that your results are in line with those of the general market. They can be counted on to closely

OVERVIEW OF THE SIX JUST-THE-BASIC PORTFOLIOS

Portion Allocated to Stocks:	Portion Allocated to Bonds:	Intl Growth	Extend Market	S&P 500	Total Bond	Your Need for Growth of Capital:	Your Need for Current Income or Protecting Capital:	15-Year Annualized Return:	Best 12 Month Return:	Worst 12 Month Return:	Volatility Compared to the Market
100%	None	20%	40%	40%	None	Maximum	None	17.6%	45.9%	−15.3%	4% More
80%	20%	16%	32%	32%	20%	High	Little	15.9%	41.5%	−10.8%	16% Less
60%	40%	12%	24%	24%	40%	Moderate	Modest	14.2%	38.4%	−6.3%	34% Less
40%	60%	8%	16%	16%	60%	Modest	Moderate	12.5%	35.4%	−1.7%	51% Less
20%	80%	4%	8%	8%	80%	Little	High	10.8%	32.3%	−2.2%	63% Less
None	100%	None	None	None	100%	None	Maximum	9.0%	29.9%	−3.4%	65% Less

Risk is usually defined in terms of the potential an investment has for wild swings up and down in its market value. The term "volatility" refers to the extent of these price swings. An investment with high volatility (meaning very wide, often abrupt, swings in its market value) is defined as high risk. An investment with low volatility (meaning narrow, usually gradual, swings in its market value) is thought of as having low risk. From following the financial news, you may already have a rough idea how volatile the overall market is on a day-to-day basis. The table shows how volatile each portfolio is in relation to the market (as measured by the S&P 500 index).

track the market at which they're targeted. If, for example, the stocks in the S&P 500 index continue to return their historical rate of around 11% annually over the next decade, it's reasonable to expect that an S&P 500 index fund will also gain roughly 11% per year during the period.

• **Lower expenses.** One of the reasons it's difficult for mutual funds to consistently outperform the averages is that they have to overcome the costs of running the fund. The operating expenses (for management fees and certain marketing expenses) for the average stock fund amount to about 1.6% a year. Plus, money spent on commissions when the fund does its buying and selling adds another 0.5% to 1.0% per year (depending on how active the portfolio manager is in buying and selling). Thus, the shareholders' profits in the typical fund are reduced by more than 2.0% per year due to operating and transaction costs. Index funds, on the other hand, have very low expenses. Management fees are nominal because the fund can essentially be run by a computer, and transaction costs are quite low because index funds require relatively little buying and selling within the portfolio. The expenses of Vanguard's index funds run less than 0.25% per year, about one-eighth of what a typical stock fund might incur.

• **Fewer taxable distributions**. Like individual investors, mutual funds aren't taxed on their "paper profits." A taxable event takes place only when securities are sold and the paper gains are realized. The fact that index funds require fewer transactions means there are fewer occasions when stocks are sold and the paper profits converted to taxable profits. This reduces the amount of capital gains taxes, a significant advantage if you're investing taxable dollars, i.e., outside a tax-deferred retirement account.

	HISTORY OF THE SIX JUST-THE-BASICS PORTFOLIOS					
	---------- Just-the-Basics Portfolios ----------					
	All Stocks	80% 20%	60% 40%	40% 60%	20% 80%	All Bonds
1985	36.7%	33.8%	30.9%	28.1%	25.2%	22.3%
1986	23.3%	21.7%	20.1%	18.6%	17.0%	15.5%
1987	3.0%	2.7%	2.4%	2.1%	1.8%	1.5%
1988	16.7%	14.8%	13.0%	11.1%	9.2%	7.3%
1989	27.1%	24.4%	21.7%	19.0%	16.3%	13.7%
1990	−9.3%	−5.7%	−2.1%	1.5%	5.1%	8.7%
1991	29.8%	26.9%	24.0%	21.1%	18.2%	15.3%
1992	6.8%	6.9%	6.9%	7.0%	7.1%	7.1%
1993	18.7%	16.9%	15.1%	13.3%	11.5%	9.7%
1994	−0.1%	−0.6%	−1.1%	−1.6%	−2.2%	−2.7%
1995	31.5%	28.8%	26.2%	23.5%	20.8%	18.2%
1996	19.1%	16.0%	12.9%	9.8%	6.7%	3.6%
1997	24.8%	21.7%	18.6%	15.6%	12.5%	9.4%
1998	18.2%	16.3%	14.3%	12.4%	10.5%	8.6%
1999	28.2%	22.4%	16.6%	10.8%	5.0%	−0.8%
15 Yrs	17.6%	15.9%	14.2%	12.5%	10.8%	9.0%
10 Yrs	16.0%	14.4%	12.8%	11.1%	9.3%	7.5%
5 Yrs	24.2%	21.0%	17.6%	14.3%	11.0%	7.6%

The 15/10/5 year annualized returns are for the periods ending December 31, 1999.

• **Easy accessibility**. Index funds, especially those based on the S&P 500, are increasingly being offered in 401(k)s and variable annuities. That makes it easier to include your retirement assets in your overall allocation strategy.

If indexing is so great, why doesn't everybody do it?

Index funds have long been used by large pension funds in a major way, yet they account for a very small percentage of the assets of stock mutual funds. Although growing in popularity among individual investors, they've still not fully embraced index funds despite their many advantages. Here are some guesses as to why that has been the case.

Index funds conflict with our desire for security. The most significant drawback is that index funds offer no protection during periods of market weakness. They are fully invested in a portfolio of stocks that reflects the index they are designed to mimic, and they *stay* fully invested at all times. If the next bear market takes stocks down 30%,

For More On Index Funds
www.vanguard.com/
educ/inveduc.html
www.fool.com/
school/13steps/stepfour.htm

index funds will fall 30% right along with it. This is a scary thought. As long as we're actively buying and selling, we hope to somehow have the insight, impulse, or just plain luck to stand aside in time to avoid the carnage.

Because they're on automatic pilot, index funds are said to be "passively managed" funds. The managers of "actively managed" stock funds, on the other hand, can take defensive measures like increasing their holdings of cash or high-dividend-paying stocks. Such efforts may or may not help cushion the fall, but at least the managers are trying.

Our Just-the-Basics strategy deals with these drawbacks by combining several index funds into one portfolio. By adding a bond fund, we hope to provide a cushion to bear market weakness. By adding Vanguard's Extended Market Index fund and the International Growth fund, we increase our diversification by adding small company and foreign stocks to the mix. These additional funds will not enhance performance every year, but they do add safety and stability to the portfolio over the long haul.

Index funds conflict with the financial interests of the investing industry. Indexing threatens the profits of most investment advisers, stockbrokers, and financial magazines and newsletters. These companies, for the most part, prosper from the public's natural desire for above-average returns. That's why there's always a sense of urgency surrounding their advertising—the emphasis is always on what's new and changes you should make *now*. If their customers began relying on indexing, buying and selling activity would greatly diminish and their profits would as well.

Index funds conflict with common sense. The success of index funds is not something you'd expect. How can doing nothing be better than doing something? How can expert advice consistently be worse than no advice at all? And more mysteriously, how can you win by refusing to even play? Yet, the facts speak for themselves. Beating the market for a single year or two is not too hard. Beating it consistently over many years, as Charles Ellis points out, "is so very difficult to do—but it's so easy, while trying to do better, to do worse."

Index funds conflict with human nature. Who wants to settle for "average" when being "above average" doesn't really seem that hard? Most people are optimistic and see themselves as having a good chance of being in that select group who can consistently outperform the market—either through their own skills or by selecting and relying on the right advisers. Contrary to their ambitions and best efforts, however, most investors are not beating the market. The market is beating them. Anyone who invested in Vanguard's S&P 500 Index fund over the past 15 years (from 9/1/1985—8/31/2000) would have earned 17.8% per year compared to 15.5% for the average stock mutual fund. In the process, such an investor would have outdistanced about 80% of the mutual fund managers who are the "experts" (see graphic, page 179).

Before ending the chapter, let's briefly discuss the pros and cons of investing in companies located outside the U.S.

For years, it's been the conventional wisdom that a well-diversified portfolio should include foreign companies. But "the times, they are a changing." The average foreign stock fund has outperformed Vanguard's S&P 500 index fund only twice in the past ten years (see table at right), and many advisers are contending that international diversification no longer makes sense. Others have taken up the challenge and argue that diversifying abroad is still an important factor in reducing risk. Here are some of the key points made by those favoring foreign holdings:

	S&P500 Index Fund	Avg Foreign Fund	Foreign Trails By
1990	–3.3%	–11.1%	–7.8%
1991	30.2%	13.6%	–16.6%
1992	7.4%	–3.7%	–11.1%
1993	9.9%	37.8%	27.9%
1994	1.2%	–1.5%	–2.7%
1995	37.4%	10.5%	–26.9%
1996	22.9%	13.8%	–9.1%
1997	33.2%	6.3%	–26.9%
1998	28.6%	12.5%	–16.1%
1999	21.1%	47.1%	26.0%
10 Yrs	18.1%	11.3%	–6.8%

Note: The average foreign fund performance is based on the results from 204 stock funds that invest outside the U.S. and are not restricted to any particular region of the world. Source: Morningstar.

❶ *"Invest abroad because the diversification will help balance out the ups and downs in your portfolio. Because stock prices in other countries are affected by local factors, they will rally and fall at different times than U.S. stocks. When the U.S. market is weak, growth in other regions will help stabilize your portfolio."* Response: As never before, governments are working together in implementing their economic and trade policies. Furthermore, many of the barriers that previously served to restrict the flow of money across national boundaries have been removed. As a result, the world markets are so interconnected now that weakness in the U.S. is contagious. One academic study of the twenty worst declines in the S&P 500 since 1970 showed that stocks worldwide (as measured by the widely-used EAFE index from Morgan Stanley) gained on only four occasions. Six times the EAFE index went down even more than the S&P 500. In short, foreign stocks may not provide much protection during the next U.S. bear market.

❷ *"Invest abroad because it gives you more exciting growth opportunities. As strong as the U.S. is, it still represents just a fraction of the world economy. The action over the next decade is going to be in Europe and the emerging markets in Asia."* The response to this is: "Are you kidding? Are you saying there's not enough opportunity right here in the U.S. when our economy leads the world in technological change, health research, and creative entrepreneurship? The average person couldn't begin to investigate all the exciting investing opportunities. Gimme a break!"

❸ *"Invest abroad because the U.S. is overvalued now, and you can get better value for your money overseas. Since the end of 1970, the Wilshire 5000 index of U.S. stocks and EAFE index have both returned 13.7% a year. That just shows that over the long-term, you can get good returns outside the U.S. If the foreign markets have been consistently outperformed in recent years, it's now time for the trend to reverse in order to maintain the long-term parity."* In my view, this is the "invest abroad" group's strongest argument.

The invest-in-the-U.S. advocates fight back with these arguments.

❹ *"Keep your money home because you should stay with what you know. Information is plentiful, analysis is easier, and you don't have to worry about currency ex-*

change rates." Response: Sure, it's hard to make good decisions without good information, but the converse isn't true—merely possessing good information doesn't automatically translate into higher profits. After all, the average U.S. stock fund, run by the most data-rich, informed money managers in history, still can't consistently outperform the "dumb" index funds.

⑤ *"Keep your money home because America has the world's strongest economy."* This is the continuation of the response to point number two. The rebuttal is a simple but powerful one: Remember Japan at the end of the 1980s? With the second largest economy in the world, Japan seemed ready to overtake the U. S. for the number one position. At that time, few Japanese investors bought shares in U.S. blue chip companies. Why bother? There seemed to be unlimited opportunity in the Japanese market. But the Japanese Nikkei index started falling, on its way from 39,000 yen to 14,000. The average return in Japanese stock funds from 1989-1998 was a loss of 3.4% per year. As we now know, diversification would have been a smart move, no matter how great things looked at home.

⑥ *"Keep your money home because the U.S. offers a better trading environment. Our accounting practices are standardized and regulated, so you'll get fuller disclosure and more accurate information. Your commissions will be lower. Because our markets are more liquid, you'll get better executions. To keep the playing field level, our brokers aren't allowed to trade for their own accounts. We offer legal protections to investors, and we've got political stability. You can't take these things for granted when you venture outside our borders."* All of this is true, which makes it even more sensible to use mutual funds and their experienced managers and analysts to navigate those potentially treacherous foreign waters.

How would the performance in a Just-the-Basics strategy be affected if you left out the foreign stock component?

The table on the left shows the results from two Just-the-Basics portfolios that are invested 100% in stocks. The first one includes the standard 20% allocation to Vanguard International Growth; the second one omits the foreign stock fund and divides the portfolio 50% in the 500 Index fund and 50% in the Extended Market Index fund. As you would expect, given the news on the previous page that foreign funds have been lagging their U.S. counterparts, the second portfolio won the performance race in recent years.

Even so, I continue to favor some international diversification, primarily because I agree with point three and the cautionary response to point five (see pros and cons above). As for point one, our foreign holdings may not fully protect us against a slide in the U.S. markets, but then neither would adding to our U.S. holdings! Finally, I find point six well taken, and it only makes me appreciate the top-performing foreign stock fund managers all the more. But I won't fault you if you prefer to omit an international emphasis. You surrender some diversification, but you've sure got the performance numbers from the 1990s on your side.

	100% Stocks Portfolio with Foreign	100% Stocks Portfolio without Foreign
1985	36.7%	31.6%
1986	23.3%	14.9%
1987	3.0%	0.6%
1988	16.7%	18.0%
1989	27.1%	27.7%
1990	–9.3%	–8.6%
1991	29.8%	36.0%
1992	6.8%	9.9%
1993	18.7%	12.2%
1994	–0.1%	–0.3%
1995	31.5%	35.6%
1996	19.1%	20.3%
1997	24.8%	29.9%
1998	18.2%	18.5%
1999	28.2%	28.6%
15 Yrs	17.6%	17.6%
10 Yrs	16.0%	17.3%
5 Yrs	24.2%	26.4%

The 15/10/5 year returns are for the periods ending December 31, 1999.

A SOUND MIND BRIEFING

A Strange Sounding Bit of Wisdom:
Make Sure Your Decision-Making Is Inside-Out

One of the more contra-intuitive propositions that I regularly put forth in these pages is the idea that one's investing decisions can usually be made with little regard for what's currently going on in the investment markets. Let me once again make my case, and then we'll apply it to the question of deciding whether now is a good time to sell some or all of your stock holdings.

Typically, where do ideas for your investment decisions originate? For many investors, the starting point of the process is found in the impersonal "outside" world of current events, magazine articles, and brokers' recommendations. <u>Their decisions are primarily guided by outside considerations.</u> As they respond to all the data thrown at them—sometimes buying, sometimes selling—their personal "inside" financial worlds take shape. Their thinking is "outside-in." They need a continual stream of news and information to provide stimulation and provoke them to action. Decision-making would be impossible without it.

For other investors, the starting point of their decision-making is "inside" information. The focus is on their own financial needs and a personalized long-term strategy designed to meet those needs. Their buy/sell decisions are made based on what's required to make sure their financial holdings are in accord with the game plan. The "outside" world of investment professionals comes into the picture only because assistance is needed in executing decisions already made. This is "inside-out" thinking, where <u>decisions are primarily shaped by inside considerations.</u> Thus, current market fads, pressures and so-called expert opinions are largely irrelevant to inside-out investors. As you have probably guessed by now, I'm encouraging you to be an inside-out thinker.

In other words, make your investing decisions like you do other consumer purchasing decisions. For example, if your family has grown to the point you need a spacious minivan to haul everyone around, you wouldn't buy a new Volkswagon Beetle instead merely because an article in <u>Money</u> magazine said they're exceptionally "hot" at the moment. Or, if you need a medicine that lowers your blood pressure, you wouldn't let a glowing recommendation from your druggist convince you to bring home the leading antihistimine for allergies instead. It would be foolish to let irrelevant external influences (outside-in thinking) steer you into making such inappropriate purchases. Instead, you make your decisions based on your needs at the time, irrespective of what the marketplace would like to sell you.

This is obvious, you say. Yet, many people have a difficult time applying this consumer mindset to their investing decisions. One of the most frequently-asked questions I receive is a variant of "The market seems overvalued, and I've read where many experts are sounding an alarm. Is this a good time to sell my stocks?" These folks may decide whether to reduce their stock holdings depending on how volatile the market has been, what the business magazines say, what the Federal Reserve may do to interest rates, or—heaven help them—what my opinion might be.

Outside-in thinking will never tell you whether it's a "good time" to sell stocks because no one knows what the market will do in coming months (as evidenced by the continual reporting of conflicting opinions from Wall Street's bulls and bears).

Here's a checklist an inside-out investor might run through in deciding the "Is it a good time to sell?" question.

☐ Is my financial foundation still rock solid? That is, am I still debt-free (Level 1) and is my contingency fund (Level 2) still sufficient? If not, I should sell enough stock to repair the cracks in my foundation.

☐ Are my earlier assumptions about my lifetime earnings, retirement and lifestyle goals, health needs, life expectancy and emotional tolerance of risk still acceptable (chapters 17,21)? If not, perhaps I should reconsider the way I have divided my portfolio between stocks and bonds.

☐ Are my protective boundaries still in place (chapter 29)? If not, what adjustments should I make at this time?

☐ Can I commit the monies I have at risk in my stock holdings for at least another five years? If not, how long can I commit? Are the risks of loss for such a time frame acceptable (see table on page 286)?

☐ Am I meeting my giving goals? Am I now in a position so I can give even more? Perhaps I should give some of my stocks that have gone up in value to my church or favorite mission organization (chapter 27).

☐ Has my portfolio grown enough so that I can now achieve my long-term goals with less risk? If so, perhaps I should convert a portion of my stock holdings into fixed-income securities (chapter 24).

Notice that the focus is on the personal needs and circumstances of the individual, not on the headlines of the day which almost never tell you anything that will enhance the quality of your decision-making. While current events may provoke you to run through your personal list of review questions, they should not dictate the answers.

From the June 2000 issue of <u>Sound Mind Investing</u>. To learn more about the monthly SMI newsletter, use the postage-paid tear-out card in this book, or visit our website at www.soundmindinvesting.com.

If you *do* want to include an international fund, why go with the International Growth fund when you could use Vanguard's Total International Stock Index fund? After all, this is an indexing strategy.

The explanation is found in the flexibility to invest in the regions of the world where the manager finds the most attractive opportunities. International Growth has it; Total International Stock doesn't. It's a "fund of funds," splitting its assets among three other Vanguard international index funds (typically using the weightings shown in the table below). This means it tends to

	Ticker Symbol	Typical Weighting	Recent 5 Years	2000 8Mos	1999 Return	1998 Return	1997 Return	1996 Return	1995 Return
Vang European Index	VEURX	45%	17.9%	−5.3%	16.7%	28.9%	24.2%	21.3%	22.3%
Vang Pacific Index	VPACX	45%	0.9%	−10.2%	57.1%	2.4%	−25.7%	−7.8%	2.8%
Vang Emerging Markets	VEIEX	10%	2.2%	−12.5%	61.6%	−18.1%	−16.8%	15.8%	0.6%
Vang Intl Stock Index	VGTSX		new	−7.6%	29.9%	15.6%	−0.8%	new	new
Vang International Growth	VWIGX		12.8%	−1.2%	26.3%	16.9%	4.1%	14.7%	14.9%

In addition to Just-the-Basics, the SMI newsletter provides two other portfolios. One is geared toward beginning investors. The other diversifies among actively-managed mutual funds selected from the current top performers. For more information, visit our Model Portfolios page at www.soundmindinvesting.com/vsection/v_model/index.htm.

be locked-in to a fixed regional mix. The International Growth fund has yet to be beaten by the index fund. Until the index portfolio can demonstrate that its fixed mix approach is preferable, I'll continue to use International Growth.

I encourage you to give the Just-the-Basics strategy a serious look, and consider using it as the foundation of your long-term strategy.

Of course, indexing need not be an "all or nothing" proposition. Many of my newsletter readers use the Just-the-Basics funds as basic all-season holdings to anchor their portfolios. For example, you could divide your portfolio between a Just-the-Basics mix of funds—perhaps two-thirds of the total value—and then be a little more flexible with the rest. You could either be more adventurous (by investing the remaining one-third in selected stock funds or individual stocks) or more conservative (by adding Treasuries, CDs, or other money market holdings). Or, you might use the more structured "Core & Explore" strategy explained on page 197. ◆

CHAPTER PREVIEW

Selecting the Portfolio Mix Best Suited to Your Risk-Taking Temperament and Current Season of Life

I. **All of us have "money personalities" that reflect our attitudes toward earning, spending, saving, and investing money.**

   A. Psychologist Kathleen Gurney has conducted nationwide surveys and found that people have a financial self and use money as a means to gain security, freedom, love, respect, power, and happiness.

   B. Gurney notes nine distinct money personality types, but I have combined several in developing the four investing temperaments in this chapter.

II. **Meet the Preserver, Researcher, Explorer, and Daredevil.**

   A. Each of these investing personalities reflects a different emotional reaction to risk taking.

   B. A series of "attitudinal snapshots" should enable you to select the one that is closest to the way you feel about financial security and the tradeoffs between risk and reward.

III. **For financial planning purposes, life can be divided into four phases.**

   A. Laying the foundation: Typically runs up into your forties.

   B. Accumulating assets: Your forties and fifties.

   C. Preserving assets: Your sixties and into your seventies.

   D. Distributing assets: Age seventy-five and beyond.

IV. **These two factors—your temperament and your current "season of life"—come together to determine how much risk is appropriate for your situation.**

   A. The "controlling your risk" matrix shows how I suggest dividing your investments between stocks (investing-by-owning) and bonds (investing-by-lending).

   B. This matrix provides a rational basis for dealing with the constant tension between the need for capital growth and the fear of capital loss that confront every investor.

"Not only do we have a physical self, an emotional self, and a social self, but we have a financial, or money, self.

"This money self is an integral part of our behavioral repertoire and influences the way we interact with our money. In other words, your money personality is a major factor in how you utilize your money. Most of us fail to realize the extent to which our money personality impacts our financial habits and affects the degree of satisfaction we get from what money we have. There is an inseparable link between our unconscious feelings about money and the way in which we earn it, spend it, save it, and invest it."

This observation is made by Kathleen Gurney in her book *Your Money Personality*. She adds that psychologists believe that money is a kind of "emotional currency" that symbolizes many of our unconscious needs and desires, among them:

> "I'm trying to find myself."
> — Common quest of popular culture

> "If you don't know who you are, the markets are an expensive place to find out."
> — Adam Smith
> The Money Game

• **Security** (If I have enough money, I'll always be safe. No person and no catastrophe can harm me.)

• **Freedom** (If I have enough money, I can freely choose my jobs or choose not to work; my options are open.)

• **Love** (If I have enough money, more people will care about me. Money makes relationships a lot easier.)

• **Respect** (If I have enough money, everyone will recognize that I have merit, that I accomplished what I set out to do.)

• **Power** (If I have enough money, nobody will ever push me around. I will be strong and have total control over my life.)

• **Happiness** (If I have enough money, I will truly be happy. I can finally relax and enjoy life.)

Dr. Gurney suggests that as many as nine different investment personality types exist (which she discusses in detail). To simplify matters, I have combined them in order to consider just four. There's nothing "official" about these. I devised them simply to help make this process easier and perhaps a little more fun. We all probably have some elements of each of the four types within us, so don't think I'm saying that any one type will fit you perfectly. But you may find that you identify with one temperament more than the other three. If so, you can learn something about yourself from this exercise.

I call the most aggressive investors "Daredevils."
They enjoy the investment "fast lane" . . .

. . . and are often found playing the markets on a short-term basis. They have plenty of self-confidence. The new issues market, stock and index options, and commodity futures would be areas of interest due to the opportunities they offer to make a lot of money quickly.

They often resist advice to diversify into more prudent, less colorful investments. Yet, even Daredevils need a solid, conservative base to counter their occasional impulsiveness and higher-risk tendencies. If they're not careful, they'll reach their retirement years with little to show for a lifetime of wheeling and dealing.

Daredevils could really benefit from the Just-the-Basics approach where we emphasize putting first things first. The use of highly diversified mutual fund portfolios, while not as high-stakes as some of their other investments, would bring a much-needed balance to their overall investment picture. It would go a long way toward countering their natural inclinations to "go for it."

"Explorers" are fascinated by the money-making potential of investing . . .

. . . but if they lack confidence in choosing the best path, they often take refuge in the safety of following the crowd. They are attracted to the latest trendy investments that are dominating the news. The "thrill of the hunt" is the fun part for them.

Explorers can be impetuous and often hop aboard a new investment without fully understanding just how serious the risks might be. As a result, their holdings are frequently a random assortment of moderate- to high-risk "good deals" collected over the years. Such a portfolio likely lacks balance and has no long-term focus. Explorers would benefit from a systematic, controlled-risk way of moving toward their long-term goals.

"Researchers" also tend toward caution, but their self-confidence enables them to overcome their concerns . . .

. . . if they feel they have done sufficient investigation. Simply reading in this book that a certain mutual fund is recommended may not be good enough for Researchers; they may want to know more about that mutual fund and why I recommend it. They are willing to immerse themselves in facts and figures in order to get a thorough understanding of the strengths and drawbacks of the investments they are considering.

They can easily postpone making commitments because they want more information. Up to a point, this caution serves them well. If overdone, their ability to make decisions is paralyzed because they will never know for sure that they have all the relevant information. Researchers appreciate the self-discipline imposed by following an objective set of guidelines. In addition, they have the long-term mind-set and patience necessary to stay with their game plan for many years in spite of occasional setbacks.

The Psychology of Investing

Most people are willing to invest time and expense in gaining a good understanding of market fundamentals (knowledge) and work at assembling that knowledge into a proven strategy (technique). Unfortunately, these are not the only attributes needed for success—if they were, we'd all be millionaires!

The quality that separates the top professionals from the rest of us is one that takes years to develop: emotional self-control. Our emotions interact with news and market events in ways that incline us to act at exactly the wrong time. We all want to "buy low and sell high," but experience shows that most investors do the opposite. That is likely because, emotionally, it's quite difficult to "buy low." The reason that prices are low is that the news is bad and people are pessimistic. They become fearful about the future. Investors feel pressured, and under pressure, emotions tend to dictate our actions.

As our fears increase, so do our anxieties, and we can become paralyzed. We know what we should do, but we "tighten up." Athletes call it "choking." A short putt to a golfer or free throw to a basketball player is no big deal in a friendly pick-up game. But with huge television audiences looking on and millions of dollars at stake, it's a far different story. Why? Emotions.

If you'd like to know more about the psychological side of investing, you might enjoy a book by market veteran Justin Mamis called The Nature of Risk. It offers interesting insights into why we behave as we do in making investing decisions. This is not casual reading, so be prepared for your thinking to be stimulated and challenged.

"Preservers" tend to worry about their investments . . .

. . . because the risk of losing their capital is very real to them. As a result, they are usually quite cautious, favoring CDs, government bonds, and only the highest quality blue-chip stocks. This approach helps them to preserve their wealth but may not provide enough growth to achieve reasonable performance goals.

Sometimes their desire to be cautious makes it difficult for them to make any investment decisions at all. If they can find advisers in whom they have confidence, they are frequently willing to rely on them heavily to assist with investment decisions. Realizing that they are safety conscious and must accept lower returns as part of the trade-off for safety, they usually have realistic expectations with regard to how much they can reasonably hope to make.

If you're a Preserver, the basic philosophy underlying all of your investing decisions is to preserve capital. You would agree with Warren Buffett, a legendary investor of our time, when he said there were only two really important rules of investing. Rule #1 is "Don't lose any money," and Rule #2 is "*Never* forget Rule #1."

You're now ready to select the investment temperament that best describes your attitudes toward . . .

. . . monetary risk-taking and its possible rewards. On the following two pages, you'll find each of the four investment temperaments listed along with their corresponding attitudes on risk and profit expressed in a variety of ways. Read each of them carefully and thoughtfully. You might want to pencil in checkmarks next to the statements that you identify with. Which of the four temperaments has the most check marks? (If you're married, you should ask your spouse to study them as well.)

It's been my experience that most people have little trouble seeing themselves in one of the four. The identification is usually almost instantaneous. However, if you narrow it down to two and have trouble deciding between them, my suggestion is to select the one on the right, the more conservative one (risk decreases as you move from left to right). Err on the side of safety and prudence rather than risk-taking.

Once you identify your money personality, I encourage you to stay within the boundaries it implies if at all possible. James Dale Davidson and Sir William Rees-Mogg, in their best-selling investment book, *Blood in the Streets,* stated well what usually happens to those who play a high-stakes game for which they are temperamentally unsuited:

Nothing is more surely condemned to failure than a high-risk strategy pursued by a low-risk man; he will always flinch at the point before the strategy has succeeded, and will throw away his potential gains in an attempt to leap back to the security he actually prefers. . . . To be a successful investor you have to be right, but in your own way. It is not only a matter of knowing yourself. It is even more important to be yourself.

There's always a tension between our *need for capital growth* **and our** *fear of capital loss.*

Obviously, it would be great if we could make all that we need on our investments without taking any risk. A relatively small number of multimillionaires might be able to live comfortably off the interest paid by their T-bills, but the rest of us aren't so fortunate. Without taking away from the importance of "being yourself" as stated above, we must sometimes learn how to live with a little more risk than we would like.

Many readers of my newsletter became so committed to their comfort levels that they were not making sufficient progress in building their capital. To remedy this, I developed guidelines for helping them decide how to balance their holdings between stocks and bonds. They're based on the "seasons of life" through which we all travel. The four temperaments still play an important role, but a new dimension has been added—the need for capital growth at various phases of life:

Phase 1: Laying the foundation. This is the starting point for most of us. We spend the greater part of our twenties and thirties acquiring transportation and a residence, paying off student and other loans, and building a contingency reserve. There may not be much in the way of monthly surplus left to invest for retirement (which is still twenty-five or more years away). The money we do put aside can be invested aggressively because we have a very long time frame in which to work. This is the phase where we can afford to take our greatest risks.

Phase 2: Accumulating assets. Most of us experience our peak earning years during our forties to fifties. At the same time, our expenses should be falling as the house gets paid for and the kids are raised. Retirement is now more than a distant concept; we see it as an economic reality that we will actually experience. Fine-tuning our financial plans and following a workable strategy takes on a new importance. We should begin reducing risk because our time horizon has shortened.

Phase 3: Preserving assets. Unbelievably, retirement is just around the corner (or already here)! Our need for preserving capital and generating current income has

CONTROLLING YOUR RISK MATRIX

| | NEED FOR GROWTH | | | FEAR OF LOSS | | | | | | |
Financial Phase	Characterized by	Typical Age	Daredevil Stock	Bond	Explorer Stock	Bond	Researcher Stock	Bond	Preserver Stock	Bond
Phase 1	Laying foundation	Under 45	100%	0%	100%	0%	80%	20%	60%	40%
Phase 2	Accumulating assets	45 to 59	80%	20%	80%	20%	60%	40%	40%	60%
Phase 3	Preserving assets	60 to 75	60%	40%	40%	60%	40%	60%	20%	80%
Phase 4	Distributing assets	Over 75	40%	60%	20%	80%	20%	80%	0%	100%

There are many theories on how best to allocate your portfolio at various stages of life. As an alternative to the above, many recommend using this rule of thumb: subtract your age from 100 and allocate at least that percentage to your holdings in stocks.

The Daredevil

❏ If I believe an investment has a chance of really paying off big, I'm willing to take the chance that I could lose a large part (maybe even all) of my money.

❏ I can accept losses in the value of my investments, even if they continue for several consecutive years. The end result is all that really matters!

❏ I almost always prefer to make my investing decisions on my own.

❏ The amount of current income I receive from an investment is not a factor in my decision making.

❏ Inflation is the number one threat. I think it's essential that you beat inflation, and that means you don't have the luxury of playing it safe all the time.

❏ I've had some super results on a few high-risk situations. Of course, I've had my share of big losers, too. To really make money, you've got to risk money.

❏ For me to risk 10% of my net worth in an investment that seemed to have a 90% chance of success, the potential profit would have to be at least equal to the amount I put at risk.

❏ I suppose I'm optimistic (and a tad impulsive at times), but I don't usually worry about my investment decisions once they're made.

❏ It's important to me, perhaps even a source of pride, that my portfolio does better than the stock market over the course of an economic cycle.

❏ If a stock doubled in price a year after I bought it, I'd buy some more shares in that company.

The Explorer

❏ I'm willing to take a greater-than-average amount of risk in return for the possibility of having my portfolio grow substantially.

❏ I can accept an occasional year where I lose money on my investments, but I wouldn't like it if I had two of them back-to-back.

❏ I occasionally make my investing decisions all on my own, but usually I prefer to let my broker bring me what he thinks are his best ideas.

❏ It would be desirable to receive some current income from my investments, but I don't insist upon it in every case.

❏ Inflation is a genuine concern, so I'm willing to invest where there's a good chance of getting a "real" return even though there's a little more risk.

❏ I think exploring new financial territory is exciting. When I hear about the latest "hot" investment area, I like to take a look.

❏ For me to risk 10% of my net worth in an investment that seemed to have a 90% chance of success, the potential profit would have to be at least twice as much as the amount I put at risk.

❏ I don't have time to bury myself in the details like some people. I keep my ear to the ground and think I have pretty good intuitive insights.

❏ I do tend to compare the results in my portfolio with what the overall stock market did. It's a good feeling to know that you "beat" the market.

❏ If a stock doubled in price a year after I bought it, I'd hold on and hope for still more gains.

The Researcher

The Preserver

❑ I'm fairly conservative, but am willing to take a greater-than-average amount of risk with part of my portfolio in order to boost its growth potential.

❑ I'm very conservative, and am much more concerned about protecting what I already have than in taking risks to make it grow.

❑ I can handle the month-to-month ups and downs of investing, but I wouldn't want to end up losing any money for the entire year.

❑ It's important to my peace of mind to have stable, consistent year-to-year results.

❑ I prefer to make my own investing decisions, but am always open to ideas from the "experts" which I search out in magazines, books, and television/radio.

❑ Making investing decisions all on my own makes me a little nervous. I tend to rely a lot on others to help me.

❑ It's fairly important that I receive current income from my investments, but I'm willing to accept some uncertainty as to the amount.

❑ The amount of current income I receive from an investment is important to me; if possible, I'd like to know the amount in advance.

❑ Inflation is a genuine concern, but gains lower than the rate of inflation are acceptable if it means I can keep my risk down.

❑ Preserving my capital and knowing how much current income I'll receive are much more important to me than beating inflation.

❑ I want to make my decisions based on a solid understanding of all the facts. I don't believe in investing in something just because everyone else is doing it.

❑ News about such things as the savings and loan closings, our trade deficits, or the losses in "junk bonds" are a little scary and confusing.

❑ For me to risk 10% of my net worth in an investment that seemed to have a 90% chance of success, the potential profit would have to be at least four times as much as the amount I put at risk.

❑ No amount of potential profit is worth risking the loss of 10% of my net worth.

❑ Once I make a decision, I have a lot of confidence in it, which enables me to stay with it even if others around me are changing their minds.

❑ Making investment decisions is hard for me; I'm never quite sure I have all the facts. I wish I could be sure what the best investments are for me.

❑ I keep an eye on what the overall stock market is doing during the year. Naturally, I'd like to do even better, but it's not a major factor in my thinking.

❑ It's irrelevant to me whether my portfolio does better than the stock market over the course of an economic cycle.

❑ If a stock doubled in price a year after I bought it, I'd sell half my shares and lock in part of my profits.

❑ If a stock doubled in price a year after I bought it, I'd sell all my shares.

risen, and if we've done our job well, our need for additional growth in our capital base has abated. Our time horizon, which used to allow us the luxury of decades to bounce back from bear market losses, has shrunk dramatically. The situation calls for more fixed income investments and fewer stocks.

THE PERSONALITY TRAITS UNDERLYING THE FOUR TEMPERAMENTS

The temperaments were developed by factoring in one's willingness to lose money in the quest to make more money. You might say it's a question of whether optimism or caution is the governing emotion.

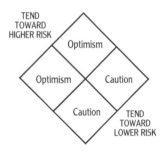

Then, we divide the diamond to show the levels of self-confidence in making one's own financial decisions versus the tendency to rely on others.

Phase 4: Distributing assets. We're in the home stretch of life, and can envision it won't be too long before we'll experience the joy of what Scripture means when it teaches that "to be away from the body" is to be "at home with the Lord." As much as prudently possible, we'll want to give away our surplus capital to our children and the Lord's work. At this point, unnecessary risk-taking should be avoided.

Locate your investing personality in the "controlling your risk" matrix on page 193. Then, select the financial phase of life that best describes your situation. Use the ages as guidelines, not laws. You might be age thirty-five and already in Phase Two, or fifty and still laying your Phase One foundation. If your recommended stock/bond mix requires a greater commitment to stocks than you've been comfortable with in the past, you've got a judgment call to make. You can use a dollar-cost-averaging approach (see chapter 19) for making the transition from where you are now to where you want to go.

The matrix reflects my personal sense of risk. Other investment advisers might feel more comfortable with less restrictive guidelines. For example, they might feel that a mix of 80% stocks and 20% bonds is acceptable even when you move into Phase 3 of life. All of us are being arbitrary to a degree. The point is that as the time to begin drawing on the investments draws ever nearer, you should move increasingly to a more conservative approach. If you've got ten or more years, you can afford to take more risk if you want to—but do you want to? It's up to you.

Another very important reminder: After you select guidelines that you feel comfortable with, *stick with them!* There will be many temptations from your broker, well-meaning friends, the media, and your own desires for higher returns that will encourage you to "make an exception" or abandon your guidelines altogether. You do so at your own peril.

Being realistic in your expectations is an important part . . .

. . . of your investment planning process. Making assumptions (often known as "wild guesses") about the future is an unavoidable part of planning and budgeting. One fundamental question that needs answering is: "How much of a return can I reasonably expect from my investment portfolio?" It's important that your answer be grounded in reality and not wishful thinking.

A SOUND MIND BRIEFING

One Portfolio that Fits All Four Temperaments:
Indexing + Fund Selection

Since 1992, I've offered readers of my SMI newsletter two approaches for putting together a diversified, long-term portfolio. One uses index funds, guaranteeing that their returns will at least be equal to those generated by the overall market (our model "Just-the-Basics" portfolios). The other strategy chooses from among the top performing funds that we provide each month on the Recommended Funds page (our "Upgrading" portfolios).

Many subscribers (Daredevils/Explorers) like the opportunities presented by the top-performing funds and hesitate to settle in to an indexing-only approach. But perhaps their spouses (Researchers/Preservers) are attracted to the many advantages of an indexing approach (as explained in chapter 16). What to do? Make them both happy. It's really not necessary to restrict yourself to either an "active" (upgrading) or "passive" (indexing) strategy. In fact, the Charles Schwab Company has published research that indicates the highest rewards appear to go to investors who use both approaches in combination.

According to The Wall Street Journal, the Schwab report concluded "there are specific blends of index funds and so-called actively-managed funds that have the best chance of accomplishing a goal held by many investors: minimizing a portfolio's risk of lagging behind the market, while increasing its probability of outperforming it." Schwab calls this a "Core & Explore" strategy, wherein index funds comprise the "core" that provides broad diversification, and actively-managed funds "explore" for higher returns.

To determine which combinations would work best, Schwab's computers observed the results from blending thousands of combinations of actively-managed and index funds. They computed the average returns and volatility of these mixtures over numerous time periods. The resulting recommendations are shown in Table A.

You'll notice that indexing has generally been the most profitable path when it comes to large company stocks. That's why Schwab suggests putting 80% of the large-cap portion of your portfolio in index funds. The recommended allocations to index funds in the small company and foreign categories, on the other hand, are much lower. This reflects the fact that actively-managed funds in these areas have a much better record of outperforming index funds.

As I've explained, an all-stock Just-the-Basics portfolio is typically invested 40% in large caps, 40% in small caps, and 20% in foreign stocks. Table B shows how those numbers would be affected by applying Schwab's findings. In the large-cap area, for example, only 32% of the portfolio would automatically be invested in the S&P 500 Index fund; the remaining 8% would be directed into an actively-managed fund which—it is hoped— would do even better than the index fund.

Of course, the $64 question becomes how to select the actively-managed funds. There are thousands of ways this could be approached. Let me give just one example, assuming you had undertaken a Core & Explore strategy and gotten results similar to those of the funds recommended in my newsletter during 1999. Follow along in Table C.

The average SMI-recommended large-cap fund gained 25.4% in 1999. This was only slightly better than the 21.1% returned by the 500 Index fund. But a real difference was made in the small-company portion of the portfolio where the non-index funds returned 56.6% compared to 36.2% in the Extended Market Index fund. Likewise, the non-Vanguard international fund gained 52.5% versus 26.3% for the International Growth fund. When you put it all together in the allocation amounts shown in Table B, the Core & Explore portfolio gained 37.1% compared to 28.2% for the generic Just-the-Basics strategy. Of course, it's unlikely you'll do so well every year compared to the indexes, but the example illustrates the possibilities. More importantly, Core & Explore provides the basis for a strategy that, because it offers something appealing to each of the four temperaments, has the potential to wear well emotionally for many years, an important consideration for the long-term investor.

Table A	Large Caps	Small Caps	Foreign Stocks
"Core" Fund	80%	40%	30%
"Explore" Fund	20%	60%	70%

Table B	Large Caps	Small Caps	Foreign Stocks
"Core" Fund	32%	16%	6%
"Explore" Fund	8%	24%	14%
Total Stock Portion	40%	40%	20%

Table C	Large Caps	Small Caps	Foreign Stocks
Just-the-Basics Funds	21.1%	36.2%	26.3%
Average SMI Funds	25.4%	56.6%	52.5%

Table D	1999 Return
Just-the-Basics Portfolio	28.2%
"Core & Explore" Portfolio	37.1%

From the December 1999 issue of Sound Mind Investing. To learn more about the monthly SMI newsletter, use the postage-paid tear-out card in this book, or visit our website at www.soundmindinvesting.com.

To this end, on page 183 I provided annual performance data for the Just-the-Basics portfolios. Bear in mind that the 1990s were an unusual time of economic growth and prosperity. The decade was hardly typical. After all, the stock market's average historical return over the past quarter century is about 11% per year. You can see that the performance numbers shown are higher than that. So, in order to provide a more realistic guide as to what you might expect in the future, I would suggest that you have performance expectations that are lower than those shown.

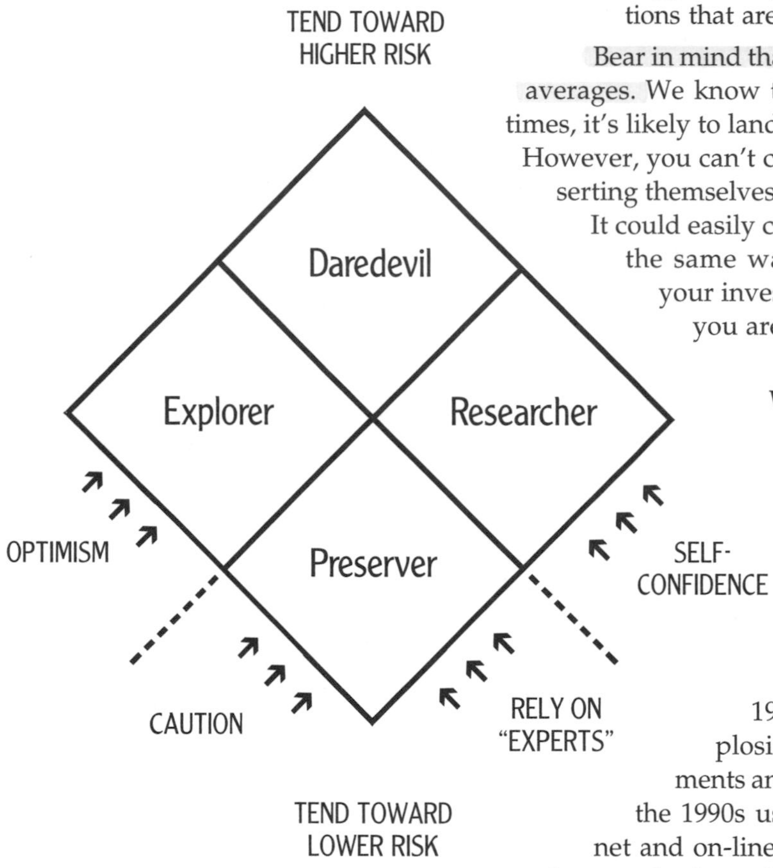

Bear in mind that the results shown are merely averages. We know that if a penny is tossed 1,000 times, it's likely to land heads up about half the time. However, you can't count on these probabilities asserting themselves if you toss a penny *only twice*. It could easily come up tails twice in a row. In the same way, the longer you stay with your investing program, the more likely you are to get these kinds of returns.

THE RESULT IS FOUR RISK PROFILES WITH DISTINCT STYLES OF INVESTMENT DECISION-MAKING

TEND TOWARD HIGHER RISK

Daredevil

Explorer

Researcher

OPTIMISM

Preserver

SELF-CONFIDENCE

CAUTION

RELY ON "EXPERTS"

TEND TOWARD LOWER RISK

What the first decade of the 21st century will produce in the way of dramatic change in the financial markets . . .

. . . is anyone's guess. The 1970s gave us listed stock options and the birth of money market funds. The 1980s produced a veritable explosion in the fixed income investments and mutual fund industries. And the 1990s ushered in the era of the Internet and on-line transactions with banks, brokers, and other sellers of financial services.

But in terms of the potential risks and rewards for the average investor, the importance of those advantages offered by the Just-the-Basics strategy—sufficient diversification for safety and a risk level designed to fit your individual situation—hasn't changed. Assemble a portfolio tailored to your individual financial personality and long-term goals, and peace-of-mind investing can become a reality for you. ◆

18

CHAPTER PREVIEW

Getting Started on the
Road to Financial Security

I. **There are six key principles I believe should be incorporated into every investment strategy, all of which are reflected in the Just-the-Basics strategy.**

    A. The foremost principle is to diversify in order to protect your capital against unexpected economic developments.

    B. Other principles include having clear-cut, objective rules for your decision making, staying within your emotional comfort zone, acknowledging your current financial limitations, and having a provision for investing in small amounts so you can get an early start.

II. **The Just-the-Basics strategy requires you to open an investing account with the no-load Vanguard Group.**

    A. I will walk you through the steps of how to do this, leading to the launch of your personalized Just-the-Basics portfolio.

    B. Tables are provided to show you how to divide your money among the Vanguard funds in order to achieve the portfolio mix and level of risk that you desire.

III. **Just-the-Basics avoids the four "red flag" traps discussed in chapter 12.**

IV. **After your Just-the-Basics portfolio is in place, it requires you to take further action only once a year.**

    A. This annual rebalancing process restores your desired portfolio allocations to their correct levels.

    B. It can be done at any time during the year which is convenient to you, but I usually recommend January as being a good time because it tends to coincide with other financial planning activities.

"The spontaneous tendency of our culture is to inexorably add detail to our lives: one more option, one more problem, one more commitment, one more expectation, one more purchase . . .

. . . one more debt, one more change, one more job, one more decision. We must now deal with more 'things per person' than at any other time in history. Yet one can comfortably handle only so many details in his or her life. Exceeding this threshold will result in disorganization or frustration. It is important to note here that the problem is not in the 'details.' The problem is in the 'exceeding.' This is called overloading."

I've been reading Dr. Richard Swenson's interesting book *Margin*. He says that margin is the space that once existed between us and our limits. It's the gap between rest and exhaustion, between peace and anxiety. He thinks most of us don't have enough margin, and he has written his book to provide a prescription for the dangers of overloaded lives. I've found it fascinating so far, and intend to finish it as soon as I can find the time.

Swenson lists twenty-three specific types of overload. I was struck by how many of the items could also appear on a list of frustrations that often overwhelm average people as they attempt to manage their financial lives. A few of them include: choice overload (too many possible investments clamoring for attention), education overload (too much to learn), expectation overload (we're told we can have "wealth without risk"), hurry overload (investing ads are presented as if it's essential to "act now"), information overload (research, articles, and opinions coming at us faster than we can possibly absorb them), and media overload (thousands of experts writing thousands of books and appearing on thousands of radio and TV programs).

It was to help eliminate this sense of overload and the paralysis it can cause that I created the Four Levels process . . .

. . . and Just-the-Basics investing strategy. To get a perspective as to where we now stand on our journey toward sound mind investing, let's briefly review what we've covered thus far.

• In Section One, we considered the first financial fitness test you should pass before using your monthly surplus to invest in the stock and bond markets—getting debt-free (chapter 1). We also discussed why having a spending plan is essential (chapter 2), the costs and dangers of credit cards and how to handle them wisely (chapter 3), and where paying off a house mortgage fits into your long-range plans (chapter 4).

• In Section Two, we looked at the second test of financial fitness—saving for future needs (chapter 5). We reviewed the best kinds of investments for your emergency fund where safety and "anytime availability" is so important (chapter 6) as well as a different set of investment options for your accumulation fund where you're saving for a large purchase (chapter 7). Finally, we considered the rising costs of college and how to plan for them (chapter 8).

• In Section Three, we moved out into the world of Wall Street, looking at what investing is and why it's actually quite simple (chapter 9). I introduced you to mutual funds and the advantages they offer the average investor (chapter 10), how they're sold and the best way to buy them (chapter 11), necessary cautions that should be understood about their risks (chapter 12), and the tax consequences of owning mutual funds (chapter 13).

• Thus far in Section Four, we've looked at some basic things you should know about the nature of bonds (chapter 14) and stocks (chapter 15). Next, I introduced you to a "no muss, no fuss" approach to putting together a long-term stock and bond portfolio that I've dubbed Just-the-Basics because of its simplicity and low maintenance requirements (chapter 16). I explained how it works and why it gives better results than the majority of professional money managers can achieve. And in chapter 17, I gave you some guidelines for personalizing the all-important decision as to how much of your Just-the-Basics portfolio should be invested in stocks versus bonds.

In this chapter, I'm going to equip you with the remaining specifics you need to launch your own Just-the-Basics strategy. I'd like to start by showing how Just-the-Basics reflects the six principles that I believe every investment strategy should follow. Whether you're single or married, young or nearing retirement, investing for college or buying your first house, this strategy is flexible enough to work well for you! Here are the six principles.

Principle #1: Success in investing comes not in hoping for the best, but in knowing how you will handle the worst.

Always remember: nobody *really* knows what's going to happen next. Some things can be predicted; most things can't. The tide tables, for example, can be prepared far ahead of time because they are governed by physical laws. The investment world is a colossal engine fueled by human emotions. Millions of people make billions of decisions all reflecting their feelings of fear or security, hardship or prosperity. To attempt to make reliable forecasts in the face of this staggering complexity is foolhardy.

Therefore, since nobody really knows what is going to happen next year, next month, or even next week, your plan must allow for the fact that the investment markets will experience some unexpected rough sledding every now and then. That's where diversification comes in. The idea is to pick investments that "march to different drummers." This means your strategy involves owning a mix of investments that are affected by different economic events. For example, you might invest in both a bond fund and a gold fund. When inflation really heats up, bonds go down (due to rising interest rates) while at the same time gold often goes up (because investors want a secure "store of value"). To the extent that the price changes in the two funds offset each other, you have added stability to your overall portfolio.

Surprisingly, it is possible to assemble some lower-risk investment combinations that give pretty much the same returns over time as higher-risk ones. When that is done, such a mix of investments is said to be more "efficient" because it accomplishes the same investment result while taking less risk. Just-the-Basics offers you portfolios that combine stocks and bonds in various combinations in order to reduce volatility and risk while still achieving attractive long-term returns.

Principle #2: Your investing plan must have easy-to-understand, clear-cut rules.

There must be no room for differing interpretations. You must be able to make your investing decisions quickly and with confidence. This means reducing your decision making to numerical guidelines as much as possible. A strategy that calls for a "significant investment" in small company stocks is not as helpful as one that calls for "30% of your portfolio" to be invested in small company stocks.

Insofar as possible, your strategy should not only tell you *what* to invest in but also offer precise guidance in telling you *how much* to invest and *when* to buy and *when* to sell. With Just-the-Basics you'll always know exactly where you stand and what you need to do to stay on course.

Principle #3: Your investing plan must reflect your current financial limitations.

Your plan should effectively prevent you from taking risks you can't financially afford. The words "higher risk" mean that there's a greater likelihood that you can actually lose part or all of your money. Every day, people who mistakenly thought "it will never happen to me" find just how wrong they were. Investing in the stock market is not a game where gains and losses are just the means of keeping score. Money is not an abstract commodity. For most of us, it represents years of work, hopes, and dreams. Its unexpected loss can be devastating.

That's why the sound mind approach sets getting debt-free and building your emergency reserve as your two top priorities. Only then are you financially strong enough to bear the risk of loss that is an ever-present reality in the stock market. I encourage you: do not invest any discretionary funds in the stock and bond markets until your debt and savings goals are fully met. At that time, you can refer to the "controlling your risk" matrix for guidelines that reflect the growth needs appropriate for your current season of life.

Principle #4: Your investing plan must keep you within your emotional "comfort zone."

Your investing plan should prevent you from taking risks that rob you of your peace. Consider the four responses given in the Attitude Check (far right). These are likely reactions from our four investment temperaments. The amount of risk you take should be consistent with your temperament. You shouldn't adopt a strategy that takes you past your good-night's sleep level! If you do, you will tend to bail out at the worst possible time. A Just-the-Basics portfolio, used in conjunction with the risk matrix shown on page 193, will reflect your investing personality and current season of life.

Principle #5: Your investing plan must be realistic concerning the level of return you can reasonably expect.

I receive letters asking me to recommend safe investments that will guarantee returns of 12%, 14%, and more. If by "safe" it is meant that there's absolutely no chance of the value of the investment falling, then I must answer that I don't know of any investments like that. The ones that I do know about that are "safe" in that sense usually pay much less than 12%.

The reason any investment offers a potentially higher rate of return is that *it has to* in order to reward investors for accepting a higher level of risk. My goal is to help you get started in the right direction, incurring the least risk possible that will still get you to your destination safely. The tables on page 183 provided the historical performance results of each of the Just-the-Basics portfolios in order to let you know ahead of time what are reasonable expectations with respect to rates of return.

Principle #6: Your investment plan must allow you to begin investing in small amounts so that you can get started right away and take full advantage of the tremendous power of compound interest.

Remember the story of Jack and Jill in chapter 5? Who would you have expected to have the larger retirement fund at age sixty-five—Jack, who put $6,600 in as a young paperboy, or Jill, who put in $80,000 over the forty years of her working life? Weren't you surprised to learn that Jack was the winner? His fund had grown to more than $1,078,000, an amount 162 times more than he put in as a child! Jack's earlier start, even with much smaller amounts and for far fewer years, was too much for Jill to overcome, thanks to the tremendous power of compounding.

That's why it's important to start investing early and to add to your program regularly. The Vanguard mutual funds recommended in this strategy offer automatic savings programs, some of which will accept amounts as low as $50 per month. Even such small amounts can grow to substantial sums over many years. Every dollar makes a difference!

ATTITUDE CHECK

When Saddam Hussein launched his surprise invasion of Kuwait in 1990, the Dow Jones Industrials fell over 6% in just three days. After stabilizing for a few sessions, it dropped another 6%. Altogether, it fell more than 17% in a little over a month. Imagine yourself watching the value of your hard-earned investment portfolio losing so much of its value so quickly! Not only that, but there was no way of knowing how long the weakness would last or what the final outcome would be. Which of these statements do you think would best reflect your reaction to what was happening in the financial markets? Your choice reflects your investment temperament (shown in parentheses).

❑ "You never know when something like this could happen. That's why I don't put much of my money in the stock market. I'm very conservative and am more interested in holding on to what I have than in taking risks that might make my money grow" (Preserver).

❑ "I realize that things like this are going to happen from time to time. That's why I'm careful to investigate before I invest. I'm fairly conservative but am willing to accept some risk of loss in return for greater growth potential. My long-term plan is still sound. I'm going to stay calm and ride this out" (Researcher).

❑ "My broker called and said he was recommending that his clients buy some call options on oil. I've never invested in options before, but this sounded like a good time. I'm willing to risk losing a fair amount of my capital in return for the possibility of having my money grow substantially" (Explorer).

❑ "What a great opportunity! Oil prices are skyrocketing, gold is moving up, and stocks are really taking a beating. By jumping in quickly, a person has a chance to double his money pretty fast. I'm willing to risk losing all of the money I put at risk if I'm convinced that the investment has a chance of paying off really big" (Daredevil).

Here's how to open your Just-the-Basics account at Vanguard.

Vanguard is one of the largest and most respected no-load mutual fund organizations in the investment industry. It offers an exceptional variety of funds from which you can choose, and you can move your money from one of its funds into another via the telephone at no cost. Vanguard has a reputation for giving excellent service while keeping administrative costs low. Accounts can be opened with as little as $3,000. As with all no-load funds, there are no commissions charged, either when you invest or when you take your money out.

Call Vanguard toll-free at (800) 662-7447. Ask them to send information on their money market funds as well as the funds you wish to use in launching your Just-the-Basics portfolio. To reduce confusion over similar sounding names, Vanguard assigns each of its funds a number—see headings, page 206. It helps if you will specify each fund by its number when asking for information or buying and selling shares. (It's possible to move your current IRA, SEP-IRA, Keogh, or 403(b) account to Vanguard. If interested, request the necessary forms at this time as well.)

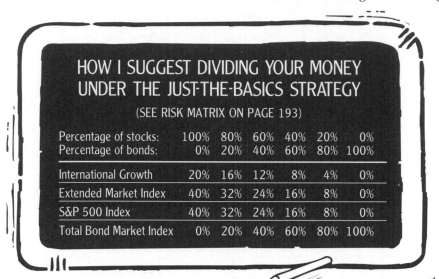

HOW I SUGGEST DIVIDING YOUR MONEY UNDER THE JUST-THE-BASICS STRATEGY

(SEE RISK MATRIX ON PAGE 193)

Percentage of stocks:	100%	80%	60%	40%	20%	0%
Percentage of bonds:	0%	20%	40%	60%	80%	100%
International Growth	20%	16%	12%	8%	4%	0%
Extended Market Index	40%	32%	24%	16%	8%	0%
S&P 500 Index	40%	32%	24%	16%	8%	0%
Total Bond Market Index	0%	20%	40%	60%	80%	100%

In the package that you will receive is an account registration form for opening a money market fund account. This is a simple form that can be completed in a few minutes. Some of the questions request that you make choices (which can be changed at any time) among different convenience options. You can call Vanguard toll-free, if you need to, for help in completing the form.

The automatic investment plan is especially helpful for automating your program. By providing the information about your local bank, you can have your bank send the amount you choose directly to your Vanguard money market account every month. Vanguard will take care of the arrangements. I also suggest that you sign where indicated and apply for check-writing privileges. Vanguard will send you checks, which will come in handy in case you need to quickly transfer your money from Vanguard to your home bank.

Initially, I suggest you deposit all of your money into the Vanguard Money Market Prime Portfolio.

It pays excellent short-term interest rates with virtually no risk. Once your account is established, your initial deposit will be sitting in your new money market account. Then, you can make a phone call with instructions to move the money out of the money market fund and into our recommended funds in accordance with the portfolio mix you have selected.

There are many different ways to achieve the various portfolio mixes. The ones shown on the chalkboard (far left) are offered as guidelines. While I've made an effort to provide a proper balance on the stock side, they are still arbitrary to a certain extent. For example, you might want to invest less in international stocks and more in the small company stocks represented by the Extended Market Index fund. So, don't feel like you have to follow my suggestions to the letter of the law—it's fine to make some small adjustments. Also, don't worry about being super-precise ("My S&P 500 fund is only 29% of my total portfolio and it should be 32%"). If you're off a little one way or the other, it's OK.

To simplify your tax accounting (for those accounts that are not tax-deferred like IRAs), I suggest you tell Vanguard that you do not wish to have all income and capital gains distributions reinvested; instead, ask that they be deposited into your money market account, where you can reallocate them among the four funds at a convenient time.

Keep in mind that the minimum for investing in any of the Vanguard funds is initially $3,000. This makes it difficult for smaller accounts to diversify among the four funds according to the portfolio allocation guidelines I've suggested. To help you reach the approximate mix you're looking for, I prepared the tables on pages 206-207. (I didn't include suggestions for portfolios with 80% and 100% bond allocations because it's unlikely anyone who is in the process of getting started with a long-term strategy would want to be that conservative.) In addition to the four Just-the-Basics funds, you'll temporarily be using a few other Vanguard funds which will help you come close to achieving the mix you desire. They include:

• **Total Stock Market Index Fund.** The goal of this fund is to imitate the performance of the Wilshire 5000 index (see pages 166-167 for basics on Wilshire and other stock indexes). Stocks in the S&P 500 index now represent about 80% of the Wilshire 5000, leaving approximately 20% of this fund invested in smaller companies. This "small cap" component has enabled the Wilshire to outpace the S&P 500 in 14 of the past 25 years. On the other hand, the Wilshire trailed the S&P 500 in six of the ten years of the 1990s, a decade when large company stocks excelled.

• **LifeStrategy Portfolios.** These are funds that invest in *other* Vanguard funds. For example, 15% of the LifeStrategy Growth portfolio is invested in the Total International Stock Index fund, 50% in the Total Stock Market Index fund, and so on (see table at right). Vanguard's Asset Allocation fund divides its investments between a stock and bond index, altering the mix between the two as the portfolio manager thinks best. There-

Vanguard LifeStrategy "Fund of Funds" Portfolios Inception: September 1994	LifeStrategy Growth	LifeStrategy Moderate Growth	LifeStrategy Conservative Growth
Total International Stock Index Fund	15%	10%	5%
Total Stock Market Index Fund	50%	35%	20%
Asset Allocation Fund	25%	25%	25%
Total Bond Market Index Fund	10%	30%	30%
Short-Term Corporate Bond Fund			20%
1995 Return	29.2%	27.9%	24.4%
1996 Return	15.4%	12.7%	10.4%
1997 Return	22.3%	19.8%	16.8%
1998 Return	21.4%	19.0%	15.9%
1999 Return	17.3%	12.0%	7.9%
2000 (Through September)	0.2%	2.3%	4.0%
Most Recent 5 Year Average Return	16.1%	14.0%	11.9%

LAUNCHING A JUST-THE-BASICS PORTFOLIO
WITH A MIX OF 100% STOCKS AND 0% BONDS

Amount of Money You Have Available to Invest	Vanguard International Growth (Fund 81) VWIGX	Vanguard Extended Market Index (Fund 98) VEXMX	Vanguard 500 Index (Fund 40) VFINX	Vanguard Total Bond Market Index (Fund 84) VBMFX	Vanguard Total Stock Market Index (Fund 85) VTSMX	Vanguard LifeStrategy Growth (Fund 122) VASGX	Vanguard LifeStrategy Moderate Grow (Fund 914) VSMGX	Vanguard LifeStrategy Conserv Grow (Fund 724) VSCGX
$3,000					$3,000			
$6,000		$3,000	$3,000					
$9,000	$3,000	$3,000	$3,000					
$12,000	$3,000	$4,500	$4,500					
$15,000	$3,000	$6,000	$6,000					
$20,000	$4,000	$8,000	$8,000					
$25,000	$5,000	$10,000	$10,000					
$30,000	$6,000	$12,000	$12,000					
$35,000	$7,000	$14,000	$14,000					
$40,000	$8,000	$16,000	$16,000					
$45,000	$9,000	$18,000	$18,000					
$50,000	$10,000	$20,000	$20,000					
Additional	20%	40%	40%					

LAUNCHING A JUST-THE-BASICS PORTFOLIO
WITH A MIX OF 80% STOCKS AND 20% BONDS

Amount of Money You Have Available to Invest	Vanguard International Growth (Fund 81) VWIGX	Vanguard Extended Market Index (Fund 98) VEXMX	Vanguard 500 Index (Fund 40) VFINX	Vanguard Total Bond Market Index (Fund 84) VBMFX	Vanguard Total Stock Market Index (Fund 85) VTSMX	Vanguard LifeStrategy Growth (Fund 122) VASGX	Vanguard LifeStrategy Moderate Grow (Fund 914) VSMGX	Vanguard LifeStrategy Conserv Grow (Fund 724) VSCGX
$3,000						$3,000		
$6,000						$6,000		
$9,000						$9,000		
$12,000						$12,000		
$15,000	$3,000	$3,000	$3,000	$3,000	$3,000			
$20,000	$3,200	$6,400	$6,400	$4,000				
$25,000	$4,000	$8,000	$8,000	$5,000				
$30,000	$4,800	$9,600	$9,600	$6,000				
$35,000	$5,600	$11,200	$11,200	$7,000				
$40,000	$6,400	$12,800	$12,800	$8,000				
$45,000	$7,200	$14,400	$14,400	$9,000				
$50,000	$8,000	$16,000	$16,000	$10,000				
Additional	16%	32%	32%	20%				

LAUNCHING A JUST-THE-BASICS PORTFOLIO
WITH A MIX OF 60% STOCKS AND 40% BONDS

Amount of Money You Have Available to Invest	Vanguard International Growth (Fund 81) VWIGX	Vanguard Extended Market Index (Fund 98) VEXMX	Vanguard 500 Index (Fund 40) VFINX	Vanguard Total Bond Market Index (Fund 84) VBMFX	Vanguard Total Stock Market Index (Fund 85) VTSMX	Vanguard LifeStrategy Growth (Fund 122) VASGX	Vanguard LifeStrategy Moderate Grow (Fund 914) VSMGX	Vanguard LifeStrategy Conserv Grow (Fund 724) VSCGX
$3,000							$3,000	
$6,000							$6,000	
$9,000							$9,000	
$12,000							$12,000	
$15,000	$3,000	$3,000	$3,000	$6,000				
$20,000	$3,000	$4,500	$4,500	$8,000				
$25,000	$3,000	$6,000	$6,000	$10,000				
$30,000	$3,600	$7,200	$7,200	$12,000				
$35,000	$4,200	$8,400	$8,400	$14,000				
$40,000	$4,800	$9,600	$9,600	$16,000				
$45,000	$5,400	$10,800	$10,800	$18,000				
$50,000	$6,000	$12,000	$12,000	$20,000				
Additional	12%	24%	24%	40%				

LAUNCHING A JUST-THE-BASICS PORTFOLIO
WITH A MIX OF 40% STOCKS AND 60% BONDS

Amount of Money You Have Available to Invest	Vanguard International Growth (Fund 81) VWIGX	Vanguard Extended Market Index (Fund 98) VEXMX	Vanguard 500 Index (Fund 40) VFINX	Vanguard Total Bond Market Index (Fund 84) VBMFX	Vanguard Total Stock Market Index (Fund 85) VTSMX	Vanguard LifeStrategy Growth (Fund 122) VASGX	Vanguard LifeStrategy Moderate Grow (Fund 914) VSMGX	Vanguard LifeStrategy Conserv Grow (Fund 724) VSCGX
$3,000								$3,000
$6,000								$6,000
$9,000								$9,000
$12,000								$12,000
$15,000								$15,000
$20,000	$3,000	$3,000	$3,000	$11,000				
$25,000	$3,000	$3,800	$3,800	$14,400				
$30,000	$3,000	$4,500	$4,500	$18,000				
$35,000	$3,000	$5,500	$5,500	$21,000				
$40,000	$3,200	$6,400	$6,400	$24,000				
$45,000	$3,600	$7,200	$7,200	$27,000				
$50,000	$4,000	$8,000	$8,000	$30,000				
Additional	8%	16%	16%	60%				

fore, the amount of the LifeStrategy portfolios invested in bonds varies depending on what's happening in the Asset Allocation fund at any given time. Due to Vanguard's low expenses, these funds seem like an attractive option for the beginning investor who wants to pursue an indexing strategy.

Keep in mind that the advantages of indexing—keeping costs low, for example—manifest themselves over time. Don't focus too much on short-term performance. Carefully review the material Vanguard sends in order to be sure you clearly understand the pros and cons of investing in index funds.

Remember the cautions concerning many of today's mutual funds which I alerted you to back in chapter 12?

At the end of that chapter, I promised to "introduce you to a special breed of mutual funds . . . that, by their very nature, avoid the red flag traps we've just discussed." Let's briefly look at how index funds and the Just-the-Basics strategy protect you from the abuses explained in chapter 12.

• Red Flag #1: You can't necessarily accept a fund's "investment objective" at face value.

You don't have to worry about an index fund broadening its investing horizons (and taking on more risk in the process), because that would be self-defeating. An index fund doesn't have any investment objective other than to replicate the performance of the index it's based on.

• Red Flag #2: You can't necessarily accept a fund's diversification claims at face value.

For an index fund to concentrate its holdings in a relatively few stocks would also be self-defeating. Unless, of course, the fund is based on an index, like the Dow Industrials, which itself encompasses a small number of stocks. In that case, the fund would be doing exactly what it is supposed to do.

• Red Flag #3: You can't necessarily accept a fund's implied performance excellence at face value.

There's no incentive for an S&P 500 index fund to claim a gain of 15% in a year when the S&P 500 gained just 10%. It would only serve to reveal that the fund manager had done a poor job of tracking the index and make the manager look inept rather than insightful.

• Red Flag #4: You can't necessarily accept a fund's rankings at face value.

Performance rankings are a function of which peer group a fund is in and how well it performs in that group. There's no disagreement among industry observers as to which peer groups the various index funds should be placed in. Relative rankings of index funds may not always be in the top quartile, but they will at least be honest.

The four red flags are all symptoms of the same problem: Mutual funds function in a highly combative marketplace, and their managers are under tremendous pressures to outperform the competition. Take away the need to outperform, and you take away the stimulus for the abuses. Index funds have the luxury of being appreciated for the fact that, while they never outperform the markets, neither do they have the misfortune of underperforming it.

One of the periodic housekeeping chores investors must deal with from time to time is "rebalancing" their portfolios. It's like four people playing a game of Monopoly.

Everybody starts out with 25% of the money, but after a few rounds of play, some are richer and some poorer. To get back where you started, you'd have to "rebalance" by taking money from some players and giving it to others. Here's how that applies here.

Assume you invest along the lines recommended for those desiring a portfolio mix of 80% stocks and 20% bonds. You divide your money among the four Vanguard funds as shown in the first column of the table below. In the months that follow, as some funds do better than others, the percentages you started with begin to change. If Extended Market does better than International Growth, for example, it may soon represent 35% of your total holdings while International Growth falls to just 12%. How long do you let this continue before you step in and sell some Extended Market in order to return its value to just 32% of your portfolio? How long, in other words, before you rebalance? I suggest the first week of each new year. Emotionally, January is a good time for new beginnings and fresh starts. Also, if you have taxable gains, waiting until January postpones paying the tax for a year.

The table shows how the rebalancing computation is made. The initial purchases were made based on a portfolio mix of 80% stocks, 20% bonds as shown in column one. At the end of the year, the account balances have changed due to market fluctuations

AN EXAMPLE OF THE ANNUAL REBALANCING PROCESS

	Desired Mix	Initial Purchases	End Of Period	Desired Balances	Changes Needed
International Growth	16%	$4,000	$3,606	$4,636	+1,030
Extended Market Index	32%	8,000	10,190	9,271	−919
S&P 500 Index	32%	8,000	9,782	9,271	−511
Total Bond Market Index	20%	5,000	5,394	5,794	+400
Total Holdings	100%	$25,000	$28,972	$28,972	

(and possibly because you added some new money during the year). Going into the new year, you want to get your portfolio back to the desired 80/20 levels. To do this, you simply multiply the percentage in column one for each fund times the new total value of your holdings (circled). In the example, the new target level for International Growth is $4,636 (16% x $28,972). To restore the fund to its proper level, you must buy $1,030 in new shares ($4,636 minus $3,606). This purchase (as well as the smaller one for the bond fund) is paid for by selling off shares in the Extended Market and S&P 500 funds.

You will notice that rebalancing takes money away from your star performers and gives it to the poorer performing groups.

A common question is: "Why are we buying more shares in last year's losers at the expense of last year's winners? Since they've done so poorly, wouldn't it be better to put less emphasis on them for the coming year?" If "better" means "more profitable," then the answer is that some years it would be better; but I think most years it would not. Market

Portfolio Diversification
Read about why it's important
and how to achieve it at
news.morningstar.com/
university/display_article/
0,1845,2938-1,00.html.

performance leaders change as the economy goes through the various stages of its cycle.

For example, in 1990, the worst performance among the four Vanguard Just-the-Basics funds was the Extended Market fund, which lost 14.0% (see page 181). If you had not rebalanced and built that portion of your portfolio back up to its recommended percent allocation, you would have been underinvested in that fund in 1991 when it turned in the best performance of the four (+41.9%). Similarly, in 1992, the worst performer was the International Growth fund, which lost almost 6%. If you had not rebalanced at the end of 1992, you would have missed out on having a full allocation in 1993's top performer among Just-the-Basics funds when International Growth soared 44.7%. This kind of thing happens all the time. If it didn't, wouldn't the markets be a great place to make easy money? ◆

CHAPTER PREVIEW

Systematic Strategies for Meeting Long-Term Investment Goals (Even if You're Starting from Scratch)

I. **Dollar-cost-averaging is a widely practiced formula strategy for investing that automates your decision making.**

   A. Dollar-cost-averaging requires investing the same amount of money in the same investment at regular time intervals.

   B. This approach forces you to do what every investor seeks to do: buy more shares when prices are low and fewer shares when prices are high.

   C. Dollar-cost-averaging is an excellent way to gradually invest a large sum.

II. **Value-averaging is an innovative improvement in the traditional dollar-cost-averaging strategy that helps assure you will reach your long-term goals on time.**

   A. Rather than making your monthly investment based on a fixed amount, value-averaging has you invest whatever amount is necessary in order to keep you on track toward your goal after taking into consideration the market gains or losses in the account for that month.

   B. This strategy generates better returns than dollar-cost-averaging, as the investor buys more than usual when prices move lower. It does, however, involve greater complexity and requires more effort on the part of the investor.

III. **A strict buy/sell discipline, as provided by formula strategies, is essential for successful investing.**

   A. Formula strategies need not be "perfect" to be highly profitable.

   B. A disciplined strategy is essential to protect you from unexpected swings in the market and your own emotions.

One knowledgeable writer called dollar-cost-averaging a long-term investment technique that "beats the market...by ignoring the market."

A consistent theme of the Sound Mind Investing philosophy is the importance of taking charge of your own financial future by becoming an "initiator" rather than a "responder." Initiators don't let others shape their course; *they* set the pace. Action is taken as a result of specific guidelines from a specific strategy coming into play. They "plan their work and work their plan."

In devising your plan, consider making use of a systematic "formula" strategy. They can be quite useful in helping you stay focused on your long-term goals because they require you to make your buying and selling decisions based solely on mechanical guidelines. There is no judgment involved; it's all automatic. They are helpful because they protect you against your own emotions and the tendency to go along with the crowd. Such strategies fit well into the disciplined framework for decision making desired by initiators.

Probably the best-known formula strategy is dollar-cost-averaging (DCA). It's not complicated. It's not time-consuming. In fact, it's simplicity personified. Here's all you do: (1) invest the *same amount* of money (2) at *regular time intervals*. For example, you might choose to invest $300 once a month. The amount and frequency are up to you. The important thing is to pick an amount you can stick with faithfully over many years.

The beauty of DCA is that it frees you from . . .

. . . the worry of whether you're buying stocks at the "wrong" time. Your constant dollar investment forces you to buy more shares when the price is low and to buy fewer shares when the price is high. In effect, you are buying more shares at bargain prices and fewer shares at what might be considered high prices. Of course, only when you look back years from now will you know when prices really were bargains and when prices were too high.

It is critically important to ignore all market fluctuations when employing a dollar-cost-averaging strategy. Most investors who obtain poor returns in the market are victims of their own emotions. Only after stock prices have been rising sharply do "responders" work up enough courage to buy stock fund shares. And about the only time they ever sell shares is when they become especially fearful after prices have plunged. The consequence is that they buy high and sell low, the very opposite of their ambition. It is important, then, not to let your emotions control you. You must exercise the discipline of maintaining your systematic investment program.

Dollar-cost-averaging doesn't protect you against losses.

It does result in your average cost per share being lower than the average price of the shares over time. But in a bear market, you still can have temporary losses.

DCA Math

The benefits of DCA can be illustrated with a simple example. Let's assume you can afford to invest $100 every month in your stock fund program. At the time of your first new investment, the fund shares sell for $10.

(I'm going to exaggerate the amount of market volatility in order to show the mathematical effects.)

The next month, the market soars and you pay $14 for your shares. Finally, the third month the market falls back, and your fund retreats to $12, midway between your two buying levels.

Ordinarily, that would put you at break-even. But look at what has happened. The first month you were able to buy ten shares at $10 per share. The second month you acquired only 7.1429 shares at $14 per share. Now, at $12 each, your 17.1429 shares are worth $205.71. Instead at being at break-even, you have a small profit.

Furthermore, DCA is a two-edged sword. It can lower your potential profits as well as losses. If your fund's share prices had risen all year long, you would obviously show greater gains if you had made a single large investment early on. In fact, academic studies have appeared in recent years purporting to show that DCA is a bad idea. Why? Because the market has a long-term upward bias. Over time, the market always moves higher. The implication is that, on average, you're going to be paying more for your shares if you stretch your buying out than if you go ahead and invest as much as you can as soon as possible.

That's all well and good when you're looking back over a forty-year period with 20/20 vision. It ignores the fact that there are bear market periods along the way when it's quite easy for investors to be frightened out of the markets altogether. If you invest your $50,000 inheritance just before a bear market wipes out $10,000 of it, who's to say you're going to have the stomach for staying around and waiting for the next bull market to recoup your losses and then some? The academics may have it right in theory, but in the real world, DCA makes it easier for investors to overcome their fears and make the difficult decision to put their limited (and therefore, precious) savings at risk.

In summary, DCA is the systematic investing of a fixed amount of money on a regular basis, usually monthly. I especially like it when used in conjunction with no-load funds and 401(k) plans for these reasons:

- It eliminates the need to ask the question, "Is this a good time to buy stocks?" As far as DCA investors are concerned, every month is a good month.

- It imposes a discipline, forcing you to make regular "installment" payments on your future financial security.

- It will cause you to buy relatively more fund shares when prices are low and fewer shares when prices are high.

- Using no-load funds allows the purchase of fractional shares, eliminates commission costs, and provides sufficient diversification to reflect the stock market at large.

Let's walk through an example of some of the decisions involved in executing a DCA strategy.

We'll assume that you've gone through the exercises in chapter 17 and determined that a "100% stocks" portfolio is appropriate for you given your current season of life and risk-taking temperament. You have $5,000 you can use to launch your program. Creating your personal versions of the worksheets shown on these pages can help you deal with adjustments for fund minimums, dividends, annual rebalancing, and the occasional need to change the funds in your portfolio. They're intended to be read from far left to far right as if they were all on the same page; it might be helpful to use a ruler to guide your eyes as you follow along with the example I've created. In what I hope will eventu-

Have a Windfall or Other Lump Sum to Invest?

The money might have come from the sale of a home, an unexpected inheritance, an IRA rollover, or from aging parents who no longer can handle the investing of their own funds. Here's how you can use DCA in combination with Just-the-Basics as your long-term growth strategy:

• Deposit the money into the Vanguard Prime money market account in order to put it to work right away. This removes any pressure on you to make decisions quickly. When you open your account, ask for check-writing privileges in order to easily transfer your funds later should an emergency arise.

• Review the suggestions for making "right" investment decisions given in chapter 20. Follow the principles given as closely as possible.

• Choose one of the six Just-the-Basics portfolios that seems best for your situation (page 182). The "controlling your risk" matrix (page 193) provides some guidelines.

• Decide to invest a certain number of dollars every month until it's all deployed the way you want it. If you have a $50,000 sum, you can invest $10,000 per month for five months, or $5,000 per month for ten months, or whatever seems comfortable. There is no particular rule of thumb as to which is best. My perspective is that it's better to lose an opportunity than to lose money. So, I tend to favor the slow-as-you-go approach.

If you're doing DCA with more than one mutual fund, ideally you should add to each of the funds each month.

ally prove reassuring, I've decided to let you begin your program at a particularly bad time—at the end of June 1998, just before the market experienced a "mini-crash" in the third quarter of that year.

❶ Since Vanguard's minimum for opening a fund account is $3,000, you can purchase only one fund initially. You look at the table on page 206 and see that the Total Stock Market Index fund is recommended for your situation—at least until you reach the $6,000 level. This fund will give you exposure to both large and small company stocks. As your account grows in value, you will be able to add new funds that will gradually move your holdings toward a more conventional Just-the-Basics "100% stocks" profile—40% large company stocks, 40% small company stocks, and 20% international growth stocks.

❷ You expect to add $300 a month during the first year with the hope of increasing your monthly deposit by $50 every twelve months. Since you only own one fund at this point, the entire $300 for

July is invested in Total Stock Market. To simplify matters, I assume your investment is made on the last trading day of the month. (Actually, you might want to do it a little earlier—see the subject of "seasonality" on page 221.) At a price of $25.36, your $300 buys another 11.83 shares.

❸ As you get ready for your end-of-the-month deposit in August, you check the value in your account and find it's fallen to $4,374. This isn't what you expected! In just two months, you've lost almost $1,000. But you know it's important to stay with your program regardless of what the market's doing, so you put in another $300. With shares down to $21.39, you get more for your money— another 14.03 shares are added to your account.

❹ Your September statement shows that your fund paid a dividend distri-

A DOLLAR-COST-AVERAGING STRATEGY IN ACTION

On The Last Day Of Month	Total Portfolio Value	Total Monthly Deposit		(1) Fund Name	(2) Share Price	(3) Shares Divds Received	(4) Total Shares Owned	(5) Value Before Deposit	(6) Amount Invested In Fund	(7) New Shares Bought	(8) Total Shares Owned
June 1998	$5,000		❶	Total Stock	$25.95	0.00	0.00	$0	$5,000	192.68	192.68
July 1998	$4,886	$300	❷	Total Stock	$25.36	0.00	192.68	$4,886	$300	11.83	204.51
Aug 1998	$4,374	$300	❸	Total Stock	$21.39	0.00	204.51	$4,374	$300	14.03	218.54
Sept 1998	$5,014	$300	❹	Total Stock	$22.76	1.78	220.32	$5,014	$300	13.18	233.50
Oct 1998	$5,714	$300	❺	Total Stock	$24.47	0.00	233.50	$5,714	($5,714)	-233.50	0.00
Oct 1998	$6,014		❻	S&P 500	$102.28	0.00	0.00	$0	$3,007	29.40	29.40
Nov 1998	$6,385	$300		S&P 500	$108.49	0.00	29.40	$3,190	$150	1.38	30.78
Dec 1998	$7,150	$300		S&P 500	$113.95	0.10	30.88	$3,519	$150	1.32	32.20
Jan 1999	$7,661	$300	❼	S&P 500	$118.74	0.00	32.20	$3,823	$150	1.26	33.46
Feb 1999	$7,618	$300		S&P 500	$115.03	0.00	33.46	$3,849	$150	1.30	34.76
Mar 1999	$8,217	$300		S&P 500	$118.90	0.21	34.98	$4,159	$150	1.26	36.24
Apr 1999	$9,034	$300	❽	S&P 500	$123.48	0.00	36.24	$4,475	($1,308)	-10.59	25.64
Apr 1999	$9,334		❾	S&P 500	$123.48	0.00	25.64	$3,167	$0	0.00	25.64
May 1999	$9,130	$300		S&P 500	$120.53	0.00	25.64	$3,091	$150	1.24	26.89
June 1999	$9,869	$300		S&P 500	$126.83	0.08	26.97	$3,421	$150	1.18	28.16
July 1999	$9,980	$350	❿	S&P 500	$122.86	0.00	28.16	$3,459	$175	1.42	29.58
Aug 1999	$10,245	$350		S&P 500	$122.25	0.00	29.58	$3,616	$175	1.43	31.01
Sept 1999	$10,416	$350		S&P 500	$118.55	0.09	31.10	$3,687	$175	1.48	32.58
Oct 1999	$11,306	$350		S&P 500	$126.05	0.00	32.58	$4,107	$175	1.39	33.97
Nov 1999	$12,312	$350		S&P 500	$128.60	0.00	33.97	$4,368	$175	1.36	35.33
Dec 1999	$13,941	$350		S&P 500	$135.33	0.25	35.58	$4,815	$175	1.29	36.87
Jan 2000	$13,812	$350	⓫	S&P 500	$128.52	0.00	36.87	$4,739	$926	7.21	44.08
Jan 2000	$14,162			S&P 500	$128.52	0.00	44.08	$5,665	$0	0.00	44.08
Feb 2000	$15,153	$350	⓬	S&P 500	$126.07	0.00	44.08	$5,557	$140	1.11	45.19
Mar 2000	$15,879	$350		S&P 500	$138.08	0.00	45.19	$6,239	$140	1.01	46.20
Apr 2000	$15,064	$350		S&P 500	$133.93	0.00	46.20	$6,188	$140	1.05	47.25
May 2000	$14,821	$350		S&P 500	$131.20	0.00	47.25	$6,199	$140	1.07	48.31
June 2000	$16,128	$350		S&P 500	$134.15	0.20	48.52	$6,508	$140	1.04	49.56
July 2000	$16,104	$400		S&P 500	$132.15	0.00	49.56	$6,549	$160	1.21	50.77
Aug 2000	$17,612	$400		S&P 500	$140.33	0.00	50.77	$7,125	$160	1.14	51.91
Sept 2000	$17,095	$400		S&P 500	$132.59	0.00	51.91	$6,883	$160	1.21	53.12

bution that was reinvested in more shares per your earlier instructions. You post your new shares to your worksheet. (If your Just-the-Basics strategy is not taking place in a tax-deferred account, you might prefer to *not* have the dividends reinvested in order to simplify the tax accounting paperwork.)

❺ By the end of October, your account has rallied to $5,714. You've put in $5,900 (the original $5,000 plus three monthly deposits of $300 each), so you're still below water, but after what you've been through, it's encouraging to almost be even! You notice that with the $300 you're about to deposit, you'll have $6,014, just enough to graduate from Total Stock Market. You sell your shares.

❻ With the proceeds and your $300, you invest $3,007 in both the 500 Index and Extended Market Index funds (per the recommendation on page 206). From this point on, you'll split your monthly deposit and invest $150 into each of your two new funds.

❼ At the end of January 1999, your account is worth $7,661. Since it's split almost evenly between your two funds (as called for), it's not necessary to go through the annual rebalancing process. You make your monthly deposit as usual.

❽ By the end of April, your total account value is over $9,000. By making withdrawals from each of your two funds, you can raise the $3,000 needed to diversify even further. You make your computations so as to rebalance between 500 Index and Extended Market Index; that is, after the transactions are completed, the two funds will be roughly equal in account value.

❾ You open your International Growth account for the $3,000 minimum ($2,700 from selling shares in the other two funds plus your $300 monthly deposit). Your goal

(1) Fund Name	(2) Share Price	(3) Shares Divds Received	(4) Total Shares Owned	(5) Value Before Deposit	(6) Amount Invested In Fund	(7) New Shares Bought	(8) Total Shares Owned
Extended Mkt	$28.58	0.00	0.00	$0	$3,007	105.21	105.21
Extended Mkt	$30.37	0.00	105.21	$3,195	$150	4.94	110.15
Extended Mkt	$30.62	8.43	118.58	$3,631	$150	4.90	123.48
Extended Mkt	$31.08	0.00	123.48	$3,838	$150	4.83	128.31
Extended Mkt	$29.38	0.00	128.31	$3,770	$150	5.11	133.41
Extended Mkt	$28.76	7.71	141.12	$4,059	$150	5.22	146.34
Extended Mkt	$31.16	0.00	146.34	$4,560	($1,392)	-44.67	101.66
Extended Mkt	$31.16	0.00	101.66	$3,168	$0	0.00	101.66
Extended Mkt	$31.03	0.00	101.66	$3,155	$150	4.83	106.50
Extended Mkt	$32.33	0.00	106.50	$3,443	$150	4.64	111.14
Extended Mkt	$31.42	0.00	111.14	$3,492	$175	5.57	116.71
Extended Mkt	$30.70	0.00	116.71	$3,583	$175	5.70	122.41
Extended Mkt	$30.44	0.00	122.41	$3,726	$175	5.75	128.16
Extended Mkt	$32.08	0.00	128.16	$4,111	$175	5.46	133.61
Extended Mkt	$34.77	0.00	133.61	$4,646	$175	5.03	138.64
Extended Mkt	$37.07	8.88	147.53	$5,469	$175	4.72	152.25
Extended Mkt	$36.52	0.00	152.25	$5,560	$105	2.88	155.12
Extended Mkt	$36.52	0.00	155.12	$5,665	$0	0.00	155.12
Extended Mkt	$42.24	0.00	155.12	$6,552	$140	3.31	158.44
Extended Mkt	$39.61	4.16	162.59	$6,440	$140	3.53	166.13
Extended Mkt	$34.91	0.00	166.13	$5,800	$140	4.01	170.14
Extended Mkt	$32.34	0.00	170.14	$5,502	$140	4.33	174.47
Extended Mkt	$36.18	0.00	174.47	$6,312	$140	3.87	178.34
Extended Mkt	$35.20	0.00	178.34	$6,278	$160	4.55	182.88
Extended Mkt	$39.12	0.00	182.88	$7,154	$160	4.09	186.97
Extended Mkt	$37.55	0.00	186.97	$7,021	$160	4.26	191.23

(1) Fund Name	(2) Share Price	(3) Shares Divds Received	(4) Total Shares Owned	(5) Value Before Deposit	(6) Amount Invested In Fund	(7) New Shares Bought	(8) Total Shares Owned
Intl Growth	$19.45	0.00	0.00	$0	$3,000	154.24	154.24
Intl Growth	$18.70	0.00	154.24	$2,884	$0	0.00	154.24
Intl Growth	$19.48	0.00	154.24	$3,005	$0	0.00	154.24
Intl Growth	$19.64	0.00	154.24	$3,029	$0	0.00	154.24
Intl Growth	$19.75	0.00	154.24	$3,046	$0	0.00	154.24
Intl Growth	$19.47	0.00	154.24	$3,003	$0	0.00	154.24
Intl Growth	$20.02	0.00	154.24	$3,088	$0	0.00	154.24
Intl Growth	$21.38	0.00	154.24	$3,298	$0	0.00	154.24
Intl Growth	$22.49	8.39	162.63	$3,658	$0	0.00	162.63
Intl Growth	$21.60	0.00	162.63	$3,513	($681)	-31.53	131.11
Intl Growth	$21.60	0.00	131.11	$2,832	$0	0.00	131.11
Intl Growth	$23.22	0.00	131.11	$3,044	$70	3.01	134.12
Intl Growth	$23.85	0.00	134.12	$3,199	$70	2.94	137.06
Intl Growth	$22.45	0.00	137.06	$3,077	$70	3.12	140.17
Intl Growth	$22.26	0.00	140.17	$3,120	$70	3.14	143.32
Intl Growth	$23.08	0.00	143.32	$3,308	$70	3.03	146.35
Intl Growth	$22.39	0.00	146.35	$3,277	$80	3.57	149.92
Intl Growth	$22.23	0.00	149.92	$3,333	$80	3.60	153.52
Intl Growth	$20.79	0.00	153.52	$3,192	$80	3.85	157.37

for this new fund is that it eventually represent 20% of your portfolio, not the 32% it does now. Because International Growth is overweighted in your portfolio, you do not add to it with any of your monthly deposit. Your $300 continues to be divided between the 500 Index and Expanded Market Index funds. (Depending on your enthusiasm for foreign holdings, you could have elected to wait and diversify later when the $3,000 minimum would have represented a smaller portion of your portfolio. For example, if you had waited until your holdings were worth $12,000, the new fund would have totaled just 25% of your portfolio; at $15,000, it would have been just 20%.)

⑩ You raise your monthly deposit by $50 as planned. You now invest $175 in each of your largest two holdings.

⑪ It's January again, time to rebalance. You calculate the current value of your three funds ($13,812) plus your $350 monthly deposit. The total is $14,162. Following your target percentages (see step one), you determine the correct theoretical values for each fund. By selling off $681 of your International Growth shares, you reduce its value to 20% of your total portfolio. This money, along with your $350 deposit, is allocated to the other two funds so that they will each be worth 40% of the total.

⑫ Starting in February, you'll divide your monthly deposit among all three funds according to their weight in the portfolio. This means putting 20%, or $70, in International Growth. The minimum deposit at Vanguard is usually $100, but it allows smaller monthly investments if you sign up for their "automatic investment plan." The investments are automatically made by a transfer from your checking or savings account.

There are hundreds of variations on how DCA investments can be made. There's no single "right" way to do this, so don't second guess yourself or let small things distract you from the big picture. *The important thing is that you get started and stay with it.* Being consistent in putting money into the market and keeping your transaction costs under control are more important factors than maintaining your allocations precisely. Mechanical strategies like DCA are designed to make investing easier for you by removing your emotions from the equation. So don't stress out over the details. Relax, and enjoy the ride!

Let's now address one problem presented by the typical DCA strategy: you have no way of knowing ahead of time . . .

. . . what your DCA portfolio will be worth in five, ten, or twenty years. You know how much you expect to be putting in each month, but you *don't know* what it will grow to over the years. This makes long-range planning difficult.

Michael Edleson, a former professor at Harvard's Graduate School of Business Administration, has proposed a change in the traditional dollar-cost-averaging approach that solves this problem. He suggests placing your focus primarily on the current value in your account each month instead of on how much you put in. He calls his approach "value averaging" (VA) and offers several different variations of how you might tailor it to your situation. Edleson claims that his research indicates VA is consistently superior to the traditional DCA approach. (For an in-depth review, try to pick up a copy of his book *Value*

Averaging, The Safe and Easy Strategy for Higher Investment Returns. Although it's now out of print, many bookstores—including the large online ones—provide a search service.)

To whet your appetite, I'm going to walk you through a simple example. Let's say I'm setting up a college education fund for Ben, my two-year old grandson. I've got 16 years before the money will be needed, and let's assume my goal is to accumulate a fund of $60,000. Here's how I proceed.

Step 1: Because the calculations require me to make an assumption about the rate of return I'll be earning on my investments, I must first decide how optimistic I want to be. To be on the conservative side, I'm going to assume an 8% average annual return. I hope it's more, but I don't want to *need it* to be more.

Step 2: I must determine how much I currently have available for launching the program. It's possible to start from scratch, of course, but then my choice of mutual fund organizations would be more limited (see page 110 for a listing of funds and their current minimums when opening an "automatic deposit account"). I decide to start with $600, a ballpark estimate of how much a typical family might be able to readily pull togther. You can make the starting amount as low as your mutual fund of choice will allow.

Step 3: Referring to Table 1 nearby, I learn that $1,000 will grow to $3,581 over 16 years assuming an 8% return. But I'm starting with just $600, so I have to make an adjustment ($3,581 divided by 1000 times 600) to learn that my initial capital will grow to $2,148 under similar circumstances.

Step 4: I subtract $2,148 from my $60,000 goal. This gives me $57,852, the amount I must accumulate via my monthly contributions.

Step 5: Now I turn to Table 2 (page 218). I find the "16 Years" column, and write down the number at the top: $2.5826. This represents the dollar amount I must set aside monthly in order to accumulate $1,000 assuming an 8% average annual return. (I've also provided Table 3 that assumes a 12% average return for those who don't wish to be quite as cautious.)

Step 6: Of course, I need to accumulate a lot more than just $1,000. I need $57,852. That's why I now multiply $2.5826 times 57.852. This gives me $149.41. In other words, if I invest $149.41 per month for 192 months (16 years times 12) and can average an 8% return, I'll have $57,852 after 16 years. To make it simpler, I decide to "round up" my monthly investment to $150.

The tables assume any taxes due on my gains will be paid from another source, that is, I will not make withdrawals from the value averaging account to pay taxes. To minimize the tax bite, setting the account up under the Uniform Gifts to Minors Act (UGMA) is an option (see chapter 8).

Now, it's time to calculate my "value path." The value path is merely the *minimum desired value* of my portfolio at each step along the way. Once I know my value path, it's simply a matter of applying my monthly contribution in a way so as to make sure that

Table 1:
Growth of $1,000

Yrs	8% Return	12% Return
1	$1,083	$1,127
2	$1,173	$1,270
3	$1,270	$1,431
4	$1,376	$1,612
5	$1,490	$1,817
6	$1,614	$2,047
7	$1,747	$2,307
8	$1,892	$2,599
9	$2,050	$2,929
10	$2,220	$3,300
11	$2,404	$3,719
12	$2,603	$4,191
13	$2,819	$4,722
14	$3,053	$5,321
15	$3,307	$5,996
16	$3,581	$6,756
17	$3,879	$7,613
18	$4,201	$8,579
19	$4,549	$9,667
20	$4,927	$10,893

TABLE 2: MONTHLY DEPOSIT AND VALUE PATH GOALS FOR BUILDING $1,000
(ASSUMES AVERAGE ANNUAL RATE OF RETURN OF 8%)

	20 Years	19 Years	18 Years	17 Years	16 Years	15 Years	14 Years	13 Years	12 Years	11 Years	10 Years	9 Years	8 Years	7 Years	6 Years
	$1.6977	1.8783	2.0830	2.3159	2.5826	2.8899	3.2465	3.6641	4.1579	4.7488	5.4661	6.3520	7.4700	8.9195	10.8666
1	21.14	23.39	25.93	28.83	32.15	35.98	40.42	45.62	51.76	59.12	68.05	79.08	93.00	111.05	135.29
2	44.03	48.71	54.02	60.06	66.97	74.94	84.19	95.02	107.83	123.15	141.75	164.73	193.72	231.31	281.80
3	68.82	76.14	84.43	93.88	104.69	117.14	131.60	148.52	168.54	192.49	221.57	257.48	302.80	361.56	440.48
4	95.67	105.84	117.37	130.50	145.53	162.84	182.94	206.47	234.29	267.59	308.01	357.94	420.93	502.61	612.33
5	124.74	138.01	153.05	170.16	189.76	212.34	238.54	269.22	305.51	348.92	401.63	466.73	548.87	655.38	798.44
6	156.23	172.85	191.68	213.12	237.66	265.94	298.76	337.19	382.63	437.01	503.02	584.55	687.43	820.82	1000.00
7	190.34	210.59	233.53	259.64	289.54	323.99	363.98	410.79	466.15	532.40	612.82	712.15	837.48	1000.00	
8	227.27	251.45	278.84	310.03	345.73	386.86	434.60	490.50	556.60	635.71	731.73	850.34	1000.00		
9	267.27	295.71	327.92	364.59	406.57	454.95	511.10	576.83	654.57	747.60	860.52	1000.00			
10	310.59	343.63	381.07	423.68	472.47	528.69	593.93	670.32	760.66	868.77	1000.00				
11	357.51	395.54	438.63	487.68	543.84	608.54	683.65	771.58	875.56	1000.00					
12	408.32	451.76	500.97	556.99	621.13	695.03	780.81	881.24	1000.00						
13	463.34	512.64	568.48	632.05	704.84	788.70	886.04	1000.00							
14	522.94	578.57	641.60	713.35	795.49	890.14	1000.00								
15	587.48	649.98	720.78	801.39	893.67	1000.00									
16	657.38	727.31	806.54	896.73	1000.00										
17	733.07	811.06	899.41	1000.00											
18	815.06	901.76	1000.00												
19	903.84	1000.00													
20	1000.00														

my portfolio keeps pace with the value path.

Step 7: Returning to Table 2, I once again locate the "16 Years" column. Since the numbers in the column represent a theoretical value path for accumulating $1,000 over the period in question, I multiply the numbers by 60 (because I want to accumulate a total of $60,000). I learn that my goal should be to have a portfolio value of at least $1,929 (32.15 times 60) at the end of year one, $4,018 (66.97 times 60) at the end of year two, and so on. I use this data when setting up my value averaging worksheet (Table 4).

Step 8: Because the table provides only *annual* value path projections, I need to extrapolate the monthly numbers. I know I have to reach $1,929 by the end of year one; dividing that by twelve means growth of about $161 each month. Year two requires growth of $2,089 ($4,018 minus $1,929) or $174 per month, and so on. To simplify matters, I'm going to ignore the head start I got from my $600 initial capital. (There's a way to be more precise than this, but it involves formulas that say things like $V_t = C \times t \times (1+R)^t$. I'm providing all these tables to spare you from boning up on your algebra!) I copy the monthly value path numbers into Column B of my worksheet.

Here's how my worksheet guides me as I invest my $150 monthly contribution. Gains and losses in the investment account each month are reflected in Column C. Let's say my stock mutual fund earned 1.5% during the first month. That's $9 on my $600 of original capital. My fund's value, therefore, has grown to $609. Thanks to my starting capital, I'm well ahead of where I need to be at this early stage ($161 as shown in Column B). Because I'm "ahead" for now, I don't need to add to my stock fund. Instead, I'll put my $150 contribution for the first month into a money market fund at the same fund organization (Column F). Ditto

TABLE 4: VALUE AVERAGING WORKSHEET

(A) End of Month	(B) Value Path	(C) Stock Fund	(D) Add to Stocks	(E) After Addition	(F) Add to MoneyMkt	(G) After Addition
1	$161	$609	$0	$609	$150	$150
2	322	621	0	621	150	300
3	482	617	0	617	150	450
4	643	624	19	643	131	581
5	804	627	177	804	−27	554
6	965	780	185	965	−35	519
12	1,929	1,804	125	1,929	25	591
24	4,018	3,921	97	4,018	53	575
36	6,281	6,214	67	6,281	83	570
48	8,732	8,487	244	8,732	−94	322
60	11,386	11,388	0	11,388	150	220
72	14,260	14,160	99	14,260	51	80
84	17,372	17,798	0	17,798	150	156

TABLE 3: MONTHLY DEPOSIT AND VALUE PATH GOALS FOR BUILDING $1,000
(ASSUMES AVERAGE ANNUAL RATE OF RETURN OF 12%)

	20 Years	19 Years	18 Years	17 Years	16 Years	15 Years	14 Years	13 Years	12 Years	11 Years	10 Years	9 Years	8 Years	7 Years	6 Years
	$1.0109	1.1539	1.3195	1.5122	1.7373	2.0017	2.3143	2.6867	3.1342	3.6779	4.3471	5.1842	6.2528	7.6527	9.5502
1	12.82	14.63	16.73	19.18	22.03	25.39	29.35	34.07	39.75	46.64	55.13	65.75	79.30	97.06	121.12
2	27.27	31.12	35.59	40.79	46.86	53.99	62.42	72.47	84.54	99.21	117.26	139.84	168.66	206.42	257.60
3	43.54	49.70	56.84	65.14	74.84	86.23	99.69	115.73	135.01	158.43	187.26	223.32	269.35	329.66	411.39
4	61.89	70.64	80.78	92.58	106.36	122.55	141.69	164.48	191.88	225.17	266.14	317.39	382.82	468.52	584.69
5	82.56	94.24	107.76	123.50	141.88	163.48	189.01	219.42	255.97	300.37	355.03	423.39	510.67	625.00	779.96
6	105.85	120.82	138.17	158.34	181.91	209.60	242.33	281.32	328.18	385.11	455.18	542.84	654.73	801.32	1000.00
7	132.09	150.78	172.42	197.60	227.01	261.56	302.41	351.07	409.55	480.60	568.04	677.44	817.07	1000.00	
8	161.66	184.53	211.02	241.83	277.83	320.12	370.12	429.67	501.24	588.19	695.22	829.10	1000.00		
9	194.99	222.57	254.52	291.68	335.10	386.11	446.41	518.24	604.56	709.44	838.52	1000.00			
10	232.54	265.43	303.54	347.85	399.64	460.46	532.38	618.04	720.99	846.05	1000.00				
11	274.85	313.73	358.77	411.15	472.35	544.25	629.25	730.49	852.17	1000.00					
12	322.53	368.15	421.00	482.47	554.29	638.66	738.40	857.21	1000.00						
13	376.25	429.48	491.13	562.84	646.62	745.04	861.40	1000.00							
14	436.79	498.58	570.15	653.40	750.66	864.92	1000.00								
15	505.01	576.44	659.20	755.44	867.90	1000.00									
16	581.87	664.19	759.54	870.43	1000.00										
17	668.49	763.05	872.60	1000.00											
18	766.09	874.46	1000.00												
19	876.07	1000.00													
20	1000.00														

for months two and three, bringing my total money fund balance to $450 (Column G). At the end of month four, the value of my stock fund trails my value path for the first time (compare Column B to Column C). I'm "behind." Value averaging calls for me to use part (or all) of my $150 monthly contribution in order to catch up. Since I'm only $19 behind, that's how much I invest in my stock fund. I deposit the remaining $131 into the money fund.

Due to stock market weakness during month five, the value of my stock fund holdings is once again behind, this time by $177. To catch up, I buy stock fund shares using all of my $150 monthly contribution plus another $27 from the money fund. I continue in this way—some months buying more fund shares, some months not—throughout the first year. At the end of twelve months, the $1,929 goal has been reached, plus there's $591 in the money market fund (not including the interest that would have been earned during the period). Due to space limitations, I can't show all 192 months. Instead, I have listed the year-end results through the first eight years of the strategy. At the half-way point of my 16-year endeavor, my portfolio is $459 ahead ($21,203 portfolio value minus $20,744 value path goal) and I have another $323 in reserve in the money fund.

The VA strategy generates better returns than conventional DCA because it doesn't just "buy more when prices are low" as with DCA. It buys *even more than usual* when prices move lower during the month. Consider months five and six when more than the "normal" $150 went into the stock fund account. And conversely, it doesn't just "buy less when prices are high" as with DCA. It *buys even less than usual* when prices are unusually strong during the month and your portfolio value moves closer to or surpasses the value path goal. So VA does an even better job of providing mechanical guidance to your buying than traditional DCA.

If you'd like to see how value averaging has worked during some difficult times in the market . . .

. . . consider the example on the next page. It assumes you began your value-averaging program at the worst possible time—near the highs just before the crash of 1987. The assumption is that you have saved $3,000 for college for your oldest child and invested it in the Vanguard 500 Index fund at the end of June 1987. Additionally, you contribute $75 per month into your VA strategy.

❶ We invest our entire $3,000 nest egg at the outset. At the time, we don't know whether it's a "good" time or a "bad" time to buy stocks. It soon turns out to be a very bad time.

❷ At the end of the first month, the gains in the stock fund have us "ahead of schedule" versus where the value path says we should be. That means we can put the entire monthly addition of $75 into the money market fund for use in the future.

❸ To our horror, the crash of '87 takes place during the fourth month. Our stock fund drops more than 20% in value, and we are now $757 behind our value path. We invest our monthly $75 plus the entire $223 from the money market fund in the stock fund account.

❹ For the past nine months, we've been investing our entire $75 each month into the stock fund, and we are now only $190 behind the value path. In the process, we've been loading up on shares at some pretty low prices.

❺ At the end of year two, gains in the stock fund portfolio (from all those shares we bought at bargain prices after the crash) have now enabled the stock fund to surpass our value path goal. We also have a $488 additional cushion in the money market fund.

❻ You can't tell it from looking at the stock fund value, but the market sold off heavily in month thirty-eight due to the Iraqi invasion of Kuwait. While other investors were selling in panic, we calmly invested our normal $75 plus an additional $378 pulled from the money market fund. In month thirty-nine, we invested another $75 plus $316. By month forty-two we were once again comfortably ahead of schedule.

❼ At the end of year five of our ten-year plan, we are $2,133 ahead of schedule (a $244 "surplus" in our portfolio plus $1,889 in the money market fund). This provides a solid cushion (and a little extra courage) to confidently face the uncertain years ahead.

The worksheet shows that, in spite of the crash of 1987 and the sell-off following the invasion of Kuwait, you'd be comfortably ahead of schedule at the half-way mark of your 10-year program. Given enough time, you will survive (and even prosper from) the occasional stock

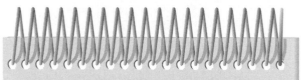

VALUE AVERAGING WORKSHEET

End of Month	Value Path	Portfolio Value	Add to Portfolio	After Addition	Left for MoneyMkt	MoneyMkt Balance
❶	$3000					
1	3073	$3147 ❷	$0	$3147	$75	$75
2	3134	3268	0	3268	75	150
3	3196	3194	2	3196	73	223
4	3259	2502 ❸	298	2800	−223	0
5	3322	2511	75	2586	0	0
6	3387	2775	75	2850	0	0
12	3791 ❹	3601	75	3676	0	0
18	4230	4193	37	4230	38	38
24	4704	4925	0	4925	75	❺ 488
30	5218	5556	0	5556	75	938
36	5772	6082	0	6082	75	1058
42	6372	6742 ❻	0	6742	75	539
48	7019	7696	0	7696	75	989
54	7717	8780	0	8780	75	1439
60	8470	8714	0	8714	75	❼ 1889

COLUMN HEADINGS

Value Path: Amount we should have at the end of each month if we are to reach $10,000 by the end of the tenth year (calculated by using the formula given in Dr. Edleson's book). Portfolio Value: The month-end market value of the stock fund account. Add To Portfolio: The amount used to purchase more stock fund shares. After Addition: Value of the stock fund after the month-end purchase of new shares is made. Left For Money Market: The amount deposited in the money market fund due to the fact that the entire $75 monthly contribution wasn't needed in the stock fund. Money Market Balance: Month-end balance after all transactions, excluding interest earned.

A SOUND MIND BRIEFING

Stock Market Seasonality

The stock market is open an average of twenty-one days each month. From 1924-1989, let's assume that your family had a strategy of owning common stocks only during a certain seven-day stretch. Let's also say your neighbors thought you were crazy and, just to prove you wrong, insisted on owning stocks only on the other fourteen days when you didn't. Both families started with $1,000. Which family did the best?

Well, lucky you! Even though you were invested only one-third of the time, your family's nest egg grew to a staggering $4,400,000! And your contrary neighbors, who were invested twice as many days each month as you were, watched with dismay as their original $1,000 shrank to a meager $433! (Commissions and taxes have been omitted to dramatize the point.) Curious? What seven days are we talking about here? The last two trading days and first five trading days of each month. From now on, I'll refer to this stretch as a "favorable period."

I first read of this tendency in the late 1970s in a book called Stock Market Logic, by Norman Fosback, who did the pioneering work in popularizing the seasonality concept. In 1990, the scholarly Journal of Finance published a paper by Joseph P. Ogden of State University of New York. He has offered an explanation of why there seems to be recurring buying activity at these times of the month that drives the market higher.

Professor Ogden's research discovered that 45% of all common stock dividends, 65% of all preferred stock dividends, 70% of interest and principal payments on corporate bonds, and 90% of the interest and payments on municipal bonds, is paid to investors on the first or last business day of each month. All this is in addition to the month-end contributions from salary checks that have been predesignated to go into various stock purchase plans. What do investors do with all this money? Dr. Ogden thinks they put a sizable portion into the stock market and believes this accounts for a significant part of the turn-of-the-month phenomena.

Yale Hirsch, publisher of the Stock Trader's Almanac, believes the growing awareness among investors of the monthly favorable period caused it to change beginning in the mid-1980s. As more investors tried to get in ahead of this monthly rally, it had the effect of causing the rally to begin sooner. Hirsch says the pattern has been altered so that the "new seasonality shifted to the last four trading days of the previous month and the first two of the current month." Meanwhile, the man who started it all, Fosback, appears unconvinced. He continues to use his traditional definition.

Who's right? For the investor using a monthly dollar-cost-averaging strategy, it doesn't matter. Just do your buying before the other month-end investors start theirs, say with at least five trading days remaining in the month. Then, whether the Hirsch theory (seasonality begins with four trading days remaining in the month) or the Fosback theory (seasonality begins with two trading days remaining in the month) is correct, you'll still

benefit from the buying that surrounds the turn of the month. Remember, the value of this strategy manifests itself over the long haul—it won't work as expected every month.

For example, assume the last seven days in April fall as follows: 24th Thursday, 25th Friday, 26th Saturday, 27th Sunday, 28th Monday, 29th Tuesday, and 30th Wednesday. Since the financial markets are closed on the weekends, the final four trading days in April would be the 25th-30th. In that event, you would want to make your investment the day before the 25th—on Thursday the 24th. If you have your money at the fund organization, a timely phone call or click of the mouse will transfer it into your stock fund on the day of your choosing each month.

On the other hand, if you've set up an automatic transfer which is executed on the same date every month, you give up a little precision because the seasonal period varies from month to month depending on where weekends fall and the number of days in the month. In that case, I would probably choose the 24th of the month. That date will be on target most of the time during months that have 30 days, and a little early in months other than February. This will be close enough to still provide a benefit.

Here are a few other ways you can use monthly seasonality to improve your long-term performance.

• Perhaps you're in retirement and part of your income derives from selling enough of your growth fund each month in order to withdraw $500. Wait until the favorable period has run its course; sell your shares on the fifth trading day of each month (or a few days earlier if observation persuades you that Hirsch is correct). A refinement of this takes into account that Friday has a tendency to be a strong market day; therefore, if the fifth trading day of a particular month falls on Thursday, wait one more day and sell on Friday instead. Over the long-term, you'll get a slightly better average price.

• Let's say that you're looking to move from one mutual fund organization to another. Sell your holdings in your present fund near the beginning of the month as a favorable period is concluded. Then, you've got time to receive your proceeds and get your account set up at the new organization. Initially, deposit your money into a money market fund. Then, near month's end just before the start of the next favorable period, make a phone call to switch into the stock fund you've selected.

• On a variation of the dollar-cost-averaging strategy, use favorable periods when investing a windfall (for example, an inheritance). If you haven't been investing regularly, it's a little scary to take a large sum and put it into the market "all at once." Divide it into several smaller amounts of equal size, depending on how long you want to stretch things out. For example, if you wanted to invest it over a period of six months, divide your total into six equal amounts. Then invest one-sixth each month just before the start of the favorable period.

From the Sound Mind Investing newsletter. To learn more about the monthly SMI newsletter, use the postage-paid tear-out card in this book, or visit our website at www.soundmindinvesting.com.

market crisis. The problem occurs if the sell-off comes too close to the end of your multi-year program. If you had been ending your program in late 1987 rather than just getting started, you would almost certainly not have attained your value path goal. That's why the threat posed by a poor market environment increases as you get ever closer to your investment goal; there's not enough time to recoup your losses. To help offset this risk, here are a few ways you can be more conservative in your VA strategy: (1) plan on meeting your target a year or two ahead of schedule; (2) set your dollar goal at a higher level than actually needed; or (3) put in more money monthly than the formulas call for. Make a point to reevaluate your program every year or two. Are your market growth assumptions still valid? Does your dollar goal still appear sufficient for your needs? Should you increase the amount of your monthly contribution?

Reviewing the market lessons of years gone by only renews my commitment to the discipline . . .

. . . imposed by having a specific, well-researched strategy in place—a strategy that has *objective* decision-making criteria. Such discipline is essential to your investment survival for four reasons.

• **Every investment strategy involves some capital risk.** There's no way around it: to live is to take risks. In the same way, financial life has risks. Investing your capital involves accepting some risk of losing part or all; not investing invites the risk of losing buying power to inflation.

• **Nobody really knows what's going to happen next.** Nobody. There are things that can be predicted. We know precisely when the sun is going to come up each morning, for instance. The investment world, on the other hand, is about people and their attitudes about money. It's primarily a world governed by human emotions and behavior and, as such, cannot be predicted with certainty by anyone or any method.

• **The market won't present a clear warning when it's time to act.** The reality is that you cannot know in advance how long a good thing is going to last. It might last a long time. On the other hand, it might end tomorrow. Systematic investing will help balance the up and down swings in your portfolio.

• **Our emotions naturally cause us to postpone committing ourselves.** First, there's our natural optimism. Second, there's simple greed. And third, there is an enormously powerful influence felt by every investor: the "fear of regret." It's this fear of doing the wrong thing that can paralyze us and prevent us from taking prompt action.

The key to successful investing is in having the self-discipline to adhere to your strategy.

It's not that any strategy is perfect: there's no such thing. But a strategy doesn't have to be perfect in order to be highly profitable over time. The value of discipline and how it can protect us, from the markets and from ourselves, cannot be overstated. Please keep that in mind as you risk your capital in what is basically a high-risk endeavor. ◆

CHAPTER PREVIEW

Making the Transition: How to Get from Where You Are Now to Where You Want to Go

I. The "right" portfolio moves can't be evaluated simply in terms of maximizing profits. Rather, they take into account your spiritual, intellectual, and emotional priorities.

  A. No investment portfolio can be consistently positioned to maximize profits from coming events.

  B. The right portfolio move is one that is consistent with a specific, biblically sound long-term strategy you've adopted.

  C. The right portfolio move is one where you've taken plenty of time to pray and to seek trusted, experienced Christian counsel.

  D. The right portfolio move is one that you understand.

  E. The right portfolio move is one that is prudent under the circumstances. It passes the "common sense" test.

  F. The right portfolio move is one that is consistent with your investing "self"—it fits comfortably.

II. A remodeling worksheet can provide an overview of how you go about making the transition.

  A. The remodeling worksheet will list current equity and fixed-income holdings and allow you to conveniently calculate the percentage allocations between the two.

  B. The worksheet will show you what changes in holdings are necessary to change your portfolio from its present structure to one that matches your investment temperament and long-term goals.

"Future shock is the disorientation that affects an individual when he is overwhelmed by change and even the prospect of change. It is the consequence of having to make too many decisions . . .

. . . about too many new and unfamiliar problems in too short a time. . . . We are in collision with tomorrow. Future shock has arrived."—Alvin Toffler

Do you ever feel like that? As if the decisions you are required to make, especially about your finances, are coming at you at an ever faster and more confusing rate? A great many people today are finding it increasingly difficult to know which is the "right" step to take. They wonder:

"Is this a good time to buy stocks?"

"Which money market mutual fund would be best?"

"Should I sell some of my employer's stock in order to diversify?"

"My CDs mature soon. Should I renew them for ninety days or a year?"

"How much of my retirement plan should I put in stocks versus bonds?"

"If I sell this losing investment and buy something else, will I be better off?"

Since we cannot know the future with certainty, it's obvious that no investment portfolio that any of us comes up with will ever be *perfectly* positioned to profit from upcoming events. As the future unfolds, it will always be possible to point to ways we could have made more money than we did—and some of them will appear incredibly obvious in retrospect! *This means that it's pointless to think of the "right" investment portfolio simply in terms of maximizing profits. If that is your approach, you will always be frustrated and second-guessing your decisions.*

The "right" portfolio is one that realistically faces where you are right now, looks years ahead to where you want to go, *and has a very high probability of getting you there on time.* As you consider "remodeling" your current holdings, let's look at some of the characteristics of the "right" steps to take.

The plans of the diligent lead to profit as surely as haste leads to poverty.
Proverbs 21:5

• The right portfolio move is one that is consistent with a specific, biblically sound long-term strategy you've adopted.

One common trait that I find among many of those I counsel is that their current investment portfolio tends to be a random collection of "good deals" and assorted savings accounts. Each investment appears to have been made on its own merits without much thought of how it fit into the whole.

I find savings accounts (because the bank was offering a "good deal" on money market accounts), company stock (because buying it at a discount is a "good deal"), a savings bond for the kids' education (because they read an article that said they were a "good deal" for college), a universal life policy (because their insurance agent said it was a "good deal" for someone their age), a real-estate partnership (which their broker said was a "good deal" for people in their tax bracket), and 100 shares of XYZ stock (because their best friend let them in on this *really* "good deal").

As we've discussed, I want you to become an *initiator* (one who develops an individual investing strategy tailored to your personal temperament and goals) rather than a *responder* (one who reacts to sales calls, making decisions on a case-by-case basis). Then you can select the appropriate investments accordingly. The right investment step is the one that *you* seek out purposefully, knowing where it fits into the overall scheme of things.

• The right portfolio move is one where you've taken plenty of time to pray and to seek trusted, experienced Christian counsel.

Because your decisions have long-term implications, you should take all the time you need to become informed. Don't be in a hurry; there's no deadline. A good friend once commented to me: "The Christian life isn't a destination; it's a way of travel." Likewise, you're not under pressure to predict the best possible portfolio for the next six months or make this year's big killing. You're remodeling in order to settle in for a comfortable investing lifestyle that will serve you well for decades.

The way of a fool seems right to him, but a wise man listens to advice.
Proverbs 12:15

Besides, prayer takes time. You need time to pray, ask for the counsel of others, and reflect. You should consider the alternatives, examine your motives, and continue praying until you have peace in the matter. If you're married, you should pray with your partner and talk it out until you reach mutual agreement. You're in this together and, rain or shine, you both must be willing to accept responsibility for the decision. The right investment step is the one that results from careful and prayerful consideration. This will add to your steadfastness during the occasional rough sledding along the way.

• The right portfolio move is one that you understand.

This typically involves at least two things. First, it's relatively simple. It's not likely that your situation requires exotic or complicated strategies. In fact, the single investment decision of greatest importance is actually pretty easy to understand. Do you know what it is? We covered it in chapter 16. It's deciding what percentage of your investments to put in stocks (where your return is uncertain) as opposed to bonds and other fixed income investments (where your return is relatively certain). *This one decision has more influence on your investment results than any other.*

The heart of the discerning acquires knowledge; the ears of the wise seek it out.
Proverbs 18:15

And second, you've educated yourself on the basics. When you're able to give a simple explanation of your strategy to a friend and answer a few questions, you've probably got at least a beginner's grasp. The right investment step is the one where you understand what you're doing, why you're doing it, and how you expect it to improve matters. That's the least you should expect of yourself before making decisions that can dramatically affect your life and the lives of those you love.

A simple man believes anything, but a <u>prudent man gives thought to his steps</u>.
Proverbs 14:15

• The right portfolio move is one that is prudent under the circumstances. Does it pass the "common sense" test?

How much of your investing capital can you afford to lose and still have a realistic chance of meeting your financial goals? The investments that offer higher potential returns also carry correspondingly greater risks of loss. The right portfolio for you is not always the one with the most profit potential.

For example, it's usually best not to have a majority of your investments in a single asset or security. For that reason, people who have large holdings of stock in the company they work for often sell some of it in order to diversify. If the stock doubles after they sell it, does that mean they did the "wrong" thing? No, they did the right thing. After all, the stock could have fallen dramatically as well as risen. What would a large loss have done to their retirement planning? The right investment step is the one that protects you in the event of life's occasional worst-case scenarios. Generally, this moves you in the direction of increased diversification.

Do not be anxious about anything, but in everything, by prayer and petition, with thanksgiving, present your requests to God. And the peace of God, which transcends all understanding, will guard your hearts and your minds in Christ Jesus.
Philippians 4: 6–7

• The right portfolio move is one that is consistent with your investing "self"—will it fit comfortably?

I originally developed the structure of the four Sound Mind Investing temperaments to illustrate that, as part of our separate God-given identities, we each have different capacities to accept risk and uncertainty. Some people actually seem to be energized by the thrill of adventure, whereas others prefer more secure, predictable surroundings. If you make investments that violate your natural temperament, you are much more likely to react emotionally when the occasional setbacks occur and objective decision making is needed.

When someone presents me with two investing alternatives and invites my opinion, I often ask, "Which one would you like to do, and why?" This is my way of learning more about that person's investing temperament. Unless I find a grievous flaw in their financial logic, I encourage them to take the course of action they intuitively prefer. They are more likely to stick with their strategy over the long term and exercise the self-discipline needed to be successful if they are comfortable with their portfolio. The right investment step is the one that enhances your ability to make calm and well-reasoned decisions.

With these points in mind, it's time to walk through a "remodeling" project that revamps an investment portfolio. I have designed it . . .

. . . to teach by example. Carefully follow the steps taken by Tom and Marilyn Randolph as they adjust their portfolio to achieve the mix that they have decided is best for them given their tolerance for risk and current stage of life—40% invest-by-owning and 60% invest-by-lending. In developing this example, I assumed that Tom's 401(k) plan offers the typical choices: company stock, blue-chip stock fund or S&P 500 index fund, long-term bond fund, and money market fund.

As you begin, keep in mind these two guiding principles:

• You don't need to *perfectly* achieve the recommended percentages for the various risk categories. It's good enough to come close; when in doubt, go with less risk.

• You don't have to change things all at once. Take it in steps over many months (or even a few years) as your comfort level grows.

Step 1: List the current values of your assets.

Basically, this means writing down the investments over which you exercise control. Divide them into two groups: investments where you are an owner and investments where you are a lender (see the notepad at right). There are two exceptions. Do not count the savings set aside for your Level Two contingency fund—they are not part of your long-term risk-taking strategy. Also, do not include money set aside for the children's education. These assets should go through their own remodeling process once you understand how to do it.

If you're married, put down both spouses' investments. Married partners are in this together— I discourage attempts to keep "his" money separate from "her" money. Also, as you can see from Tom and Marilyn's list, you don't need to distinguish between retirement or current savings, or when you bought them or what you paid. Nor do you care whether the investment is held in a normal brokerage account, an IRA, a 401(k), a variable annuity, or any other legal structure in which investments are placed. The goal is to list on paper your various investments and the amount you would expect to receive if you sold or exchanged them.

When you're finished, add up the totals and calculate what percentage each group represents in your total holdings. This is your first insight into how much risk you're

INVESTMENT HOLDINGS OF TOM AND MARILYN RANDOLPH

INVESTMENTS WHERE WE ARE OWNERS

$6,000	Marilyn's pension plan invested in a growth fund
8,300	Tom's 401(k) at work invested in the "S&P 500" portfolio
15,800	Tom's 401(k) at work invested in G.E. stock
4,300	Goodyear shares inherited from Marilyn's mother
3,300	Utility shares inherited from Marilyn's mother
$37,700	Equity portion is 62% of total holdings

INVESTMENTS WHERE WE ARE LENDERS

$1,900	Tom's 401(k) at work invested in long-term govt bonds
6,200	Marilyn's pension plan invested in long-term corp bonds
3,000	IBM bond inherited from Marilyn's mother
4,600	Tom's 401(k) at work that's invested in the money market
2,400	Credit union passbook joint savings account
2,600	Tom's IRA invested in a bank money market account
2,600	Marilyn's IRA invested in a bank money market account
$23,300	Fixed income portion is 38% of total holdings
$61,000	Total Investment Holdings

taking in your portfolio. If you're like most people, your investments carry a higher overall risk level than you expected.

Step 2: Determine what dollar changes are needed.

Now that the Randolphs know their current mix (62% equity and 38% fixed income), they can compute the dollar amount of the change needed to achieve the mix they seek (40% equity and 60% fixed income). Obviously, they will need to decrease the equity portion and increase the fixed income portion.

Here's how they calculate the dollar amount. They take the total value of their holdings of $61,000 and multiply it times 40% to arrive at the equity portion goal—$24,400. They then subtract this from their current equity portion of $37,700 to learn how much of a decrease is needed.

This tells them that they need to sell $13,300 worth of securities from the equity side and reinvest it over on the fixed income side. This will decrease their equity portion to $24,400 (current $37,700 less sales of $13,300) while increasing the fixed income portion to $36,600 (current $23,300 plus new investments of $13,300). Once this is done, their desired mix will have been accomplished.

Step 3: Decide which holdings to sell in order to meet your dollar goal.

They say that "timing is everything." When it comes to investing, the timing of buy orders gets all the attention. Many forces work to incline us toward making an investment (e.g., friends, relatives, brokers, and financial planners), but very few of these sources return with the message "It's time to sell that stock I told you about!"

The Randolphs now know they need to liquidate $13,300 worth of their equity holdings—but which ones? Here are a few rules of thumb that might be of help in deciding.

• Keep in mind any limitations imposed by your pension holdings. For example, if Tom sells some of his 401(k) equity holdings, he can only reinvest the money in *other* 401(k) offerings. This limits the number of possible ways he can accomplish his goal.

• Move toward increased diversification. This means that Tom's large holding in his employer's stock (G.E.) could prudently be reduced.

• Sell the losers. The alternative is to sell the winners—the strong companies that have fulfilled your hopes and expectations. Why would you want to unload the winners and hang on to the disappointments? Go ahead and acknowledge that they didn't work out. If the stock is not being held in a tax-deferred account, you can take advantage of the loss for tax purposes.

• Sell a stock when the reason you bought it is no longer valid. For whatever reason (the expected new product didn't pan out, the merger was called off, they didn't land the big government contract, etc.), the original case for investing in the stock no longer holds true.

• Sell stocks whose earnings have fallen. Any company looks bad if it reports lower earnings, so its management will go to great lengths (and accounting mischief) to avoid doing so. Only when they exhaust all their options for disguising their deteriorating profits will management generally report earnings that are down (for the most recent twelve-month period compared with the previous twelve months). It may be a good time to exit.

• Don't worry. Many people fear "being wrong" and selling something that later goes higher. They're right to expect it, but wrong to think there's anything they can do about it. You can't know the future, so be realistic and accept your limited vision—don't let it paralyze you.

The Randolphs decide to sell their Goodyear and utility stocks plus however many of Tom's G.E. shares are necessary in order to reach a total of $13,300. These moves are steps toward achieving greater diversification.

Step 4: Decide in which risk categories to make your new purchases.

Now that they've raised the $13,300 to add to their fixed income portion, how do they decide *exactly* where to put it? Again, there are no absolute rules that govern this. There isn't just one "right" way to do your portfolio fine-tuning.

Let's assume that Tom and Marilyn decide to deal with the risk of rising interest rates by having roughly equal portions of their fixed income holdings in long-term bonds (over ten years), medium-term bonds (over four years but less than ten years), and money market funds and savings accounts. That means allocating $12,200 (one-third of their fixed income portfolio of

LEVELS OF INVESTMENT RISK

Investing by Lending (your fixed income holdings)	Investing by Owning (your equity holdings)
Zero coupon bonds	Oil and gas partnerships
High yield "junk" bond funds	Gold/silver coins/bars
Long-term high quality bond funds	Real-estate partnerships
Long-term tax-free bond funds	Individual shares in small
High yield "junk" tax-free bond funds	companies
Fixed annuities	Sector funds
Medium-term high quality bond funds	Small company/growth funds
Medium-term tax-free bond funds	International stock funds
Govt-backed mortgage bond funds	Rental property
Short-term high quality bond funds	Small company index funds
Short-term tax-free bond funds	Small company/value funds
Money market mutual funds	Individual shares in large companies
Bank CDs/money market accounts	Large company/growth funds
U.S. Treasury bills	S&P 500 index fund
	Large company/value funds
Volatility and risk is lowest at the bottom.	Volatility and risk is lowest at the bottom.

$36,600) to each of the three categories. The targets were attained as follows:

❶ They raised $7,600 by selling the Goodyear and utility stock, then invested in a new medium-term no-load bond fund at Vanguard.

(Note that once the Randolphs knew the *kind* of investments they wanted to make, they selected a no-load mutual fund organization *that offered funds with demonstrated performance excellence in their area of interest*—bonds.)

❷ The $3,000 IBM bond was sold and the proceeds were added to the new Vanguard bond fund account also. This increases the diversification.

❸ They withdrew $1,600 from their credit union savings and also added to the new Vanguard bond fund account, making the total $12,200.

❹ In Tom's 401(k) plan, he sold $5,700 worth of G.E. shares, transferring $4,100 of it into the long-term bond fund and $1,600 into the money market fund. Note that none of this money actually left the 401(k), but it was moved around *within* it.

The "remodeling" worksheets the Randolphs used are shown on pages 232-233. Each of the above numbered steps is shown in the "changes needed" columns. The final result is summarized on the notepad at the far right. Notice they didn't feel they needed to follow my allocation suggestions "to the letter of the law." They had the flexibility of adjusting their bond holdings to fit their personal situation and preference.

To help you begin your own remodeling project, you'll find some blank forms on pages 234-235. Feel free to make all the copies you need.

It's at this stage that investors often "freeze up."
Many people seem to find investing to be a nerve-racking . . .

. . . if not downright scary experience. Making investment decisions, and then watching the results unfold, can be stressful. Do you become anxious when circumstances compel you to make important investing decisions? Most of us do to one degree or another. If my mail is any indication, a great degree of financial fretting is common. Three recurring comments lead the list of ways my readers express their concerns.

• "There's so much at stake. I'm afraid I'll make the wrong decision."

• "I don't have much experience. I'm afraid I'll make the wrong decision."

• "My savings aren't making enough now, but if I make a change I'm afraid I'll make the wrong decision."

What is the "wrong" decision, anyway? If you feel a wrong decision is like saying 2+2=5, then you're off track; such thinking implies investing decisions can be made with mathematical certainty. They can't. This doesn't mean the economy and investment markets are completely random, only that you're dealing with *probabilities*, not certainties and predictable events. Scientists can predict with great accuracy when the next eclipse of the sun will occur decades into the future, yet they can't tell you if the sun will be eclipsed by clouds and ruin next week's picnic.

All of this is actually good news. It means anybody can play. It's like learning to drive a car. After a couple of lessons, you know enough to travel around town if you follow a few basic safety guidelines. After all, you're not trying to qualify for the Indy 500—you just want to reach your destination. In the same way, once you understand the concepts in this book, you're fairly well equipped for making whatever decisions you face.

Pretend you're in a contest where . . .

. . . you are to travel from coast to coast before the current interstate system was built. You can choose any route (but they're almost all two-lane roads), travel any speed, and take as much time as you want. There are no extra bonus points for getting there first—the only goal is to arrive safely. Everybody who does that "wins."

As you drive along, you constantly must make decisions. Should you take the route to the left or to the right? Is there construction or traffic up ahead? Will there be a motel with a vacancy? There are no scientific answers to these questions. Every decision requires some powers of observation, the ability to learn from your experiences, and a little common sense. You rarely come to a point where the decision is obvious. It would always be helpful to have "just a little more" information—but the challenge of the trip is the necessity of making choices *without having all the information. Nobody ever has all the relevant information.*

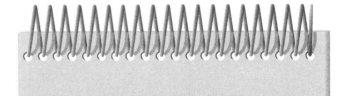

**INVESTMENT HOLDINGS OF
TOM AND MARILYN RANDOLPH
AFTER REBALANCING**

INVESTMENTS WHERE WE ARE OWNERS

$6,000	Marilyn's pension plan invested in a growth fund
8,300	Tom's 401(k) at work invested in the "S&P 500" portfolio
10,100	Tom's 401(k) at work invested in G.E. stock
$24,400	Equity portion is 40% of total holdings

INVESTMENTS WHERE WE ARE LENDERS

$6,000	Tom's 401(k) at work invested in long-term govt bonds
6,200	Marilyn's pension plan invested in long-term corp bonds
12,200	Vanguard Intermediate-term corporate bond fund
6,200	Tom's 401(k) at work that's invested in the money market
800	Credit union passbook joint savings account
2,600	Tom's IRA invested in a bank money market account
2,600	Marilyn's IRA invested in a bank money market account
$36,600	Fixed income portion is 60% of total holdings
$61,000	Total Investment Holdings

Investing is a lot like such a contest. You can't know for certain what lies ahead; anyone who would have you believe otherwise is lying to you. It's *because* we can't know the future that we diversify and stay flexible. This brings us to one of the few rules that investing has: protect your capital! That's the

INVEST-BY-OWNING
(Risk Generally Decreases as You Move Down the Page)

What Goes Here	Your Current Holdings	Current Value	Changes Needed	After Rebalancing
Include in this section any investments that are not specifically named in the SMI strategy				
Total				
Special purpose equity investments				
Total				
International equity investments				
Total				
Investments that fall into Stock Risk Category 4: Small companies + "growth" characteristics	Marilyn's pension plan	6,000		6,000
Total		$6,000 9.8%		$6,000 9.8%
Investments that fall into Stock Risk Category 3: Small companies + "value" characteristics				
Total				
Investments that fall into Stock Risk Category 2: Large companies + "growth" characteristics	Tom's 401(k) S&P 500 portfolio	8,300		8,300
	Tom's 401(k) G.E. stock	15,800	❹ −5,700	10,100
	Goodyear shares	4,300	❶ −4,300	
Total		$28,400 46.6%		$18,400 30.2%
Investments that fall into Stock Risk Category 1: Large companies + "value" characteristics	Utility shares	3,300	❶ −3,300	
Total		$3,300 5.4%		
	INVESTING BY OWNING	$37,700 61.8%	−$13,300	$24,400 40.0%

INVEST-BY-LENDING (Risk Generally Decreases as You Move Down the Page)				
What Goes Here	Your Current Holdings	Current Value	Changes Needed	After Rebalancing
Include in this section any investments that are not specifically named in the SMI strategy				
	Total			
Special purpose bond investments				
	Total			
Investments that fall into Bond Risk Category 4: Lower quality high-yield (junk) bonds				
	Total			
Investments that fall into Bond Risk Category 3: Long-term bonds of generally high quality	Tom's 401(k) long-term govts	1,900	❹ +4,100	6,000
	Marilyn's pension plan	6,200		6,200
	Total	$8,100 13.3%		$12,200 20.0%
Investments that fall into Bond Risk Category 2: Medium-term bonds of generally high quality	Vanguard Intermed-term Corp		❶ +7,600	
	Vanguard Intermed-term Corp		❷ +3,000	
	Vanguard Intermed-term Corp		❸ +1,600	12,200
	Total			$12,200 20.0%
Investments that fall into Bond Risk Category 1: Short-term bonds of generally high quality	IBM bond (matures 6/2004)	3,000	❷ −3,000	
	Total	$3,000 4.9%		
Cash-equivalent investments like savings accounts, CDs, T-bills, and money market funds	Tom's 401(k) money market	4,600	❹ +1,600	6,200
	Credit union joint savings	2,400	❸ −1,600	800
	Tom's IRA bank money market	2,600		2,600
	Marilyn's IRA bank money market	2,600		2,600
	Total	$12,200 20.0%		$12,200 20.0%
	INVESTING BY LENDING	$23,300 38.2%	+$13,300	$36,600 60.0%

INVEST-BY-OWNING
(Risk Generally Decreases as You Move Down the Page)

What Goes Here	Your Current Holdings	Current Value	Changes Needed	After Rebalancing
Include in this section any investments that are not specifically named in the SMI strategy				
	Total			
Special purpose equity investments				
	Total			
International equity investments				
	Total			
Investments that fall into Stock Risk Category 4: Small companies + "growth" characteristics				
	Total			
Investments that fall into Stock Risk Category 3: Small companies + "value" characteristics				
	Total			
Investments that fall into Stock Risk Category 2: Large companies + "growth" characteristics				
	Total			
Investments that fall into Stock Risk Category 1: Large companies + "value" characteristics				
	Total			

INVEST-BY-LENDING
(Risk Generally Decreases as You Move Down the Page)

What Goes Here	Your Current Holdings	Current Value	Changes Needed	After Rebalancing
Include in this section any investments that are not specifically named in the SMI strategy				
	Total			
Special purpose bond investments				
	Total			
Investments that fall into Bond Risk Category 4: Lower quality high-yield (junk) bonds				
	Total			
Investments that fall into Bond Risk Category 3: Long-term bonds of generally high quality				
	Total			
Investments that fall into Bond Risk Category 2: Medium-term bonds of generally high quality				
	Total			
Investments that fall into Bond Risk Category 1: Short-term bonds of generally high quality				
	Total			
Cash-equivalent investments like savings accounts, CDs, T-bills, and money market funds				
	Total			

only prerequisite for "arriving safely." When in doubt, take the safe route.

You control the level of risk you take by deciding how you divide your money between the two choices—to invest by lending (lower risk) and to invest by owning (higher risk). Don't make decisions in isolation (e.g., should I renew this CD? or, should I change the mix in my 401(k) plan?) without taking into account how the decision affects your overall mix.

Scripture teaches that *"to the Lord your God belong the heavens, even the highest heavens, the earth and everything in it"* (Deuteronomy 10:14). God has ownership rights; we have management responsibilities. That's why, whether you have many or few investments, doing your best to manage them in a God-pleasing manner is a task that must be taken seriously. It's a lifelong calling. ◆

SECTION

5

PREPARING FOR THE HIGH COST OF PRIME TIME

Retirement Countdown

Go to the ant, observe her ways and be wise, which
having no chief, officer or ruler, prepares her food in
the summer and gathers her provision in the harvest.

Proverbs 6:6-8

"The Social Security system calls it quits.
Details at 11:00. And now, sit back and enjoy tonight's movie . . ."

CHAPTER PREVIEW

The High Cost of Living in Prime Time

I.   As the baby-boomer generation moves into retirement, the sixty-five-and-over age group will grow from 12% at present to 20% of the total population. The need for adequate retirement planning will grow too.

   A.   Today's retirees are the wealthiest in U.S. history. With life expectancies of about fifteen years following retirement, the vast majority of them live out their lives quite comfortably.

   B.   As life expectancies continue to increase, the baby-boomer generation can reasonably expect to live twenty to twenty-five years past retirement.

   C.   Longer life expectancies and the increasing cost of health care indicate that today's workers must plan carefully to be sure of financial security during retirement.

II. Projecting your financial needs for a secure and comfortable retirement involves making many financial assumptions concerning inflation, future rates of return, and your life expectancy. Worksheets are included that will help you through the process.

III. The truth about Social Security is that it is a wealth-transfer program, much like welfare. It takes money from one group of citizens (active workers) and gives it to another group of citizens (inactive workers).

   A.   It is not an "insurance" program because the amount you put in has no correlation to the amount you receive back. It does not "entitle" you to benefits because Congress can legally reduce them any time it chooses. Workers do not make "contributions" that "earn" them protection. Workers pay taxes that earn them nothing.

   B.   When the baby-boomer generation enters retirement, there will be an inadequate number of active workers to tax. To balance the books, changes will be needed. There will be a continuing national dialogue in coming years on various reform proposals. It's in your financial interest to become educated on the issues and actively participate in the debate.

When I was a small child, perhaps five or so, it used to fascinate me to think that someday I'd be "old" like my parents.

My mother was twenty-one when I was born, and I used to say to her (proud of my newly acquired ability to add numbers), "Mom! When I'm twenty-one, you'll be forty-two!" And she'd answer back, "And when you're forty-two, I'll be sixty-three!" Knowing it was my turn to go next, I would usually begin giggling at what to me was a really silly idea; namely, that I would *ever* be sixty-three or that she would *ever* be eighty-four!

I could imagine being old enough to go to high school someday, and maybe college after that. I could almost imagine being old enough to get married, although I wasn't at all sure why I would ever want to. But picturing myself as being over sixty, like my grandparents, was simply incomprehensible, beyond the limits of my youthful imagination.

I recalled my little childhood game recently as I read some fascinating statistics on what has been called "the graying of America." Did you know that today's generation of retirees (I'll call them "prime-timers") are the wealthiest in U.S. history? They participated in the postwar economic boom, watched their homes greatly escalate in value during the inflationary 1970s, and paid far less into pension plans and Social Security than they are now taking out in indexed benefits. At the same time, their cash flow needs are past their peak—the children are grown and out on their own, most mortgages are paid off, and work-related expenses are no longer a drag on the family budget.

The majority of Americans sixty-five and older are living relatively comfortably. According to the most current data . . .

. . . available, they had an average net worth of around $86,300 per household, well above the U.S. average of $37,600. Their median income was $31,600 (including Social Security and other government transfer payments), and almost 80% own their own homes.

The number of those joining the ranks of the retired is increasing at twice the rate of the overall population. By the year 2030, the post-WWII "baby boomers" will raise the prime-timer population to 64 million. This translates to about one out of every five Americans, up from only one in every eight now. What will retirement be like for us newcomers? (Although I was born a year too early to officially be a boomer, I'm taking a little editorial license and including myself.) Will we have it as good? The trends are not encouraging.

Somewhat paradoxically, the problem has to do with the fact that life expectancy continues to make remarkable gains. This increasing longevity is due mainly to the continuing improvements in health care; also contributing to longer lives is the American public's discovery of the benefits of nutrition, physical fitness, and healthier lifestyles. About 80% of prime-timers consider their health excellent, good, or fair. A significant decline in activities and interests doesn't generally occur until age 85 and later.

It now seems that moving into the 85-plus group has the "elderly" connotation formerly associated with the 65-plus group. One expert refers to them as "old-olds" to distinguish them from the "young-olds" who are *only* 65 to 84. The old-olds population is growing fast, projected to exceed 8 million by 2030. The odds of living to age 100 are now down to just eighty-seven to one. The number of centenarians will triple in the next ten years; more than 35,000 are now at least age 100.

In short, we'll all be living longer. And let's face it: living costs money. Of course, the longer the life, the greater the likelihood that support services will be needed; families now stand a greater chance than ever before of having a disabled elderly relative to support. More than 80% of us will enjoy reasonably good health, but even so, it's estimated that health care for prime-timers costs three to four times what it costs the rest of the population. Then there are the other niceties of everyday life, such as food, shelter, clothing, and recreation.

A fundamental fact of retirement life is that you don't want your money to run out before you do! For a reasonable guess as to how long you'll live in retirement, let's consider the case of 65-year-old males as shown in the table at right. On average, a man who lives to age 65 goes on to live another 19 years. Roughly half of this age 65 group will live more than 19 years and half will live less. To be on the safe side, financially speaking, you have to assume you'll be in the surviving group. If you make it to age 85, your expected life span is increased another seven years. That means, in the absence of health reasons to the contrary, your goal should probably be to have enough money to support yourself (and your spouse, if married) into your nineties.

LIFE EXPECTANCIES		
Age	Men	Women
30	50 more years	55 more years
35	45 more years	50 more years
40	40 more years	45 more years
45	36 more years	40 more years
50	31 more years	35 more years
55	27 more years	31 more years
60	23 more years	26 more years
65	19 more years	22 more years
70	15 more years	18 more years
75	12 more years	14 more years
80	9 more years	11 more years
85	7 more years	8 more years
90	5 more years	6 more years
95	4 more years	4 more years

So that brings us to the big question: how much is all this going to cost, anyway?

If you're feeling a sense of urgency about learning the answer, good! I've got your attention. Now you're ready to make the effort needed to come up with a reasonable approximation of how much you should be budgeting for your own prime-time experiences. My goal is to help you understand what it will take to get you "in shape" financially in preparation for your retirement years. The process will involve making a series of assumptions. As we go along, I will explain the reasoning for the ones I make, but feel free to change them to fit your own sense of what is appropriate.

Getting in shape is not a particularly enjoyable process. It requires us to consistently sacrifice *certain* enjoyments now in return for *uncertain* benefits in the future. Watching my diet and scheduling regular workouts is, for me, extremely easy to postpone. Retirement planning, and the goal of getting in shape financially, is similar. It's no fun, it requires short-term sacrifice with little immediate positive reinforcement, and the benefits can seem a long way off. That may explain why too many of us arrive in our sixties ill-prepared—in both body and bank account—to get the most from our retirement years. You need not let this happen to you and your family.

We'll now turn to a step-by-step process that will help you see where you are now in relation to your long-term retirement needs.

The series of worksheets on the following pages is designed to serve only as a very general tool to help you think through your personal retirement planning responsibilities. It is based on a variety of assumptions concerning inflation and the rates of return you will earn on your investments. The closer you are to retirement, the more accurate it is likely to be. It's a good idea to run the numbers anew every year or two to keep them reasonably on target.

Unless noted, I've made no special attempt to take one's normal annual income tax obligations into consideration. All the financial goals and standard of living assumptions are based on "before tax" dollars. My hypothetical couple, the Millers, have a current income of $50,000 before income taxes. The dollars they have remaining after they pay their income taxes are sufficient to support a certain standard of living. I assume the same will be true during their retirement. That is, they will have to pay their income taxes out of their projected retirement income just as they do their other living expenses. I took this approach because it was impossible to accommodate all of the various state and federal income tax rates currently in effect, let alone guess what they might be years into the future.

Let me warn you ahead of time that you might be tempted to feel discouragement when you complete step 11. That's the point at which you discover how much money you'll need in order to live comfortably for the rest of your life once you retire (based on assumptions you will have made regarding lifestyle costs, inflation, and your life expectancy). It will be a huge number. But don't stop there. By the time you factor in Social Security and your other pension and retirement assets, you'll likely find that the amount you need to save between now and retirement (step 45) is manageable.

But given Social Security's widely-publicized short-comings, is it realistic . . .

. . . to count on receiving your Social Security retirement benefits? That depends on how close *you personally* are to the day you switch teams—leaving the ranks of the people paying in and joining those in that happy state of grace where you receive monthly income for life far in excess of your earlier contributions. If you are planning to retire in the next ten years, you're in pretty good shape. There may be minor adjustments to your benefits along the way, but congressional hypocrisy and cowardice is probably good for another decade of failure to face up to Social Security's monumental problems.

The rest of us are probably going to be pretty unhappy about whatever "fix" Congress finally comes up with (see page 253), and the younger we are now, the more unhappy we're likely to be. In the past, each generation of workers was asked to support the benefits for the previous generation. But it is falling to the baby-boomer generation and their children to pay for the retirement of not only the earlier generations but also to provide trillions in additional taxes for their own retirement as well.

According to government figures, the Social Security "trust fund" had a surplus on hand of $896 billion at the end of 1999. This is supposed to be reassuringly good news, but it's not. The surplus is a drop in the bucket compared to the level of benefits already promised. Here's the coming scenario according to the 2000 *Annual Report of the Board of Trustees of the Federal Old-Age and Survivors Insurance Fund.*

• **From now through 2014.** At the present time, the taxes being paid into the system by current workers is more than enough to pay the promised benefits to retirees. The money that's not needed for paying benefits gets invested in U.S. Treasury IOUs and carried over to future years, increasing the surplus. Think of it as a family that is able to live within its income and save for the future.

• **From 2015 through 2024.** Matters are projected to continue in this way until 2015, at which time the money going out (to an ever-larger number of retirees) will exceed the money coming in (from an ever-smaller number of workers). At that point, Social Security will have to use some of the interest income it receives from its Treasury IOUs to make up the difference. Our family is now spending all its income, and needs to use part of its interest income to support its standard of living.

• **From 2025 until 2037.** In 2025, the interest income is no longer sufficient to make up the difference. To continue making payments, Social Security will need to draw on the surplus. This has two important implications: (1) the Treasury will need to begin paying off its IOUs, and (2) as the IOUs are paid off and the money distributed to retirees, there are fewer IOUs left in the Social Security fund to earn interest for the

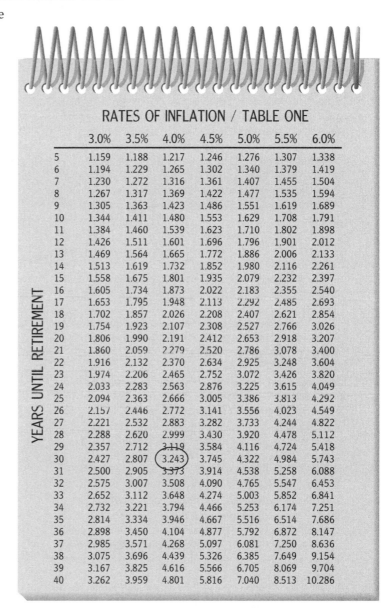

| | RATES OF INFLATION / TABLE ONE | | | | | | |
YEARS UNTIL RETIREMENT		3.0%	3.5%	4.0%	4.5%	5.0%	5.5%	6.0%
	5	1.159	1.188	1.217	1.246	1.276	1.307	1.338
	6	1.194	1.229	1.265	1.302	1.340	1.379	1.419
	7	1.230	1.272	1.316	1.361	1.407	1.455	1.504
	8	1.267	1.317	1.369	1.422	1.477	1.535	1.594
	9	1.305	1.363	1.423	1.486	1.551	1.619	1.689
	10	1.344	1.411	1.480	1.553	1.629	1.708	1.791
	11	1.384	1.460	1.539	1.623	1.710	1.802	1.898
	12	1.426	1.511	1.601	1.696	1.796	1.901	2.012
	13	1.469	1.564	1.665	1.772	1.886	2.006	2.133
	14	1.513	1.619	1.732	1.852	1.980	2.116	2.261
	15	1.558	1.675	1.801	1.935	2.079	2.232	2.397
	16	1.605	1.734	1.873	2.022	2.183	2.355	2.540
	17	1.653	1.795	1.948	2.113	2.292	2.485	2.693
	18	1.702	1.857	2.026	2.208	2.407	2.621	2.854
	19	1.754	1.923	2.107	2.308	2.527	2.766	3.026
	20	1.806	1.990	2.191	2.412	2.653	2.918	3.207
	21	1.860	2.059	2.279	2.520	2.786	3.078	3.400
	22	1.916	2.132	2.370	2.634	2.925	3.248	3.604
	23	1.974	2.206	2.465	2.752	3.072	3.426	3.820
	24	2.033	2.283	2.563	2.876	3.225	3.615	4.049
	25	2.094	2.363	2.666	3.005	3.386	3.813	4.292
	26	2.157	2.446	2.772	3.141	3.556	4.023	4.549
	27	2.221	2.532	2.883	3.282	3.733	4.244	4.822
	28	2.288	2.620	2.999	3.430	3.920	4.478	5.112
	29	2.357	2.712	3.119	3.584	4.116	4.724	5.418
	30	2.427	2.807	3.243	3.745	4.322	4.984	5.743
	31	2.500	2.905	3.373	3.914	4.538	5.258	6.088
	32	2.575	3.007	3.508	4.090	4.765	5.547	6.453
	33	2.652	3.112	3.648	4.274	5.003	5.852	6.841
	34	2.732	3.221	3.794	4.466	5.253	6.174	7.251
	35	2.814	3.334	3.946	4.667	5.516	6.514	7.686
	36	2.898	3.450	4.104	4.877	5.792	6.872	8.147
	37	2.985	3.571	4.268	5.097	6.081	7.250	8.636
	38	3.075	3.696	4.439	5.326	6.385	7.649	9.154
	39	3.167	3.825	4.616	5.566	6.705	8.069	9.704
	40	3.262	3.959	4.801	5.816	7.040	8.513	10.286

coming years. Our family is now beginning to spend the capital that has been providing the essential interest income. A downward spiral has begun.

		Millers	Yourself
RETIREMENT PLANNING WORKSHEET: SECTION 1			
How much annual income will you need during prime time?			
Overview	Step by Step	Millers	Yourself

Overview	Step by Step	Millers	Yourself
In order to project the amount of annual income you are likely to need each year during retirement, we start by considering how your income needs will change as you enter retirement. The good news is that you can expect to maintain approximately the same standard of living you have now in spite of the fact you will have a lower income after you retire. There are several reasons for this:	1. Enter <u>your current before-tax annual income</u>, or if you wish to plan for a higher standard of living than you now enjoy, enter an amount that you believe would provide that standard of living.	$50,000	
1. You won't have work-related expenses such as commuting, eating away from home, and wardrobe maintenance.			
2. You won't have the children to feed, clothe, transport, and educate.	2. Enter <u>your lifestyle maintenance assumption</u>.	×90%	
3. You won't have to pay Social Security and other payroll taxes.			
4. You won't be contributing to your personal and employer's retirement plans.	3. Multiply Item 1 by Item 2. This provides an estimate of how much <u>annual income (before taxes) you will need during retirement</u> to maintain your standard of living.		
5. And, assuming you arrive at retirement debt-free, you won't have home mortgage payments, car payments, or credit card payments to make.			
Of course, as I've already pointed out, you'll be facing increased health care costs, and since you'll have more free time, you're also likely to spend more on recreation. But all in all, most experts say that if your retirement income is around 80% of what you're earning now, you'll be in good shape; however, they warn that you're likely to face financial difficulties if it drops below 50% of what you're now making.		= $45,000	
Let's see how this works. I'm going to pick a family out of the mid-range of the census data and assume we are preparing a projection for them. Let's call them the Millers. The husband and wife are both thirty-five years old and have current income (before taxes) of $50,000 per year. What will their annual income needs be when they retire? To be on the conservative side, I'm going to use 90% as their "lifestyle maintenance" assumption; that is, the Millers' retirement income needs will be equal to 90% of their current level of income. By multiplying the lifestyle maintenance assumption times their current income (90% x $50,000), we learn that the Millers will need to generate $45,000 per year in income (before taxes) during their prime-time years.			
Of course, that's in today's dollars. How can we adjust this number so that it will have the same buying power during retirement that is does today? Continue on to the next page.			

	RETIREMENT PLANNING WORKSHEET: SECTION 2		
	What about the effects of inflation?		
Overview	Step by Step	Millers	Yourself
The Millers' $45,000 will not always buy for them what it can buy today. We must take the $45,000 per year we projected as the amount of annual income the Millers will need during retirement and translate that to a higher number to allow for the fact that the value of the dollar shrinks a little every year. To do that, we refer to the inflation chart on page 243. I'm assuming that long-term inflation will average 4% per year. That's what it was for the 20 years ending in December 1999. You're free to change the inflation assumption if you wish. Because your family's spending pattern is unique, your personal inflation experience will be different from any theoretical number computed for the "typical" American family. Choosing a higher rate, for example, is for the extra cautious person who wants to be doubly careful to arrive at retirement with a sufficient nest egg built up. Choosing a lower rate is for those who think I'm being too pessimistic—after all, inflation averaged just 2.9% annually for the ten years ending in 1999. Since the Millers have thirty years to go before they retire at age sixty-five, we look down the left-hand column until we come to the number "30." Then, we go over three columns to find the number listed under the 4% heading. The number we find is 3.243. Now, here comes the scary part. We multiply $45,000 times 3.243 to learn what the Millers' income will need to be when they retire in thirty years in order to maintain the standard of living they enjoy today. The answer is $145,935 per year! Sort of overwhelming, isn't it? It's difficult to imagine that the day will come when a family would need that much money every year just to maintain a modest lifestyle.	3. From page 244. 4. Enter the rate of inflation assumption which you are making for planning purposes. 5. Enter the number of years remaining until you retire. 6. Using the table on page 243, enter the inflation adjustment factor which reflects your assumption concerning the rate of future inflation and the years remaining until you retire. 7. Multiply Item 3 by Item 6. This is an estimate of the amount of income you will need during your first year of retirement to sustain your desired standard of living.	$45,000 4% inflation 30 years x 3.243 = $145,935	

Will you have enough to sustain you through a normal life expectancy?

Overview	Step by Step	Millers	Yourself

Overview

An essential part of your planning is to come up with a reasonable estimate of how long you (and, if married, your spouse) will live. The table of life expectancies on page 241 is a good starting point. You can make adjustments based on your current state of health and family history.

We use this information to project how much income you'll need during the whole of your retirement years. This is a function of your standard of living, life expectancy, and the rate of inflation after you retire.

The table below has been designed to do the math for you. In the Millers' situation, I'm being cautious and assuming they will live to be ninety. This means their life expectancies after retirement at age sixty-five are another twenty-five years. Continuing to assume inflation of 4%, the table gives us a factor of 43.31.

RATES OF INFLATION / TABLE TWO

LIFE EXPECTANCY AFTER RETIREMENT

Years	3.0%	3.5%	4.0%	4.5%	5.0%	5.5%	6.0%
1	1.03	1.04	1.04	1.05	1.05	1.06	1.06
2	2.09	2.11	2.12	2.14	2.15	2.17	2.18
3	3.18	3.21	3.25	3.28	3.31	3.34	3.37
4	4.31	4.36	4.42	4.47	4.53	4.58	4.64
5	5.47	5.55	5.63	5.72	5.80	5.89	5.98
6	6.66	6.78	6.90	7.02	7.14	7.27	7.39
7	7.89	8.05	8.21	8.38	8.55	8.72	8.90
8	9.16	9.37	9.58	9.80	10.03	10.26	10.49
9	10.46	10.73	11.01	11.29	11.58	11.88	12.18
10	11.81	12.14	12.49	12.84	13.21	13.58	13.97
11	13.19	13.60	14.03	14.46	14.92	15.39	15.87
12	14.62	15.11	15.63	16.16	16.71	17.29	17.88
13	16.09	16.68	17.29	17.93	18.60	19.29	20.02
14	17.60	18.30	19.02	19.78	20.58	21.41	22.28
15	19.16	19.97	20.82	21.72	22.66	23.64	24.67
16	20.76	21.71	22.70	23.74	24.84	26.00	27.21
17	22.41	23.50	24.65	25.86	27.13	28.48	29.91
18	24.12	25.36	26.67	28.06	29.54	31.10	32.76
19	25.87	27.28	28.78	30.37	32.07	33.87	35.79
20	27.68	29.27	30.97	32.78	34.72	36.79	38.99
21	29.54	31.33	33.25	35.30	37.51	39.86	42.39
22	31.45	33.46	35.62	37.94	40.43	43.11	46.00
23	33.43	35.67	38.08	40.69	43.50	46.54	49.82
24	35.46	37.95	40.65	43.57	46.73	50.15	53.86
25	37.55	40.31	(43.31)	46.57	50.11	53.97	58.16
26	39.71	42.76	46.08	49.71	53.67	57.99	62.71
27	41.93	45.29	48.97	52.99	57.40	62.23	67.53
28	44.22	47.91	51.97	56.42	61.32	66.71	72.64
29	46.58	50.62	55.08	60.01	65.44	71.44	78.06
30	49.00	53.43	58.33	63.75	69.76	76.42	83.80

Step by Step

7. From page 245. — **$145,935**

8. Using the life expectancy table on page 241 as a guide, enter the number of years of life after retirement that you have decided to use for financial planning purposes. — **25 years**

9. Enter the inflation assumption that you are making for planning purposes. It can be the same assumption you used in Item 4, or you can raise or lower it if you have a different outlook for the more distant years. — **4% inflation**

10. Using the table at left, enter the inflation adjustment factor that reflects your inflation assumption as well as the years of life expectancy after retirement. — **x 43.31**

11. Multiply Item 7 by Item 10. This is the approximate total spending you anticipate during all of your retirement years. Let's call it your "prime-time wealth." In the Millers' case, this would be the total expected spending for the twenty-five years following retirement. — **$6,320,445**

RETIREMENT PLANNING WORKSHEET: SECTION 4

How much of your "prime-time wealth" will Social Security provide?

Overview	Step by Step	Millers	Yourself
For years, workers have been paying much more in Social Security taxes than was needed to fund the current level of benefits. That's because a surplus was needed in order to take care of the baby-boomers when they retire beginning around 2010. Projections made at the time of the 1983 "reforms" predicted the surplus would peak at a huge $16 trillion before the baby-boomer drawdown began.	12. Enter the amount of your combined annual Social Security benefits as projected in your Social Security Statement (in today's dollars).	His: $15,696 + Hers: $7,848 = $23,544	
Eleven years later the projected surplus had almost vanished. Critics of the 1983 changes said at the time that the surplus was based on several unrealistic assumptions having to do with birth rates, life expectancies, and economic growth. They were proven correct, and the reality is that the benefits will have to be substantially scaled back.	13. Enter the inflation adjustment factor used in Item 6.	x 3.243	
Once a year, an updated Social Security Statement is mailed automatically to workers age 25 or older who are not yet getting Social Security benefits. Your Statement provides you with a record of the contributions credited to your account (be sure to check it for accuracy) and an estimate of what your retirement benefit will be. If you will be retiring in the next ten years, it will likely be fairly accurate. The further you go beyond ten years, however, the more you might want to adjust the estimate downward to allow for economic and political realities.	14. Multiply Item 12 by Item 13. This is the approximate amount of your Social Security benefit during your first year of retirement.	$76,353	
You should get your Statement a few months before your birthday. If you'd rather not wait, you can request a Statement at any time. Call (800) 772-1213 or visit www.ssa.gov to get the ball rolling. While you're there, you can check out the "Benefit Calculators" at www.ssa.gov/oact/anypia/ which will give you an immediate online estimate of what your Statement will show.	15. Enter Social Security's annual cost-of-living increase. You might assume an increase less than the inflation assumption (made in Item 9) in order to reflect the possibility of benefit cutbacks.	3% annual increases	
	16. Using Table Two on the opposite page, enter the inflation adjustment factor that reflects the inflation assumption in Item 15 as well as the years of life expectancy shown in Item 8.	x 37.55	
	17. Multiply Item 14 by Item 16. This is the approximate total amount of Social Security you can anticipate receiving during all of your retirement years.	$2,867,062	

RETIREMENT PLANNING WORKSHEET: SECTION 5
How much of your prime-time wealth will your company's pension provide?

Overview	Step by Step	Millers	Yourself
There are two different varieties of pension plans (which we'll review in chapter 22). One kind is called a "defined-benefit" plan because the focus is on the lifetime benefit you'll ultimately receive. These plans promise to pay you, when you retire, a certain dollar amount every month for as long as you live. If you participate in a defined-benefit plan, your employer is required by law to offer you a summary of the plan that's written in layman's terms. This is called a "summary plan description," and should be readily available from your personnel department. Many companies also provide a personalized employee benefit statement once a year that provides an estimate of how much your monthly retirement check will be. (Plans in the other major category of employer-sponsored retirement benefits are called "defined-contribution" plans because they place their emphasis on how much the employer will put into the plan for you each year. They should not be included in the worksheet at this point—we'll get to those on the next page.) When you reach retirement and the time comes for your monthly pension benefit to be paid, you have several choices as to how you wish it to be calculated. See pages 266-268. If you are currently a participant in a defined-benefit plan, make an appointment with the appropriate person at your company to get your specific questions answered. If you have participated in such a plan in the past at another company, you may have earned vested benefits there as well. Be sure to include them here also unless you have already moved them into a rollover IRA. In that case, enter the value of that account in Step 31.	18. Enter the <u>amount of your annual pension benefit</u>. See your most recent employee benefit statement. 19. If your benefit is "<u>indexed for inflation</u>," enter the factor used in Item 16. Or, if your benefit is <u>not</u> "indexed for inflation," enter the factor used in Item 8. 20. Multiply Item 18 by Item 19. This is the approximate <u>total amount of pension income you can anticipate receiving during all of your retirement years</u>. 21. Enter the <u>amount of your spouse's annual pension benefit</u> from his or her employee benefit statement. 22. If your <u>spouse's benefit</u> is "<u>indexed for inflation</u>," enter the factor used in Item 16. Or, if your spouse's benefit is <u>not</u> "indexed for inflation," enter the factor used in Item 8. 23. Multiply Item 21 by Item 22. This is the approximate <u>total amount of pension income your spouse can anticipate receiving during all of his or her retirement years</u>.	$3,312 25 $82,800 none N/A none	

RETIREMENT PLANNING WORKSHEET: SECTION 6
How much of your prime-time wealth must you provide?

Overview	Step by Step	Millers	Yourself

Overview

In step 27, we learn the amount that you must supply from your own retirement investment strategy. Of course, you don't need to have all your prime-time wealth available on your first day of retirement. After all, it's going to take the rest of your life to spend it all. The question is: How much of your prime-time wealth do you need to have at the outset (knowing that your investments will continue to earn a respectable rate of return after you retire)?

Table Four, shown below, will help you ascertain that amount. It assumes not only that your retirement capital earns a return (see headings which range from 6% to 10%), but also that withdrawals are made from your investment accounts each month to meet current spending needs. The withdrawals are designed to exhaust the investment account by the end of your life expectancy. For example, when you have a remaining life expectancy of twenty-five years, you can withdraw 4.00% of the account value during that year (1 divided by 25). The next year, when you have twenty-four years of life expectancy, you can withdraw 4.17% of the account value (1 divided by 24). And so on. In the Millers' example, I assumed a 7% long-term return during retirement. This is lower than the 9% expected return prior to retirement because they should be taking less risk at this stage of life.

You should understand that this provides only a rough blueprint of what each year's cash flow will be like. The 7% return is an average over a twenty-five-year period. You might start off with a 15% return the first year, or a loss. If a given year's scheduled withdrawal is insufficient to cover that year's needs, you might have to "borrow" from next year and wait for your investment returns to catch up.

RATES OF RETURN DURING RETIREMENT
TABLE FOUR

	Years	6%	7%	8%	9%	10%
LIFE EXPECTANCY	5	0.8368	0.8126	0.7891	0.7665	0.7445
	10	0.7157	0.6764	0.6392	0.6039	0.5704
	15	0.6080	0.5579	0.5115	0.4687	0.4292
	20	0.5129	0.4559	0.4047	0.3587	0.3175
	25	0.4299	0.3694	0.3166	0.2708	0.2311
	30	0.3580	0.2968	0.2452	0.2019	0.1658
	35	0.2963	0.2366	0.1881	0.1489	0.1174
	40	0.2438	0.1873	0.1430	0.1086	0.0822

Step by Step

24. Enter the amount from Item 11. I've been calling this your prime-time wealth. — **$6,320,445**

25. Enter the amount from Item 17. This is the approximate total amount of Social Security you anticipate receiving during all of your retirement years. — **$2,867,062**

26. Enter the sum of Items 20 and 23. This is the approximate total amount of pension income you anticipate receiving during all of your retirement years. — **$82,800**

27. Subtract Items 25 and 26 from Item 24. This is the total amount of your prime-time wealth that you must provide. — **$3,370,583**

28. Enter the average annual rate of return you are assuming your investments will earn during retirement. — **7% rate of return**

29. Enter the factor from Table Four that reflects the life expectancy during retirement (Item 8) and the expected return on investments (Item 28). — **× .3694**

30. Multiply Item 27 by Item 29. This is the amount of capital you should have on hand as you enter retirement. — **$1,245,093**

RETIREMENT PLANNING WORKSHEET: SECTION 7

How much will your current tax-deferred portfolio be worth when you retire?

Overview	Step by Step	Millers	Yourself

Overview

Now that we know your prime-time wealth goal, let's see how far along you are toward achieving it. In this section, we project the current values in any tax-deferred accounts you may have into the future. For the Millers, I'm assuming a 9% average annual rate of return. If you'd like to use a different assumption, see the table below. Using a lower percentage assumption implies a more cautious view, and may require a higher level of savings between now and retirement.

RATES OF RETURN / TABLE FIVE

Years	6%	7%	8%	9%	10%	11%	12%
5	1.34	1.40	1.47	1.54	1.61	1.69	1.76
6	1.42	1.50	1.59	1.68	1.77	1.87	1.97
7	1.50	1.61	1.71	1.83	1.95	2.08	2.21
8	1.59	1.72	1.85	1.99	2.14	2.30	2.48
9	1.69	1.84	2.00	2.17	2.36	2.56	2.77
10	1.79	1.97	2.16	2.37	2.59	2.84	3.11
11	1.90	2.10	2.33	2.58	2.85	3.15	3.48
12	2.01	2.25	2.52	2.81	3.14	3.50	3.90
13	2.13	2.41	2.72	3.07	3.45	3.88	4.36
14	2.26	2.58	2.94	3.34	3.80	4.31	4.89
15	2.40	2.76	3.17	3.64	4.18	4.78	5.47
16	2.54	2.95	3.43	3.97	4.59	5.31	6.13
17	2.69	3.16	3.70	4.33	5.05	5.90	6.87
18	2.85	3.38	4.00	4.72	5.56	6.54	7.69
19	3.03	3.62	4.32	5.14	6.12	7.26	8.61
20	3.21	3.87	4.66	5.60	6.73	8.06	9.65
21	3.40	4.14	5.03	6.11	7.40	8.95	10.80
22	3.60	4.43	5.44	6.66	8.14	9.93	12.10
23	3.82	4.74	5.87	7.26	8.95	11.03	13.55
24	4.05	5.07	6.34	7.91	9.85	12.24	15.18
25	4.29	5.43	6.85	8.62	10.83	13.59	17.00
26	4.55	5.81	7.40	9.40	11.92	15.08	19.04
27	4.82	6.21	7.99	10.25	13.11	16.74	21.32
28	5.11	6.65	8.63	11.17	14.42	18.58	23.88
29	5.42	7.11	9.32	12.17	15.86	20.62	26.75
30	5.74	7.61	10.06	13.27	17.45	22.89	29.96
31	6.09	8.15	10.87	14.46	19.19	25.41	33.56
32	6.45	8.72	11.74	15.76	21.11	28.21	37.58
33	6.84	9.33	12.68	17.18	23.23	31.31	42.09
34	7.25	9.98	13.69	18.73	25.55	34.75	47.14
35	7.69	10.68	14.79	20.41	28.10	38.57	52.80
36	8.15	11.42	15.97	22.25	30.91	42.82	59.14
37	8.64	12.22	17.25	24.25	34.00	47.53	66.23
38	9.15	13.08	18.63	26.44	37.40	52.76	74.18
39	9.70	13.99	20.12	28.82	41.14	58.56	83.08
40	10.29	14.97	21.72	31.41	45.26	65.00	93.05

YEARS UNTIL RETIREMENT

Step by Step

31. Enter the current values of any tax-deferred investment accounts you and your spouse have:
    a. IRAs
    b. 401(k)
    c. 403(b)
    d. Variable annuity
    e. Other
    f. Other

32. Enter the sum of all the accounts listed in Item 31. This is the total amount of tax-deferred capital that you and your spouse currently have working for you.

33. Enter the average annual rate of return you are assuming your investments will earn between now and the year you retire.

34. Using the table at left, enter the rate of return factor that reflects your assumption concerning the future annual rate of growth of your long-term capital (Item 33) over the period of time between now and retirement (Item 5).

35. Multiply Item 32 by Item 34. This is an estimate of the value of your current tax-deferred capital when you reach retirement.

Millers

31. a. $14,552
    b. $32,460

32. $47,012

33. 10% rate of return

34. x 17.45

35. $820,359

RETIREMENT PLANNING WORKSHEET: SECTION 8			
How much will your current taxable holdings be worth when you retire?			
Overview	Step by Step	Millers	Yourself

Now, we calculate the current value in your taxable holdings and estimate their value at the time of your retirement. We will take into account the taxes due on your gains under the assumption they will be paid with funds from these accounts. For the Millers, I'll use the same estimated rate of return of 9% as before. You can use the table below to select another one if you wish. This table differs from the one on page 250 in that it assumes a 34% combined state/federal income tax rate.

RATES OF RETURN / TABLE SIX

Years	6%	7%	8%	9%	10%	11%	12%
5	1.21	1.25	1.29	1.33	1.38	1.42	1.46
6	1.26	1.31	1.36	1.41	1.47	1.52	1.58
7	1.31	1.37	1.43	1.50	1.56	1.63	1.70
8	1.36	1.44	1.51	1.59	1.67	1.75	1.84
9	1.42	1.50	1.59	1.68	1.78	1.88	1.99
10	1.47	1.57	1.67	1.78	1.89	2.02	2.14
11	1.53	1.64	1.76	1.89	2.02	2.16	2.31
12	1.59	1.72	1.85	2.00	2.15	2.32	2.50
13	1.66	1.80	1.95	2.12	2.30	2.49	2.69
14	1.72	1.88	2.06	2.24	2.45	2.67	2.91
15	1.79	1.97	2.16	2.38	2.61	2.86	3.14
16	1.86	2.06	2.28	2.52	2.78	3.07	3.39
17	1.94	2.16	2.40	2.67	2.96	3.29	3.65
18	2.01	2.25	2.52	2.83	3.16	3.53	3.94
19	2.09	2.36	2.66	2.99	3.37	3.79	4.26
20	2.17	2.47	2.80	3.17	3.59	4.06	4.59
21	2.26	2.58	2.95	3.36	3.83	4.36	4.96
22	2.35	2.70	3.10	3.56	4.08	4.67	5.35
23	2.44	2.83	3.27	3.77	4.35	5.01	5.77
24	2.54	2.96	3.44	3.99	4.64	5.38	6.23
25	2.64	3.09	3.62	4.23	4.94	5.77	6.72
26	2.74	3.24	3.81	4.48	5.27	6.19	7.26
27	2.85	3.39	4.01	4.75	5.62	6.63	7.83
28	2.97	3.54	4.22	5.03	5.99	7.12	8.45
29	3.08	3.71	4.45	5.33	6.38	7.63	9.12
30	3.21	3.88	4.68	5.65	(6.80)	8.19	9.84
31	3.33	4.06	4.93	5.98	7.25	8.78	10.62
32	3.47	4.24	5.19	6.34	7.73	9.42	11.46
33	3.60	4.44	5.46	6.71	8.24	10.10	12.37
34	3.75	4.64	5.75	7.11	8.79	10.84	13.35
35	3.89	4.86	6.05	7.54	9.36	11.62	14.41
36	4.05	5.08	6.37	7.98	9.98	12.47	15.55
37	4.21	5.32	6.71	8.46	10.64	13.37	16.78
38	4.37	5.56	7.07	8.96	11.34	14.34	18.11
39	4.55	5.82	7.44	9.49	12.09	15.38	19.54
40	4.73	6.09	7.83	10.06	12.89	16.50	21.09

YEARS UNTIL RETIREMENT

Step by Step

36. Enter the current values of any taxable investment accounts that you and your spouse may have that are not part of your contingency fund or set aside for a special purpose like college or house purchase:
   a. Bank savings/CDs
   b. Money market funds — **$ 3,188**
   c. Mutual funds
   d. Brokerage accounts — **$ 8,524**
   e. Other
   f. Other

37. Enter the sum of all the accounts listed in Item 36. This is the total amount of taxable investments that you and your spouse currently have working for you. — **$ 11,712**

38. Using the table at left, enter the rate of return factor that reflects your assumption concerning the future annual rate of growth of your long-term capital (Item 33) over the period of time between now and retirement (Item 5). — **× 6.80**

39. Multiply Item 37 by Item 38. This is an estimate of the value of your current taxable holdings when you reach retirement. — **$79,642**

How much should you save each year to meet your retirement goal?

Overview	Step by Step	Millers	Yourself

Overview

Your final step is to calculate how much you need to save in the future in order to arrive at retirement day with the amount of capital needed. If the amount computed in step 43 is a positive number, you're already in great shape. Unfortunately, most of us need to continue adding to our retirement savings. Table Seven will help you determine the annual amount which you need to add each year to a tax-deferred account (it assumes no taxes are paid on the returns earned).

RATES OF RETURN / TABLE SEVEN

Years	6%	7%	8%	9%	10%	11%	12%
5	17.22%	16.80%	16.39%	15.99%	15.60%	15.22%	14.85%
6	13.92%	13.51%	13.11%	12.72%	12.34%	11.98%	11.63%
7	11.57%	11.16%	10.78%	10.40%	10.04%	9.69%	9.35%
8	9.81%	9.42%	9.04%	8.68%	8.33%	7.99%	7.67%
9	8.45%	8.07%	7.70%	7.35%	7.01%	6.69%	6.38%
10	7.37%	6.99%	6.64%	6.30%	5.98%	5.67%	5.38%
11	6.48%	6.12%	5.78%	5.45%	5.14%	4.85%	4.57%
12	5.76%	5.40%	5.07%	4.75%	4.45%	4.17%	3.91%
13	5.14%	4.80%	4.47%	4.17%	3.88%	3.62%	3.37%
14	4.62%	4.28%	3.97%	3.68%	3.40%	3.15%	2.91%
15	4.17%	3.84%	3.54%	3.26%	3.00%	2.75%	2.53%
16	3.78%	3.46%	3.17%	2.90%	2.65%	2.42%	2.21%
17	3.44%	3.13%	2.85%	2.59%	2.35%	2.13%	1.93%
18	3.14%	2.84%	2.57%	2.32%	2.09%	1.88%	1.69%
19	2.88%	2.58%	2.32%	2.08%	1.86%	1.66%	1.49%
20	2.64%	2.36%	2.10%	1.87%	1.66%	1.48%	1.31%
21	2.43%	2.15%	1.91%	1.69%	1.49%	1.31%	1.15%
22	2.24%	1.97%	1.73%	1.52%	1.33%	1.17%	1.02%
23	2.07%	1.81%	1.58%	1.38%	1.20%	1.04%	0.90%
24	1.91%	1.66%	1.44%	1.25%	1.08%	0.93%	0.80%
25	1.77%	1.53%	1.32%	1.13%	0.97%	0.83%	0.71%
26	1.64%	1.41%	1.20%	1.03%	0.87%	0.74%	0.63%
27	1.52%	1.30%	1.10%	0.93%	0.79%	0.66%	0.56%
28	1.42%	1.20%	1.01%	0.85%	0.71%	0.59%	0.49%
29	1.32%	1.11%	0.92%	0.77%	0.64%	0.53%	0.44%
30	1.23%	1.02%	0.85%	0.70%	(0.58%)	0.48%	0.39%
31	1.14%	0.95%	0.78%	0.64%	0.52%	0.43%	0.35%
32	1.07%	0.88%	0.72%	0.58%	0.47%	0.38%	0.31%
33	1.00%	0.81%	0.66%	0.53%	0.43%	0.34%	0.28%
34	0.93%	0.75%	0.61%	0.49%	0.39%	0.31%	0.25%
35	0.87%	0.70%	0.56%	0.44%	0.35%	0.28%	0.22%
36	0.82%	0.65%	0.51%	0.41%	0.32%	0.25%	0.19%
37	0.76%	0.60%	0.47%	0.37%	0.29%	0.22%	0.17%
38	0.71%	0.56%	0.44%	0.34%	0.26%	0.20%	0.15%
39	0.67%	0.52%	0.40%	0.31%	0.24%	0.18%	0.14%
40	0.63%	0.48%	0.37%	0.28%	0.22%	0.16%	0.12%

YEARS UNTIL RETIREMENT

Step by Step

40. Enter the amount from Item 35. This is the estimated value of your current tax-deferred investments when you reach retirement. — **$820,359**

41. Enter the amount from Item 39. This is the estimated value of your current taxable investments when you reach retirement. — **$79,642**

42. Enter the amount from Item 30. This is the amount of your prime-time wealth that you must provide from your retirement investment strategy. — **$1,245,093**

43. Add Items 40 and 41 and subtract Item 42. This is your estimated shortfall if you do not continue adding to your retirement savings in future years. — **– $345,092**

44. Using the table at left, enter the annual savings growth factor that reflects your assumption concerning the future rate of growth of your capital (Item 33) over the period of time between now and retirement (Item 5). — **x .58%**

45. Multiply Item 43 by Item 44. This is an estimate of the amount of new savings you need to add to your tax-deferred accounts each year. — **$2,002**

• **2037 and later.** The surplus is gone; the trust fund is empty. All the IOUs have all been paid (don't ask me where the Treasury got the money) and the money spent. There is no interest income. And the tax money coming in covers only about three-fourths of the need. Our spendthrift family is broke.

Numerous reforms are being floated as ways to remedy the system.

• **Increase payroll taxes again.** A former chief actuary for the Social Security Administration estimated that individual payroll taxes would have to be raised from their present 12.4% rate to more than 40% just to pay all the benefits currently being promised. Is it realistic to think that the next generation will tolerate increases of that magnitude? Should they? Not a chance.

• **Slowing benefit growth.** Social Security is already a terrible investment for today's workers under age fifty. Reducing benefits would make it even worse. According to the *Wall Street Journal*, eliminating the deficit without increasing taxes would require that "Social Security would pay out 14% less across-the-board compared with what is currently promised by 2020 and up to 30% less by 2070."

• **Means testing.** This involves requiring individuals to pass a test concerning their annual income before granting them full benefits. One such proposal suggests that benefits should start being reduced for anyone who enjoys an annual retirement income of $40,000, and eliminated entirely if the income exceeds $120,000. This is a truly terrible idea because it would: (1) undermine public support for the Social Security program by making it clear that it is just another welfare program where only the "needy" would receive full benefits; (2) discourage hard work, saving, and an attitude of self-reliance because your other retirement accounts would be used against you to deprive you of benefits that would be available only to those who weren't as frugal or farsighted; and (3) summarily break the promises of the past sixty years, further undermining respect for the law. It's an evil thing to force people to pay all their working lives into such a system, continually reassuring them that their benefits will be there when they retire, and then defrauding them at the last minute.

• **Privatization.** There have been several proposals that would allow workers to divert part of their Social Security taxes to an account similar to an IRA where they would have control over how it is invested. In return, they would surrender part of their future Social Security benefits. Chile pioneered this years ago when faced with a similar dilemma, and it has worked well there. Many other countries are studying Chile's results with an eye toward applying a similar strategy. There are many variations on this theme, and while the details differ, it seems inevitable that some form of privatization will be included in any long-term solution. Since this is where the action will likely be, I encourage you to read carefully any articles you see on this topic in order to stay informed.

Recommended Resource

<u>Social Security, Medicare, and Pensions: The Sourcebook for Older Americans</u>

by Joseph L. Matthews

This helpful book guides you through the maze of federal income and benefit programs. In plain language, it explains how to keep from missing out on income and coverage and how to collect all benefits due. It describes the changes in the Medicare system now that the Catastrophic Coverage Act has been repealed, and explains all the rules senior citizens need to know.

Pastors and Social Security

"The decision to withdraw from the Social Security system must be made solely on the basis of a pastor's conscientious objection to Social Security as a form of government welfare or assistance, and is not allowed under any other circumstances. There are also financial ramifications from that decision, and although they cannot be part of the decision, must be dealt with as a result of withdrawing. If a pastor elects to withdraw from Social Security, he needs to discipline himself and save and invest in an alternate retirement plan, as well as provide disability insurance in case he becomes unable to perform his duties for medical reasons."
– Larry Burkett

**Online Retirement
Planning Aids**

www.soundmindinvesting.com/
vsection/v_tools/index.htm

university.smartmoney.com/
Departments/Retirement401k/
index.cfm?microsite=retire

www.quicken.com/
retirement/planner/

moneycentral.msn.com/
retire/home.asp

www.financialengines.com/

Today's workers carry the triple burden of (1) paying far more in Social Security taxes than any previous generation, (2) waiting longer to collect than any previous generation, and (3) retiring with lower after-tax benefits than any previous generation. As unfair as this is, tomorrow's workers, our children, might have to pay even more, wait even longer, and receive even less. And that's why the truth about Social Security is indeed outrageous.

In light of the uncertainties surrounding the level of Social Security benefits after 2014, receiving significant support from the private retirement plans sponsored by your employer is all the more critical. A basic understanding of their strengths and weaknesses is essential if you are to plan realistically. We begin our look at such plans in the next chapter.

Bear in mind that the projections in the worksheet . . .

. . . are based on the assumption that you will live to a specific age. If the end of your (earthly) life comes earlier than you had assumed, there will be money on hand that you won't need. It can be left to your heirs and the Lord's work. If you die "on schedule," you and your money will run out at the same time. If you live longer than you had expected, you'll have a problem. There are two ways to deal with this "risk." One is to pick a very long life expectancy (e.g., 95 or 100). That way, you would be less likely to outlive your money. A second way, assuming you own your house, is to sell it or take out a "reverse mortgage" in order to create additional cash flow.

If all this seems a bit overwhelming, don't despair.

Inflation can be harnessed to work for you as well as against you. Before Section Five is completed, you'll have been given enough information to enable you to overcome three of the four most common elements of financial failure:

•**A failure to inquire.** Many are ignorant of the serious financial implications of our changing society and how they will be affected.

•**A failure to learn.** Once made aware, they may still lack the know-how needed to begin putting their financial house in order.

•**A failure to plan.** Even informed, knowledgeable people can let years go by without formulating goals and a strategy for achieving them.

But after I inform you of the seriousness of the situation, teach you the basics of survival, and lead you through the planning process, there's still one element that only you can overcome:

•**A failure to act.** Procrastination can be the greatest deterrent to reaching your financial goals. If you're like I was as a child, acting as if you'll never grow old, you've been losing valuable time. Commit yourself now to making the sacrifices needed to put your family's finances on a solid foundation. ◆

CHAPTER PREVIEW

Your Pension at Work

I. **Employer-sponsored pension plans that promise to pay a specific dollar amount when you retire are called "defined benefit" plans.**

   A. There are usually eligibility requirements to be met in terms of the length of time you've been with the company before you can participate in the plan.

   B. The amount of your retirement benefit is computed according to a formula that takes many variables into account. Among them are your salary, age at retirement, years with the company, Social Security benefits, and the survivors' benefit you select.

   C. You should fully understand the circumstances under which you will receive a retirement benefit and how the benefit will be computed.

II. **Employer-sponsored pension plans that pay specific dollar amounts into your retirement account each year are called "defined-contribution" plans.**

   A. These plans make no promises as to how much your benefit will be when you retire. Your retirement benefit will ultimately be determined by the amount and frequency of annual contributions and the investment performance experienced in your account.

   B. Under such plans the risk of poor investment returns rests with the employee rather than the employer. That's why employees generally have significant control over the investment portfolios.

   C. There are a variety of these plans with differing contribution requirements, limitations, and employer matching features. The 401(k) plan is by far the most common. We discuss the key features of the major kinds of plans.

   D. When you are ready to withdraw your benefits, these plans provide three alternative methods. Each has its own advantages, depending on your personal income and tax situation at that time.

Additional Information on
Defined Benefit Plans
www.pueblo.gsa.gov/
cic_text/money/secure-4life/
secure-pension.htm

Although the government itself can change its rules anytime it wants and arbitrarily reduce . . .

. . . the Social Security benefits you've been "contributing" to for a working lifetime, it won't let *your employer* do that to you. After all, that wouldn't be fair. So let's look at employer-sponsored pension plans to see what help you can expect from your company. First, you should understand that there are two different kinds of pension plans. One kind promises only to put a certain amount aside for you each year and makes no projections as to the amount of your ultimate monthly benefit. This kind is called a "defined-contribution" plan, and it comes in a bewildering array of alphabet-like names such as SEP-IRA, MPP, 401(k), and 403(b). We'll look at these plans later in the chapter.

For now, let's concentrate on the other type of pension plan, the kind that has historically covered the greatest number of employees. According to U.S. government numbers, they covered about 43 million American workers and retirees in 2000.

These plans promise to pay you, when you retire, a certain dollar amount every month for as long as you live . . .

. . . however, they promise nothing about how much money your company will put aside each year to accomplish this (other than to observe certain minimum federal requirements). These plans are called "defined benefit" plans because the focus is on the *lifetime monthly benefit* you'll ultimately receive. Under this arrangement, the employer carries the burden of where the money for the contributions comes from as well as how well the investments do between now and your retirement.

The first barrier standing between you and your monthly pension check is meeting the eligibility requirements. Just because you've been hired doesn't mean you immediately qualify for a company's retirement plan. Usually they require (1) that you've reached a certain age, and (2) that you have been with the company for a certain period of time before you qualify to join the plan. It is customary that an employee must be at least twenty-one years old and have been with the company at least one year.

Once you're eligible, what you really want to know is . . .

. . . how much is my monthly benefit going to be when I retire? That depends on several factors. Each is fairly simple; let's take them one at a time.

• **Salary formula.** The goal of a monthly pension check is to help replace the earnings lost when you retire. That means your benefit is based primarily on the amount of your annual earnings while you were still working. Some formulas take an average of your earnings from all the years you worked for the company. Presumably, the earlier years were not as well paying, so this is not as favorable to you as a plan that uses a formula based on your final year(s) of service.

• **Years of service.** People who spend their entire career with the same company receive more than those who come along later. Your benefit is affected by the number of years you work for your employer. But how many hours are needed to constitute a "year of service"? Some plans may require 500 hours in a twelve-consecutive-month period, whereas others require 1,000 hours. Or what if you worked for twenty years, left for two years, and returned for another eighteen years? Do you get credit for thirty-eight years or just the last eighteen years? And does it matter why you left for those two years? There are countless variations on this theme that can affect your benefit.

• **Vesting requirements.** When can you know for sure that you're guaranteed to receive at least some pension benefit from your employer? The day you start to work? The year you qualify to join the plan? After three years with the company? That's where the concept of "vesting" comes in. It means you have an absolute right to receive some money from a retirement plan, even if you resign or are fired. You're entitled to it no matter what.

Some plans call for "graded vesting," where you receive a right to a pension gradually (for example, 20% after three years, 40% after four years, and so on). Others provide for what is called "cliff vesting," an all-or-nothing approach where, for example, you could become 100% vested after five years but be entitled to nothing if you leave before then. The most favorable is "vesting upon entry" where you must wait for two years before qualifying to participate in the plan, but are immediately 100% vested upon entry. This is especially helpful to working women who, on average, change jobs more frequently than men.

• **Normal retirement age.** Most plans use formulas that consider sixty-five as the normal retirement age. If you choose to work past sixty-five (federal law prohibits age discrimination rules that would *require* you to retire before age seventy), will your plan give you credit for the additional years worked? Or what if you wanted to take early retirement—how much will that reduce your monthly pension check? The rules governing these matters vary from plan to plan.

• **Social Security considerations.** So-called "integrated plans" deduct a portion of your monthly Social Security check from your monthly benefit check. Remember that your employer has already paid hefty Social Security taxes. From his point of view, it seems reasonable that the company retirement plan formula recognize that you are receiving Social Security benefits to which the company has already contributed.

• **Survivors' benefits.** As an alternative to the basic "monthly check for life" benefit, federal law requires most plans to offer you another approach:

a joint and survivor annuity. If this is selected, the monthly benefit check doesn't stop coming when you die; it goes instead to your spouse (or whoever you have named in the annuity). The trade-off is that your pension will be 10%–20% lower than it otherwise would be—after all, it has to last for two lifetimes now instead of just one—and the amount of the monthly check is cut in half when you pass on. Even so, it's good to know that your spouse will still be provided for.

Armed with this information, you might now be wondering how the plan at your company . . .

. . . measures up in these various areas. If you aren't sure, it's time to find out! And don't worry about how you'll ever get your thoughts together in order to ask the right questions. Your employer is required by law to offer every participant a summary of the plan that's written in layman's terms. This is called a "summary plan description" and should be readily available from your personnel department. Ask for one. It will explain all of the above and lots more.

Many companies also provide a personalized "employee benefit statement" once a year that explains the amount of benefits you've earned to date and provides an estimate of how much your monthly retirement check will be. Other items that you're entitled to receive upon request include: the "summary annual report" (your plan's balance sheet), the Form 5500 (your plan's tax return and an excellent source of information concerning its financial health), and the retirement plan document itself (in case you happen to enjoy digging through page after page of mind-numbing legalese).

So far, we've been talking about retirement plans that promise to pay, upon retirement, a certain dollar amount every month for as long as you live. Under that arrangement, the employer makes all the contributions into the plan plus carries the burden of how well the investments perform until your retirement.

GOOD QUESTIONS TO ASK YOUR COMPANY ABOUT YOUR BENEFITS

❑ What do I have to do to participate in the plan?

❑ Do I contribute money, and if so, does the company match my contributions?

❑ What is the vesting schedule? That is, when will I be partially versus fully vested?

❑ What are the investments in the plan?

❑ Do I get to decide how the investments in my account are allocated among the various options?

❑ How do I make changes to the allocations?

❑ How quickly is my contribution deposited in my account?

❑ If a defined-benefit plan, is it federally insured?

❑ Can I borrow or withdraw money before I retire?

❑ Does the plan include death or disability benefits?

❑ What happens if I take early retirement?

❑ What happens if I work past the normal retirement age?

There is another major category of employer-sponsored retirement plans. They are called "defined-contribution" plans because . . .

. . . they place their emphasis on how much (if any) the employer will put into the plan for you each year. No promises are made with respect to how much your account will be worth when you retire. In this respect, they are like IRAs.

The advantage to employers of this approach is that *you* bear the investment risk between now and retirement rather than your company. If the investments do great, you'll have a healthy amount in the plan at retirement; if they perform poorly, you must make do with a lesser amount. This shift of the investment risk from the employer to you is significant; you no longer can "count on" having a specific monthly income. You should look at it as an opportunity! Here is another area that is now under your control where your Sound Mind strategy can help shape a balanced long-term portfolio that will be personalized to your specific goals and risk tolerance.

Over the years, Congress has created several varieties of defined contribution plans. I've listed them in a table on the next page to give you an overview of the possibilities. Many companies have more than one of these plans in place in order to help you take the fullest advantage of the tax-sheltering possibilities. Though I cannot review all the complexities, the table will provide a general idea of the kinds of plans your employer may offer. Make an appointment with the appropriate person at your company to get your specific questions answered.

By far the most popular of these is the 401(k) plan.

About 75% of companies with 100 or more employees sponsor a 401(k) plan. In such a plan, employees elect to contribute (via payroll withholding) a portion of their paycheck to a tax-deferred investment account set up in their name. Here are the primary features:

• Contributions are tax-deductible in the year they're made.

However, there are limits imposed that affect the maximum amount you can contribute. According to current IRS guidelines (periodically adjusted for inflation), the most a 401(k) plan can permit you to contribute is $10,500, or 15% of your salary, whichever is less. Your employer can elect to apply even more stringent limitations.

• Employees control how their money is invested.

However, they usually must choose from among a lineup of stock, bond, and money market funds selected by the employer. This limits the flexibility of the employee to invest in the funds or securities of his or her choice. To offset this drawback, many plans are beginning to offer a "self-directed" option which allows you to enter buying and selling instructions through a broker, thus opening up a vast range of investment choices.

Employee Stock Ownership Plans

ESOPs are similar to profit-sharing plans except you receive shares in your company's stock rather than a portion of company profits. The number of shares you receive is based on your salary, typically ranging in value from 5% to 25% of your annual compensation. Taxes usually aren't due until you leave the company or sell the shares.

403(b) Plans

A 403(b) plan is a retirement plan for employees of non-profit or tax-exempt organizations such as schools, hospitals, churches, charities, and ministries. They are sufficiently similar to 401(k) plans that eligible participants in these plans can learn much about how best to use them by reading the information in this chapter. Before investing money, however, it would be best to read the plan description for your 403(b). Both plans take their names from the section in the tax code in which they are regulated.

401(k) Web Resources
www.401kafe.com/index.html

www.smartmoney.com/retirement/401k/

www.quicken.com/retirement/401k/advice/

www.timyounkin.com/

AN OVERVIEW OF THE MAJOR KINDS
OF DEFINED-CONTRIBUTION PLANS

Your company may offer one or more of the following defined-contribution pension plans. These are the most common types; however, there are many variations depending on the way your company's plan was initially structured. This is a highly technical area, and this table is merely intended to provide an overview. For more information on your specific rights and benefits, contact your company's Human Resources department.

Type of Plan	Money Purchase	Profit Sharing	SEP IRA	401(k) Plan	403(b) Plan
Brief summary	Your company agrees to contribute a certain percentage of your salary every year (even in unprofitable years). Can be either a corporate plan or, if employer is not incorporated, can be a Keogh plan.	Your company annually contributes a portion of its profits, if any, into a fund for employees. Can be either a corporate plan or, if employer is not incorporated, can be a Keogh plan.	Simplified Employee Pensions use a form of employee IRAs rather than set up a separate company plan. Primarily funded by your employer, these accounts are highly portable if you change jobs.	A salary reduction plan where you decide how much of your salary to put in (up to a maximum level that is raised annually for inflation).The amount you contribute is not counted as taxable income.	Similar to the 401(k) plan, but limited to employees of public schools, government agencies, hospitals, religious organizations, and other nonprofit institutions.
What is the most you can put in each year?	You don't contribute.	You don't contribute.	You don't contribute.	$10,500	$10,500
What is the most your employer can put in each year?	25% of compensation or $30,000, whichever is less.	15% of compensation or $25,500, whichever is less. Your contribution plus employer's can't exceed $30,000 or 25% of your salary (after deducting your contribution), whichever is less.	15% of compensation or $25,500, whichever is less. See sidebar on page 261 for mention of a second kind of IRA that has salary reduction features similar to a 401(k).	Can match a percentage of your salary deferral. Your contribution plus employer's can't exceed $30,000 or 25% of your salary (after deducting your contribution), whichever is less.	Can match a percentage of your salary deferral up to 100%. Your contribution plus employer's can't exceed $30,000 or 25% of your salary (after deducting your contribution), whichever is less.
Are annual contributions fixed at a certain amount?	Yes. The salary contribution formula must be followed each year.	No. The amount contributed can change from year to year.	No. The amount contributed can change from year to year.	No. The amount contributed can change from year to year.	No. The amount contributed can change from year to year.
When do you receive ownership rights to your pension?	Typically 3-7 years.	Typically 3-7 years.	Immediately.	Immediately on your contributions, but at the employer's discretion on any matching amounts.	Immediately on your contributions, but at the employer's discretion on any matching amounts.
Can you borrow from your account?	Some plans allow borrowing at the employer's discretion.	Some plans allow borrowing at the employer's discretion.	No.	At the employer's discretion, but generally yes.	At the employer's discretion.

• All investment income and capital gains in the account grow tax-deferred.

However, withdrawals are taxed at ordinary income tax rates in the year they're made. Thus, capital gains ultimately lose their advantageous tax status when occuring within a 401(k) account.

• Payroll deduction provides a disciplined, consistent approach to saving for retirement.

However, once you put the money in, you normally can't get it out before age 59½ without paying a 10% early withdrawal penalty (plus the customary income taxes due on plan withdrawals as mentioned above). Most plans, however, do allow employees to borrow from their 401(k) accounts.

• Most employers (over 90%) match their employee's contributions to some degree. For example, a company might contribute 50 cents for every $1 the employee puts in. This is the feature that makes 401(k)s so attractive; the employer match provides an automatic and immediate profit on your contribution.

However, employers who offer matching programs put a ceiling on the amount they will match, say up to 6% of the employee's income. Thus, money contributed above the ceiling will not be matched. Furthermore, many plans require employees to remain with the employer for a certain number of years before the matching contributions *vest*, that is, become the property of the employee. They do this to discourage employee turnover.

The 401(k) is becoming the bedrock of our private pension system.

At the end of 1999, 34 million American workers had investments worth $1.7 trillion in their 401(k) accounts. Based on those numbers, the average 401(k) account was worth about $50,000. According to a study by the Profit Sharing/401(k) Council of America, about 80% of those eligible to participate in a 401(k) do so. Yet, it's been estimated that 95% of those who participate in a 401(k) plan contribute less than they are allowed.

If possible, I encourage you to participate in your company's 401(k) plan at least to the point where you take full advantage of any employer-matching funds. If you're still working on getting your consumer debt paid off (Level 1) or building your emergency fund (Level 2), that may not be possible immediately, but it should be one of your intermediate-term financial goals. If your 401(k) plan doesn't offer a matching feature, or if you can afford to contribute beyond the maximum matching percentage, then you will want to weigh the remaining advantages of 401(k)s versus the pros and cons of IRAs (see next chapter) before deciding which should have the priority in your retirement planning.

What happens to your 401(k) account should you change jobs?

Your first priority should be to repay any money you may have borrowed from your 401(k) plan account. Otherwise, it will be considered a distribu-

SIMPLE–IRAs

Firms with fewer than 100 employees that do not otherwise offer a retirement plan can establish a Savings Incentive Match Plan for Employees IRA. These are not to be confused with the regular SEP IRAs described in the graphic on page 260. In a SIMPLE-IRA, employees may make tax deductible contributions up to a maximum of $6,000 annually. The employer must agree to one of two matching formulas: (1) matches 100% of the employee's contribution (up to 3% of their total compensation), or (2) contributes 2% of employee's compensation, whether they contribute or not (up to $3,200 maximum per year). Other than the higher contributions allowed, SIMPLE-IRAs are governed by the same rules as a traditional IRA. Furthermore, employees who participate in a SIMPLE-IRA can also contribute to a traditional or Roth IRA, subject to the income limitation tests.

Separation From Service

While most withdrawals from a 401(k) prior to age 59½ result in a 10% penalty, there is one important exception. If you are 55 or older and leave your employer (voluntarily or otherwise), you can withdraw part or all of your 401(k) money penalty-free. However, if you roll the money into an IRA, you lose the ability to make these earlier-than-usual withdrawals. This is an important and often overlooked difference between 401(k)s and IRAs, so plan carefully before rolling the money over to an IRA if you're 55 or older.

tion and applicable taxes and penalties will be assessed. Check with your current employer immediately to see how much time you have to repay the loan and avoid this.

As for the longer-term considerations, you have several options and they can vary dramatically in terms of the investment and tax consequences. Two of them should be avoided if at all possible because they immediately bring the tax man into the picture:

• **Cash it out in a lump sum.** You'll have to pay income taxes on the entire amount, plus a 10% penalty for premature withdrawal if you're not at least 59½. (There's an exception—see sidebar at bottom of previous page.) As a down payment on your tax bill, 20% of the account will be withheld and forwarded to the government.

• **Annuitize it.** This means to sign up for a series of regular withdrawals, usually monthly, based on your life expectancy using IRS tables. The withdrawals are designed to last through retirement, but if you change your mind and prefer to leave the money in your retirement account for further tax-deferred compounding, they can be discontinued after five years or upon reaching age 59 ½, whichever is later. You'll still owe income taxes, but you'll avoid the 10% penalty even if you're younger than 55. For more on annuitizing, see page 279.

The remaining options avoid any immediate tax liability. They leave the money in a tax-deferred account where it can continue to be invested and grow tax-deferred. The primary difference is where the account is.

• **Move it to an IRA.** This is usually your best option. It gives you the most flexibility in terms of investment choices and tax planning. You can transfer it to either an existing IRA into which you've been making contributions, or to a Rollover IRA (also called a Conduit IRA). Moving to an IRA preserves the option of converting to a Roth IRA should that be advisable in years to come. A Rollover IRA also preserves the right to later move the funds back into a future employer's 401(k). Why might you want to do that? Three possibilities: (1) If you were born before 1936, 401(k) withdrawals qualify for forward averaging, a potential tax advantage when large amounts are involved; (2) You can borrow from a 401(k) account (not that I encourage *that*!); (3) Creditors cannot come after assets in a 401(k) account. None of the above applies to IRAs (although some states do extend creditor protection to IRAs).

If you choose this route, it's best if you carry out a trustee-to-trustee transfer where the money goes straight from the old plan to the IRA without passing through your hands. This avoids the possibility that you might end up with an unexpected tax bill by running afoul of the rules governing transfers where the employee temporarily takes possesion of the money (see page 268).

• **Leave it in your former employer's 401(k) plan.** If your account is worth $5,000 or more, you have this option. You wouldn't elect this, of course, if you've been unhappy with the investment choices available. Nor if you contemplate borrowing from the plan in the future, because borrowing by former employees is typically not permitted. The advantage of this approach is its simplicity. It also is the only way to keep the tax deferral going on any after-tax contributions you might have made.

• **Move it to your new employer's 401(k) plan.** The biggest consideration is whether you find the investment choices in the plan to be attractive. If so, check to see if there's a waiting period before new employees are allowed to transfer in. Again, use the trustee-to-trustee transfer approach rather than personally taking possession of the money.

Federal workers participate in a retirement plan . . .

. . . similar to a 401(k) arrangement—the Thrift Savings Plan. Those hired after 1983 are covered by the Federal Employees Retirement System (FERS), which means, among other things, that the government matches employee contributions to the Thrift Plan in a very generous way.

First, the government automatically contributes an amount equal to 1% of salary. Second, for every dollar employees contribute up to 3% of their salary, the government matches it with a dollar. Third, for every dollar employees contribute above 3% of salary (up to 5%), the government puts in 50 cents. By contributing 5%, therefore, employees have doubled their money just by virtue of the government's matching funds. Finally, employees can contribute another 5% of salary (raising their total contribution to 10%, but not to exceed $10,000) which, although not matched by the government, does provide an additional tax deduction and long-term tax-deferred compounding of investment returns.

According to government figures, 15% of FERS participants don't contribute to the Thrift Plan. In light of the generous matching provisions, this is surprisingly shortsighted behavior. Their goal should be to contribute 3% of their salary at a minimum, and 5% if at all possible. Federal workers hired in 1983 and earlier fall under the Civil Service Retirement System (CSRS). While that plan doesn't offer matching funds for the Thrift Plan, it does

MANAGING THRIFT PLAN ALLOCATIONS

For Federal Workers	For Purposes of Assessing Risk When Rebalancing SMI Portfolio
Proposed New I Fund To invest in common stocks of foreign companies. Would be similar in performance to: Morgan Stanley EAFE Index	Treat as International Stock
Proposed New S Fund To invest in common stocks of smaller, emerging growth companies. Would be similar in performance to: Vanguard Index Extended Market	Treat as Stock Category 4.
The C Fund Invests in common stocks of large, blue chip companies. Similar in performance to: Vanguard Index 500	Treat as Stock Category 2.
The F Fund Invests in corporate, government, and mortgage-backed securities. Similar in performance to: Vanguard Bond Index / Total Bond Market	Treat as Bond Category 2.
The G Fund Invests in short-term Treasury securities. Similar in performance to: Money market funds listed in Level Two column.	Treat as Bond Category 1.

allow workers to contribute to it. Check to see when the next open season for signing up or raising your contribution arrives.

Other points of interest concerning the Thrift Plan: You can borrow from your account for purposes of buying a house, paying education or medical expenses, or alleviating a temporary financial hardship. When you leave your job with the government, you can roll your Thrift account assets into your personal IRA.

In 2000, the Thrift Plan offered just three investment choices; however, the government was scheduled to add two excellent new options—a fund that invests in the stocks of small companies as well as one that invests internationally—in 2001. If you want to change the way your money is currently allocated, you can authorize transfers by phoning (504) 255-8777, or via their website at www.tsp.gov. You're allowed to make transfers between your investments monthly. To make sure you're getting the most from your Thrift Plan opportunities, get a copy of *Your Thrift Savings Plan,* a privately produced, comprehensive guidebook for both FERS and CSRS employees. The cost is $17.95 postage-paid. Call (800) 989-3363.

For purposes of controlling risk, it's important to include your retirement plan investments as part of your overall portfolio.

This requires that you understand where the various choices in your retirement plan fit in terms of SMI's risk categories—see graphic below. (It might also be good to review the basics on pages 156-158, 169-172, and 229-236.) The SMI philosophy is that all of your long-term investments go into the same "pot," and it is the portfolio mix *of the entire pot*

MANAGING 401(K) OR 403(B) ALLOCATIONS

Investment Choices	For Purposes of Assessing Risk When Rebalancing Portfolio
International Stock Fund Invests primarily in foreign stocks, but many also allow some U.S.	Treat as Stock Category 5.
Growth Fund Invests primarily in stocks chosen for their potential to rise in price.	Treat as Stock Category 2 or 4.
Stock Index Fund Usually designed to give results identical to S&P 500 stock index.	Treat as Stock Category 2.
Equity Income Fund Invests primarily in stocks chosen for their dividend-paying potential.	Treat as Stock Category 1.
Balanced Fund Invests in a fixed combination of stocks and bonds.	Treat as Stock Category 1.
Government Bond Fund Invests primarily in long-term IOUs of U.S. Treasury.	Treat as Bond Category 3.
Money Market Fund and Guaranteed Investment Contracts Short-term IOUs of businesses, banks, government, insurance companies.	Treat as Bond Category 1.

that matters. That means you should consider all of the investments over which you have decision-making authority, including those in your retirement accounts, as you analyze how best to diversify your holdings to achieve the portfolio allocation you desire. By shifting some of your retirement plan holdings from stocks to bonds or vice versa, you can achieve the right balance between equity and interest-earning investments.

Much has been said concerning the tendency of investors to be too conservative in their retirement plan investments. The SMI philosophy is that you should be guided by the mix appropriate to your season of life and investing temperament (see risk matrix on page 193). However, just so you'll know, many others recommend using a common rule of thumb: subtract your age from 100 and allocate at least that percentage to your holdings in stocks. This formula gives younger workers, who can afford to take more risk, a greater opportunity for long-term capital growth.

A warning: Don't overcommit to your company's stock.

A 1996 study by the Institute of Management and Administration, a newsletter that monitors the investments in retirement plans, contained a bombshell. It was based on a survey of the retirement plan holdings of over ten million workers at 246 of the country's largest companies. The study revealed that workers were investing a towering 42% of the money in their 401(k) and similar retirement plans in the stock of just one company—their employer. This is significantly more than the previous prevailing view that suggested approximately 25% of retirement assets were invested this way.

You may recall that if a mutual fund wishes to meet the diversification standards of the Securities and Exchange Commission, it can invest no more than 5% of its holdings in the stock of any one company. The workers in this study, therefore, are eight times more concentrated than the government's standard of prudence would suggest. Is this higher level of commitment to one security appropriate? The answer depends on another question: How much of your total retirement holdings are contained in your retirement plan at work?

For example, assume that all of your retirement plan assets are worth $100,000, but only $20,000 of that is in your 401(k). If you invested 42% of that $20,000 in your company stock, your holdings would amount to $8,400. This is a reasonable amount in a $100,000 portfolio. On the other hand, if $80,000 of your $100,000 was in your 401(k), then a 42% allocation would mean that $33,600 was invested in your employer's stock. This is, in my opinion, too high.

How is it that more and more employees are building such a significant stake in their company's future? The four most common ways this happens are: stock-purchase plans that let employees buy shares at a discount, stock-options being given to employees, company stock offered as an option in

Getting Your Money Out Early

Withdrawing funds from your tax-deferred plans prior to turning 59½ should be a last resort.

The tax consequences are severe—a 10% premature withdrawal penalty plus income taxes on any pre-tax contributions or earnings you take out. There are other ways to meet a temporary cash squeeze:

• Stop contributing to the plan. This may sound obvious, but many workers become so accustomed to having their contribution automatically deducted from each paycheck that they forget it's their choice.

• Borrow from your account. Most profit-sharing and 401(k) plans permit employees to borrow against their retirement account, often up to 50% of its value. Repayments typically must begin immediately and be completed within three to five years.

• If you have made after-tax contributions, withdraw them first. You'll have to pay the 10% penalty and income tax only on the interest earned while your money was in the plan. Or you may be able to avoid the taxes and penalty entirely by rolling the qualified plan balance to an IRA while taking out only your after-tax contributions.

401(k) retirement savings plans, and using company stock to match employee contributions into 401(k) plans. All of these avenues have one thing in common—the employee gets a "good deal" on the company stock, either receiving a discount from current market value or, in the case of 401(k) matching programs, getting shares "for free."

Obviously, there are pitfalls that arise from being dependent on a single company for one's income, health and life insurance, *and* retirement investments. Consider the risk of those in troubled industries during a possible recession—not only would many lose their jobs and health benefits, but they would also watch the value of their retirement assets fall as the stock market value of their company's stock dropped. Even in good times, there are no guarantees that an employer's stock will do well. The *Wall Street Journal* reported on the plight of the 23,000 employees of International Paper, one of the companies that makes up the Dow Jones Industrial Average. For a five-year period in the 1990s, the stock of International Paper averaged just a 5.4% a year return at a time when the overall DJIA was returning a healthy 16% a year.

The reasons that many fail to prudently limit their investments in their company stock are primarily emotional. They include the fear of being considered disloyal, fear of "missing out" if the company stock does well, peer pressure from co-workers, greed in wanting to accumulate stock at discount prices, and blind optimism concerning the company's future. From a strictly financial view, diversification is the more prudent strategy.

How much company stock is too much? There is no hard and fast rule concerning this because individual situations can vary widely. However, a general range that is useful is to limit your investing in any one stock (whether it's your company or not) to 5%-15% of your total investable assets. The smaller the value of your total portfolio, the more you should gravitate to the lower end of the range.

If you find yourself in a situation where you need to diversify, read the sidebar on page 268 first, and make sure you understand the implications of giving up employer securities in your plan. If you decide to sell, consider spreading out the selling over several years. This minimizes both the tax impact (for shares held outside your retirement plan) as well as the risk of selling too much during a period of market weakness. If your company uses its stock to match your 401(k) contribution, make sure you don't compound the problem by investing your contributions the same way.

All retirement plans have one thing in common:
at some point, you're going to want to take your money out!

Your decision as to how to do this will be one of the most important and far-reaching ones of your financial life. You shouldn't make it hurriedly; in fact, you should begin thinking about it years ahead of time. Make sure you understand the laws (which Congress has succeeded in making complicated and confusing by changing them from time to time) and how they affect your range of options.

With defined-contribution plans, your options are clear cut. Most people choose to roll the money into an IRA, although some of the other options listed on page 262 may also be available. With defined-benefit plans however, the choices become more complex. Some of the factors that will influence your decision include your age at retirement, birth year, health and life expectancy, income tax bracket, other sources of retirement income, inflationary expectations, desire for certainty versus desire for greater potential future income, and the list goes on.

Basically, you have three choices: to take all your money out in one large payment, to transfer your account value to an IRA Rollover where you can continue to invest it on a tax-deferred basis, or to take it in the form of monthly payments spread over the remainder of your life. Here are some guidelines to consider as you go about making your decision. After finding out from your employer the amounts of both your lump-sum benefit and your monthly income benefit, ask yourself these questions:

• **How long do I expect to live?** Obviously, you can only make a guess based on your health at the time and your family history. The reason this comes into play is that the monthly payment option is usually computed based on a life expectancy of age eighty. The longer you live past eighty, the greater the value of your total monthly pension and the better off you are versus taking the lump-sum.

• **How dependent are my spouse or heirs on my estate?** If your spouse is dependent on you, you might prefer the "joint and survivor" pension. It provides a monthly payment to you for life (about 10%–20%

THE THREE PRIMARY CHOICES FOR RECEIVING YOUR RETIREMENT BENEFITS FROM A DEFINED BENEFIT PLAN

	Take your money in one large payment	Transfer your money to an IRA rollover account	Take your money in monthly payments
How do you receive your money?	Your employer pays your retirement benefit to you all at one time.	Your employer sends your entire retirement benefit directly to your new IRA account.	You choose the combination of amount and duration of guaranteed monthly payments.
What taxes will you pay?	The entire amount is taxed at ordinary income rates in the year it is received.	None until you begin making withdrawals (which will be taxed as income the year they are received).	The money you receive will be taxed as income the year it is received.
What other factors come into play?	A special tax formula that can reduce your taxes may apply. Depending on your birth year, income averaging over five- or ten-year periods may be permitted. Early withdrawal penalty could apply if you are under age 59½.	You lose the option of reducing your tax burden by income averaging over a ten-year period. Your investments continue to grow tax-deferred and are under your direct supervision.	Early withdrawal penalty could apply if you are under age 59½ and do not choose the lifetime income option. If your employer provides your monthly payments by buying an annuity for you, a financially strong insurance company is of great importance.

lower than it would otherwise be), with an ongoing monthly payment (reduced by half) to your spouse after your death. If providing for your spouse is a primary consideration, these and other options should be explored fully with your pension administrator. If providing for heirs is important, then the lump-sum option is the way to go.

Sometimes It Pays to Take Your Company Stock Out When Leaving a Retirement Plan

Employer stock can be an exception to the wisdom of rolling retirement plan assets into an IRA.

If you have appreciated company stock, you may be better off walking away with some or all of the actual stock certificates instead. You'll owe taxes on the value of the shares at the time you purchased them (or they were added to your account), and, if you're under age 55, you'll have to pay the additional 10% early withdrawal penalty as well.

But here's the advantage: if the shares have gone up a lot in value since you acquired them, you'll be taxed on those gains at the favorable long-term capital gains rate when you later sell the stock. Otherwise, if you roll the shares into an IRA, all of your gains on the stock will eventually be taxed as ordinary income at your regular marginal tax rate.

It takes some number crunching to figure out which route will be more profitable in the long run, but it's worth the effort.

• **How do I feel about inflation?** Unless your monthly benefit provides for adequate cost-of-living increases, you may find it difficult keeping up with inflation over the longer term. The lump-sum approach burdens you with the responsibility and risk of investing, but following our Sound Mind portfolio recommendations should keep you ahead of inflation.

• **What other sources of income will I have?** Both options have their risks: the lump-sum has the risk of doing your own investing, and the monthly payment has the risk of not keeping ahead of inflation. You should also consider what additional help you can expect from Social Security and your investments.

The table on page 267 summarizes the tax implications and other important features of each of the three alternatives. For additional help, I encourage you to contact some of the leading no-load fund organizations. Just tell them you are facing this very important decision of whether to take your retirement in a lump-sum or roll it into an IRA. They've developed some user-friendly explanatory material (Schwab, Fidelity, Price, and Vanguard have done especially good jobs), which will walk you through the technical aspects. No-load fund organizations offer their help free of charge because they're hoping to win you over as a long-term customer during your retirement years.

Be careful when "rolling out" of your company's retirement plan.

Prior to 1993, you were given sixty days to deposit your lump-sum benefit check into a Rollover IRA in order to avoid any tax bite and preserve your tax-deferred program. Under current law, though, your benefit check will be hit with a 20% withholding rate *if it's made out to you*. This is a form of withholding similar to what your employer takes out of your paycheck. So, even if it's your intention to deposit it into a Rollover IRA, you're going to be 20% short!

Say you have $50,000 in your employer's plan. They're going to withhold $10,000 (which they'll turn over to the IRS where it will be applied as a credit against your total tax liability for the year) and give you $40,000. But in order to avoid any penalty, you've got to deposit $50,000 in the Rollover IRA. See the problem? Unless you've got an extra $10,000 you can spare to make up for what was withheld, you're going to get hit with a 10% penalty (if you're under 59½) and taxes.

You can avoid this potential problem by removing yourself from the transfer process. Arrange in advance for your employer to send your money directly to your new IRA rollover account. This is called a trustee-to-trustee transfer (see page 277).

Why did Congress change the old way, which was working fine? Perhaps to discourage workers from electing the lump-sum option (where they might spend it rather than save it). According to one survey, 68% of the people who change jobs cash out their 401(k) account. It also didn't hurt that the new law raised new tax revenues. The government says it expected to gather in more than $2 billion from those unsuspecting citizens who were unaware that the rules had, once again, been changed. ◆

Your Personal Pension:
The Ins and Outs of IRAs

I. **Individual Retirement Accounts can play a key role in your retirement investing strategy. Their are two primary kinds you should know about:**

   A. The traditional "Deductible IRA" offers a potential tax deduction if you meet certain tests. All the investment earnings in it compound tax-*deferred* until you begin taking them out at retirement. At that point, you pay taxes at ordinary income rates on the money as it's withdrawn.

   B. The newer "Roth IRA" offers no current tax deduction; however, all the investment earnings in it compound tax-*free*. In order to qualify for contributing to a Roth in a given year, your income must be below certain levels for that year.

   C. We look at the factors to consider in deciding whether a Deductible or Roth IRA is best for you.

II. **The control you have over your IRA makes it very flexible.**

   A. You select the financial organization with which you do business and control how its assets are invested.

   B. You decide whether to contribute each year, and if so, how much.

   C. You select the timing and amount of your withdrawals.

III. **In this chapter, I answer several general questions concerning the use of IRAs.**

   A. What are some of the drawbacks of investing through an IRA?

   B. If you have access to a 401(k) plan, what priority should it be given?

   C. What rules govern the conversion of a traditional IRA to a Roth IRA?

   D. What is an IRA rollover?

   E. What is the best way to move your IRA?

   F. What are the rules for taking money out of an IRA?

   G. Which financial firms offer the most attractive terms for opening an IRA?

IV. **A variable annuity is another way to build a personal pension. We look at its pros and cons as well as some guidelines for when to invest in one.**

IRA Laws May Change
The material in this chapter was correct as of mid-2000. Proposals for changing aspects of the laws governing IRAs are announced from time to time. Be sure to familiarize yourself with the current regulations before making important planning decisions.

IRA Resources
www.quicken.com/
retirement/IRA/

www.estrong.com/strongweb/
strong/jsp/planning/ret/ira/
index.jsp

www.rothira.com/

**Should You Convert
to a Roth IRA?**
www.troweprice.com/
retirement/
troweretireIRAHome.html

For Updated Information
The Internet is constantly changing, and the above sites may have moved or ceased operations by the time you read this. For an up-to-date list of the better online resources related to IRAs & 401(k)s, visit the SMI website at www.soundmindinvesting.com/
vsection/v_planning/
s_irasand.htm.

Your retirement income rests on what has been referred to as a three-legged stool.

Social Security has traditionally been regarded as the first of the three legs; however, the problems with Social Security make it impossible to project with confidence the level of monthly benefits twenty years and more into the future. Historically, the program has provided 35%-45% of retirees' monthly income; to be on the conservative side, investors under age fifty should use a lower assumption to reflect the uncertainty.

Private employer-sponsored retirement plans are the second leg (see chapter 22) and provide about 15%-20% of retirees' monthly income on average, according to the Social Security Administration. But there's a lot of room for variation here. For workers who spend most of their careers with the same company, it would not be unusual to receive a pension equal to 30%-40% of what they were making at the time of retirement. On the other hand, corporate America has been strongly moving away from defined-benefit plans in recent years, so your employer might not even offer a plan that pays a guaranteed monthly pension.

In any event, it is obvious that the third leg of personal savings and retirement funds will continue to play a very important role in providing adequate retirement incomes. And one of the best ways to go about building your personal retirement funds is by using an Individual Retirement Account (IRA).

What we might call the "Deductible IRA" first appeared . . .

. . . on the financial scene in 1974 when Congress voted to allow certain working persons—those not covered by a pension plan at work—to put away up to $2,000 a year for retirement *and deduct it* from their federal income tax return. Not only did they enjoy immediate tax-savings, but they also were excused from paying any income taxes on the investment profits they made. Until they began withdrawing the money upon retirement, they had the pleasure of watching their money grow tax-deferred. After the deductibility of home mortgage interest, it was the best tax break available to the middle class.

Not many were able to take advantage of it, however, because a relatively small percentage of the work force lacked a work-related pension benefit of some kind. In 1980, six years after IRAs were first introduced, only 2.6 million federal tax returns included deductions for IRA contributions

In 1981, Congress liberalized the law, making Deductible IRAs available to all wage earners, regardless of whether they participated in a retirement plan at work. This is when the IRA concept really took off. By 1985, the number of tax returns claiming an IRA deduction had soared to 16.2 million. Congress soon decided it had been too generous in allowing taxpayers to keep so much of their income. In passing the Tax Reform Act of 1986, the law was changed to eliminate the tax deduction on contributions to Deductible IRAs for wealthier taxpayers—namely, those whose adjusted gross incomes exceeded the levels specified in the so-called "phase-out range" (more on this shortly). There was one exception to this change: Taxpayers who were not active participants in an employer-sponsored retirement plan could still make fully deductible contributions to their IRAs regardless of their level of income.

The new complexity left taxpayers confused concerning the deductibility of their contributions. The result was predictable—the use of IRAs plummeted. In 1987, the first year under the new law, the number of tax returns claiming IRA deductions fell by more than half. By 1994, only 4.3 million returns reflected IRA contributions.

The IRA landscape grew even more complicated in 1997 when Congress gave us the "Roth IRA."

Named for Senator William Roth, a consistent supporter of IRAs, this new option was an effort to reinvigorate the IRA concept and encourage middle-income folks to save more for their retirement. It differs from the Deductible IRA primarily in the way taxes are handled—do you want to pay them now or pay them later? In a Deductible IRA, you receive a tax deduction for the amount you contribute (save on taxes now) and eventually pay income tax on all contributions and gains when money is taken out down the road (pay taxes later). With a Roth IRA, your current contributions are not deductible at all (no tax savings now) but all of your future withdrawals, even your investment gains, are tax-free (no taxes to pay later, ever).

Along with the Roth came new regulations that govern who qualifies for one—not everyone does. But assuming you qualify, is a Roth a better bet than a traditional IRA? You have a decision to make because *your total IRA contributions are still limited to $2,000.* The big question is which kind will give you the best long-term result. It can be a confusing analysis to make, and the outcome will vary depending on the assumptions you make.

Let's pretend we're in IRA school . . .

. . . and, as teacher, I'm going to lead you through some general principles that will help guide your decision as to the best place to invest your retirement money. The first is this: If you participate in a 401(k) where your contributions are matched, and you're currently not contributing up to the full amount that would be matched by your employer, you don't even need to consider IRAs at this point. If this describes you, your homework assignment is to channel your efforts into taking full advantage of the employer matching opportunity in your 401(k). Meanwhile, you're dismissed for the rest of the chapter. You can stay if you want, but I'm going to be giving all my attention to the other students.

IRA Phase Out Ranges

In the coming years, those at higher income levels will increasingly be eligible for tax deductions on contributions to traditional IRAs. The first number shown is the highest Modified AGI permitted in order to receive a full deduction. Above those levels, the phase-out kicks in. The second number is the limit for receiving any tax deduction.

Single Taxpayers

2001	$33,000-$43,000
2002	$34,000-$44,000
2003	$40,000-$50,000
2004	$45,000-$55,000
2005+	$50,000-$60,000

Married, Filing Jointly

2001	$53,000-$63,000
2002	$54,000-$64,000
2003	$60,000-$70,000
2004	$65,000-$75,000
2005	$70,000-$80,000
2006	$75,000-$85,000
2007+	$80,000-$100,000

What Is Modified Adjusted Gross Income?

Modified AGI is your "adjusted gross income" as shown on your 1040 tax return modified as follows:

• subtract any income resulting from a conversion of an IRA to a Roth IRA

• add back your traditional IRA deduction

• add back any student loan interest deduction

• add back any foreign earned income deduction

• add back any foreign housing exclusion or deduction

• add back any exclusion of qualified bond interest shown on Form 8815

• add back any exclusion of employer-paid adoption expenses shown on Form 8839

– IRS Publication 590

Now, I want to divide the rest of you into five groups according to your annual income. But not your gross income. Instead, Congress has complicated the task by making us use what they call "modified adjusted gross income" (MAGI). Groan! I know, but don't blame me. I'm just trying to help you sort through your options. So, with MAGI in mind (see sidebar on page 271 for details on how to calculate yours), look on the blackboard below to see which of the five groups you belong to. Be sure to read the small print, especially Footnote 2. Now consider the following general guidelines:

• Group 1: You have the greatest flexibility. You can choose to make either a fully deductible contribution to a traditional IRA or a non-deductible contribution to a Roth IRA. Later we'll have a "Deductible versus Roth" discussion that will be helpful in making your decision.

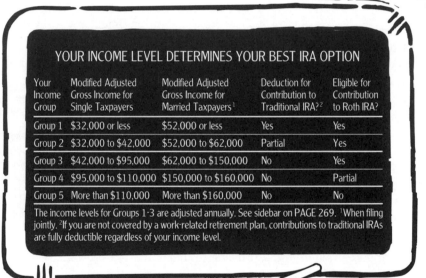

YOUR INCOME LEVEL DETERMINES YOUR BEST IRA OPTION

Your Income Group	Modified Adjusted Gross Income for Single Taxpayers	Modified Adjusted Gross Income for Married Taxpayers[1]	Deduction for Contribution to Traditional IRA?[2]	Eligible for Contribution to Roth IRA?
Group 1	$32,000 or less	$52,000 or less	Yes	Yes
Group 2	$32,000 to $42,000	$52,000 to $62,000	Partial	Yes
Group 3	$42,000 to $95,000	$62,000 to $150,000	No	Yes
Group 4	$95,000 to $110,000	$150,000 to $160,000	No	Partial
Group 5	More than $110,000	More than $160,000	No	No

The income levels for Groups 1-3 are adjusted annually. See sidebar on PAGE 269. [1]When filing jointly. [2]If you are not covered by a work-related retirement plan, contributions to traditional IRAs are fully deductible regardless of your income level.

• Group 2: You're in the "phase-out range" where the government begins taking away your tax deduction for contributing to a traditional IRA. Because your family income is more than $52,000 but less than $62,000, only a portion of your contribution is tax-deductible. (Single taxpayers have a lower threshhold at each step along the way as can be seen on the board.) As a rough rule of thumb, you lose $200 in tax deductions for every $1,000 in income above the $52,000 threshhold. You'll also want to pay attention during the "Deductible versus Roth" discussion.

One quick note—mixing deductible and non-deductible contributions in the same IRA can *greatly* complicate your tax situation when you finally withdraw the money. If possible, set up separate IRAs to keep these different types of contributions separate.

• Group 3: You're over the limit. Because your income is $62,000 or more, you receive no deduction ☹ unless you're a Footnote 2 person. You could make a non-deductibile contribution to a traditional IRA, but why do that with the Roth option available? You're Roth material all the way.

• Group 4: Like Group 3, Roths are your best option. But you're in the "phase-out range" where the government begins taking away your right to make a full $2,000 Roth contribution (it falls about $200 for every $1,000 in income above the threshhold). Still, take what you can get.

• Group 5: What can I say? You've been too successful and Congress figures you don't need any tax incentives to save for retirement. You're on your own—no IRAs for you. Well, that's not strictly true. You could make a non-deductible contribution to a traditional IRA and, considering your lack of other options, you might want to do just that. At least you get tax-deferred growth on your investments, and you pay taxes only on your investment gains when withdrawals are made, not on the amount of the entire withdrawal. You may also want to review page 281 for information on variable annuities.

Now, all you Footnote 2 folks who aren't covered by a retirement plan at work, pay attention. You're the exception to the rule. No matter what group you're in and no matter what I just said, you are entitled to a full tax deduction for any contributions you make to a Deductible IRA. And unless you're in Group 5, a Roth IRA is also an option.

Okay, that covers the basic "who qualifies for what?" question.

Now let's look at three questions that will help you decide what's best when choosing between a Roth and a Deductible IRA.

The first question to consider is: Do you expect to be in a lower tax bracket when you retire than you are now? If so, choose a Deductible IRA. You get a tax benefit now while your rates are higher, and pay tax later when they're lower. Conversely, if you anticipate a higher bracket in retirement, take your tax lumps now and put the money in a Roth. It'll sure feel good coming out tax-free in the future.

Having said that, this question is probably useful only if you anticipate retiring and beginning IRA withdrawals within 10-15 years. Beyond that it's too hard to predict what might happen to tax rates, not to mention personal circumstances. Plus, the longer your time horizon, the greater the tax-free advantages of the Roth become. So, throw the first question out of the equation if your time horizon is longer than 15 years.

The second question is: Would you like to postpone withdrawals beyond age 70½, or possibly leave the IRA intact for your beneficiaries? If so, opt for the Roth, which has no mandatory withdrawal requirements.

The final question is: Can you afford to put the full $2,000 into a Roth? Remember, those are after-tax dollars. Assuming you're in the 28% tax bracket, you'll have to actually set aside $2,778—$2,000 for your Roth and $778 for federal taxes. If you can do that, you'll get a better deal with the Roth. See the sidebar at right for the details.

Going Head to Head: Comparing a Roth to a Deductible IRA

Assume Ben and Caleb have $2,778 pretax dollars to invest each year in an IRA strategy, that they earn 10% a year, and that they're in the 28% tax bracket, both before and during retirement.

Ben chooses a Roth IRA. He pays $778 in taxes and puts the remaining $2,000 in his Roth each year. After 20 years, he has $126,000 which he can withdraw tax-free.

$2,778 pre-tax dollars	
−$778 tax going in @ 28%	
$2,000 net into Roth	
@ 10% annual compounding	
$126,000 net after-tax dollars	

Caleb chooses a traditional IRA. He puts $2,000 in his IRA and has $778 remaining. To obtain tax-deferred growth on that portion, he invests it in a variable annuity (see page 281). However, only $560 would be available to invest because taxes of $218 (28% of $778) would have to be paid first.

After 20 years, Caleb has a combined accumulation of $161,280 but has to pay taxes as the money is withdrawn. After tax, he receives $119,258. This is $6,742 less than Ben's $126,000 (which equals the tax Caleb had to pay on his annuity profits).

$2,000 into Traditional IRA	
@ 10% annual compounding	
$126,000 gross accumulation	
−$35,280 tax coming out @ 28%	
$90,720 net after-tax dollars	

$778 pre-tax dollars	
−$218 tax going in @ 28%	
$560 net into variable annuity	
@ 10% annual compounding	
$35,280 gross accumulation	
−$6,742 tax on gain	
$28,538 net after-tax dollars	

So the Roth has an advantage—while the $2,000 limit appears to be the same for both the Roth and traditional IRAs, the Roth actually maximizes the use of $2,778 pre-tax dollars whereas the traditional represents only $2,000 pre-tax dollars.

To sum up, unless retirement will be arriving shortly and with it the expectation that you'll be in a lower tax bracket, the Roth IRA is the superior choice for most retirement savers.

If you're still considering a Deductible IRA, be sure you take these drawbacks into consideration.

It's easy to become so impressed with the power of tax-deferred compounding that we can overlook a few of the disadvantages of the traditional IRA. One is that it turns lower-taxed capital gains into higher-taxed ordinary income. That's because when you begin taking your money back out, it *all* gets taxed the same way—as ordinary income— even though a sizable portion of your growth came in the form of capital gains.

Another drawback are the rules governing how much you must take out each year. If you run afoul of them, the penalties are unbelievable (see page 279).

And third are the estate tax implications. These are the taxes we Americans pay for the privilege of dying and leaving what wealth we may have attained to our loved ones. (The first $675,000 is currently exempt, and the exemption rises to $700,000 in 2002, $850,000 in 2004, $950,000 in 2005, and tops out at $1 million in 2006.) This tax has always struck me as outrageous because the estate that we leave behind is comprised of wealth that, by and large, has already been taxed at the local, state, and federal level. It seems criminal for the government to come back for more. Yet, federal estate taxes start at 18% and gradually rise to 55%. Thus, in the lives of some taxpayers, the government demands for itself an equal standing with their heirs—one-half for the family, and one-half for the government. Congress killed the tax in 2000 only to have the legislation vetoed by the president; hopefully a future Congress will try again and estate tax complications will become a thing of the past.

The question is: How does the Deductible IRA fit into all this? It suffers the same fate as most other tax-deferred retirement accounts. According to the *Wall Street Journal:*

> *Death is brutal for retirement accounts, because the government still insists on collecting all the income taxes owed. Sure, your heirs may be able to delay the impact, but eventually a combination of income taxes and estate taxes will wreak their havoc. With larger estates, you can get 60% or 70% of the retirement plan going to taxes. . . . By contrast, if you die with your money in a regular taxable account, only estate taxes get levied.*

Roth IRAs are better in regard to all three of the above concerns: (1) all monies taken out of a Roth are tax-free; (2) there are no mandatory distribution requirements; and (3) estate taxes still apply but no income taxes or penalties come into play.

What about converting my traditional IRA to a Roth?

First things first—are you eligible to convert? To be eligible, your modified AGI (not including the converted IRA income) needs to be $100,000 or less, and you can't be using the "married filing separately" status. If you meet those criteria, some of the questions are the same as the ones we looked at on page 273: How does your current tax bracket compare with your anticipated tax bracket in retirement? Is postponing withdrawals and/or being able to pass the account to your heirs important to you?

There are also two new factors that come into play. If you convert your IRA, you will have to pay income tax on any gains in the account, plus any deductible contributions you've made over the years. It all comes due on this year's tax return, which can add a sizeable sum to your tax bill. If you have the resources to pay those extra taxes without having to raid any of your retirement accounts for cash, then you might want to consider converting. If you will have to pull money out of the account just to pay the tax bill, chances are converting is not a good move for you. Not only will you lose out on future appreciation on these funds, but you'll pay a stiff early withdrawal penalty if you're under age 59½.

If you have the cash on hand to pay the tax bill, and converting looks good to you, a final question to consider is how far off is your retirement? At a bare minimum, you should have at least five years before you'll need to tap the converted IRA. That's because you'll face early withdrawal pen-

WHEN YOU HAVE A CHOICE, SHOULD YOU CONTRIBUTE TO A 401(K) OR AN IRA?

	401(k) Plan	Deductible IRA	Roth IRA
Are you eligible?	❏ Your company offers a 401(k) plan. ❏ You meet the customary eligibility requirements.	❏ You're not a participant in a retirement plan at work, or ❏ You have Modified AGI of less than $62,000.[1] At least one of these boxes must be checked. Also, you must be under 70½ years old and have earned income during the year.	❏ You have Modified AGI of less than $160,000. ❏ You have earned income during the year.
What is the most you can put in each year?	$10,500	$2,000 per spouse in all IRAs combined.	$2,000 per spouse in all IRAs combined.[2]
Will you receive matching funds from your employer?	Generally yes. See page 260.	No.	No.
Are contributions tax-deductible?	Yes.	Yes, but reduced for those with income in the phase-out range.	No.
Can you borrow from your account?	At the employer's discretion, but generally yes.	No.	No.
Investment options?	Generally limited.	Vast.	Vast.
How are withdrawals taxed once you reach age 59½?	Contributions and gains are taxed as ordinary income.	Contributions and gains are taxed as ordinary income.	Contributions are tax-free. Gains are tax-free assuming the plan has been in place 5 years.
When do you have to begin taking distributions?	No later than age 70½ unless still working.	No later than age 70½.	No mandatory distribution age.

[1] A sliding scale comes into play to determine how much of your contribution is deductible. See pages 271-272. [2] For those with income between $150,000 and $160,000, a sliding scale comes into play to determine the amount that can be contributed. See page 272.

alties if the Roth is not established for five years before withdrawals begin. Note that when *any* Roth IRA of yours passes the five year mark, *all* of your Roths clear that hurdle together, regardless of whether the other Roths are brand new or not. A five year horizon is a minimum, not an automatic signal to proceed. The Roth's advantages build with time, so the longer the Roth will be intact, the better your chances that the conversion will be worthwhile.

How should you invest the money you put into your IRA?

An IRA is not, in and of itself, an investment. It's merely a tax shelter that you put your investments in. IRAs can contain a wide variety of investments of your choosing. To get the most from the tax-deferred advantage, put your fixed-income higher-yielding investments in your IRA (because a large part of their total returns is interest income, which is taxed at your highest marginal tax rate). Investments where you expect a large part of your total return will be from growth should be put in your regular accounts because the tax on long-term capital gains is limited to 20%.

Don't invest in tax-exempt securities like municipal bonds and annuities in your IRA. There's no point in putting investments that are already tax-exempt into an IRA; there's no additional tax savings. With municipal bonds, you're lowering your investment potential as well as because they yield significantly less than corporate or government bonds.

What is an IRA rollover?

A rollover is a tax-free distribution of cash or other assets from one retirement program that you then contribute to another retirement program. The amount you roll over tax-free is generally taxable later when the new retirement program makes distributions to you (or your beneficiary).

There are two kinds of IRA rollovers. In one, the money you're putting into your new IRA comes from a qualified employer plan (like those discussed in chapter 22). In the other, the money you're putting into your new IRA comes from another IRA. In this second kind of rollover, you must complete the transaction within sixty days of receiving the check (although completing it within sixty days of the date on the check is safer because you can prove you complied with the time limit). If you miss the sixty-day deadline, you might be assessed income tax and early withdrawal penalties on the full amount of the check.

Also, such a change can be done only once in any one-year period (the period begins on the date you receive your money from the old IRA, not on the date you roll it over into your new one). You may, however, roll over assets from separate IRAs during a one-year period. In other words, each "old" IRA has its own one-year period, and if you have several IRA accounts, it's

OK if they overlap. You must roll over into your new IRA the same amount (the same "property") you received from your old one.

What is an IRA asset transfer (sometimes called a trustee-to-trustee transfer)?

There's another way to move your IRA—have the trustee/custodian of your new IRA do it for you. A transfer of funds at your request from your old IRA *directly* to your new one is not only simpler but it avoids any potential problems associated with missing the sixty-day deadline. Also, it is not affected by the one-year waiting period mentioned above.

I recommend using either a no-load fund organization or one of the leading discount brokers that also offer no-load mutual funds. Once you sign the authorization forms they provide, they will take care of the paperwork in what is called a trustee-to-trustee transfer. It couldn't be easier!

If you have more than one IRA account, you might consider combining them into one. It's not unusual for people to have many different IRAs spread around various places that were offering the "best deal" at the time their contribution was made. By combining them into one account at a no-load mutual fund organization, you'll save on annual account fees and cut your paperwork. More important, you'll have a much easier time managing your investments and tracking their performance.

As always, there's an exception: be sure to keep IRAs of different types separate. Putting an IRA with non-deductible contributions together with one containing deductible contributions is not only confusing, it can cost you down the road if you can't distinguish which withdrawals should and should not be taxed.

It's worth moving your IRA where it can get better returns even if they amount to only 2%-3% a year. For example, someone with $10,000 in his IRA who earns 8% a year will have $68,485 in twenty-five years. But if he could earn 10% instead, he'd have $108,347. That extra $40,000 provides additional months of income once he retires.

Concerning IRA Fees
Many advisers suggest that you pay any fees associated with your IRA account directly rather than allowing them to be deducted from the account. This preserves the capital in the IRA for futher tax-deferred growth.

For More on the Technical Aspects of IRAs
Request IRS Publication 590. To obtain a free copy, call the IRS Forms Distribution Center at (800) 829-3676, or download it from www.irs.ustreas.gov.

The longer you wait before withdrawing money from your IRA, the longer it can continue to grow tax-deferred.

Since it's your money, you might think that it's up to you to decide when to start tapping your IRA account and how much to withdraw each year. Naturally, because the federal government is involved, it's not that simple.

The IRS imposes very strict rules that dictate how long you can postpone making withdrawals from your IRA, as well as the minimum amount you must withdraw each year. (They want you to start taking your money out so you will begin paying some of those long deferred income taxes.) The minimum withdrawal amounts are called "required minimum distributions," and the latest you can wait to begin making them is April 1 of the year after you reach age 70½. If you violate the IRS guidelines, there are some horrendous penalties awaiting you. Here are the basics.

• **Up to age 59½—Take it and pay a penalty.** The general rule is that IRA withdrawals are taxed as ordinary income in the year you receive them. If you withdraw money before reaching age 59½, you are also hit with a 10% penalty that is in addition to any income tax you owe. The penalty does not apply if you have a disability, or if you begin a series of scheduled annuity payments based on your life expectancy (see next page).

Things get slightly more complicated if you've made nondeductible contributions, because they've already been taxed. In that case, part of your withdrawal is taxed and part of it is treated simply as a return of your nondeductible contribution. The 10% penalty is applied to the taxable amount of your withdrawal. This is true of both Deductible and Roth IRAs.

• **Age 59½ to age 70½—Take it or leave it.** You have the greatest flexibility in your sixties. You can take out as much as you like, or nothing at all. The amounts you withdraw are no longer subject to the 10% penalty tax. Of course, normal income taxes apply. If they can afford it, most people are inclined to make no withdrawals during this period in order to make the most of the benefits of tax-deferred growth.

• **Age 70½ and over—Leave it and pay a penalty, unless you've got a Roth.** You've gotten the most from the tax deferral, and the IRS now insists you make a withdrawal whether you need the money or not. Listen carefully: The law says that you must take your first minimum annual distribution no later than April 1 of the year *after the year* you reach 70½. The IRS calls this your "required beginning date." Furthermore, you must take additional minimum annual distributions no later than December 31 of each year after you attain age 70½.

For example, if you were born on March 15, 1950, you'll turn 70½ on September 15, 2020. You must make your first minimum withdrawal on or before April 1, 2021. Then you must make your second minimum withdrawal by December 31, 2021. These deadlines are for people who have resisted taking their distributions. You don't have to wait this long. In fact, most people would benefit from taking their first required distribution three months early to avoid having their first two distributions occur in the same tax year.

If you wish, you can begin making penalty-free withdrawals as soon as you turn 59½. Remember that when you begin withdrawing IRA funds, you'll pay taxes at that time. *Being tax-deferred is not the same as being tax-free.* Don't think of a traditional IRA in the same category as a truly tax-free investment like municipal bonds or a Roth IRA.

How is the minimum annual withdrawal calculated?

We've been discussing the concept of "required minimum distributions," but don't let that give you the impression that you are restricted to taking small amounts out of your IRA. You're free to empty the entire account anytime you want (of course, the penalty tax applies before age 59½, and the income tax applies regardless of your age). But assuming you want to minimize your withdrawals, how is the required minimum calculated?

The law requires that withdrawals must be made in "substantially equal amounts" over a period that does not extend beyond your life expectancy (as determined according to IRS tables). Or, you may elect a longer period—which would result in smaller withdrawals—that involves using the "joint life and last survivor" expectancy of you and the beneficiary that you name.

The minimum amount that must be withdrawn annually is calculated by dividing your account balance (as of December 31 of the previous year) by the applicable life expectancy. The table at right shows the value to use if the calculation is based on the life expectancy of the owner of the IRA. For example, a 70-year-old person with a year-end IRA value of $250,000 would be required to withdraw at least $15,625 the following year (250,000 divided by 16.0).

What if you fail to withdraw the minimum? That's where the "horrendous" penalty I referred to previously comes in—a 50% nondeductible excise tax is assessed on the shortfall, that is, on the difference between what you should have withdrawn and what you actually withdrew. If the 70-year-old retiree in the above example withdrew $6,000 the following year, the excise tax would amount to $4,813 (50% of the difference between $15,625 and $6,000). And the excise tax would not be deductible on that year's income tax return.

The moral of this is that it's really important to pay close attention to the details when you're planning how you want to use your IRA during retirement. The rules can be complicated, especially those that relate to what's best in terms of naming a beneficiary. The articles I've read on this subject make clear that the choices you make prior to your "required beginning date" have extremely important long-term implications. As that date approaches, make sure you have adequate tax planning counsel and plenty of time to make your decisions.

Roth's offer more flexibility than traditional IRAs if you face a cash crunch.

In a Roth, you always have access to the principal you've contributed without income taxes or penalties. In addition, earnings can generally be withdrawn early without penalty if the distributions are for death or disability, high medical expenses, qualified higher education expenses for you, a spouse, child or grandchild, or first time home buyer expenses. Naturally there are many details to each of these exceptions, so you'll have to do some re-

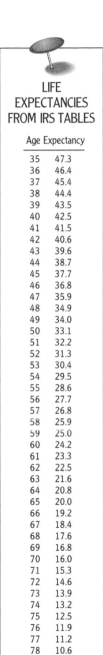

LIFE EXPECTANCIES FROM IRS TABLES

Age	Expectancy
35	47.3
36	46.4
37	45.4
38	44.4
39	43.5
40	42.5
41	41.5
42	40.6
43	39.6
44	38.7
45	37.7
46	36.8
47	35.9
48	34.9
49	34.0
50	33.1
51	32.2
52	31.3
53	30.4
54	29.5
55	28.6
56	27.7
57	26.8
58	25.9
59	25.0
60	24.2
61	23.3
62	22.5
63	21.6
64	20.8
65	20.0
66	19.2
67	18.4
68	17.6
69	16.8
70	16.0
71	15.3
72	14.6
73	13.9
74	13.2
75	12.5
76	11.9
77	11.2
78	10.6
79	10.0
80	9.5

search to find out more specifics, but generally you can get away with just paying income taxes and no penalties in these cases. With traditional IRAs, if you touch any of it early, you pay dearly.

If you need to tap your traditional IRA before reaching age 59½, there is a way around the 10% early withdrawal penalty. It involves invoking the annuity option.

You don't read much about the strategy I'm about to describe. Possibly it's because financial advisers don't want to encourage the investing public to spend their IRA funds prematurely. I certainly can understand that. On the other hand, on those occasions where the need for cash is so great that a decision to withdraw it from an IRA has already been made, wouldn't it be good to know there's a way to do it without paying the 10% penalty? Here's the key as explained in IRS Publication 590:

> *Generally you cannot withdraw assets from your IRA until you reach age 59½ without having to pay a 10% additional tax. However, there are a number of exceptions to this rule. . . . You can receive distributions from your IRA that are part of a series of substantially equal payments over your life . . . without having to pay the 10% additional tax even if you receive such distributions before you are age 59½. You must use an IRS-approved distribution method and you must take at least one distribution annually for this exception to apply. . . . The payments under this exception must continue for at least five years, or until you reach age 59½, whichever is the longer period.*

In essence, you can decide to temporarily treat your IRA as an annuity. The amount of your annual withdrawal depends on your life expectancy at the time, and all withdrawals are taxable as income in the year you receive them. Once you begin your withdrawals, you must continue taking them for at least five years, or until you reach 59½ if that period is longer. The table at left illustrates how this could work for a 52 year old who is temporarily unemployed, but has a $300,000 IRA that resulted from a rollover out of his previous employer's retirement plan.

His withdrawal schedule is designed so that, even though his payments increase each year as he ages, they are calculated based on his life expectancy so as to last the remainder of his lifetime. Upon reaching age 59½, he has the option of stopping the payments and once again working to rebuild his IRA account with additional tax-deductible contributions.

There are other IRS-approved distribution methods that result in higher

Age	Value of IRA	IRS factor	Annuity withdrawal	IRA after withdrawal	Assume 9% return	IRA at end of year
52	$300,000	31.3	$9,585	$290,415	$26,137	$316,553
53	316,553	30.4	10,413	306,140	27,553	333,692
54	333,692	29.5	11,312	322,381	29,014	351,395
55	351,395	28.6	12,287	339,109	30,520	369,628
56	369,628	27.7	13,344	356,284	32,066	388,350
57	388,350	26.8	14,491	373,859	33,647	407,507
58	407,507	25.9	15,734	391,773	35,260	427,032
59	427,032	25.0	17,081	409,951	36,896	446,847
60	446,847	24.2	18,465	428,382	38,554	466,936

A SOUND MIND BRIEFING

Look Before You Leap:
A Primer on Variable Annuities

Variable annuities (VAs) are mutual funds wrapped up in a tax-sheltered package. Unlike a fixed annuity, where you are essentially loaning money to the insurance company and, in return, agree upon a rate of return up front, the returns in a variable annuity aren't locked in ahead of time. They vary depending on how well the investments perform—that's why they're called "variable."

The VA has one major advantage over the fixed kind—you have control over the investments. Insurance companies typically offer a range of investment choices in their variable annuities, and let you decide how much of the money you give them goes into each category. Your eventual return is affected by three things.

• Your allocation decisions. If you decide to put all your money into the stock market just before a major sell-off, you'll get off to a slow start. On the other hand, if you play it safe in the money market fund, you're giving up the reason for choosing a VA in the first place—greater profit potential.

• Investment fund performance. It could be that even though you make excellent allocation decisions, the funds offered by your particular insurer just don't perform well. Just like mutual funds, some finish in the top ranks year after year, whereas others are perennial also-rans. Check out the track records of the funds in the variable annuity being offered to you. How do they compare with other variable annuity funds over the same period?

• Fees, fees, and fees. There are three kinds of fees you have to pay with most VA products. First, there are the sales fees, usually disguised as "surrender charges." In the most common arrangement, there are no up-front sales charges; instead, the cost of commissions paid to the brokers and insurance agents is recovered by penalties paid if investors take their money out of the annuity in the first seven years.

Next come the "contract fees," which include annual administrative and insurance fees. Among their other purposes, these fees guarantee that your beneficiaries won't get back less than you put in, regardless of how poorly your investment choices perform. According to Morningstar, these fees average about 1.3% per year. You pay these every year you own the annuity.

Finally there are the fees paid to the investment managers who make the portfolio decisions in the funds. These are similar to the management fees paid by shareholders of regular mutual funds and typically run about 0.9% per year. These also are ongoing.

So, you can see how the overhead expenses cut into your returns by about 2.2% each and every year, even assuming you hold your annuity longer than seven years and avoid the surrender charges. Another drawback is the loss of liquidity. Annuities are designed for retirement planning and are intended as long-term investments. Once you put your money into one, you're supposed to leave it there until at least age 59$^1/_2$. If you take it out sooner, you get hit with a 10% penalty from the government, just as with IRAs.

Are variable annuities worth the cost, red tape, and possible tax headaches down the road?

Because of the high costs and the possible tax disadvantages, many financial planners recommend VAs only as a "last resort," that is, after all the other options have been explored and exhausted. Their unique characteristics create a situation where it's difficult to decide which kinds of investments would be appropriate within a variable annuity:

On the one hand, if you invest in equities with growth potential, you're going to end up paying ordinary income tax rates on what would otherwise qualify for long-term capital gains

tax treatment. If the capital gains rate is lowered from its present 28% level, the problem becomes even worse.

On the other hand, if you put your VA money in fixed income investments, then the high fees become particularly burdensome. Do you really want to pay 2% a year and more just to invest in bonds (which have historically returned about 8% a year)? The same investment in a low-cost, no-load mutual fund (like those at Vanguard) would cost only about 0.3% per year.

From a planning point of view, a VA makes the most sense if:

1. You are in one of the higher tax brackets now (28% and up) and have a reasonable expectation that your tax bracket will be lower after you retire, and

2. You expect to make withdrawals in regular, systematic payments to supplement your other retirement income, and

3. You got a late start contributing to other retirement accounts and are using an annuity as a means for making up lost ground, and

4. You anticipate that your regular monthly withdrawals will exhaust the assets in your annuity in your lifetime. (Due to tax laws, an annuity is not a good vehicle for accumulating capital to leave to your heirs.)

Before investing in a VA, I suggest you should be able to pass all the following tests:

❑ You're already making the full tax-deductible contribution to your IRA.

❑ You're already paying the maximum permitted into an employer-sponsored 401(k) plan.

❑ You've got investment money you're willing to lock away for at least ten years, which is the time needed to make up for the fees.

❑ You've set aside an amount of cash sufficient to cover major expenses and emergency needs so that you'll have no need to withdraw your money before age 59$^1/_2$.

From the Sound Mind Investing newsletter. To learn more about the monthly SMI newsletter,
use the postage-paid tear-out card in this book, or visit our website at www.soundmindinvesting.com.

yearly withdrawals for a fixed number of years, at the end of which his IRA would have been completely emptied. Consult a professional for guidance and a discussion of your options.

Even after you know which kind of IRA you want, the question still remains: Where should you open your account?

All the major banking, brokerage, and mutual fund institutions offer IRAs. I've provided the list below as a starting point as you look for a home for your IRA. The competition for your IRA business is fierce, as can be seen by the willingness of the firms to waive their annual fees if your account is large enough. Many discount brokers (like E*Trade, TD Waterhouse, etc.) charge no annual fees for IRA accounts. They often offer huge numbers of mutual funds, many as no-transaction-fee options. As long as you aren't tempted by the easy access to trade more within your account,

WHO'S OFFERING THE MOST FAVORABLE TERMS ON IRAs?

Fund Organization	Annual Fee For Each Fund Held	Minimum To Avoid Annual Fees	Minimum To Open Account	Minimum Subsequent Deposit	Minimum Automatic Deposit[1]	For More Information
Amer Century	$10 ($30 max)	$10,000 total account	$1,000	$50	$50	800-345-2021
T. Rowe Price	$10	$5,000 per fund [2]	None [3]	$50	$50	800-541-6592
Vanguard	$10	$5,000 per fund [2]	$1,000	$100	$50	800-847-2999
Schwab	$29 [4]	$10,000 total account	None	None	$100	800-472-4922
Fidelity	$12 ($60 max)	$2,500 per fund	$500	$250	$100	800-544-3922

FOOTNOTES: This schedule is the result of a telephone survey by SMI staff in 1999. Additional fees may apply if you also open a discount brokerage account. [1] Monthly automatic investments can be made directly from your checking or savings account, a good way to be sure you save as well as benefit from dollar-cost-averaging. [2] If your combined IRA assets exceed $50,000, all fees are waived regardless of the balances in your individual fund accounts. [3] You must set up automatic monthly deposits to qualify; otherwise the minimum is $1,000. [4] Until your account value exceeds $10,000, Schwab charges a flat $29 annual fee.

they can be a good deal worth investigating. The "deals" being offered change frequently, so these may be outdated by the time you read this. Check with these and other no-load fund organizations for their current policies.

Investors are fee-sensitive, as evidenced by the fact that financial organizations give such great emphasis to their low fees in their advertising. However, when selecting a home for your IRA, I would suggest that you give greater weight to having a large number of investment alternatives from which you can choose. After all, what good are low fees if you have only a few average performing funds to select from? And you can't go simply by how many funds an organization offers because many of them aren't suitable for an IRA. For example, you wouldn't want to invest in tax-exempt securities like municipal bonds in your IRA because there would be no additional tax savings. You especially want good fund choices from the risk categories which figure most prominently in your personal portfolio. Use the Internet or the fund performance rankings in the SMI newsletter to get an overview of how well the various organizations are represented in the categories of interest to you. ◆

CHAPTER PREVIEW

Lowering Your Investment Risk as You Approach Retirement

I. **Because nobody knows what the future holds for the investment markets, we can never know in advance which combination of investments will minimize our risk while maximizing our gains.**

    A. This uncertainty makes it difficult to decide with confidence how much to cut back your investment risk as you near retirement. To a large extent, your decision will reflect your personal investing temperament.

    B. The risk matrix contains my suggestions as to what is an appropriate allocation between stocks (higher risk) and bonds (lower risk) given your age and temperament. Other professionals may offer different suggestions. There is no universally agreed upon "right" allocation for a retired person.

II. **A study of historical returns since 1926 shows how various combinations of stocks and bonds have performed in the past.**

    A. A table is presented that is useful for gaining an understanding of the potential risks and rewards from holding six different stock/bond allocations over various time periods ranging from one year to thirty years.

    B. A similar table is presented that is useful for gaining an understanding of the potential risks and rewards from holding shares in large companies versus those of small companies.

    C. There are no "sure things." It is inevitable that you must make decisions that involve trade-offs between the risks you're willing to take and the rewards you hope to reap.

Like all the other kids, I wanted to see *Jurassic Park* when it came out in the summer of 1993.

As I expected, it turned out to be an action-packed, nerve-wracking tale overflowing with amazing special effects. Having read the book, I enjoyed the intellectual stimulation and the way the story got me to thinking about the critical importance of boundaries.

Boundaries exist for safety reasons; breaking through them can be dangerous. The film is scary because the prehistoric creatures break through *physical boundaries* and attack the people. And it provokes us to weigh the risks before breaking through *scientific boundaries* and playing with the building blocks of life. It may even have something to say to societies that are breaking through *moral boundaries* and removing limits on personal freedoms that have characterized civilized societies for thousands of years.

Because I'm a person who thinks a lot about how to help people invest more successfully, the film caused me to also reflect on the risks taken by those who willfully ignore *time boundaries*. We are quite limited as to what we can know of the future with certainty.

My favorite character in *Jurassic Park* is Malcolm, the "chaos theory" scientist. In the book, I particularly liked the passage where he is describing to a co-worker why many events are inherently, inescapably unpredictable:

"Computers were built because mathematicians thought that if you had a machine to handle a lot of variables simultaneously, you would be able to predict the weather. Weather would finally fall to human understanding. And men believed that dream for the next forty years. They believed that prediction was just a function of keeping track of things. If you knew enough, you could predict anything.

"Chaos theory throws it right out the window. It says that you can never predict certain phenomena at all. You can never predict the weather more than a few days away. All the money that has been spent on long-range forecasting is money wasted. It's a fool's errand. It's as pointless as trying to turn lead into gold. We've tried the impossible — and spent a lot of money doing it. Because in fact there are great categories of phenomena that are inherently unpredictable."

"Chaos says that?"

"Yes, and it is astonishing how few people care to hear it."

Consider that last line: "*. . . it is astonishing how few people care to hear it.*" How well that applies to people when they're making investment decisions! We refuse to believe that the markets, like the weather, cannot be accurately predicted. Throughout my advisory career I've seen people suffer financially because they look to the forecasts and opinions of gurus and experts to guide their decisions.

I was slow in accepting this limitation myself. But it's very important we learn to admit, "I don't know what the future holds. The financial commentators in the media don't know. Investment experts don't know. Nobody knows. So, I must face the fact that I can never know in advance which investment alternatives will make the most money, lose the most money, or do little at all."

This uncertainty makes it difficult to know how much to cut back our investment risk—and the potential gains we're hoping for— as we near retirement.

In chapter 17, I offered my opinion on how this might best be done. The risk matrix (see pages 193–197) balances the two competing influences in your investment planning—your fear of loss and your need for growth. On the one hand, I believe that you should "be yourself" as you make investing decisions. The quiz I designed helps you select the investing temperament best suited to your personality by probing the intensity of your fear of losing money (an ever-present possibility in the markets). It's important that you be emotionally comfortable with your strategy. Otherwise, it's questionable if you'll develop the confidence and discipline needed to hang in there when the periodic storms of market turbulence blow through.

On the other hand, your investing strategy must face the realities of your present stage of life—how much time remains before you reach retirement, and what financial goals do you hope to achieve by that time? If you structure your portfolio too conservatively, your investment capital may not grow by the needed amount. But if you take too great a risk, you could suffer a large loss just before you need to withdraw capital for living expenses.

In the matrix, I offer suggestions on how much to invest-by-owning (typically in stocks and stock funds) versus how much to invest-by-lending (in savings accounts, bonds and bond funds, and other fixed income holdings). As I pointed out at the time, however, "This matrix reflects my personal sense of risk. Other investment advisers might feel more comfortable with less restrictive guidelines." In fact, most do.

After reviewing several of the books in my library on the subject of how to adjust your stock-to-bond mix as you grow older, it's clear that the guidelines I offer are somewhat conservative.

For example, if you're 65 years old (in what I call "phase three" of your financial life), the matrix indicates that the stock portion of your holdings not exceed 60% in stocks. The recommendations of other advisers called for portfolios with stock allocations ranging from 40% to as high as 75%. Their argument for higher stock holdings is that, although stocks are subject to occasional major setbacks, they are needed to keep ahead of inflation. The response to that argument is that, while it's true that stocks have always recovered from previous bear markets, older investors may have a need to withdraw their money

HISTORICAL INVESTMENT RETURNS
OF VARIOUS PORTFOLIO COMBINATIONS

Portfolio Consists of >>>	Stocks: 100% Bonds: 0%	Stocks: 80% Bonds: 20%	Stocks: 60% Bonds: 40%	Stocks: 40% Bonds: 60%	Stocks: 20% Bonds: 80%	Stocks: 0% Bonds: 100%
Average of 589 1-Year Periods	14.5%	12.9%	11.3%	9.7%	8.0%	6.5%
Best 1-Year Period	(1) 61.0%	(2) 54.2%	(3) 47.3%	(4) 40.4%	(5) 33.6%	(6) 32.7%
Worst 1-Year Period	−38.9%	−30.8%	−22.6%	−14.5%	−6.3%	−5.6%
Result two-thirds of the time	−1.4% to 30.4%	−0.1% to 25.9%	1.0% to 21.6%	1.6% to 17.7%	1.5% to 14.6%	0.0% to 12.9%
Average of 565 3-Year Periods	13.2%	12.0%	10.7%	9.3%	8.0%	6.5%
Best 3-Year Period	(7) 33.4%	(8) 29.9%	(9) 26.3%	(10) 22.7%	(11) 20.2%	(12) 18.4%
Worst 3-Year Period	−10.6%	−7.0%	−3.7%	−0.7%	1.5%	−0.4%
Result two-thirds of the time	5.1% to 21.3%	5.3% to 18.6%	5.3% to 16.1%	4.9% to 13.8%	3.9% to 12.0%	2.2% to 10.8%
Average of 541 5-Year Periods	12.7%	11.6%	10.4%	9.2%	7.9%	6.5%
Best 5-Year Period	(13) 29.7%	(14) 26.9%	(15) 24.0%	(16) 21.0%	(17) 20.0%	(18) 18.0%
Worst 5-Year Period	−4.1%	−1.5%	1.0%	2.0%	2.3%	0.7%
Result two-thirds of the time	6.1% to 19.2%	6.2% to 17.0%	6.0% to 14.9%	5.5% to 13.0%	4.4% to 11.4%	2.7% to 10.4%
Average of 481 10-Year Periods	11.7%	10.9%	10.0%	9.0%	7.9%	6.8%
Best 10-Year Period	(19) 19.4%	(20) 18.1%	(21) 16.8%	(22) 15.7%	(23) 14.8%	(24) 13.7%
Worst 10-Year Period	0.5%	1.6%	2.6%	3.4%	4.0%	1.3%
Result two-thirds of the time	7.0% to 16.5%	6.8% to 15.0%	6.4% to 13.5%	5.8% to 12.2%	4.9% to 11.0%	3.6% to 10.0%
Average of 421 15-Year Periods	11.3%	10.6%	9.8%	8.9%	7.9%	6.9%
Best 15-Year Period	(25) 19.7%	(26) 18.0%	(27) 16.2%	(28) 14.4%	(29) 12.7%	(30) 11.4%
Worst 15-Year Period	4.1%	4.5%	4.8%	4.8%	4.1%	2.4%
Result two-thirds of the time	7.2% to 15.3%	7.0% to 14.1%	6.6% to 12.9%	6.0% to 11.8%	5.1% to 10.8%	4.0% to 9.9%
Average of 361 20-Year Periods	10.7%	10.1%	9.4%	8.7%	7.8%	6.9%
Best 20-Year Period	(31) 17.9%	(32) 16.4%	(33) 14.8%	(34) 13.2%	(35) 11.5%	(36) 10.1%
Worst 20-Year Period	6.4%	6.3%	6.0%	5.5%	4.6%	2.4%
Result two-thirds of the time	7.6% to 13.7%	7.4% to 12.8%	6.9% to 11.9%	6.3% to 11.0%	5.5% to 10.1%	4.5% to 9.3%
Average of 301 25-Year Periods	10.6%	10.1%	9.4%	8.6%	7.8%	6.9%
Best 25-Year Period	(37) 17.2%	(38) 15.7%	(39) 14.1%	(40) 12.5%	(41) 10.8%	(42) 9.3%
Worst 25-Year Period	7.3%	7.1%	6.7%	5.9%	5.1%	3.5%
Result two-thirds of the time	8.5% to 12.3%	8.1% to 11.6%	7.6% to 11.0%	6.8% to 10.3%	6.0% to 9.5%	4.9% to 8.8%
Average of 241 30-Year Periods	10.6%	10.1%	9.4%	8.6%	7.8%	6.9%
Best 30-Year Period	(43) 13.7%	(44) 12.9%	(45) 12.0%	(46) 11.0%	(47) 9.9%	(48) 8.7%
Worst 30-Year Period	9.1%	8.5%	7.7%	6.6%	5.2%	3.6%
Result two-thirds of the time	9.7% to 11.6%	9.1% to 11.0%	8.4% to 10.4%	7.5% to 9.7%	6.5% to 9.1%	5.4% to 8.3%

Notes: The source for performance data was <u>Stocks, Bonds, Bills, and Inflation 2000 Yearbook</u> published by Ibbotson Associates in Chicago. The data for stocks are based upon total returns (capital appreciation and dividend income) of the Standard & Poor's 500 index. The data for bonds are based on Ibbotson's "intermediate-term government bonds" total return (capital appreciation and coupon interest income) index, which uses bonds of approximately 5 years maturity. The period covered runs from 1950 (after the atypical events of the Depression and WWII) through 1999. Portfolios were rebalanced to their original allocations every twelve months.

before stocks have time to rebound. Interest income from bonds is certain; good returns from stocks in the short run are not. A guiding principle should be that you take as little risk as possible in attaining your income goals. For example, if a 20% stocks, 80% bonds mix will generate adequate investment income, then a 65-year old should move in that direction even if they have a temperament that would suggest a higher stocks allocation.

So, it's a matter of balance. You need stocks for growth and bonds for income, but, putting your emotions aside, how much of each would be best given your current age and the amount of time before you'll need to begin cashing in your portfolio?

To help put that question into historical perspective, I've prepared the table on the left. The six columns correspond to the different approaches for organizing your investments that are found in the risk matrix. They range from a very aggressive strategy of investing all your money in blue chip stocks to a more conservative strategy of investing only in government bonds. For each of the six portfolio combinations, the historical results over the past half century are shown.

Let's start at the top (scenarios one through six) with a look at "rolling" one-year periods. Market results are usually stated in terms of calendar years. For instance, an analyst might claim that a search of the historical data since 1950 revealed that the single worst twelve-month performance for a portfolio of large-company stocks was a loss of 26.5%. What the analyst has done is to look at the year-by-year results and picked 1974 as the twelve months with the worst performance. But investors don't invest only on January 1, so that report is somewhat misleading as to the potential risk. That's where the use of "rolling" periods can be helpful. Here's how I ran the calculations.

After looking at the results from buying on January 1, 1950, and holding for twelve months, I then "rolled" to the next month to see what happened if the stocks had been purchased on February 1 and held for twelve months. Then I moved to March 1 and did the same thing. And so on. Continuing in this way, I computed the results for all of the 589 twelve-month holding periods from 1950 through 1999. This is in contrast to just 50 periods when only calendar years are considered. Using this more exhaustive process provides a more accurate picture of the degree of volatility and level of returns that can be expected from different blends of stocks and bonds. In our example, I found that the worst-case one-year performance for the large-company stocks in the S&P 500 index was actually a loss of 38.9% (October 1973–September 1974), as shown in scenario 1.

The forty-eight different scenarios shown in the table reflect the basic risk-reward relationships we have discussed in previous chapters.

If you study the numbers you'll see once again that:

• **The shorter your holding period, the higher the risks and potential rewards.** Over a thirty-year holding period (scenarios 43-48), the range of *likely* results is relatively narrow. They are shown on the line where it says "result two-thirds of the time." Even in an all-stock portfolio (such as scenario 43), this range of likely results is less than two percentage points per year from low to high. As you move up the table to shorter holding periods, the range broadens, that is, it becomes more volatile. By the time you get to a one-year holding period in the all-stock portfolio (scenario 1), there is almost a 32 percentage point difference from low to high in the range of likely results.

   • **The more you allocate to stocks, the higher the risks and potential rewards.** As you move from right to left across the table, the "best" and "worst" results become more exaggerated. These extremes don't come along very often, so you can't weigh them too heavily in your decisions, but it's good to keep in mind the full range of possibilities (as unlikely as they may seem). The numbers illustrate the extent to which blue chip stocks carry greater risks than intermediate-term government bonds.

   • **There's no sure thing.** Pretend you watched the companies in the S&P 500 index return an average of 14.5% per year, every year, for five years. This is what happened from October 1960–September 1965. You say to yourself, "I want to get in on this!" and in October 1965 you invest your retirement money in those very same stocks. Imagine your disappointment as the next five-year period unfolds and your average annual returns are just 2.0% per year. You didn't earn the "average" double-digit gain typical of a five-year holding period (scenario 13). Nor did your returns fall within the range of results that investors who held on for five years received two-thirds of the time. You, unfortunately, were invested during one of the five-year periods that was an uncharacteristic underachiever. You knew it could happen; scenario 13 shows that stocks actually have lost money during some five-year periods, the worst being a fall of 4.1%. You were hoping it wouldn't happen to you. But it can, and it did. That's why Wall Street is always reminding you that "past performance is no guarantee of future results."

Let me share with you how I might apply the data in the table to come up with an allocation strategy for my personal retirement investing.

   I'm presently 55 years old. Based on normal life expectancies, an argument could be made for assuming a retirement age of seventy or even seventy-five, but in keeping with tradition, let's assume I select a time frame of ten years, which coincides with my reaching age 65. I have two goals: (1) to earn average returns of 10% per year, and (2) to do it with as little risk as possible. The risk matrix suggests that Daredevils/Explorers (like me) consider an 80% stocks, 20% bonds allocation. With a time frame of 10 years, that leads me to scenario 20.

   An 80/20 mix returned 10.9% per year during the average 10-year holding period over the past 50 years. That's slightly higher than my goal (nice to have a little cushion), but not so far off that I feel I should move down to 60/40 (scenario 21). The range of 6.8% to 15.0% represents what actually happened two out of three times The remaining one-third of the time, the result was outside the "likely" range. That means I have roughly one chance in six of averaging less than 6.8% per year (that's the scary part), and a one in six chance of doing better than 15.0% per year (too good to be true).

Emotionally, the difficult part of this will be to stay with my 80% stock allocation as I get closer to age sixty-five, especially if I've "fallen behind" the pace I need to maintain. As I consider the probable results for the final three years, I will need to remind myself that those negative one- and three-year numbers (scenarios 2 and 8) are *already reflected* in the ten-year calculations that I based my asset allocation strategy on initially. So, hopefully my overall ten-year results will still fall within the likely range.

Resources To Check As You Approach Retirement
www.soundmindinvesting.com/vsection/v_planning/s_nowthat.htm

www.smartmoney.com/consumer/index.cfm?story=20000609retire

There's one wrinkle I can add to minimize the risk that poor results in the final few years will sabotage my strategy. If at any point along the way, I find I could reach my ten-year target with a dramatically lower stock allocation, I would make the change. For instance, investing $193,000 on a tax-deferred basis for ten years at 10% gets you to $500,000. Assume this is my plan. But if I averaged 15% annually during the first six years, my portfolio would already be up to $446,000. At that point, I would need to average only 2.9% during the final four years to reach my goal. So why not move everything into a money market fund, thus guaranteeing my success? Some would hesitate, saying I could make more by staying with my 80/20 allocation. Perhaps. Perhaps not. Nobody knows. The important thing is to reach my goal, not "make more money."

One way to continue using a relatively high stock allocation as you enter retirement (if that's your wish) is to extend your time horizon. You can do this by investing a portion of your capital in a money market fund. Pick an amount that, along with your Social Security and any pension you receive, will absolutely ensure you can live comfortably over the next five years. Then, knowing your liquidity needs are met, you can commit to a five-year holding period and the higher stock allocations that such a time frame permits. Short-term fluctuations won't be a concern.

How much should you invest in small company stocks versus those in larger companies?

Because the table on page 286 uses the Standard & Poor's 500 index to represent stock market returns, it implicitly assumes that all of your stock investing is done in larger companies. But shares in smaller companies also offer significant profit opportunities. They have the potential to grow to ten, twenty, or fifty times their present size. Of course, they also carry higher risk because they are more easily devastated by economic setbacks. Let's look at the historical risks and rewards of investing in small companies versus large ones.

The first data column in the table below shows the historical results from the S&P 500 index, and the column on the far right shows similar data for a portfolio consisting solely of small company stocks. These are the kinds of stocks that "micro-cap" funds invest in—by today's standards, they're not just small, they're *very* small, typically having market values of $250 million or less. The middle column shows the results from having your stock allocation split evenly between large and small companies. You can observe that:

• The *average* returns from small companies are higher than those of large companies over every time period measured.

• For holding periods of less than ten years, the risk of loss from investing in smaller companies is greater. This holds true in both the worse-case scenario as well as the lower end of the range of results that occur two-thirds of the time.

• For holding periods of ten years and more, the results clearly favor smaller companies over large ones.

• A reasonable case is made for having a significant portion of your stock allocation, perhaps 50% for starters, diversified among micro-cap stocks or mutual funds that specialize in them.

One group is not "better" than another. They offer different strengths that are suitable for different investing needs. Large companies typically offer higher dividends and greater price stability; smaller companies offer higher long-term growth potential.

HISTORICAL INVESTMENT RETURNS OF LARGE COMPANIES VS. SMALL COMPANIES

Portfolio Consists of >>>	Large: 100% Small: 0%	Large: 50% Small: 50%	Large: 0% Small: 100%
Average of 589 1-Year Periods	① 14.5%	② 15.7%	③ 16.8%
Best 1-Year Period	61.0%	79.3%	97.6%
Worst 1-Year Period	−38.9%	−36.2%	−45.9%
Result two-thirds of the time	−1.4% to 30.4%	−2.3% to 33.6%	−6.2% to 39.9%
Average of 565 3-Year Periods	④ 13.2%	⑤ 14.4%	⑥ 15.3%
Best 3-Year Period	33.4%	32.0%	44.5%
Worst 3-Year Period	−10.6%	−13.0%	−16.7%
Result two-thirds of the time	5.1% to 21.3%	5.9% to 22.8%	−3.1% to 27.5%
Average of 541 5-Year Periods	⑦ 12.7%	⑧ 14.1%	⑨ 15.3%
Best 5-Year Period	29.7%	28.0%	39.8%
Worst 5-Year Period	−4.1%	−7.9%	−12.2%
Result two-thirds of the time	6.1% to 19.2%	7.4% to 20.9%	5.4% to 25.1%
Average of 481 10-Year Periods	⑩ 11.7%	⑪ 13.4%	⑫ 14.7%
Best 10-Year Period	19.4%	23.4%	30.6%
Worst 10-Year Period	0.5%	2.4%	3.2%
Result two-thirds of the time	7.0% to 16.5%	9.2% to 17.7%	9.0% to 20.4%
Average of 421 15-Year Periods	⑬ 11.3%	⑭ 13.3%	⑮ 14.9%
Best 15-Year Period	19.7%	20.8%	23.8%
Worst 15-Year Period	4.1%	5.5%	5.9%
Result two-thirds of the time	7.2% to 15.3%	10.3% to 16.4%	11.6% to 18.1%
Average of 361 20-Year Periods	⑯ 10.7%	⑰ 13.0%	⑱ 14.7%
Best 20-Year Period	17.9%	18.0%	20.3%
Worst 20-Year Period	6.4%	7.8%	8.2%
Result two-thirds of the time	7.6% to 13.7%	10.7% to 15.4%	12.3% to 17.2%

Notes: The source for performance data was Stocks, Bonds, Bills, and Inflation 2000 Yearbook published by Ibbotson Associates in Chicago. The data for large company stocks are based upon total returns (capital appreciation and dividend income) of the Standard & Poor's 500 index. The data for small company stocks are based on the total returns of those companies listed on the New York Stock Exchange that fall in the bottom 20% in terms of market capitalization. The period covered runs from 1950 through 1999. Portfolios were rebalanced to their original allocations every twelve months.

A SOUND MIND BRIEFING

Once You Reach Retirement, Which Assets Should You Draw From First?

by Eric Reinhold, CFP, MBA

Once you reach retirement and begin drawing from that storehouse of wealth you've worked so hard to accumulate, the question naturally arises: Which asset accounts should you withdraw from first? This is an often overlooked question, since most banks, mutual fund companies and brokers are more focused on how to solicit and where to invest your money.

Let's look at four of the most common retirement vehicles: traditional tax-deductible IRAs, Roth IRAs, tax-deferred annuities and taxable investments. For purposes of this discussion, I'll assume that any pension plan assets from your place of employment have been rolled over into a traditional IRA at retirement. The starting point is to answer this question: "Are my intentions to pass a significant portion of these assets to my family, or will I be utilizing them for myself?"

• To favor your heirs, withdraw from your annuity and traditional IRAs first. Let's suppose that your desire is to maximize what you can pass along to your family at the time of your death. This means you want to minimize the tax consequences to your heirs even though it would cost you a little more in income taxes in the meanwhile. With this in mind, you'll not want to generate income by selling assets that receive a "step-up in basis" at your death. For example, if you purchased Micro Inc. at $5.00 a share (your "basis"), and Micro is priced at $50.00 a share on the date of your death, $50.00 a share becomes the new tax basis enjoyed by your heirs (and the capital gains tax on the $45.00 per share profits is completely avoided).

Even better than the "stepped-up basis" deal is the treatment of Roth IRAs. These are passed to your children with their tax-free advantages intact, meaning the account can continue to grow tax-free over the beneficiary's life expectancy if they elect to make only the minimum required withdrawals each year. Over time, this can be an incredible benefit.

For passing on wealth, it is to your advantage, then, to initially draw from your annuities or traditional IRAs where there is no step-up in basis at your death. In the case of an annuity, a portion will be taxable upon withdrawal (the amount above what you invested), and in the case of a traditional IRA, all of the withdrawal will be taxable. If left to your heirs, however, these assets would be subject to income tax on *your* basis. If they are in the highest tax bracket, this would be almost 40%. In addition, estate taxes can take as much as 55% of what's left. When all is said and done, your children may only be inheriting 30 cents on the dollar from your tax-deferred retirement accounts.

• To increase your giving. If your tax bracket situation is such that your heirs might receive only 30 cents on the dollar from your annuity and IRA retirement accounts, you might want to consider leaving a portion of them to charity. One of the simplest ways to do this is by making your spouse the first beneficiary and a church and/or charities your secondary beneficiary. Your spouse is taken care of, but upon his/her death, the charity would get 100% of the remainder. The government would not receive its customary 70%, and your children's inheritance would only be reduced by 30% of that value. Since annuities and IRAs pass outside of probate, you do not have to change your will or trusts. You simply have to ask for a "change of beneficiary form" from the company at which you have your investment and update it to reflect your desires. Over the course of time, if the Lord leads you to pass this money along to different organizations, you can easily update your beneficiary form again.

• To maximize your lifetime income, withdraw from your taxable investments first. If your priority is not maximizing inheritance but rather maximizing your retirement income, then you would want to first withdraw from your taxable investments in order to prolong the tax-deferral aspects of your annuity and IRAs for as long as possible. The compounding of tax-deferred dollars is hard to beat. For a traditional IRA, you can postpone making withdrawals until age $70\frac{1}{2}$; in the case of an annuity, it will vary from company to company. To postpone your withdrawals even further, you might want to consider a Roth IRA which requires no minimum distributions ever. Upon your death, the assets provide tax-free income to your children when annuitized over their lifetimes, as mentioned previously.

Depending upon your desires, an ideal strategy may be to combine both concepts. Let your tax-deferred investments continue to grow and designate your spouse as the first beneficiary and church/charities as the secondary beneficiary while utilizing your taxable investments as a source of income. Meanwhile, you could make annual gifts to family members so they are able to enjoy the benefit in their younger years when it is most often needed.

From the Sound Mind Investing newsletter. Eric Reinhold is the Regional V.P. and branch manager for
Academy Financial in Orlando, Florida. To learn more about the monthly SMI newsletter, use the
postage-paid tear-out card in this book, or visit our website at www.soundmindinvesting.com.

How you react to the data in this chapter depends largely on your temperament.

Preservers will tend to focus on the worst-case scenarios, thinking if it has happened before, it might happen again. Daredevils will look at the best-case numbers, ignoring the downside risks. Nothing in this chapter is meant to sway you toward a certain class of investments. Rather, it was written to help you better understand that there is no single "right" way to arrange your portfolio when nearing retirement, and that you must make trade-offs between the risks you're willing to take and the rewards you hope to reap.

Let's return to the opening theme of this chapter—nobody knows what the future holds or which investments will do best in the coming year. That's why our Sound Mind portfolios are based on a strategy of diversification—spreading out your money into several different areas so that you won't be overinvested in any single hard-hit area *and* you'll have at least some investments in the more rewarding areas.

As you consider your investing strategy, let me encourage you to:

• **Acknowledge your limited vision.** "Now listen, you who say, 'Today or tomorrow we will go to this or that city, spend a year there, carry on business and make money.' Why, you do not even know what will happen tomorrow. . . . As it is, you boast and brag. All such boasting is evil" (James 4:13-14, 16).

• **Look to God, not man, for wisdom.** "If any of you lacks wisdom, he should ask God, who gives generously to all without finding fault, and it will be given to him" (James 1:5).

• **Diversify your risks and stay flexible.** "Give portions to seven, yes to eight, for you do not know what disaster may come upon the land" (Ecclesiastes 11:2).

• **And above all, let the Lord be your treasure.** "Delight yourself in the Lord and he will give you the desires of your heart" (Psalm 37:4).

This counsel from Scripture is a guide for all of us, not just during these uncertain economic times but as a way of life. It is my belief that it's ultimately impossible to self-destruct financially if our decision-making is pointed in the direction of God's glory. It's to that theme we turn in the next section. ◆

Investing That Glorifies God

A Biblical Blueprint for Building Your Financial House on Solid Rock

The awesome beauty of nature. The innocence of childhood. The security of a world at peace. The exuberance of romantic love. The joy of living life freely and fully.

All of these are noble themes. Great literature, art, and music have all been inspired by them. They capture our emotions and imaginations. They challenge our values and influence our priorities. They reflect universal longings of the human spirit. But although uplifting, they fall short of the noblest and greatest theme of all.

A grander theme runs through all of human history, from the beginning of recorded history to this very moment. This theme explains why we're here, why things happen as they do, where the world is headed, and why the world, as we know it, must eventually end. It underlies everything that is, and is the reason for everything that is not.

It is the incomparable glory of our God, surely the greatest theme in all the universe! In his book *Keys to Spiritual Growth*, John MacArthur describes it this way:

> *God possesses intrinsic glory by virtue of who He is. This is not given to Him. If man had never been created, if the angels had never been created, would God still be a God of glory? Certainly! If no one ever gave Him any glory, any honor, or any praise, would He still be the glorious God that He is? Of course! That is intrinsic glory—the glory of God's nature. It is the manifestation and combination of all His attributes. . . . It is His being, as basic as His grace, His mercy, His power, and His knowledge. All we do is recognize them. So we say, "Yes, it's true; God is glorious!"*

The theme of God's glory is a continuous golden thread which is woven throughout Scripture. We see it operative from the opening story of creation through the triumphal establishment of Christ's kingdom. The infinite worth of God's glory is emphasized over and over again. We should, therefore, be mindful that in all of our daily decision-making, including that small part that has to do with our financial and investing decisions, our primary goal must always be kept uppermost in mind—that of glorifying our wonderful God. In this section, we will explore what investing "for the glory of God" might involve.

CHAPTER PREVIEW

Investing That Glorifies God Acknowledges His Sovereignty

David praised the Lord in the presence of the whole assembly, saying, "Praise be to you, O Lord, God of our father Israel, from everlasting to everlasting. Yours, O Lord, is the greatness and the power and the glory and the majesty and the splendor, for everything in heaven and earth is yours. Yours, O Lord, is the kingdom; you are exalted as head over all. Wealth and honor come from you; you are the ruler of all things. In your hands are strength and power to exalt and give strength to all. Now, our God, we give you thanks, and praise your glorious name."

(1 Chronicles 29:10-13)

"Who has known the mind of the Lord? Or who has been his counselor? Who has ever given to God, that God should repay him?" For from him and through him and to him are all things. To him be the glory forever! Amen. Therefore, I urge you, brothers, in view of God's mercy, to offer your bodies as living sacrifices, holy and pleasing to God—this is your spiritual act of worship. Do not conform any longer to the pattern of this world, but be transformed by the renewing of your mind. Then you will be able to test and approve what God's will is—his good, pleasing and perfect will.

(Romans 11:34-12:2)

Shortly after my twenty-fifth birthday, my father passed away and I inherited my share in a million-dollar restaurant business. Think about it . . .

. . . only twenty-five and already having just about everything you could reasonably hope for in life. I was financially secure and young enough to enjoy it! I was married to my college sweetheart, the girl of my dreams, and we had two healthy boys. In a world that values position, I was the head of six businesses employing two hundred people. In a world that values freedom, I could go places I wanted to go, pursue interests I wanted to pursue, be any kind of person I wanted to be. And yet, somehow, in some way, something was missing. In spite of it all, I wasn't really fulfilled.

Well, why not? If you had asked me, I couldn't have told you. Instead of feeling peace, I felt pressure to achieve further success in a business I didn't really enjoy. Instead of feeling happy, I felt guilt. In looking back, I can now identify two major areas of stress.

First, there was my time. Eighty-hour weeks are common in the restaurant business; I awoke at 4:30 A.M., arrived at the store by 5:30, and worked through breakfast, lunch, and dinner, leaving around 8:00 P.M. after taking the evening inventory. I would do this six days a week and take Tuesday off. When my friends with regular jobs would call on weekends to see if I could play, I'd say "No, I've gotta work. Would you like to do something on Tuesday?" No one ever did.

So, when I had two weeks off, I really appreciated it. But before I could really catch my breath, the two weeks were up and it was time to go back. What if you're twenty-five with a life expectancy of seventy-five and you've got fifty years to fill? Did I want to spend them running restaurants? For the first time, I began thinking about not only what I would do with my life, but also about what was *worth* doing.

I started really wondering about such things as . . .

. . . What's life all about? Where did I come from and where am I going? Where do I fit in now that I'm here? Mortimer Adler, the famous educator, said that the driving force behind human behavior is a search for significance. I could relate to that. Don't we all want it to somehow matter that we were born, that we worked and played, that we laughed and cried, that we visited this place? I wanted a purpose that had credibility, that would be adequate to take me all the way in life. Though a Christian, I did not realize my key purpose in work and play was to glorify God.

Then, there was my inheritance. I really hadn't made peace with it. My pride said I should make it on my own! Have you ever read the life story of a real financial achiever—someone who started out with nothing much, but who through force of will and intellect and creativity and courage established a business empire? When you finished reading, your response probably was respect, perhaps inspiration. That's how I felt.

I wanted to feel adequate in my own right—not just as the caretaker of my father's business. Years earlier, I had graduated in the upper tenth of my class with a major in banking and finance. Now I found myself attracted to the investment world. I thought that if I could set meaningful goals, and achieve them, in an area where my father had not been very proficient, at least I'd feel better about myself and maybe some of the other pieces would fall into place.

So I'll tell you what I did. I decided to try to make my fortune in the stock market.

(You can see what an original thinker I was.) But, hey—this was 1970, one of the exciting "go-go" years on Wall Street. Everyone seemed to be making money, even amateur upstarts like me. Well, I threw myself into it all the way! I subscribed to all the leading investment industry publications and began reading. Although I was working hard running the family business, I made time to teach myself the various trading and charting techniques. I began trading, and I kept meticulous records of my successes and failures. At one point, I had four brokers—simultaneously! (They loved me because I churned my accounts continuously. A few more like me and they would have been the office superstars.) Eventually I had a ticker installed right there in my office so I could get instant quotes from the New York and American Stock Exchanges. It was great! I was trading, making a little money in spite of myself, and having fun at it.

Then, one of my brokers introduced me to . . . (imagine the ominous soundtrack to *Jaws* playing in the background) . . . commodities futures. Given my propensity for trading, this was probably a criminal act on his part. In those volatile and emotional markets, I was soon swimming with the sharks. Surveys have indicated that nine out of ten commodities speculators lose money. It was said that you needed ice water in your veins to stay calm under the daily pressures. The leverage, the risks, and the rewards are great.

Think of the attraction this held for me as I sought to prove myself: I could make more money, make it faster, and make it under greater stress. What an arena! If you're up for playing Russian roulette with your self-esteem and your bank account, you should check it out. Personally, I loved it!

For a time, commodities became my driving purpose. You know, everyone has a driving purpose.

Everyone is driven by something. What drives you? I'll tell you how to find out. Ask yourself these questions. How do you spend your most precious resource, your time? What successes excite and exhilarate you the most? What defeats irritate and frustrate you the most? The ones tied to your driving purpose.

Well, for a time, commodities was it for me. I remember making and losing $10,000 (in 1970 dollars!) in a single day of trading. I remember driving along the Pennsylvania Turnpike on a summer getaway with Susie and ruining the whole effect by stopping every 75 miles to call my broker back in Louisville. Every hour I stopped. Can you believe it? Susie couldn't: "You mean we're stopping again?!" She just didn't understand. I had left town still holding a heavy short position in frozen pork bellies and I had to be careful. (For you laymen, that means that I had sold 200 tons of bacon I didn't own to a buyer I had never met for a price one of us would soon regret. Obviously, I was hoping it wouldn't be me.)

I remember that I made more money in commodities than I ever made in stocks.

But to my surprise, in spite of this success, I was not any deep-down happier. The up and down emotions . . .

. . . from running a restaurant chain and speculating in the markets was no foundation upon which to build a fulfilling life or a healthy marriage. I was searching, trying to fill the emptiness but not really knowing how. Pascal, the scientist and philosopher, said: "There's a God-shaped vacuum in the heart of every man placed there by God that only He can fill."

But I didn't know that. To be sure, Susie and I had Christian upbringings. I have a loving mom who took me to church when I was a boy, and I learned about God: how He had visited earth in the person of Jesus Christ, had died on a cross and in so doing had somehow accepted the penalty for my own personal sins, and had come back to life again and was seen by more than five hundred people. At least that's what they taught me, and I accepted those teachings. But somehow, in the process, I never developed a full picture of a personal God.

In the Sunday school where I grew up, there were all these colored drawings of Jesus and His disciples. They were walking through the desert, and He was teaching and heal-ing people and feeding the multitudes. Miraculous things! And I used to think: "Boy, I wish I could have been there and seen *that*! To see an honest-to-goodness miracle!" Did you ever wish that? To see something undeniably supernatural? Well, I did. But Jesus lived two thousand years ago—a long, long, *long* time ago. So remote, so far away, that it almost wasn't even real. And it made God seem far away, because you never hear of those kinds of miracles anymore.

So I had gradually gotten the impression that you couldn't really know God now. He was there, but . . .

. . . seemed too far away. I didn't see any way to relate to Him in any meaningful, practical, relevant way. When I got to heaven, whatever and wherever that is, I could learn more about God. But until then, in this life, I assumed it was completely up to me to find my own way, to make my life count.

About this time, one of my very best friends came to town for a visit. We'd gone through high school together and were as close as brothers. He'd gone off to Ohio State to study engi-neering and had become involved with one of those Christian student organizations. He mar-ried a girl he met there, and they became really enthusiastic about spiritual things.

They came home about once a year and always wanted to talk about the Bible and the Christian life when we were together. Now you know, when you're not into that, a little bit goes a long way—so once a year was just about right for them!

Well, sure enough, Bob and Carole called to ask if they could stop by. I really wasn't up for it. I asked Susie, and she wasn't up for it. But he was a dear friend, so what can you do? After reluctantly concluding there was no gracious way out of it, I returned to the phone and said, "Great, we'd love to see you! How soon can you get over here? How about staying for dinner?"

After dinner, it wasn't long before Bob shifted the conversation to spiritual matters. He saw us living the comfortable life and asked Susie at one point: "Susie, are you happy?"

And she answered, "We've really got a lot to be thankful for." He said: "I can see that. But are you happy?" And she paused, then simply said, "No."

Well, I was surprised. I didn't know she was unhappy. And I was embarrassed! You just don't want your wife . . .

. . . to go around admitting she's unhappy. Before I could jump in and try to salvage the situation ("What Susie really meant by that was . . ."), Bob asked one of the most surprising questions I'd ever heard. He asked: "Have you ever considered asking Jesus Christ to take control of your life?"

Bob really took me off guard, because no one had ever suggested to me that Jesus was even remotely interested in assisting in the everyday management of my life, let alone asked if I would be willing to let Him. Anyway, Susie responded: "This may sound egotistical, but I don't think I want anyone running my life or telling me what to do."

The question scared her because, in our limited understanding of what it meant to give God "control" of our lives, it might mean that we had to go to the mission fields of Africa or something else equally traumatic. As for me, I certainly wasn't attracted to the idea of God telling me what to do. I suppose I imagined that He would rob my life of any fun, or joy, or excitement.

Besides, as a man I felt it would be a sign of weakness to depend on anyone else. Is there a higher, more masculine ethic . . .

. . . than absolute self-sufficiency? Remember William Henley's words from "Invictus"?

It matters not how strait the gate, How charged with punishments the scroll, I am the master of my fate: I am the captain of my soul.

Isn't that why James Bond and Indiana Jones are so appealing—they're overwhelmingly adequate for any conceivable situation. As a man, I especially wanted to be completely in control of my own destiny.

But even so, Bob and Carole shared some things that night that shed new light on the basics of the Christian faith that we had learned as children. The first point they made was that God is, after all, a personal God, that He loves us as individuals, and that He offers a wonderful plan for our lives. Christ said, "*I have come that they may have life, and have it to the full [that it would be abundant and meaningful]*" (John 10:10). I said this was hard to understand because it was obvious that the world is terribly messed up and that everyone is not experiencing an abundant life.

They responded with words something like: "The reason for that is we're the ones who choose to go our own independent ways and separate ourselves from God. Generally we don't give Him much thought. He's irrelevant to the important decisions we make everyday. So, with that attitude, how *can* we know or experience God's love and plan for our lives?

"Although we were created to have fellowship with God, we have chosen to pretty much do our own thing, and fellowship with God has been broken off. Our independence, which may be characterized by either active rebellion or just passive indifference, is evidence of what the Bible calls sin. The consequences of our living independently from God is that we have been spiritually separated from Him.

"It's obvious that we sense this and try to bridge the separation and reach God. But we usually want to return to Him on our own terms of reference: a relatively moral life, some charitable work here and there, going to church regularly, perhaps even giving some money to charity. But these things aren't enough."

Bob continued: "The truth is, we must approach God on *His* terms of reference. That's fair, isn't it? After all, He is God. But what exactly. . .

. . . are God's terms of reference as to how we should bridge this gulf of separation? That's where Jesus comes in. God has made a special provision for our rebellion against Him. It's through Jesus that we're reconciled to God. The Scriptures say, 'God demonstrates his own love toward us in this: while we were still sinners, Christ died for us.'

"There's nothing we can add to this—we can only accept it as one would accept a gift. Ironically, that's the hardest part. Our pride says we should contribute our fair share to this arrangement. Unfortunately, in this case, we have nothing to negotiate with. God looks at our meager efforts at righteousness, compares them to His holiness, and says in His book, 'All have sinned and fall short of the glory of God.'

"Since we're helpless to save ourselves, God took the initiative and provided the way back in Jesus Christ, who died in our place to pay the penalty for our rebellion and gives us right standing with God once more."

As I was listening, I was thinking, "Bob, I've heard most of this since we were kids. We used to go to church together all the time. This isn't what I really want to know. What I really am curious about is why do you and I believe pretty much these same things about who Christ was, but you're so excited about it, so fired up, and I'm not? What has happened to make you so different now?"

After they left, Susie and I continued to talk. I can still remember lying on our bed with arms outstretched . . .

. . . reading a little blue booklet they had left us, and sharing how we felt about what they had said. We eventually came to a prayer at the end of the booklet, which read:

> *Dear Father, I need You. I acknowledge that I have been directing my own life and that, as a result, I have sinned against You. I thank You that You have forgiven my sins through Christ's death on the cross for me. I now invite Christ to again take His place on the throne of my life. Fill me with the Holy Spirit as You commanded me to be filled, and as you promised in Your word that You would do if I asked in faith. I pray this in the name of Jesus.*

Then, right under the prayer was the suggestion that, if the prayer expressed the desire of our hearts, why didn't we pray "right now." I started to turn the page, but Susie said to wait, and asked, "What do you think of this prayer?" I said it was a nice prayer. She said,

"Why don't we pray it right now?" I was surprised that she was so intense.

But as we talked, my mind returned to Bob and how, to him, Christ was so real and so personal. It was obvious to me that his relationship with Christ was on a much more intimate level than mine. I recognized that if the claims Jesus made about Himself were true, He offered a significance and purpose to life that the world could never match; that, as God, He was truly worthy of first place in my life.

After all, when you think it through to its logical conclusion, if the claims of Jesus are true, knowing Him is worth everything. Think about it . . .

. . . If He's worth anything, He's worth everything. What I mean by this is that if Jesus *was* who He claimed to be, then He's worthy of our complete devotion. If He *was not* who He claimed to be, then Christianity is a cruel hoax and illusion.

There's no doubt that 2000 years ago, there appeared a Jew who went about talking as if he were divine. His claims sound like the ravings of a madman. After all, He claimed to be without sin, to be the judge of the world, to be able to give eternal life, to be the only way to salvation, and to be able to satisfy the deepest needs and longings of the human heart.

These are not comments that can easily be written off as minor boasts. Those who saw and heard him were said to be astonished and amazed. One of the strangest aspects of Jesus' story is that even his enemies, when they read his teachings, don't come away with the impression that he was deranged or a megalomaniac. Even they admit that he was perhaps the greatest teacher on love and human relationships that the human race has yet produced. And when he said he was "humble and meek," they find it easy to believe him. How can his astonishing claims of divinity be reconciled with the fact that he is held in high regard by non-believers the world over? They can't. C.S. Lewis put it well:

> "I am trying here to prevent anyone from saying the really foolish thing that people often say about Him: 'I'm ready to accept Jesus as a great moral teacher, but I don't accept His claim to be God.' That is the one thing we must not say. A man who was merely a man and said the sort of things Jesus said would not be a great moral teacher. He would either be a lunatic — on a level with the man who says he is a poached egg — or else he would be the Devil of Hell. You must make your choice. Either this man was, and is, the Son of God; or else a madman or something worse. You can shut Him up for a fool, you can spit at Him and kill Him as a demon; or you can fall at His feet and call him Lord and God. But let us not come with any patronizing nonsense about His being a great human teacher. He has not left that open to us. He did not intend to."

That's why if Jesus is worthy of any obedience, He's worthy of total obedience. If Jesus is worthy of any of our worship, He's worthy of all of our worship. In other words, if Jesus is worth anything, He's worth everything!

And I decided, lying there on the bed next to my wife, that I wanted to know Christ the way my friend did.

I wanted to share in his excitement of knowing God personally if that were possible. If it required me to make Him sovereign in my life, so be it.

In my heart, I confessed my sins to God, and there were a whole lot of them. Maybe the greatest sin of all was being indifferent to God—being what you might call a casual Christian—professing some sort of belief in God but really not treating it seriously. So Susie and I prayed together that night. Not because we were in church, not because everyone else was praying, but because we wanted to know God as never before.

God is sovereign. Being sovereign means "possessed of supreme power that is unlimited in extent, enjoying autonomy, having undisputed ascendancy." We see this aspect of God portrayed in Scripture repeatedly.

> *I am God, your God. . . . I have no need of a bull from your stall or of goats from your pens, for every animal of the forest is mine, and the cattle on a thousand hills. I know every bird in the mountains, and the creatures of the field are mine. If I were hungry I would not tell you, for the world is mine, and all that is in it. (Psalm 50:8-12)*

> *Remember the former things, those of long ago; I am God, and there is no other; I am God, and there is none like me. I make known the end from the beginning, from ancient times, what is still to come. I say: My purpose will stand, and I will do all that I please. (Isaiah 46:9-10)*

> *His dominion is an eternal dominion; his kingdom endures from generation to generation. All the peoples of the earth are regarded as nothing. He does as he pleases with the powers of heaven and the peoples of the earth. No one can hold back his hand or say to him: "What have you done?" (Daniel 4:34-35)*

Amazingly, although God is sovereign over all He has made and could dictate our every thought and movement, He tolerates pockets of resistance to His reign. He allows us to make a decision of monumental importance: whether to willingly embrace Christ's rule in our lives and affections or to continue exercising our own self-rule and independence. We are allowed the audacity of challenging His "undisputed ascendancy" in our own lives.

What makes the choice so difficult is that the results are counterintuitive.

If we should abdicate control of our lives and invite His Spirit to guide us according to His purposes, we would expect a loss of freedom, power, and happiness. *The actual result is just the opposite.* We are never more free, never have more strength to reach our potential, and never experience more fulfillment than when we acknowledge His sovereignty over our lives. The reason for this is that only when we place our faith in Christ does He come to live within us, and it is His actual presence—the personal presence of the omnipotent Creator God of the universe—that raises our daily existence to a higher, entirely new level of existence.

On the other hand, we can choose to continue living independently, doing as we think best. We expect that way of living to give us the best chance of building a future that will be the most satisfying. But again, the result is just the opposite of what we expect. We find that achieving our goals provides only short-lived fulfillment. The thrill of acquiring material possessions wears off. Fame has a short shelf life, and perversely it creates greater anxiety than emotional security. A famous Hollywood producer, when asked how fame, fortune, and immense popularity had changed his life, gave this startling reply: "Success means never having to admit you're unhappy." His success did not end his unhappiness; it just allowed him to deny it.

Investing that glorifies God has a requisite first step: first we must invest ourselves. We do this by . . .

. . . willingly trusting His sovereignty—not only over the physical universe, but over our very lives as well. We asked Christ to take our lives and make us the kind of people He wanted us to be. Susie and I gave Him our lives. God says: "If you'll give Me your life, I'll give you My life." It has been called "The Great Exchange." In light of who He is and all that He offers, what could be more reasonable?

> *"Who has known the mind of the Lord? Or who has been his counselor? Who has ever given to God, that God should repay him?" For from him and through him and to him are all things. To him be the glory forever! Amen. Therefore, I urge you, brothers, in view of God's mercy, to offer your bodies as living sacrifices, holy and pleasing to God—this is your spiritual act of worship. Do not conform any longer to the pattern of this world, but be transformed by the renewing of your mind. Then you will be able to test and approve what God's will is—his good, pleasing and perfect will. (Romans 11:34–12:2)*

It should go without saying that when we present ourselves to God as "living sacrifices," our material possessions are included. After surrendering all that we are and ever hope to be to His eternal sovereignty, the idea that we're also acknowledging God's ownership of the world's wealth (including ours) shouldn't be surprising. When we made The Great Exchange, part of the transaction involved exchanging ownership privileges for management responsibilities. It's called stewardship.

God owns it all. He doesn't need our help or our money. The fact is we have nothing He needs . . .

. . . and He has everything that we need. Bob Benson, one of my favorite writers, had a way of telling humorous stories in simple ways that revealed great truths. I'm grateful to him for putting things into perspective for us:

> *Do you remember when they had old-fashioned Sunday School picnics? I do. As I recall, it was back in the "olden days," as my kids would say, back before they had air conditioning.*

> *They said, "We'll all meet at Sycamore Lodge in Shelby Park at 4:30 on Saturday. You bring your supper and we'll furnish the iced tea."*

> *But if you were like me, you came home at the last minute. When you got ready to pack your picnic, all you could find in the refrigerator was one dried up piece of baloney and just enough mustard in the bottom of the jar so that you got it all over your knuckles trying to get to it. And just two slices of stale bread to go with it. So you made your baloney sandwich and wrapped it in an old brown bag and went to the picnic.*

> *When it came time to eat, you sat at the end of a table and spread out your sandwich. But the folks who sat next to you brought a feast. The lady was a good cook and she had worked hard all day*

Recommended Resource

The Journey Home: A Walk with Bob Benson

Selected & Edited by R. Benson and others

God gifted Bob Benson with a skill for communicating great truths in simple and humorous ways. This book is a collection of stories from among his several books, gathered by his son after his father went to be with the Lord. You'll laugh, and perhaps shed a tear, and learn a few new ways to think about our God.

The Journey Home: A Walk with Bob Benson, R. Benson, Copyright 1997, Beacon Hill Press, pp. 108-110. Used by permission.

to get ready for the picnic. And she had fried chicken and baked beans and potato salad and homemade rolls and sliced tomatoes and pickles and olives and celery. And two big homemade chocolate pies to top it off. That's what they spread out there next to you while you sat with your baloney sandwich.

But they said to you, "Why don't we just put it all together?"

"No, I couldn't do that. I couldn't even think of it," you murmured in embarrassment, with one eye on the chicken.

"Oh, come on, there's plenty of chicken and plenty of pie and plenty of everything. And we just love baloney sandwiches. Let's just put it all together."

And so you did and there you sat, eating like a king when you came like a pauper.

One day, it dawned on me that God had been saying just that sort of thing to me. "Why don't you take what you have and what you are, and I will take what I have and what I am, and we'll share it together." I began to see that when I put what I had and was and am and hope to be with what he is, I had stumbled upon the bargain of a lifetime.

I get to thinking sometimes, thinking of me sharing with God. When I think of how little I bring, and how much he brings and invites me to share, I know that I should be shouting to the housetops, but I am so filled with awe and wonder that I can hardly speak. I know that I don't have enough love or faith or grace or mercy or wisdom, but he does. He has all of those things in abundance and he says, "Let's just put it all together."

Consecration, denial, sacrifice, commitment, crosses were all kind of hard words to me, until I saw them in the light of sharing. It isn't just a case of me kicking in what I have because God is the biggest kid in the neighborhood and he wants it all for himself. He is saying, "Everything that I possess is available to you. Everything that I am and can be to a person, I will be to you."

When I think about it like that, it really amuses me to see somebody running along through life hanging on to their dumb bag with that stale baloney sandwich in it saying, "God's not going to get my sandwich! No, sirree, this is mine!" Did you ever see anybody like that—so needy—just about half-starved to death yet hanging on for dear life. It's not that God needs your sandwich. The fact is, you need his chicken.

Well, go ahead—eat your baloney sandwich, as long as you can. But when you can't stand its tastelessness or drabness any longer; when you get so tired of running your own life by yourself and doing it your way and figuring out all the answers with no one to help; when trying to accumulate, hold, grasp, and keep everything together in your own strength gets to be too big a load; when you begin to realize that by yourself you're never going to be able to fulfill your dreams, I hope you'll remember that it doesn't have to be that way.

You have been invited to something better, you know. You have been invited to share in the very being of God. ◆

CHAPTER PREVIEW

Investing That Glorifies God Values His Majesty

O God, you are my God, earnestly I seek you; my soul thirsts for you,
my body longs for you, in a dry and weary land where there is no
water. I have seen you in the sanctuary and beheld your power and
your glory. Because your love is better than life, my lips will glorify
you. I will praise you as long as I live, and in your name I will lift up
my hands. My soul will be satisfied as with the richest of foods; with
singing lips my mouth will praise you. On my bed I remember you;
I think of you through the watches of the night. Because you are
my help, I sing in the shadow of your wings.

(Psalm 63:1-7)

The God who made the world and everything in it is the Lord of
heaven and earth and does not live in temples built by hands. And he
is not served by human hands, as if he needed anything, because he
himself gives all men life and breath and everything else. From one man
he made every nation of men, that they should inhabit the whole earth;
and he determined the times set for them and the exact places where they
should live. God did this so that men would seek him and perhaps reach
out for him and find him, though he is not far from each one of us.

(Acts 17:24-27)

**I can remember only one time during my childhood when
I was asked "the" question that all kids face . . .**

. . . "What do you want to be when you grow up?" I was probably around
ten years old and was out with my mom doing some routine shopping. We were
riding along when suddenly she popped the big question. She was visibly
amused when I immediately replied, "A disc jockey!" In my formative radio-
listening, rock-and-roll years, being a disc jockey must have seemed like it would
be all the fun in the world. Mom's reaction, however, communicated that while
being a disc jockey might be fun, it didn't reflect a highly developed sense of
ambition. Neither of my parents ever asked me the question again, and to play
it safe, I never brought the subject up either.

So as I moved through my teen years, an only child and obvious "heir apparent," it became the accepted wisdom that I would someday run the family business. In many respects, this greatly simplified things. I always knew that I had a
summer job and what it would be—learning some new facet of restaurant operations (from the ground up). When I enrolled in college, I didn't agonize over a
major—I went to business school and majored in finance. When I graduated, I
didn't worry about job interviews—I simply returned home and went to work.

There was only one problem with all of this. I hated the restaurant business!
I had no interest in food or cooking. I had poor people skills and felt inadequate
as a leader. Rare was the morning I didn't dread getting up and going to work.
But get up I must, and that's exactly what I did the morning after Bob and Carole's
visit. I went off to work without giving the events of the night before—the talking
with Susie, the soul-searching, the prayer of surrender—much thought at all. We
had a special evening, sure, but it was now Monday morning and my life in what
I thought of as "the real world" had resumed.

For Susie, it was an entirely different story. The little booklet our friends had
left with us said that faith was the "engine" of the Christian life and that "feelings"
were the caboose. We should not be controlled by our feelings, but as we exercise
faith and obedience, feelings would follow. So she had whispered her prayer of surrender on that basis, and we went to sleep not "feeling" any different.

**The next morning, however, she awoke with great joy.
She now understood—truly "knew"—for the first time . . .**

. . . that her forgiveness was based on placing her faith in Christ alone. It was
not a matter of her trying to be good and holy for God, but rather just giving every
area of her life over to Him *so He could be holy through her*. He would supply the
strength. She felt totally accepted by God and had peace beyond question that
she would be with Him in heaven for eternity. This was the way to relate to God
that she had been looking for her whole life! She was so joyous over this that she
began calling her friends and family to tell them this incredibly great news.

You can imagine my surprise at coming home from another routine day at the office to find this exuberant evangelist in our house. I don't recall exactly what was said that evening; I only remember that Susie "took off" in her spiritual growth and that it took a long time for me to catch up.

(Perhaps if the truth be known, I never have. The Lord has blessed me with many wonderful friends and teachers who have guided, corrected, and encouraged me in my Christian growth—I am indebted to them all. But there is also a secret life of the believer where our fears and hopes, joys and sorrows are rarely made known to others. It is only in the intimacy of the daily life in Christ between husband and wife where these matters can be shared or exposed. The "outside world" has little grasp of how married partners refresh each other and provide a desperately needed source of balance, wisdom, role modeling, inspiration, and challenge. Susie has been all these things and more to me. Without question, she has been the greatest single influence in my Christian life. We've been married for more than 35 years, and I've never appreciated her more, respected her more, or loved her more than I do today. That's the kind of marriage God has built in us as we have trusted daily in His plans and in His power to live the Christ-centered life.)

Through the years, I had put my work and other family-related demands ahead of her needs, yet she remained committed to me and the sacred aspects of our marriage. As I gradually developed a new awareness of God in my life, I began to learn how to love Susie in a deeper, purer, and more protective kind of way. I finally began to see that my wife and children have a higher call on my time and attentions than my bread-winning activities. Let me tell you—there's nothing finer that can happen to a man, a husband, a father, than to be able to sit and listen to his wife and children pray to a God whom they know in a personal way.

As we sought to know our God better, our interest in spiritual matters grew. We were introduced to Christian ministries that were devising creative new ways for taking the message of God's love and forgiveness to people in all walks of life. One of them was Campus Crusade for Christ. Through a series of events too lengthy to detail here, we received an invitation from Crusade's president, Dr. Bill Bright, to join his staff at the ministry's headquarters. It required a move to southern California, one that was made possible when the Lord answered our heartfelt prayers to send someone to run the family business in my absence. We loaded up the station wagon, our two boys, Tre and Andrew, the cat and bird, and headed west for a "mission trip" that was to last almost two years.

I can still remember what it was like "reporting for work" that first week in California. I was thrilled . . .

. . . that for the first time in my life I would be doing work that *I* had picked out, that I would enjoy, and that had a challenge and purpose that I found ful-

Recommended Resource

The Secret: How to Live with Purpose and Power

by Bill Bright

This book contains much of Campus Crusade's excellent teaching concepts, including the essence of the material that Bob and Carole left with us that night. In chapter four, "What Does It Mean to Be Filled with the Spirit?" you will find a simple way of understanding how God wants to work through the life of every one of His children. It will be a life-changing truth if you take God at His word and apply it. It was for us.

Campus Crusade has made a great deal of material available for free on their website. Check it out at www.ccci.org/.

filling. It was an unforgettable, incredibly stimulating experience. We formed friendships that are warmly treasured to this day. We joined expository Bible studies that opened up Scripture in new and personally relevant ways. We saw answers to prayers that radically changed our views of God's willingness—no, make that eagerness—to meet the needs of His children. We went to give, yet received more back than we could have ever imagined.

In the summer of 1974, Susie and I traveled to Fort Collins, Colorado, for an annual event within Crusade known as staff training. The staff had gathered together for a week of vision-building workshops and seminars. We heard many inspirational speakers, but one in particular quickly captured everyone's attention. To say that Ronald Dunn's messages were well received would be to greatly understate his impact. I have talked with Crusade staff who, fifteen and twenty years later, still recall with great appreciation (as I do) how his words were so encouraging to them that summer.

It was one of those rare times in life when "you just had to be there" to understand why it was special. His messages were really quite basic, just reminders of some of the "old truths" that we might have forgotten along the way, yet they were so meaningful to his audience. I still remember, vividly, the question he posed as he set the stage for one of his primary points:

"What is it, do you believe, that God wants from you more than anything else?" It was a sobering question.

I knew God wanted my obedience, my service, my thanksgiving, and much more. But what did He want *the most*? I really didn't know how to answer. What would you have said? From my notes, Ron's answer went something like this:

> *I believe it is the testimony of the word of God, in both the Old and New Testaments, that the primary thing, the ultimate thing, that God wants from us is not our service. He wants our searching! That we would seek the Lord. That we would seek the Lord.*

In Acts 17, Paul leaves no doubt that *the* primary purpose behind all of God's creative work is that we would seek Him.

> *The God who made the world and everything in it is the Lord of heaven and earth and does not live in temples built by hands. And he is not served by human hands, as if he needed anything, because he himself gives all men life and breath and everything else. From one man he made every nation of men, that they should inhabit the whole earth; and he determined the times set for them and the exact places where they should live. God did this so that men would seek him and perhaps reach out for him and find him, though he is not far from each one of us.*

More than anything else, the Lord wants us to seek Him. He wants to be the object of our affection and the focus of our attention. He wants to draw us to seek Him. If this is the case, then it shouldn't be surprising to think that God will negotiate circumstances or engineer certain events in order to bring us to the place where we come to the end of ourselves and are compelled to seek Him.

Now some may ask how the idea of "seeking the Lord" applies to Christians who have already sought Him out and placed their faith in Him. Ron's response was tremendous:

> When the apostle Paul wrote to the church at Philippi, he recounted his conversion experience, saying: "But whatever was to my profit, I now consider loss for the sake of Christ. What is more, I consider everything a loss compared to the surpassing greatness of knowing Christ."

> If I'd been writing that I might have said "the surpassing greatness of serving Christ." You know, he's had about every experience a fellow could have. There's not been anybody that has been able to serve in the magnificent magnitude that the apostle Paul has. Yet he comes to the end of this life and he says "I am continually giving up everything and counting everything but loss that I may . . . know Him."

> Well, now Paul, I thought you already knew Him. You met Him on the road to Damascus thirty or forty years ago. What do you mean you're counting everything but loss that you may know Him?

> Paul would say: "Well, you can know Him, and then you can know Him some more." You can know Him, and you can know Him, and you can know Him, and you can know Him some more. You see, my friends, the Christian life is not starting with Jesus, and then graduating to something better. It is starting with Jesus, staying with Jesus, and ending up with Jesus.

> I tell you I get excited when I realize that the Bible over and over again makes it clear that Jesus Christ is God's "everything." In Colossians, we read that all the fulness of the Godhead dwells in Him bodily, and we are complete in Him. All the fullness of the Godhead dwells in Jesus bodily, and I like the way Williams translates it "And you are filled with it too through union with Him." I mean, Jesus is everything.

> He's the Means to the end, and He's the End. He's the Door, and He's what you find on the other side of the door. He's the Light of the world, and He's what you see when that light shines. He's the Fountain, and He's also the Living Water that comes out of the fountain. He's the Alpha and the Omega. He's all that you need.

> And so to seek the Lord means that we seek for nothing else. We find in Jesus Christ our all in all. And so Paul is saying that the quest of the Christian life is not "How can I trust Him more? or How can I serve Him more?" but "How can I know Him better?"

> The goal of the Christian life is not service. The goal of the Christian life is Jesus. And our service is the overflow of our fellowship with the Lord Jesus Christ. So it means we need seek for nothing else, but it also means that we should settle for nothing less.

> I'll tell you what I think is happening in evangelical circles today: that we are settling for something less than the Lord Jesus Christ. We were on our way with Jesus, and we met something else along the way that caught our attention, and we settled for that. I started out with the Lord. My heart was filled with the joy of the

Recommended Resource
<u>Don't Just Stand There, Pray Something!</u>
by Ronald Dunn

This is the most helpful and practical book about prayer that I've had the pleasure to read. Ron Dunn is a gifted teacher who is great at communicating through the use of stories about everyday life. Much of the material that I found so life-changing in the summer of 1974 is here. I enthusiastically recommend this book!

Lord. I just wanted Him, that's all! I was seeking the Lord, but in my seeking the Lord, along the way I found service. And I find that often I end up settling for that.

Let me encourage you in something. As you seek the Lord, if you meet service, or a gift, or a doctrine along the way, don't stop and settle for that. Please, you must keep on going and seek the Lord. Constantly seek the Lord. Don't settle for anything less than Jesus, and the fullness of fellowship with Him day by day.

As I listened to Ron, it was immediately clear to me that I had taken a wrong turn somewhere. My serving God was a well-intentioned "living sacrifice," which I desired would please Him, but it also represented a kind of detour. I so desired to serve Him, to "invest" my life for Him, that I no longer had time to seek Him. I resembled the workaholic husband who had little time for his wife, and when she pointed this out he claimed he was "doing it all for her." This error can be quite a subtle thing; it seems to happen in the smallest of increments. You are not even aware of it until one day God works through your circumstances to get your undivided attention, and you "awaken" to find yourself miles off course.

If not consciously resisted, the spirit-sustaining pleasure of spending time alone with Him each day is easily lost to the "tyranny of the urgent." And this tendency to get caught up in the physical and visible world around us often surfaces in an even more compelling way in the area of our stewardship. If we don't guard against it, our financial goals, projects, and ambitions inevitably capture an ever-increasing share of our thought life and physical energies.

In addition to acknowleding His sovereignty, investing that glorifies God has a second indispensable precondition—it never loses sight of the fact . . .

. . . that He is the pearl of great price, causing us to joyfully set aside all that we have (and all that competes for our time) so that we may experience the priceless treasure of fellowship with God in Christ Jesus. We value His majesty and our communion with Him above all earthly ambitions and wealth. There is no greater thrill, no greater joy than to walk away from a time of prayer and meditation having met God.

It is as Jonathan Edwards has written:

The enjoyment of God is the only happiness with which our souls can be satisfied. To go to heaven, fully to enjoy God, is infinitely better than the most pleasant accommodations here. . . . [These] are but shadows; but God is the substance. These are but scattered beams; but God is the sun. These are but streams; but God is the ocean.

Jonathan Edwards, The Works of Jonathan Edwards [Edinburgh: Banner of Truth Trust, 1974], p. 244.

To glorify God, we must see Him as our great treasure. Our hearts and lives must be kept centered in Him. Christian service, although done in His name, is no substitute. Obtaining, securing, and increasing our store of wealth, although used for family support and kingdom purposes, is no substitute.

To invest more time, thought, energy, research, and emotional energy in these areas than we invest in enjoying His presence is to grieve His Father's heart. There are at least three reasons this must be true.

• **It reveals that our pleasures are misplaced.**

To delight more in the companionship of the creation around us than in the Creator who made us is idolatry. Even to delight more in the gifts we offer Him than in the gift His presence offers us is to elevate our glory above His. Our pleasure is to be in Him.

> *O God, you are my God, earnestly I seek you; my soul thirsts for you, my body longs for you, in a dry and weary land where there is no water. I have seen you in the sanctuary and beheld your power and your glory. Because your love is better than life, my lips will glorify you. I will praise you as long as I live, and in your name I will lift up my hands. My soul will be satisfied as with the richest of foods; with singing lips my mouth will praise you. On my bed I remember you; I think of you through the watches of the night. Because you are my help, I sing in the shadow of your wings. My soul clings to you; your right hand upholds me. (Psalm 63:1-8)*

• **It reveals that our confidence is misplaced.**

Isn't our security, whether spiritual, physical, emotional, or material, to be found in His loving promises rather than our human efforts and disciplines? Our confidence is to be in Him.

> *One thing I ask of the Lord, this is what I seek: that I may dwell in the house of the Lord all the days of my life, to gaze upon the beauty of the Lord and to seek him in his temple. For in the day of trouble he will keep me safe in his dwelling; he will hide me in the shelter of his tabernacle and set me high upon a rock. (Psalm 27:4-5)*

> *Keep your lives free from the love of money and be content with what you have, because God has said, "Never will I leave you; never will I forsake you." So we say with confidence, "The Lord is my helper; I will not be afraid. What can man do to me?" (Hebrews 13:5-6)*

• **It reveals that our gratitude is misplaced.**

To whom or what do we owe our successes? The free-enterprise system that rewards hard work? The company we labor for? The government programs that provided needed assistance? Our investment counselor or broker who helped us have a good year? No, God is the source of our blessings and "the giver of every good gift." Our gratitude should be toward Him.

> *David praised the Lord in the presence of the whole assembly, saying, "Praise be to you, O Lord, God of our father Israel, from everlasting to everlasting. Yours, O Lord, is the greatness and the power and the glory and the majesty and the splendor, for everything in heaven and earth is yours. Yours, O Lord, is the kingdom; you are exalted as head over all. Wealth and honor come from you; you are the ruler of all things. In your hands are strength and power to exalt and give strength to all. Now, our God, we give you thanks, and praise your glorious name." (1 Chronicles 29:10-13)*

The kingdom of heaven, and the King who reigns over it, are "like treasure hidden in a field. When a man found it, he hid it again, and then in his joy went and sold all he had and bought that field."

Do our daily lives—the decisions we make and the dreams we pursue—reflect that Christ is our treasure?

It's in this very area that Sam Storm's words lift my spirit. In *Pleasures Evermore, The Life-Changing Power of Enjoying God*, he put it this way:

> *Falling in love with the Son of God is the key to holiness. I want to be attuned to God's heart, to be of one mind, one spirit, one disposition with Him. If this occurs, it will only occur as the fruit of fascination with all that God is in Himself and all that He is for me in Jesus. The ability to walk with consistency in the things you know please God ultimately will only be overcome when your heart, soul, mind, spirit, and will are captivated by the majesty, mercy, splendor, beauty, and magnificence of who God is and what He has and will do for you in Jesus.*
>
> *I must confess that I have ransacked the dictionary for words to describe what I have in mind. Here is what I mean by falling in love with Jesus. I, you, we were made to be* enchanted, enamored, *and* engrossed *with God;* enthralled, enraptured, *and* entranced *with God;* enravished, excited, *and* enticed *by God,* astonished, amazed, *and* awed *by God;* astounded, absorbed, *and* agog *with God;* beguiled *and* bedazzled; startled *and* staggered; smitten *and* stunned; stupefied *and* spellbound; charmed *and* consumed; thrilled *and* thunderstruck; obsessed *and* preoccupied; intrigued *and* impassioned; overwhelmed *and* overwrought; gripped *and* rapt; enthused *and* electrified; tantalized, mesmerized, *and* monopolized; fascinated, captivated, *and* exhilarated *by God;* intoxicated *and* infatuated *with God!*
>
> *Does that sound like your life? Do you want it to? This is what God made you for. There is an eradicable, inescapable impulse in your spirit to experience the fullness of God in precisely this way—and God put it there!*

It is my earnest hope and prayer that I would faithfully seek the majesty of His companionship daily. My practice is, however, that too often I settle for too little. Perhaps you can identify with me in this. If so, may God grant us that we increasingly glorify Him in our seeking. ◆

Recommended Resource

Pleasures Evermore, The Life-Changing Power of Enjoying God

by Sam Storms

This compelling and highly readable book presents a fresh and liberating perspective on why a relationship with God is not only possible but irresistibly pleasurable. Storms explains that a life devoted to God should also be a life devoted to the pleasure of reveling in Him and all He has done.

CHAPTER PREVIEW

Investing That Glorifies God Builds His Kingdom

Remember this: Whoever sows sparingly will also reap sparingly, and whoever sows generously will also reap generously. Each man should give what he has decided in his heart to give, not reluctantly or under compulsion, for God loves a cheerful giver. And God is able to make all grace abound to you, so that in all things at all times, having all that you need, you will abound in every good work. As it is written: "He has scattered abroad his gifts to the poor; his righteousness endures forever." Now he who supplies seed to the sower and bread for food will also supply and increase your store of seed and will enlarge the harvest of your righteousness. You will be made rich in every way so that you can be generous on every occasion, and through us your generosity will result in thanksgiving to God.

(2 Corinthians 9:6-11)

Command those who are rich in this present world not to be arrogant nor to put their hope in wealth, which is so uncertain, but to put their hope in God, who richly provides us with everything for our enjoyment. Command them to do good, to be rich in good deeds, and to be generous and willing to share. In this way they will lay up treasure for themselves as a firm foundation for the coming age, so that they may take hold of the life that is truly life.

(1 Timothy 6:17-19)

Frankly, I was completely unqualified for the task . . .

. . . I was asked to undertake for Campus Crusade (see page 307). I had no previous hands-on experience. I lacked the innate personal temperament that it seemed to call for. I had no sphere of influence that could be tapped for guidance or assistance. In short, I was in over my head.

What was my job? I was to bring all of Crusade's fund-raising efforts under one umbrella. The goal was to make staff members more sensitive to the feelings and interests of the ministry's supporters, which would (hopefully) also make the process of raising financial support more productive over the longer term. When I started, my department had one person in it—me! This indicated to me that, far from Crusade spending too much time and attention on fund-raising (a charge made against many parachurch ministries), it spent very little.

So there I was in a job for which I was ill-equipped. As a businessman back home, I had experienced what it was like to be asked to make large contributions, but I had no experience in doing the asking. It required me to think through what biblical principles should guide me in formulating a strategy. Eventually, I saw the challenge primarily as one of evangelism and discipleship. Here's why.

It had been my experience that, as a donor, I would tend to make a token contribution to help others with "their" favorite causes while I thought nothing of making much larger gifts to *my* favorite causes. I was now volunteering time with Crusade because the Great Commission had become one of my favorite causes. How had this happened? As I had grown in my faith, my desires to tell everyone about the abundance of the Christian life had greatly increased, as had my desires to be obedient to the Lord's commands. Both of these desires found consummation in the Great Commission. Therefore I reached this conclusion: lead others to Christ and help them grow, and in due course they will also want to see the Great Commission being fulfilled. To the extent they see that happening through the ministries of Campus Crusade, they will happily and generously give. The strategy also aligned our motivations properly (how can we help these people grow?) rather than as manipulators (how can we get these people to give to us?).

The primary strategy I proposed led to a series of Executive Seminars for business and professional couples. These events featured a heavy emphasis on knowing Christ, understanding the Spirit-filled life, and the importance of sharing your faith with others. Fully one-fourth of the program was devoted to building healthy marriage relationships. There was also free time for recreation, socializing, or just plain relaxing. In the entire four-day seminar, we presented the financial needs of the ministry in only one forty-five-minute session. We trusted the Lord to prompt people to give—only He knew who was spiritually ready and how large a gift was appropriate for them. It was an exceptionally low-key approach.

A Confession

While I'm on the subject of working with Bill Bright, it's probably time I make a confession. Part of the reason that I wanted to serve with Crusade was the opportunity of working closely with Bill because, among other things, it would give me the opportunity to see if the private life and public persona were one and the same. I had often wondered about some of our best-known Christian leaders—are they truly the kind of people they appear to be? Would an honest "behind the scenes" look that caught their unguarded moments enhance or diminish my respect for them? Cynical of me, I know, but what can I say? It was something I wondered about. I discovered that Bill and Vonette Bright *are* authentic. When I think of them, the characteristic that comes to mind first is the love they have for our Savior and for His people. That is what motivates their passions for reaching the world for Him. Susie and I left our time of service with great affection for them personally and deep respect for their faithful role modeling of the life in Christ and their sincere commitment to bring glory to His name and to His name alone.

Was it successful? Absolutely! We saw hundreds of men and women give their lives to Christ. Marriages were healed; parents and children were reconciled. Christians were emboldened to share their faith as a way of life in their home communities. Thousands of participants looked back on the event as a meaningful stepping-stone in their spiritual growth.

The strategy also was successful in raising money, though in ways we did not anticipate. When Christians develop a conviction about relinquishing their lives for Christ and His gospel, they do give generously as never before. But large amounts did not stream into Campus Crusade. Most of the people who began giving more did so back where they lived—to their churches, mission boards, and local parachurch outreaches. It's to Bill Bright's credit that he continued to enthusiastically support the Executive Seminar ministry for many years, far beyond the time when it had become apparent that Crusade was not the primary financial beneficiary. He had often said publicly that he wanted Crusade, whenever possible, to be a servant to local churches and other Christian ministries. Privately, he was as good as his word.

I placed this chapter third in this section because you can't appreciate the wisdom of "laying up treasure in heaven" until . . .

. . . you've settled two other issues. We are made in God's image for God's glory, and our lives should be pointed in the direction of that foundational truth. The only way we can reflect His glory is by making The Great Exchange, giving Him our lives so that He can give us His life—so that it is His life in us that is shining forth (chapter 25). God is the treasure hidden in a field—we joyously go and surrender all that we have in order that we might know Him (chapter 26).

Now we move from discussing the treasure hidden in a field to treasure hidden in the heavenlies. Randy Alcorn, in his excellent book *Money, Possessions, and Eternity*, helps us make the transition.

> *In the greatest sermon ever preached, Jesus masterfully defined the believer's proper relationship to money and possessions: "Do not store up for yourselves treasures on earth, where moth and rust destroy, and where thieves break in and steal. But store up for yourselves treasures in heaven, where moth and rust do not destroy, and where thieves do not break in and steal. For where your treasure is, there your heart will be also" (Matthew 6:19-23).*

> *We must understand that Christ's basic position on wealth is not that it should be rejected but that it should be pursued. According to Jesus, God has an investment mentality. Our Creator and Savior agrees wholeheartedly with us—"Wealth is worth seeking." There is just one difference—He is talking about seeking true wealth.*

> *Jesus vividly described what it is like when we discover true wealth: "The kingdom of heaven is like treasure hidden in a field. When a man found it, he hid it again, and then in his joy went and sold all he had and bought that field" (Matt. 13:44).*

**Recommended
Resource**

The excerpt on the
right was taken from

Money, Possessions,
and Eternity

by Randy Alcorn

Published by Tyndale
House, copyright 1989.
Used by permission.

I found this book
challenging on many
levels and have received
excellent comments back
from others to whom I
have recommended it.
Warren Wiersbe said
about it, "The Christian
who wants a balanced
survey of the Bible's
philosophy of wealth will
not be disappointed. The
pastor who wants to
teach his people and
parents who want to train
their children will get
great help from it."

Take A Longer View

Randy Alcorn provides
solid teaching on
stewardship and many
other topics on the
Eternal Perspective
Ministries website. Visit it
at www.epm.org.

Of course, the great Treasure is Christ himself. To gain Christ—this was what made everything else seem comparatively worthless to Paul (Phil. 3:7-11). But part of gaining Christ was the prospect of eternal reward, symbolizing Christ's stamp of approval on his faithful service while on earth.

What does it mean to lay up treasure in heaven instead of on earth? It means that Christ offers us the incredible opportunity to trade earthly goods and currency for eternal kingdom rewards. By putting our money and possessions in his treasury, we assure ourselves of eternal rewards beyond our comprehension.

Imagine for a moment that you are alive at the very end of the Civil War. You are living in the South, but your home is really in the North. While in the South, you have accumulated a good amount of Confederate currency. Suppose you also know for a fact that the North is going to win the war and that the end could come at any time. What will you do with all of your Confederate money?

If you were smart, there is only one answer to the question. You would cash in your Confederate currency for U.S. currency —the only money that will have value once the war is over. You would keep only enough Confederate currency to meet your basic needs for that short period until the war was over and the money would become worthless.

The believer has inside knowledge of an eventual major change in the worldwide social and economic situation. The currency of this world—its money, possessions, fashions, and whims—will be worthless at our death or Christ's return, both of which are imminent. This knowledge should radically affect our investment strategy. For us to accumulate vast earthly treasures in the face of the inevitable future is equivalent to stockpiling Confederate money despite our awareness of its eventual worthlessness. To do so is to betray a basic ignorance of or unbelief in the Scriptures.

Let me assume the role of "eternal financial counselor" and offer this advice: choose your investments carefully; compare their rates of interest; consider their ultimate trustworthiness; and especially compare how they will be working for you a few million years from now. If the nonbeliever sees with what Jesus called the "bad eye," the Christian's view of finances will be, must be, radically different than his. True, we may participate in some of the same earthly investments, our strategies may appear to overlap at times, and occasionally our short-term goals will be similar. But our long-term goals and purposes will be, must be, fundamentally different. As Christians we must not take our cue from the world but from the Word.

Although acting on the hope of future reward is a legitimate motivation, I believe that generous giving is essentially an affair of the heart.

Here at SMI, teaching financial management skills and investing strategies have never been ends in themselves. No, my friends, the brutal truth is that stronger financial foundations mean little to me if they're not accompanied by increased generosity on your part. What motivates me is a driving desire to see our wonderful God glorified as the message of salvation in His Son is carried around the world to people He loves, people who are lost without Him. And that, more often than not, requires money. *That's* why I want you to have more—so you can give more.

However, to only help you increase the *amount* of your giving would be to miss the major emphasis of Scripture—that God looks at the *attitude* of the giver rather than the gift. That's why I say that giving is an affair of the heart. Consider with me a few principles from 2 Corinthians 8-9, the longest passage in the New Testament on the subject of giving.

• **God is pleased when we give with eager hearts**, understanding the privilege God extends when He allows us to be used in His work. (*"Entirely on their own, the Macedonian churches urgently pleaded with us for the privilege of sharing in this service to the saints..."* 8:3-4.)

• **God is pleased when we give with pure hearts**. Our gifts are acceptable only when we are acceptable, i.e., when we have repented from our sin and accepted God's forgiveness in Christ. (*"And they did not do as we expected, but they gave themselves first to the Lord and then to us in keeping with God's will..."* 8:5.)

• **God is pleased when we give with grateful hearts**. In light of what Christ has done for us, how can we ever be too generous with him? (*"I am not commanding you, but I want to test the sincerity of your love by comparing it with the earnestness of others. For you know the grace of our Lord Jesus Christ, that though he was rich, yet for your sakes he became poor, so that you through his poverty might become rich..."* 8:8-9.)

• **God is pleased when we give with expectant hearts**, recognizing that He can multiply even our small gifts like loaves and fishes and use them to help change the world. (*"If the willingness is there, the gift is acceptable according to what one has, not according to what he does not have..."* 8:12.)

• **God is pleased when we give with happy hearts**, simply for the joy of expressing our love for Him. (*"Each man should give what he has decided in his heart to give, not reluctantly or under compulsion, for God loves a cheerful giver..."* 9:7.)

• **God is pleased when we give with trusting hearts**, counting on Him to provide for the daily necessities of life. (*"And God is able to make all grace abound to you, so that in all things at all times, having all that you need, you will abound in every good work..."* 9:8.)

• **God is pleased when we give with humble hearts**. We want the praise to go to God, not to us. It is the Lord who we wish to see receive the glory. (*"This service that you perform is not only supplying the needs of God's people but is also overflowing in many expressions of thanks to God. Because of the service by which you have proved yourselves, men will praise God..."* 9:12-13.)

When you pray about your giving, may I encourage you to remember that God looks at the giver more than the gift. Give to the full measure of your eagerness, gratitude and cheerfulness. And continue to ask God to enlarge the capacity of your heart toward Him.

Investing that glorifies God is motivated by a desire to see *His* kingdom grow. May I share with you some of the truths from Scripture that . . .

. . . I try to keep in mind as I carry out my small role in the growth of God's kingdom and the accomplishment of His purposes? Consider these truths:

Since I have nothing that was not given to me, I have no basis for pride, only gratitude.

For who makes you different from anyone else? What do you have that you did not receive? (1 Corinthians 4:7)

And my God will meet all your needs according to his glorious riches in Christ Jesus. (Philippians 4:19)

Wealth comes with management responsibilities, not ownership rights. Being a steward is a lifelong calling that requires me to continually live with one eye on eternity.

So if you have not been trustworthy in handling worldly wealth, who will trust you with true riches? And if you have not been trustworthy with someone else's property, who will give you property of your own? (Luke 16:11-12)

If anyone would come after me, he must deny himself and take up his cross and follow me. For whoever wants to save his life will lose it, but whoever loses his life for me will find it. What good will it be for a man if he gains the whole world, yet forfeits his soul? (Matthew 16:24-26)

My primary management responsibility is to be available to God for Him to think, act, speak, and give through me so that His will is accomplished and His name is glorified.

If you remain in me and my words remain in you, ask whatever you wish, and it will be given you. This is to my Father's glory, that you bear much fruit. (John 15:7-8)

So whether you eat or drink or whatever you do, do it all for the glory of God. (1 Corinthians 10:31)

My giving, insofar as possible, is done primarily in the sight of God rather than in view of men. It belongs to the "secret life" of the believer so that God will receive the glory.

Be careful not to do your "acts of righteousness" before men, to be seen by them. If you do, you will have no reward from your Father in heaven. . . . But when you give to the needy, do not let your left hand know what your right hand is doing, so that your giving may be in secret. Then your Father, who sees what is done in secret, will reward you. (Matthew 6:1,3)

Wealth is exceedingly dangerous and has a history of spiritually devastating those who seek it. It must be handled with great care.

People who want to get rich fall into temptation and a trap and into many foolish and harmful desires that plunge men into ruin and destruction. For the love of money is a root of all kinds of evil. Some people, eager for money, have wandered from the faith and pierced themselves with many griefs. (1 Timothy 6:9-10)

Command those who are rich in this present world not to be arrogant nor to put their hope in wealth, which is so uncertain, but to put their hope in God, who richly provides us with everything for our enjoyment. (1 Timothy 6:17)

I'm called to live fully in each day, not in the future. Therefore, God evaluates the faithfulness of my management based on what I do with what I have now, not what I might do someday if I had more.

But seek first his kingdom and his righteousness, and all these things will be given to you as well. Therefore do not worry about tomorrow. (Matthew 6:33-34)

His master replied, "Well done, good and faithful servant! You have been faithful with a few things; I will put you in charge of many things. Come and share your master's happiness!" (Matthew 25:21)

I should manage with a sense of urgency. This inclines me toward giving what I can now rather than saving up in order to give more later. Later may be too late. This has implications for how much of my wealth I leave my children or put aside in charitable foundations.

Do you not say, "Four months more and then the harvest"? I tell you, open your eyes and look at the fields! They are ripe for harvest. Even now the reaper draws his wages, even now he harvests the crop for eternal life. (John 4:35-36)

As long as it is day, we must do the work of him who sent me. Night is coming, when no one can work. (John 9:4)

The Lord is not slow in keeping his promise, as some understand slowness. He is patient with you, not wanting anyone to perish, but everyone to come to repentance. But the day of the Lord will come like a thief. (2 Peter 3:9-10)

God has built the law of sowing and reaping into the fabric of the universe. He can be trusted to pay me the perfectly appropriate wage for my work.

Remember this: Whoever sows sparingly will also reap sparingly, and whoever sows generously will also reap generously. (2 Corinthians 9:6)

We speak of God's secret wisdom, a wisdom that has been hidden and that God destined for our glory before time began. None of the rulers of this age understood it, for if they had, they would not have crucified the Lord of glory. However, as it is written: "No eye has seen, no ear has heard, no mind has conceived what God has prepared for those who love him." (1 Corinthians 2:7-9)

Giving Resources

For a variety of articles and resources related to giving and stewardship, visit SMI's Giving Back page at www.soundmindinvesting.com/ vsection/v_ethics/ s_givingback.htm.

**I'd like to close this chapter with the story of Andrew.
In 1848, his mother worked as a shoemaker to support . . .**

. . . the family. At the age of thirteen, Andrew went to work in a textile mill to help ease the financial burdens. He worked twelve hours a day; he was paid $1.20 a week. He decided to go to night school to learn bookkeeping so he would qualify for a better job. The next year Andrew got a job as a messenger for a telegraph company. Wanting to advance, he returned to night school to study telegraphy. His diligence paid off with a promotion to telegraph operator two years later. He continued to improve at his work and soon became one of the few people who could "read" the sound of telegraph clicks without looking at the readout. This brought him to the attention of a railroad executive who offered him a job as his personal telegrapher and secretary. He was seventeen years old and earning $8.10 a week.

Andrew continued to study as he worked, learning how railroads operated. He borrowed money to invest in the first "sleeping car" company; then he convinced his boss to buy sleeping cars for the railroad. By the time he was twenty-eight, Andrew's earnings had risen to $1,250 a week from his salary and investment income.

In 1865, he left his job and went to Europe to sell securities in the new American railroad companies. While in England, he learned of Bessemer's new process of steelmaking. When he returned to the U.S. in 1872, he gave up his other businesses and concentrated on steel. He was eventually able to persuade railroad managers to replace iron rails with steel ones. By 1889, his mills were producing more than a half-million tons of steel per year. At the turn of the century, he employed more than twenty thousand people. His was the largest industrial concern the world had ever known. When he sold his company to J. P. Morgan in 1901, he netted more than $200 million (roughly $4 billion in today's dollars). On that day, Andrew Carnegie became the richest man in the world.

He was fond of saying, "The man who dies rich, dies disgraced." Once he retired, he spent the rest of his life trying to give away his entire fortune, most of it for educational purposes. He largely succeeded. How different a view from today's philosophy of life, which is so forthrightly proclaimed on bumper stickers saying: "Whoever dies with the most toys wins."

What is a proper motivation for our ambition and hard work? Carnegie, although a generous man, nevertheless devoted his life to building his own kingdom. Christians follow One who is building another kind of kingdom.

Jesus went through all the towns and villages, teaching in their synagogues, preaching the good news of the kingdom and healing every disease and sickness. . . . Then he said to his disciples, "The harvest is plentiful but the workers are few. Ask the Lord of the harvest, therefore, to send out workers into his harvest field." (Matthew 9:35-38)

And what is the mission of these workers? Consider the final command Jesus gave to His disciples just before His ascension. It has been called "The Great Commission."

All authority in heaven and on earth has been given to me. Therefore go and make disciples of all nations, baptizing them in the name of the Father and of the Son and of the Holy Spirit, and teaching them to obey everything I have commanded you. And surely I am with you always, to the very end of the age. (Matthew 28:18-20)

It couldn't be much clearer. Whose kingdom are you building? ◆

CHAPTER PREVIEW

Investing That Glorifies God Upholds His Righteousness

I will listen to what God the Lord will say; he promises peace to his people, his saints—but let them not return to folly. Surely his salvation is near those who fear him, that his glory may dwell in our land. Love and faithfulness meet together; righteousness and peace kiss each other. Faithfulness springs forth from the earth, and righteousness looks down from heaven. The Lord will indeed give what is good, and our land will yield its harvest. Righteousness goes before him and prepares the way for his steps.

(Psalm 85:8-13)

What man is wise enough to understand this? Who has been instructed by the Lord and can explain it? Why has the land been ruined and laid waste like a desert that no one can cross? The Lord said, "It is because they have forsaken my law, which I set before them; they have not obeyed me or followed my law." . . . This is what the Lord says: "Let not the wise man boast of his wisdom or the strong man boast of his strength or the rich man boast of his riches, but let him who boasts boast about this: that he understands and knows me, that I am the Lord, who exercises kindness, justice and righteousness on earth, for in these I delight," declares the Lord.

(Jeremiah 9:12-13, 23-24)

The commencement speaker at the University of California School of Business had these words of advice: *"Greed is all right. Greed is healthy.*

"You can be greedy and still feel good about yourself. Greed works." The comments reportedly received with laughter and applause by the new graduates. The speaker was Ivan Boesky, a man of vast wealth. Not too many months later, he was sent to prison for violating securities laws in his relentless quest to acquire even more.

How much is enough, anyway? Obviously, for some, there's no such thing as ever having "enough." It's not because they have material wants that are left unmet; Ivan Boesky couldn't possibly have spent, no matter how extravagant his personal lifestyle, all the money he had. There are those for whom money represents success, status, superiority, and power. They are pursuing it in a doomed attempt to fill an inner emptiness. But that emptiness is like a black hole; no matter how much you put in, it never fills with light. Ironically, Boesky's very life gave the lie to his words. Greed, it turns out, doesn't work after all.

Fortunately, we Christians already understand this. Greed may be something to watch out for . . .

. . . when doing business with "the world," but followers of Christ are not like that. We can relax with them. *They* would never take advantage of us, right? . . . Right? . . . Hello? . . .

Perhaps I imagine that my question is being received with less than thunderous agreement because I have received many letters from readers of my newsletter that contain horror stories of the various financial atrocities committed against them by people they trusted to have their best interests at heart. They met these people at church, in a couples' Bible study, through a Christian friend, or through some other association that would lead them to believe the person was trustworthy. Unfortunately, limiting your business transactions solely to Christians is no assurance that everything will work out happily ever after.

That reminds me, have I ever told you about my $100,000 tennis racket?

During my tenure with Campus Crusade, the idea struck me how great it would be if I found competent Christian people to invest with. They would perform the day-to-day work of the investment projects, and eventually we could live off the income and be free to continue devoting our time to ministry pursuits.

Well, it wasn't long (wouldn't you know it?) before I was approached about investing in a real estate project. I was introduced by a co-worker to a friend of his who was a developer (let's call him Dugan) in the greater San Diego area. He and his partner Roberts needed temporary financing on one of their projects until their permanent construction loan was approved. They were willing to pay a healthy rate of interest, personally guarantee the loan, plus pledge some stock Dugan owned as additional collateral. They had done other projects previously and had development experience. I verified with the lending institution that their loan request had, indeed, received approval, pending receipt of their pro forma financial statements.

Dugan and his wife were super people; you couldn't help but like them. They entertained us at their country club. They invited us over for friendly tennis (Dugan gave me one of his rackets so I could practice regularly). Since we were living away from Kentucky, they even included us in their plans for Thanksgiving dinner. We were practically family! So everything seemed to line up pretty well. And what seemed to confirm it was that the opportunity to invest with a Christian had come along just when it seemed the natural direction to go.

You know something went wrong, or I wouldn't own a tennis racket that cost me $100,000. Here's the sorry sequence of events.

• Through negligence, Dugan missed the deadline for submitting the financial statements to the lender, and they lost their construction loan.

• The economy was going through a downturn, and they could not get another loan commitment. The project never got off the ground. Fortunately, I still had the personal guarantees of the Dugans and the Robertses.

• Roberts died suddenly of a heart attack. Being a sensitive guy who doesn't want to invade a widow's grief, I let some time go by before asking for her share of my money. While I was being noble, her late husband's attorney was helping her hide her assets; she eventually produced a financial statement that made her appear penniless. Curiously, six months after the sudden departure of Mr. Roberts, the former Mrs. Roberts overcame her grief and married the helpful attorney.

• Mr. Dugan and his wife filed for protection under the bankruptcy laws and moved to northern California. I never heard from them again.

• The stock Dugan pledged was in a land development company that was operated and controlled by his brother. The brother later told me that things were going so well that my stock holdings would be worth $1 million within three years. This was a little optimistic; the company expanded too quickly, eventually lost its land holdings, and disappeared into bankruptcy never-never land. I never heard from the brother again.

What did I learn from this misadventure? I learned not to make certain unwarranted assumptions . . .

. . . when dealing with fellow Christians. First, I assumed that because Dugan had experience and seemed to know what he was doing, he was competent. I didn't really check him out. It turned out that his personable style

**PRYOR'S RULES
FOR EVALUATING
INVESTMENTS THAT
SEEK YOU OUT**

Rule #1
Assume the investment is being offered to you by a representative of Ivan Boesky. It's not that the person soliciting your investment is likely to be as greedy or dishonest as Boesky. I just want to help you to stay alert and not repeat the mistake of making unwarranted assumptions. All the remaining rules logically follow from this one.

Rule #2
Apply all decision-making guidelines for making the "right" decisions that I gave in chapter 20 (pages 224-226). All of them.

Rule #3
Ask the individual to put everything of importance (like representations of risk, how much money you're guaranteed to make, how long it's all going to take) in written form. Assume nothing; verify everything.

Rule #4
Check his facts out thoroughly. Ask someone you trust, who has nothing to do with the deal, to help you. Assume nothing; verify everything.

Rule #5
Investigate his track record. Contact other investors with whom he's done business. Assume nothing; verify everything.

Rule #6
Ask for personal character references, including one from his pastor. Then call the people and talk with them personally. Assume nothing; verify everything.

Rule #7
If you decide to go ahead, put the entire deal in writing, signed by all concerned, so that you have a legally enforceable position. Handshake deals are out.

Rule #8
Make absolutely, positively no exceptions to Rules #1 through #7. And, oh yes, assume nothing and verify everything.

made him competent only as a promoter. It was little help in the nitty-gritty of day-to-day details. Second, I assumed that these were people of integrity. They seemed so *sincere!* Yet they readily hid behind the bankruptcy laws to avoid repaying the money they had so earnestly besought me to loan them. Boy, had I learned an important lesson! I wouldn't make *those* mistakes again. I would make *new* ones.

This brings me to the story of my $50,000 Swiss army knife key ring.

Jack, a good Christian friend, brought it back as a souvenir from one of the frequent business trips to Europe he made for a business deal we were in together. I won't go into all the details here. I'll just skip to the new lessons I learned about *other* unwarranted assumptions you shouldn't make. First, I assumed that all the facts of the deal were exactly as Jack had represented them to me. (By the way, note that I no longer needed go-betweens to introduce me to people like Dugan—by this time I was going directly to my close personal friends to lose my money.) I know that Jack truly believed—evidently too optimistically—everything he was telling me. The point is that I would never have accepted the story just on the word of a stranger. I would have expected documented proof of all the facts. With Jack, my guard was completely down.

Second, I assumed that because I could trust my friend, the usual precautions didn't apply. In chapter 20, I gave you five guidelines for making investment decisions (see pages 224-226). In this one deal, I broke the first four of the guidelines without hesitation.

Guideline 1: The deal wasn't consistent with my long-term strategy because I didn't have one.

Guideline 2: I didn't take much time to pray about it or seek counsel from others.

Guideline 3: I never really understood the logistics of the deal or why it was supposed to work the way it was.

Guideline 4: The investment totally failed the common sense test of prudence.

In retrospect, it's so improbable that it could have worked that I'm too embarrassed to even tell you what it was about.

In short, my trust was totally in the knowledge and experience of my friend. The reason I didn't give the guidelines a thought is that I hadn't learned to apply biblical principles to financial decision making at that point. (Larry Burkett was just getting his ministry started in those days. Larry, where were you when I needed you?) This happened in 1976, and I was still flying on gut instinct.

I hope you appreciate the "school" I went to in learning these lessons that I'm passing on to you for the unbelievably low price of just $21.99. The tuition for this one cost me $50,000 (or just $49,990 if you want to count the $10 value of my Swiss army knife key ring).

Well, enough about evaluating the advisability of investment opportunities that come seeking *you* out. Let's look at the flip side—investments where you are the one taking the initiative.

Is it advisable to buy mutual funds that invest in companies without paying heed to the moral issues surrounding their products, services, or policies?

This matter of examining the ethical implications of where we invest our money has been popularly called "socially responsible" investing. Socially responsible investing (SRI) continues to gather momentum as a force in the investment world. According to research from the Social Investment Forum, the amount invested in the U.S. under various forms of SRI now exceeds more than $2 trillion.

All practitioners of SRI create a set of portfolio guidelines, called "screens," which reflect the ethical values they wish to see represented in their investments. It's generally agreed that SRI falls into three main camps:

❶ **Avoidance investing (penalize the bad guys).** Investors in this category develop screens designed to weed out companies engaged in activities or practices that they find objectionable. This is probably the most common approach, and is what most individual investors mean when they say they are interested in "ethical" investing.

❷ **Advocacy investing (convert/replace the bad guys).** This is the opposite of avoidance investing because it seeks to invest in companies with the intention of changing objectionable corporate behavior by exercising one's ownership privileges. Because this strategy calls for an ongoing effort after the investment is made, it is sometimes known as activist or interventionist investing.

❸ **Alternative investing (reward the good guys).** This is a proactive strategy where investment opportunities are sought in companies that are working to achieve those societal goals that the investor believes are important. Companies that underwrite community housing projects, search for alternative energy sources, manufacture pollution-control products, or have "nondiscriminatory" employment and promotion practices are examples of areas targeted for proactive investing.

Historically, SRI proponents have generally been in favor of: affirmative action, animal rights, environmental protection, gay and lesbian rights, gun

**Socially Responsible
Investing Resources**
www.soundmindinvesting.com/
vsection/v_ethics/
s_ethicalinvesting.htm

www.crosswalk.com

news.morningstar.com/news/
MS/Article/
0,1299,3564,00.html

www.socialinvest.org

www.socialfunds.com

**Socially Responsible
Mutual Funds**
Unlike most SRI funds, these
three groups have screens that
eliminate investments in
abortion and pornography-
related products and services:

The Timothy Plan
(800) 846-7526
www.timothyplan.com

The Noah Fund
(800) 794-6624
www.noahfund.com

Shepherd Values Funds
(888) 346-8258
www.shepherdvalues.com

control, low income housing, so-called women's issues, and nondiscrimina-
tion against people with AIDS. They have generally opposed: air pollution,
alcohol, defense and weapons contractors, gambling, nuclear power, tobacco
products, and South Africa.

This list of concerns shows that SRI activists hold, for the most part, politi-
cally liberal views concerning the way society, business, and government should
be organized and operated. This is slowly changing as greater numbers of investors from the "conservative" ranks are using their influence in support of values
they believe are important. Still, in 2000, only four out of 38 SRI stock funds listed
abortion as a screening criteria, and only two listed pornography (see sidebar).

Obviously, what constitutes social responsibility is in the eye of the beholder.

The *Wall Street Journal* has pointed out that there are key differences
among SRI mutual funds in how they define "responsible" behavior. Among
the 50 largest U.S. companies, three prominent SRI funds—Vanguard Calvert
Fund, Domini Social Equity Fund, and Citizens Index Fund—disagree on the
ethical merits of 20 of them.

While the three funds evaluate stocks using several of the same criteria,
the application of those screens "gets down to judgment calls," says John
Shields, president of Citizens Funds. Wal-Mart is one of the largest stocks on
which the three funds disagree. Calvert rules it out because it excludes retailers who sell firearms; therefore, it will not be eligible for purchase by the new
Vanguard fund linked to the Calvert Social Index. Citizens Funds has a different complaint—it doesn't like the way Wal-Mart treats its employees nor
the devastating impact it can have on local merchants when a Wal-Mart store
opens in a small rural community. But Wal-Mart passes muster at Kinder,
Lydenberg, Domini & Co., which assembles the Domini 400 Social Index. The
lesson is clear: If you're interested in an "ethical" fund, be sure the fund you
select reflects *your* moral values.

There has been an ongoing debate within investing circles as to whether an SRI strategy hurts performance.

Obviously, when you add ethical screening criteria to the list of factors
that investors normally consider when selecting stocks (such as revenue and
earnings growth, valuation, competitive position, and industry fundamentals),
you reduce your investment options. All things being equal, this should make
it more difficult to get better results than your neighbor who has hundreds
more companies to choose from.

Aaah, but all things aren't equal claim the SRI proponents. They would
say that it pays to be a good corporate citizen. Perhaps, but studies have yet

to prove a link between stock performance and any of the most commonly applied social screening criteria. In fact, the majority of SRI funds were notorious underperformers during most of the 1990s. A 1999 study by Morningstar, however, did seem to indicate things were looking up by decade's end:

> *Of the SRI funds that have a five-year record (35 in all), a total of 19 have outperformed their category peers over the trailing five years while 16 underperformed. That doesn't mean social screens add value, but it's hard to make the case that they subtract it. . . .*

> *Screening certainly has something to do with SRI funds' recent performance. Screening out tobacco companies and nuclear power utilities has kept the funds away from some of the market's worst performers over the past few years. Avoiding these and other firms with poor environmental records leaves the typical SRI domestic-equity fund underweighted in value stocks and overweighted in growth stocks. That proved to be a potent combination in 1997 and 1998 when large-growth stocks fueled the stock market's rise. . . .*

> *That's not the entire explanation, though. Some of the SRI success owes to the impact of two socially screened indexes, which together are tracked by six of the top-rated funds. The Domini Social index and the Citizens index have prospered for the same basic reason that the S&P 500 index has over the past couple of years: The stocks at the top of these capitalization-weighted indexes were those that led the market's rise.*

Whether the recent improvement can be sustained remains to be seen. In any event, performance considerations have not been a factor in why I have not placed a major emphasis on SRI funds (which primarily engage in "avoidance investing" strategies) in my monthly investment newsletter. There are two reasons that are more fundamental.

Reason #1: Because most investors tend to idealize their goals, ethical investing becomes an impossible mission.

I receive more questions asking for suggestions on where to find ethical investments than on any other single topic. I believe that the people writing have a genuine desire to please the Lord in the way they handle their finances. They are seeking investments that adhere to the righteous standards of Scripture. They sincerely strive to be faithful stewards, and they believe they have a responsibility to be sure they do not lend economic support to those forces in opposition to what they see as biblical values. I respect their heartfelt concerns. Unfortunately, I must tell them I can't be of help. Why not? Because I know of no investments that are guaranteed to meet their criteria. There are no morally pure investments, either in the mutual fund world or anywhere else. Consider:

• **Bank savings accounts and certificates of deposit.** It's possible that your bank has loaned money to help build such businesses as the local newspaper that aggressively attacks Christian home-schooling in its editorials, the

---

Helping Others While Saving at South Shore Bank

Established in 1973 as the country's first "community development" bank, the mission of South Shore Bank has been to lend financial support to those in its community (an inner-city neighborhood of Chicago) who are willing to help themselves by obtaining skills, jobs, and better housing.

South Shore Bank welcomes investors from all over the country. Here are a few of the ways you can participate in this mission while at the same time satisfying your own financial needs.

1. Money Market Max Savings and Checking. With a minimum of $2,500 each, these FDIC-insured savings or checking accounts offer competitive money market rates and flexibility.

2. Certificates of Deposits. Five different CDs are offered. Depending on length of maturity and investment amount, they are linked to providing special housing, job retention, and environment programs.

3. South Shore Bank Mastercard℠ and Visa℠. Both regular and gold are available with competitive interest rates and no annual fee. A portion of the bank's profits will be shared with five nonprofit affiliates, including The Neighborhood Institute, which offers services on the south side of Chicago. The affiliates use the funds to create jobs in their communities.

For more information on South Shore or any of the services mentioned, call (800) 669-7725.

chemical company that illegally dumps its waste, or the bookstore that has several racks of pornographic magazines right by the front door where even young children can see them. Or your bank may have loaned money to the abortion clinic that has become the largest in your state, the engineering company whose PAC contributions perpetuate corruption in local government, or the music store in the local mall that promotes music and videos that glamorize sexually destructive and drug-addicting lifestyles. The possibilities are almost limitless; let your imagination run a little. Almost every business has bank loans to some degree. The question is not *if* your bank has made loans to businesses engaged in practices abhorrent to you, but rather *how many and for how much*. And where do the banks get the money to make these loans? From the savings put on deposit by trusting folks like you and me.

• **United States government bonds, notes, and Treasury bills.** These are the investments that make it possible for our government to run the huge budget deficits that make inflation an ever-present fact of American life. Many who write on economics from a biblical perspective consider inflation to be a great evil because it constitutes theft by the government. Much has been written on that subject alone. In addition, however, start considering the many ways that government spends our money. Whether promoting abortion, supporting artists who produce blasphemous or pornographic exhibits, or undermining traditional family values through humanistic education and welfare programs, there is much for Christians to be concerned about. The one exception would be the bond mutual funds that invest only in government-backed GNMA mortgages (which provide capital for people to purchase homes). Other than these, are government securities ethical investments?

• **Common stocks.** How many of the Fortune 500 companies do you believe are operated according to Christian principles from top to bottom? That would mean the application of a biblical moral ethic in *all* of the following: their hiring and firing decisions, employee pay schedules, environmental impact policies, the way they price their products or services, their borrowing and lending decisions, and the whole of their advertising and marketing strategies. I doubt you can find even one.

It's interesting to me that many Christians question concerning the ethics of investing in stock funds, yet don't give a second thought . . .

. . . to the morality of building sizable bank savings account and Treasury bill holdings. Consistency would call for demanding ethical purity in those investments as well. Let's look at your bank, for example. Assume that it has $100 million in loans outstanding, and that you would find $2 million of them seriously objectionable if you knew about them. Further assume that you have a $5,000 CD on deposit there. Your CD represents 1/200 of 1% of the bank's total loans outstanding. That means that for every $10,000 your bank loans out, you "contribute" 50¢ to the loan. Is your CD an ethical investment? If you are looking for absolute purity, then it doesn't qualify, because 2% of the loan portfolio fails your ethics test. But is your meager role statistically meaningful? Obviously not. That's why I would consider the CD investment acceptable.

I won't spend time reviewing the extent to which investing in U.S. securities (T-bills, notes, bonds, and government-only money market funds) support the federal government's spending programs. The relatively miniscule size of an individual's holdings in relation to the absolutely massive size of the federal budget is obvious.

My point is that investors have limited choices. Whether you invest in a bank certificate of deposit, U.S. Treasury securities, or selected common stocks, you have virtually no control over the specific uses to which your money is put *once you turn it loose.* We are "in the world" and must function in it. Paul writes in 1 Corinthians 5:9-10, "I have written you in my letter not to associate with sexually immoral people—not at all meaning the people of this world who are immoral, or the greedy and swindlers, or idolaters. In that case you would have to leave this world." Paul recognizes the impossibility of completely avoiding contact with the corrupt world we inhabit. My conclusion: You can't altogether avoid incidental financial contact with disagreeable causes in the course of your investing.

Well, perhaps not, you might be thinking, *but we can at least avoid giving them meaningful support.* True, which brings me to the second reason I have not emphasized avoidance investing.

Reason #2: Because companies don't directly profit when you buy their shares through a mutual fund, ethical investing becomes an ineffective mission.

Many investors are under the false impression that a company benefits when you invest in a mutual fund that owns its stock. It's important that you understand that the money spent by a mutual fund to acquire shares in, say, a tobacco company did *not* go to the tobacco company. The shares were purchased in what's called the "secondary market," and the money paid for them went to the previous owners. It's the same as if you bought a used Pontiac from a friend. Your money would not go to General Motors, which got its money a long time ago and couldn't care less whether you buy the Pontiac or whether your friend continues to own it. SRI funds are no different from "regular" funds in this regard.

True, it is to the advantage of a company if overall market demand for their stock drives share prices up (and vice versa). I am merely trying to make the point that, *in terms of one's personal resources,* the buying of a mutual fund

A SOUND MIND BRIEFING

Building Your Own Socially Responsible Portfolio

by Mark Biller

While SMI has long touted the advantages of mutual fund investing, we're not blind to their disadvantages either. Want to index the S&P 500 but don't want to own Disney and Philip Morris? Sorry. Didn't sell any fund shares this year but still have to report a big gain on your taxes? Too bad.

Recently though, the fund landscape shifted a bit with the launch of Folio[*fn*], a new online service promising to do away with these and other disadvantages of mutual fund investing. Folio[*fn*]'s primary product is a personalized basket of stocks—like a "mini mutual fund"—called a FOLIO. For a flat fee of $295 per year, you can have as many as three FOLIOS, each holding up to 50 stocks. You can build your own, or choose from more than 50 preset FOLIOS, categorized by risk, sector, and so on. So it's easy to grab a pre-assembled FOLIO of small-cap growth stocks, or large-cap value stocks, or one that will track a specific market index. Folio[*fn*] founder Steve Wallman puts it this way, "We've combined the diversification benefits of mutual funds with the customized service of a brokerage to rethink how you invest."

If you like, you can select one of the preset FOLIOs as your starting point, then fine tune that basket of stocks to your liking by dropping one, adding another. One of the neat tools offered is the ability to back test your modifications and see how the resulting basket of stocks would have performed historically compared to an index or specific mutual fund.

The ability to fine-tune each FOLIO in this way is a major advantage over traditional funds. Let's examine some additional strengths and weaknesses of this unique service.

• Strength #1: Values-based investing possibilities. Unlike a conventional mutual fund, swapping an offensive stock out of a FOLIO is a piece of cake. Used alongside a screening tool like Crosswalk's Investigator (www.crosswalk.com), you can easily screen your FOLIO for companies that act contrary to your values and replace them.

• Strength #2: The ultimate in tax efficiency. The average domestic fund has a turnover rate of 90%, and every one of those transactions has tax implications that the fund passes on to you. That's why you can get a tax bill despite not selling any shares, even if the fund price declines. Since a FOLIO is not a mutual fund, and because you make all the buy/sell decisions, you won't get hit with unexpected tax bills. You decide when to take gains and losses using tools designed to help you achieve your tax goals.

• Strength #3: Potentially lower expenses. Annual expenses for the average stock mutual fund run about 1.6% of your account balance, so a $25,000 account would pay $400 annually. In contrast, the annual cost of running up to three FOLIOs is a flat $295. The higher your account balance, the greater the savings.

• Strength #4: Pay expenses by credit card. In an IRA or other tax-deferred vehicle, paying expenses out of your fund balance really hurts performance. How much difference does this make? A $20,000 IRA that grows 11% for 30 years will be worth $296,176 if 1.6% in fees are deducted annually as a regular stock mutual fund would do. That same account is worth $457,846 if $295 is paid to Folio[*fn*] with outside funds each year instead. After subtracting the $8,850 in total FOLIO fees paid, that's a difference of $152,820!

FOLIO investing is not without flaws, so let's examine those as well.

• Weakness #1: Not cost-effective for small accounts. The flat annual fee of $295 represents an expense ratio of 1.47% for a $20,000 account. Balances less than that are paying a hefty price for the benefits received. If you're a pure indexer, only accounts of roughly $150,000 or more would save money with FOLIO due to their typically lower expenses.

More than one account type can be included in your three FOLIOs though, which may help justify the expenses. For example, a taxable account, an IRA, and a child's custodial account could each be set up as a separate FOLIO under one $295 annual fee.

• Weakness #2: FOLIOs require more "hands-on" attention than mutual funds. The advantages of Folio[fn] come from the ability to manage your "mini mutual fund," so if taking a more active role isn't appealing, this probably isn't for you. It doesn't require a lot of extra work, but it is more involved than purchasing a regular mutual fund. And FOLIOs are only available online, so having an Internet connection is a must.

Who should consider using Folio[*fn*]? First, those who have a strong desire to add a "socially responsible" emphasis to their investing strategy. Initially, FOLIOs could be used to supplement your core holdings of individual stocks or SMI's model Upgrading and Just-the-Basics portfolios. Over time, as your comfort grows with using FOLIOs in combination with Crosswalk's Investigator, you might reach the point where you use them exclusively. The result—your own values-based portfolio personally tailored to your moral convictions.

A second investor who might enjoy Folio[*fn*] is the person who wants to "dabble" in a few individual stocks without disrupting his primary fund strategy. Creating your own FOLIO gives an outlet to that creative investing energy without risking major damage to your overall portfolio. And third, any investor with a fairly complex tax situation could gain from the tax benefits available through this service.

Folio[*fn*] is the pioneer in this space, and you can find them online at www.foliofn.com. With an idea this good though, don't be surprised to see imitators offering competition before long. It takes a sizeable sum to make it worthwhile, but there's a lot to like in this blend of stock picking and mutual fund investing.

As appeared in the Sound Mind Investing newsletter in October 2000.
Mark Biller is the editor of SMI NOW, the web home for the Sound Mind Investing family of readers.

that might hold some GM stock does not put money into GM's pockets.

I believe that mutual funds are acceptable investing vehicles for the same reason that bank savings accounts and T-bills are acceptable: The role your investment plays is absolutely insignificant in relation to the size of the problem areas. In fact, it is too small to even be called "support" at all in the usual sense. Consider this. A mutual fund rarely owns even one-tenth of 1% of a given company's stock. Furthermore, few investors would ever hold as much as one-tenth of 1% of any one mutual fund's assets. Therefore, owning a mutual fund limits the average investor to holding *less than one one-millionth of any one company's shares.* The ownership effect is nil.

Here's an example of how this works. One of the Vanguard funds recommended in my newsletter held 366,000 shares of stock in Philip Morris, the huge tobacco company with more than 925 million shares outstanding. This means that the fund owns about 1/2,500 of Philip Morris. Let's assume you invest $5,000 in this Vanguard fund; how much ownership in Philip Morris would this give you? You would own 1/70,000 of a fund which owns 1/2,500 of Philip Morris. Congratulations! That makes you the owner of 1/175,000,000 (that's one part in 175 million!) of Philip Morris. Such investment hardly qualifies as support.

We want our drinking water to be clean, but we don't demand that it be sterile. We all would like clean air, but we don't walk around wearing oxygen masks. If we accept 99.9% purity when it comes to matters of life and health, doesn't it seem reasonable to apply the same standards to material pursuits like investing?

My argument, of course, approaches the issue in terms of *effectiveness* rather than *conscience.* If it is our goal, as a matter of personal conviction, to never invest in a company or institution, directly or indirectly, that operates in a manner contrary to biblical standards, we are certain to be frustrated (as I outlined in Reason #1).

You may be concluding that I am unconcerned about corporate ethics and using one's economic influence to battle immoral forces. If so, you misunderstand my point. It's not that I want you to be less radical in this area. I want you to become *more* radical.

To do an effective job of withholding support from objectionable companies, we must be ready to boycott—*not merely their securities, but more importantly, their products and services.***

Companies primarily profit from our spending, not our investing. Targeting our routine daily spending can be a potent force for change, as we saw in the American Family Association's five-year battle with Kmart over its subsidiary's pornography sales. I encourage you to spend strategically in order to reward those companies that enhance the quality of life from a Judeo-Christian perspective and avoid rewarding those whose activities undermine the health of the family and children. If a company's behavior is offensive to your deeply held convictions, why reward it with your patronage?

For *most* of us, strategic thinking regarding our routine daily spending is a more potent force for change than the threat of withholding our investing. Let me explain why, using the boycott of Disney by the AFA and the 16 million-strong Southern Baptists as an example:

• **Everyone can participate.** All of us are consumers; not all of us have investment portfolios. Even if we do, they might not hold shares in the offending companies we are trying to influence. If you believe the value of your involvement is directly tied to the size and makeup of your investment portfolio, what do you do if your investments are modest in size and/or include no holdings, directly or indirectly, in Disney? You may conclude that there's no role for you to play.

• **Ease of recruitment.** There are millions of families who would be quite upset with Disney if they knew the facts. But in our society it can be quite awkward to talk to your friends about personal money matters concerning their investments and how they can/should use them to stand for biblical values. On the other hand, it's relatively easy to hand them an article on the subject and ask that they take this information into account before doing any further business with Disney or its many entertainment subsidiaries.

• **Ease of implementation.** To work for change through your investing requires adding an activity to already busy schedules: research who holds the shares and communicate your requests that they divest their holdings. But to work for change through your spending adds no new time demands. It merely requires a change in one's spending patterns. This makes it easier for each of us to get involved as well as making it easier to ask others.

• **Concentration of forces.** We can more readily join together and make our influence felt when we are all directing our efforts at a single decision-maker—Disney's top officer. In contrast, consider the challenge of influencing hundreds of fund managers and institutional investors, who do not share the same concerns, to sell a significant amount of their Disney stock.

• **Disney needs our spending, not our investing, for its success.** Even if a million like-minded families decided to sell their mutual fund shares in protest, Disney would have only a *public relations* problem. The influence of those families is diluted because their investments are scattered across thousands of mutual funds and pension accounts. But if a million families who previously supported Disney's movies, videos, theme parks, etc., took their Disney spending elsewhere, Disney would begin to notice a decline in *profits*. That's a far more serious problem.

Ethical Spending
Resources
www.soundmindinvesting.com/
vsection/v_ethics/
s_ethicalspending.htm

Don't let anyone tell you your opposition, as expressed through a boycott, is censorship. Censorship takes place only when the force of government is used to prevent or punish publication. Publishers are free to publish what they wish within the obscenity laws upheld by the Supreme Court. In the above example, Disney is free to make the movies, videos, and television programming it wishes to make, and to generally conduct its business in a way it believes will most advance its sales and profits. And you are free to do business with the companies you choose. While the First Amendment guarantees freedom of expression, it does not guarantee that every form of expression will meet with public acceptance or commercial success.

Let me make it clear that I am also in favor of taking action on the investment side as well. I am not saying that divestiture of Disney stock by Christian institutions is not desirable. These are important symbolic gestures that make a statement about our values and concerns. The drawback is they have no direct effect on Disney's finances. In a typical week, $4-$5 *billion* of Disney stock changes hands. The market can swallow up sales of Disney shares—even those amounting to tens of millions—with ease and little effect on the price.

Investing that glorifies God upholds His righteousness.

So far in this section, we have discussed why investing that glorifies God acknowledges His sovereignty (God owns it all), values His majesty (He is the treasure), and builds His kingdom (we are to manage His wealth for achieving God-given goals). If you are committed to making money-management decisions that reflect your firm convictions about those first three truths, you will have no problem understanding why our investing should also uphold His righteousness.

> *This, then, is how you should pray: "Our Father in heaven, hallowed be your name, your kingdom come, your will be done on earth as it is in heaven." (Matthew 6:9-10)*

It naturally follows that you will feel a solemn obligation to use your financial leverage to the maximum in order that His righteousness is revealed and upheld. No one will need to persuade you that it is a good thing. You will be grieved to think it would be otherwise.

> *Righteous are you, O Lord, and your laws are right. The statutes you have laid down are righteous; they are fully trustworthy. My zeal wears me out, for my enemies ignore your words. Your promises have been thoroughly tested, and your servant loves them. (Psalm 119:137-140)*

Far be it from us as Christians, who are responsible for handling God's wealth for God's glory, that we should provide essential financial support to the very people and institutions whose activities are undermining the biblical values we hold dear. Consider how the moral foundations of our society have been shaken in recent decades—can you doubt that we are under attack? We are in a war over whose values will prevail in America. The battle is not just for our children, but for their children as well. Yet some of us routinely and indifferently subsidize those who most despise us.

Our God is righteous. He does not need to conform to a righteous standard; He is the standard. Because He is righteous, we must regard what belongs to Him, such as the money we manage, as consecrated for righteous purposes. The thought of turning God's wealth over to His enemies, to use against His glorious name and His church, should be abhorrent to the faithful steward. We must take care to avoid financing activities that lead others into temptation and sin.

> *Whoever welcomes a little child like this in my name welcomes me. But if anyone causes one of these little ones who believe in me to sin, it would be better for him to have a large millstone hung around his neck and to be drowned in the depths of the sea. Woe to the world because of the things that cause people to sin! Such things must come, but woe to the man through whom they come! (Matthew 18:5-7)*

Because the Lord is righteous, we have an obligation to withhold support, insofar as possible, from those businesses whose corporate activities either actively mock or passively undermine the biblical values that God has given as the basis for righteousness in society. This can be done most effectively by boycotting their products and services. Withholding investment support from their stocks and bonds can also be helpful if done in a concerted fashion. I believe both of these strategies can play a role in the spending and investing decisions of every follower of Christ. ◆

CHAPTER PREVIEW

Investing That Glorifies God Seeks His Wisdom

The heavens declare the glory of God; the skies proclaim the work of his hands. Day after day they pour forth speech; night after night they display knowledge. There is no speech or language where their voice is not heard. Their voice goes out into all the earth, their words to the ends of the world. In the heavens he has pitched a tent for the sun, which is like a bridegroom coming forth from his pavilion, like a champion rejoicing to run his course. It rises at one end of the heavens and makes its circuit to the other; nothing is hidden from its heat.

The law of the Lord is perfect, reviving the soul.
The statutes of the Lord are trustworthy, making wise the simple.
The precepts of the Lord are right, giving joy to the heart.
The commands of the Lord are radiant, giving light to the eyes.
The fear of the Lord is pure, enduring forever.
The ordinances of the Lord are sure and altogether righteous.

They are more precious than gold, than much pure gold; they are sweeter than honey, than honey from the comb. By them is your servant warned; in keeping them there is great reward. Who can discern his errors? Forgive my hidden faults. Keep your servant also from willful sins; may they not rule over me. Then will I be blameless, innocent of great transgression. May the words of my mouth and the meditation of my heart be pleasing in your sight, O Lord, my Rock and my Redeemer.

(Psalm 19:1-14)

The last out. The eighteenth hole. The final buzzer. The checkered flag. The runner's tape. Match point.

In sports, all the players know where the "finish line" is. They can then train themselves and compete accordingly. But in the world of investing, very few clear rules are acknowledged by all the players. It's a kind of come-as-you-are, no-holds-barred event. You're free to participate without any preparation, training, or study of any kind. You don't need a doctor's certificate showing you're financially "fit" and able to afford the risk. Nor do you need a diploma as proof you've studied the disciplines involved and may actually know what you're doing. If you show up with a few dollars, you're almost invariably invited in.

This ease of entry usually makes people feel qualified to play. The financial media assures you that others with investment training similar to yours (that is, little or none) are making large sums with just minutes a day of effort. Surely, it can't be all that difficult. So you begin your playing days. That's what I was drawn to in the late 1960s, and it's what I returned to in the late 1970s.

Susie and I returned home to Kentucky just in time for Christmas 1974. We had reached a point in the growth and staffing of the new department I had helped build . . .

. . . that one of my assistants could now take over. The ministry-wide fund-raising activities, such as direct mail, had been brought together under one coordinated strategy, and the Executive Seminars were going very well. Meanwhile, we were getting a little homesick for family and friends, not to mention Kentucky's cold winters and green summers. I wasn't eager to return to the restaurant business, but industry trends and cultural changes were beginning to threaten our long-term profitability—a hard look at our future plans and prospects was in order. Bill and Vonette Bright thoughtfully gave us a "going away" party at their home. The pictures we still have of that evening always generate warm memories of the many friends we made on Crusade staff during our time there.

The next few years of my business life were primarily devoted to selling the family business. In one sense, it was a difficult decision to make. I was the third generation of our family to operate restaurants in Louisville; my grandfather had opened the first one in 1922. A family tradition that spans more than half a century is not easily abandoned. Yet, it was increasingly obvious that smaller "chains" like ours (we operated six restaurants) could not long survive against the money and marketing muscle of the large national companies. It was quickly becoming an uphill battle to maintain our market share. Add to the equation that my heart wasn't really in it, and it seemed the most prudent course was to sell the business while it was still performing well. With the consent of my mother (who owned one-half of the stock), we began a process that took almost three years to complete.

On the day in 1977 when I walked away from closing the final sale of the last of the restaurants . . .

. . . I was a happy man. I was young. I was deeply in love with my wife and three boys (God gave us Matthew while we were living in California). I still had a fair amount of money in the bank (despite my past errors of judgment). I was healthy. And I was unemployed.

I took advantage of my free time to pursue my ministry interests. I enjoyed serving on the founding board of directors of Crusade's Christian Embassy project in Washington, D.C. I was invited to be part of a group of businessmen and professional athletes who were starting a new training ministry—Pro Athletes Outreach—which was designed to "win, build, and send" pro players from the major sports. I started a Christian Business Men's Committee in Louisville. I had a lot of fun, and seeing the results from these efforts has been extremely satisfying. But our financial resources weren't so great that we could simply live off our investment income; I knew that I soon needed to make a career decision.

Initially, I didn't know what new direction my business life should take, but I did have a few thoughts as to the general framework. First, I recognized that my innate personality (according to the widely used Performax personal profile test) had a "perfectionist" bent. I'm the kind of person who gives attention to detail, has high quality standards, and likes to have an orderly working environment. Second, I considered my entrepreneurial background—I had always worked for my family or myself. Once I make a decision, I like to see it implemented quickly and efficiently. I wasn't sure how well I would function within a slow-moving bureaucracy. Third, I determined that I would never again participate in any project where my success or failure primarily resided with someone else. I would never forget my $100,000 tennis racket and other souvenirs. If I was going to fail, it would be entirely due to my own shortcomings. Finally, I still had an interest in finance and the investment markets. *Is that appropriate?* I wondered. *Last time I had gotten involved, it had almost taken over my life. Would I be like an alcoholic opening a tavern?*

As Susie and I prayed about these matters, our thoughts eventually came together in a decision that I should form an investment advisory firm . . .

. . . with one of my closest friends, Doug Van Meter, as my partner. We had become fascinated with a style of investing known as "market timing." The idea is to sell all of your stock holdings and move to the safety of money

Why do you call me "Lord, Lord," and do not do what I say? I will show you what he is like who comes to me and hears my words and puts them into practice. He is like a man building a house, who dug down deep and <u>laid the foundation on rock</u>. When a flood came, the torrent struck that house but could not shake it, because it was well built. But the one who hears my words and does not put them into practice is like a man who built a house on the ground without a foundation. The moment the torrent struck that house, it collapsed and its destruction was complete.
Luke 6:46–49

<u>All Scripture is God-breathed</u> and is useful for teaching, rebuking, correcting and training in righteousness, so that the man of God may be thoroughly equipped for every good work.
2 Timothy 3:16–17

For <u>the Lord gives wisdom</u>, and from his mouth come knowledge and understanding.
Proverbs 2:6

market funds when significant market weakness is anticipated. If you're correct, you not only pocket the interest earned while waiting out the downturn, but you get to buy back in at lower prices. In theory, it sounds great. In practice, it's very tough to do consistently well. (For more on market timing, see pages 173-175.)

Our company had a modest beginning. Doug moved into my existing office, bringing a few small accounts with him. We worked hard, traveling far and wide to sell our services to anyone willing to listen. Just as importantly, the market was kind to us. Our timing system worked very well—our average client account gained more than 32% annually during our first three years (compared to about 18% for the S&P 500). On the strength of that performance, we were able to move into deluxe quarters in the downtown financial district. We were on our way.

That was over 20 years ago. Since that time, my understanding of the investing process has been shaped by the books and financial periodicals I have read, the up and down markets I have experienced, and the mistakes I have made (will they never end?). Most of this book has been devoted to laying down for you a foundational understanding of how investments and the various markets work. Unavoidably, the emphasis has been on the technical and logistical basics. In this chapter, I want to focus almost exclusively on what is needed in terms of attitude and practice to be successful. It has been fascinating for me to discover that these principles, many of which I learned the hard way, were to be found in God's Word all along if only I had known where to look! Wisdom for investments, and all of life, can be found in the Bible.

Perhaps the most difficult aspect of applying what follows is trying to erase from your mind the preconceived ideas you have about what it means to be a "savvy" investor. If you're like most people . . .

. . . you have accumulated years of impressions concerning financial wizardry from the secular world. Most of them, however, are nothing more than a collection of contradictions, misconceptions, and false assumptions. You must try to forget what you *think you know* so you can learn what you *need to know.*

As you read this chapter, I am hoping to change more than your opinions; I am hoping to begin changing your convictions. An opinion is merely your preference when choosing among several alternatives. It's when you prefer one type of vacation over another or prefer one music style over another music style. An opinion is merely a personal preference. But a conviction is rooted in your core value system. Your convictions will not change without your values changing also. And the values you hold are what you draw from when setting personal boundaries. In *Changes That Heal*, psychologist Henry Cloud describes boundaries this way:

> *Boundaries, in a broad sense, are lines or things that mark a limit, bound, or border. In a psychological sense, boundaries are the realization of our own person apart from others. This sense of separateness forms the basis of personal identity. It says what we are and what we are not, what we will choose and what we will not choose, what we will endure and what we will not, what we*

feel and what we will not feel, what we like and what we do not like, and what we want and what we do not want. Boundaries, in short, define us. In the same way that a physical boundary defines where a property line begins and ends, a psychological and spiritual boundary defines who we are and who we are not.

So when I say I want to help change your convictions, I'm talking about a foundational part of your identity—how you see yourself spiritually and your moral responsibilities. It all follows from the earlier chapters in this section: because God is the glorious Creator/Sovereign and we are the creature/stewards, we see knowing Him as the true treasure, and because we cherish Him, it is our heart's desire to build His kingdom and uphold His righteousness.

What convictions do I hope to change? The ones that have crept in from worldly "wisdom." Convictions that say it's OK . . .

. . . or merely a matter of personal preference whether you borrow to invest, invest in limited partnerships that involve cosigning for debt, frequently adjust your portfolio in response to changing world events, always seek the maximum return, or invest for short-term results. Such tactics may occasionally be profitable, but more often they are self-destructive. In any event, they go against God's wisdom as given to us in His Word. We need to learn to think with new minds in order to understand His will.

I urge you, brothers, in view of God's mercy, to offer your bodies as living sacrifices, holy and pleasing to God—this is your spiritual act of worship. Do not conform any longer to the pattern of this world, but be transformed by the renewing of your mind. Then you will be able to test and approve what God's will is—his good, pleasing and perfect will. (Romans 12:1-2)

As we renew our minds, we not only see more clearly who God is; we also gain insight into our own natures.

As investors, we are our own worst enemies. This observation stems not only from my many years of practical experience, but also is confirmed by God's Word. Given our fallen natures, it would be surprising if we *weren't* the primary problem we face when investing. Consider for a moment the kind of people we are. The failings of our wisdom, our motives, our emotions, and our clarity of vision are well documented in the Scriptures.

- **Our wisdom is flawed.**

  Let no person deceive himself. If any one among you supposes that he is wise in this age—let him discard his [worldly] discernment and recognize himself as dull, stupid and foolish, without [true] learning and scholarship; let him become a fool that he may become [really] wise. For this world's wisdom is foolishness—absurdity and stupidity—with God. (1 Corinthians 3:18-19, Amplified)

- **Our motivations are impure.**

  The heart is deceitful above all things, and it is exceedingly perverse and corrupt and severely, mortally sick! Who can know it [perceive, understand, be acquainted with his own heart and mind]? (Jeremiah 17:9, Amplified)

• **Our emotions are powerful.**

For I know that nothing good dwells within me, that is, in my flesh. I can will what is right, but I cannot perform it. I have the intention and urge to do what is right, but no power to carry it out. (Romans 7:18, Amplified)

• **Our vision is limited.**

Come now, you who say, "Today or tomorrow we will go into such and such a city and spend a year there to carry on our business and make money." Yet you do not know [the least thing] about what may happen tomorrow. . . . You boast [falsely] in your presumption and your self-conceit. (James 4:13-14, 16, Amplified)

As we renew our minds, we can begin to put proper boundaries in place that not only define our Christian priorities and values but *will also serve to protect us from the markets and ourselves.* The reason for having an individualized investment strategy is to provide these needed boundaries.

You begin by acknowledging that you need help. Your financial life has no central focus. You make decisions as situations arise based on what you've read is best, what a friend says is best, or just by throwing a dart and hoping for the best. You find yourself pulled in all directions, looking something like this:

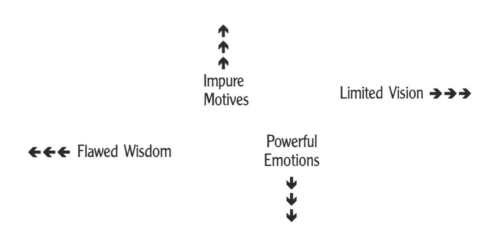

Having a specific strategy in place helps *contain and focus* your impulses by providing boundaries. It boxes you in and takes away your freedom to do what you might want. But it offers a new kind of freedom—the freedom to do what you should. It gives you a sense of perspective and a new way of knowing what's "right" for you. The illustration on the next page shows four biblically based boundaries to a focused investment strategy: objective, mechanical criteria for decision making; a portfolio that is broadly diversified; a long-term, get-rich-slow perspective; and a manager's (rather than owner's) mentality. Let's now look at how these boundaries come into play in practical ways in everyday situations.

Boundary One:
Using mechanical guidelines rather than your own intuition and judgment.

He who trusts in himself is a fool, but he who walks in wisdom is kept safe. (Proverbs 28:26)

But the fruit of the Spirit is . . . self-control. (Galatians 5:22-23)

Mechanical guidelines require that you develop objective criteria to follow for your buying and selling decisions. One example would be to use the risk matrix (page 193) to select a specific mix of stocks and fixed income investments. The allocations that are laid out for you provide explicit, objective boundaries to help you diversify according to your risk tolerance and age. They help make your investment shopping purposeful. Such boundaries protect you from giving in to sales presentations on some "really attractive" investment that you don't need at present.

Another example would be setting value criteria for timing your stock buying and selling. Using the price/earnings benchmark explained on page 175, you might decide to take profits in any stock once its P/E ratio reaches a certain predetermined level. Or you might look to buy underpriced stocks when the P/E is near the low end of its historical range.

Guidelines can help you control your losses. When you buy a stock or fund that doesn't perform as you hope, it can be difficult emotionally to admit it didn't work out. People often hold onto weak companies for years hoping to sell when they can "get even." This is a form of denial; the loss has already taken place. This emotional trap can be avoided by a mechanical guideline that says, "I'll sell if it drops x% from where I bought it because if it gets that low, there's a probability I misjudged the situation."

The dollar-cost-averaging and value-averaging strategies (see chapter 19) use mechanical guidelines to help you know how much to invest and when. The discipline imposed by these programs is helpful because our judgment tends to be unduly influenced by news events of the moment. There will always be bad news, but news is rarely as bad or good as it might first appear. These guidelines protect you from overreacting (along with everyone else) to the crisis or euphoria of the moment.

The markets go to extremes because they are driven by emotions, not reason. Also, professional money managers are afraid of getting left behind and looking bad (they want job security too, you know), so they go along with the crowd and panic like everyone else. Mechanical guidelines help you harness the powerful emotions that often cause investors to do precisely the wrong thing at precisely the wrong time. Mechanical rules may appear dull, but that's actually a virtue—the most successful market strategies tend to be dull because they are measured, not spontaneous.

Before leaving the subject of emotions, may I suggest another idea about how to remain objective? Don't give investment advice to friends and family, and don't tell them what your investment holdings are. It's not a question of secrecy; it's the tendency you'll have to lose your objectivity about the investments in question. It's important to remain flexible and follow your guidelines, right? But how can you take a loss in this great stock or fund that you've told everybody about? You might find yourself thinking, *This is humiliating. Everybody will think I'm an idiot. Better to at least wait until I can get out at "break-even" so I can save face.* Oops, that's exactly the kind of emotional decision-making you want to avoid.

Boundary Two:
Building a broadly diversified portfolio to protect against the uncertainties of the future.

> *Give portions to seven, yes to eight, for you do not know what disaster may come upon the land. (Ecclesiastes 11:2)*

> *But the fruit of the Spirit is . . . peace. (Galatians 5:22)*

Acknowledging our limited vision is to remember the reality check from *Jurassic Park* (page 284). Be honest with yourself and say, "Not only do I not know what the future holds, none of the experts do, either." Since we don't (and can't) know the future, we can never know in advance with certainty which investments will turn out most profitably. That is the rationale for diversifying—spreading out your portfolio into various areas so that you won't be overinvested in any hard-hit areas and you'll have at least some investments in the most rewarding areas.

Once you accept that "nobody knows," it makes a lot of sense to diversify and relax. Then, here are some of the things you're free to do:

• **Ask hard questions of anyone trying to sell you an investment.** Make them support and document every assertion, promise, or guarantee. You don't need to let them intimidate you anymore, because you know the truth: nobody knows for sure, no matter how confident they sound, whether what they're recommending will truly turn out to be the best for you. Then, before you act, review the decision-making guidelines I suggested on pages 196-198.

• **Ignore all forecasts by the "experts." They're guessing.** There's a kind of Newton's Law of Motion for economics: For every forecast by a group of experts with impressive credentials, there's an equal and opposite forecast by another group of experts with equally impressive credentials. Besides, if you've ever noticed, most forecasts seem to assume that the current trends (whatever they are) will continue. If they *were* to have any value, we'd need to know when the current trends will be reversed.

• **Ignore the media's explanations for why the markets are acting as they are. They're rationalizing.** Almost every item of economic news has both positive and negative implications, depending on what you want. For example, lower interest rates are good news if you're a borrower, bad news if you're a saver; a strong dollar is good news for importers, bad news for exporters. When the news is released, the media watch the markets' reactions. The next day, they merely emphasize *that aspect of the news* that the markets paid most attention to. If lower rates cause the stock market to go up, the media say it's because low rates are good for the economy; if the market goes down, the media say it's because low rates encourage renewed inflation. You should recognize that the media's explanations of market behavior are merely after-the-fact rationalizations.

• **Ignore most of the direct mail that you receive promoting an investment advisory letter. They're grossly exaggerating.** I'm talking primarily about the ones with the bold-letter "hype" that promise easy or guaranteed profits due to their consistent accuracy in making predictions about the markets. Such claims are deceptive—every newsletter writer is correct in some of his expectations and wrong about others. Some are right more than they're wrong, but nobody is consistently right. There's always a possibility that you can lose your money in the markets—it's irresponsible to imply otherwise. Such claims by any newsletter writer (or broker or anyone else) should immediately raise a red flag in your mind and call his credibility into question.

Boundary Three:
Developing a long-term, get-rich-slow perspective.

Dishonest money dwindles away, but he who gathers money little by little makes it grow. (Proverbs 13:11)

But the fruit of the Spirit is . . . patience. (Galatians 5:22)

Fewer things cause investors more losses than a short-term, get-rich-quick orientation to decision making. Patience, a fruit of the Spirit, is in short supply among investors today. Many have the attention span of a strobe light. A long-term view is extremely productive when investing; such a perspective has three major benefits:

❶ **It allows you time to do first things first.** I've already discussed the importance of being debt-free before proceeding into stocks, bonds, and other investments (other than those in your retirement plans). Once that foundation is laid, you can handle market risk with greater confidence. In the face of market setbacks, a long-term view says, "I'm investing with my surplus funds. This sell-off is no threat to my immediate well-being. I've got time to be patient and wait for the recovery."

❷ **It allows you to let those "once-in-a-lifetime, you-don't-want-to-miss-this-one-but-you-must-act-now" deals go by.** You've got plenty of time, and you don't want to invest in anything you haven't had time to carefully investigate and pray about. Trust me—there's always another day and another "great deal."

❸ **It allows you to be more relaxed when your judgment turns out less than perfect (surprise!).** For example, those times when the stock you just bought goes lower (which it always will) or the one you just sold goes even higher (which it always will). Why let that frustrate you? In your saner moments, you know it's extremely unlikely you're going to buy at the exact low or sell at the exact high. Taking the long view says, "It doesn't matter whether I bought at $14 when I could have bought at $12. The important thing is that I followed my plan. Over time, I know my plan will get me where I want to go."

Boundary Four:
Accepting management responsibility for your decisions, which leads you to study the basics and seek counsel when making important decisions.

Every prudent man acts out of knowledge, but a fool exposes his folly. (Proverbs 13:16)

But the fruit of the Spirit is . . . faithfulness. (Galatians 5:22)

Ultimately, you are accountable for what happens. You have been given a stewardship responsibility that you cannot delegate away. You can delegate authority to someone else to make certain investment decisions, but you cannot delegate your responsibility for the results that come from those decisions.

Once you "own" this fact, you will take your management obligations even more seriously. Many Christians do not see themselves as "investors" simply because they don't have large stock portfolios. I believe they have a misconception as to what investing involves. As I pointed out earlier, *investing decisions involve deciding what you will do without today in order that you might have more of something later.*

Cutting back on your spending (sacrifice convenience/luxury) in order to get debt-free (gain peace of mind and freedom) is an investing decision. Buying a used car rather than a new one (sacrifice status and ego) in order to start saving for a house someday (gain shelter and security) is an investing decision. Keeping your savings in money market funds instead of bond funds (sacrifice yield) in order to have your principal safe (gain stability and flexibility) is an investing decision.

Knowing that managing this part of your life responsibly is a God-given task will help you to become more realistic about your needs in four areas:

• **More realistic about your need for additional knowledge.** You accept that you must learn certain financial and investing basics. You can't just say, "Oh, I don't have the time (or interest or intellect) for that." You understand that some study will be necessary.

• **More realistic about the limitations of what investing can accomplish for you.** As you study, you learn that rates of return over the long haul tend to be in the 8%-12% range, not 15%-20% as many imagine. The idea that you will readily make large returns to bail you out of your problems is a dream. And mixed in that 8%-12% average will be good years (gains of 20% to 30%) and bad years (losses of 10% to 20%). It's not a smooth road.

• **More realistic about the strengths and weaknesses of the investment industry.** It does not have your best interests, first and foremost, at heart. It is awash in conflicts of interest (brokers get paid for selling securities, publishers get paid for selling magazines, financial networks get paid for attracting viewers). Your naïveté will diminish as you develop a healthy skepticism. On the plus side, America is still a land of great economic opportunity for those who are willing to diligently apply themselves and who do not easily give up.

• **More realistic about the markets themselves.** You'll no longer believe that "the pros" know something you don't, and you'll see the widely erratic swings as being evidence of emotionalism rather than calm reason. You'll discover there are few absolutes, other than preservation of your capital and survival, to guide you as you navigate the tumultuous storms and cross-currents.

These doses of realism will be very, very good for you.

We can't avoid taking risks.

Life is filled with uncertainties. Even getting out of bed in the morning and driving to work is not without its risks. But we can manage our financial affairs so that when the unexpected comes along, we can isolate the damage it does. The blueprint for planning in this manner is given to us in the Scripture, and it is incorporated into the strategies taught in this book. Know where you're going. Avoid debt. Spend less than you earn. Save for the future. Diversify your investments. Exercise self-control and stay with your plan.

In his book *Storm Shelter*, financial planner Ron Blue points out that while economic uncertainty is certain, God's principles are adequate for our protection. They've been tested through the centuries and never found wanting.

> *The picture is as clear in my mind as it was nearly thirteen years ago. As I pulled off the interstate en route to my office, I did not see the road markers; instead my eyes swam with the signs of the times.*

> *The year was 1982. Interest and inflation rates had soared to all-time highs, investors faced crushing 70 percent tax brackets, and the price of gold leapfrogged daily. Taking stock of the situation, most analysts warned of a devastating financial explosion within the next few years.*

> *As I drove to work that day, the economic consequences seemed both crippling and inevitable. I had just launched our investment and financial counseling firm. How, I wondered, were we supposed to respond to the clients who came to us for advice? Could anyone afford to purchase a home with 15 to 20 percent interest rates? Which kinds of investments and tax plans could stand up to double-digit inflation? And if the predicted monetary collapse did occur, would the resulting political turmoil uproot even the best-laid financial plans?*

> *One of my fears as I navigated the interstate highway that day was that we faced a "worst-ever" economic climate. Yet economic uncertainty—and its accompanying effects on our sense of security and well-being—are nothing new.*

> *Ten years earlier, in 1972, we had been saddled with Watergate and an oil crisis that threatened to throttle the world's economy. Who can forget the lines at the gas stations or the rationing of fuel oil that winter? Then, too, I remember being hit with wage and price controls for the first time since World War II. And for the first time in my memory, the prime rate hit ten percent. Economic security seemed an elusive, if not impossible, dream.*

> *Ten years before that, in 1962, the specter of economic and political uncertainty had hovered in every corner of the world. Our amazement at seeing a shoe-pounding Nikita Khrushchev vow to "bury" us turned to horror as the Cuban missile crisis unfolded. At that point a nuclear holocaust seemed at least possible, if not imminent. And Vietnam lay just around the corner . . .*

> *In 1952, in the shadow of the spread of Communism, amid the mud and blood of the Korean War, bomb shelters were among the best-selling items in the United States. In 1942, we faced Pearl*

Harbor and felt the full force of our entry into World War II. In 1932 we awoke to the nightmare of the Great Depression.

And on and on and on. The point is that we will always face uncertainty. Suddenly, I felt the subconscious click of the proverbial light bulb: The biblical principles of money management I had been teaching and using for years would work under any economic scenario. Armed with these concepts, I knew exactly how to help our clients weather the coming storm, no matter how hard the financial winds blew.

The predicted financial blowout never did occur. Yet as our business grew in the years that followed, we faced a thousand different financial situations that seemed specially tailored to test the worth and endurance of the money-management concepts our firm espoused. But in each and every case the biblical principles held fast, strengthening our clients' economic positions—and bringing them peace and security in the bargain.

Investing that glorifies God seeks His wisdom.

The wisdom found in God's Word is there for our protection and His glory. In financial matters, it points to God Himself as our true treasure and helps us see that *we* are the ones who suffer when we seek our treasure elsewhere.

Let's not settle for the creation when we can have the Creator.

Let's not settle for the temporal when we can have the eternal.

Let's not settle for knowing man's wisdom when we can know God's wisdom—Christ Himself.

Where is the wise man? Where is the scholar? Where is the philosopher of this age? Has not God made foolish the wisdom of the world? For since in the wisdom of God the world through its wisdom did not know him, God was pleased through the foolishness of what was preached to save those who believe. Jews demand miraculous signs and Greeks look for wisdom, but we preach Christ crucified: a stumbling block to Jews and foolishness to Gentiles, but to those whom God has called, both Jews and Greeks, Christ the power of God and the wisdom of God. For the foolishness of God is wiser than man's wisdom, and the weakness of God is stronger than man's strength.

Brothers, think of what you were when you were called. Not many of you were wise by human standards; not many were influential; not many were of noble birth. But God chose the foolish things of the world to shame the wise; God chose the weak things of the world to shame the strong. He chose the lowly things of this world and the despised things—and the things that are not—to nullify the things that are, so that no one may boast before him. It is because of him that you are in Christ Jesus, who has become for us wisdom from God—that is, our righteousness, holiness and redemption. Therefore, as it is written: "Let him who boasts boast in the Lord." (1 Corinthians 1:20-31)

May God grant us the grace to know Him. To seek for nothing else, and to settle for nothing less. ◆

CHAPTER PREVIEW

Investing That Glorifies God
Enjoys His Blessings

Delight yourself in the Lord and he will give you the
desires of your heart. Commit your way to the Lord; trust
in him and he will do this: He will make your righteousness
shine like the dawn, the justice of your cause like the noonday sun.

(Psalm 37:4-6)

As the Scripture says, "Anyone who trusts in him will never
be put to shame." For there is no difference between Jew and Gentile—
the same Lord is Lord of all and richly blesses all who call on him.

(Romans 10:11-12)

(The gifts you sent) are a fragrant offering, an acceptable sacrifice,
pleasing to God. And my God will meet all your needs
according to his glorious riches in Christ Jesus.
To our God and Father be glory forever and ever. Amen.

(Philippians 4:18-20)

I have concluded that I have very little ability to discern what is valuable in life and what isn't.

I don't always see clearly which experiences are blessings and which ones do me harm. In fact, it's probably safe to say that I really don't even know—with complete certainty—what I truly want.

That being the case, one of the most exciting steps I can take is to pray and ask God for things. I neither know which requests He'll grant nor have the slightest insight into how He'll work through circumstances in granting those requests He does. But I'm learning it's usually in the most improbable and unexpected ways.

After about five years of hard work, Doug and I had built our advisory business to what could fairly be called a "successful" level. Our investment performance results had frequently placed in the top 5% among advisers nationwide. Money goes where it's treated best, and we had attracted enough clients to the point that we were both taking home six-figure incomes. Plus, I still had time for my ministry interests. All in all, things were working out pretty well.

Then, starting around 1985, I entered a period where I seemed to have the reverse Midas touch. In about a three-year span, my financial roof fell in thanks to a variety of unrelated events: a home that took three years to sell, unprecedented losses in my personal futures trading account, and a costly business venture in South Carolina, to name a few.

The summer of 1987 was the worst period of my business life. In April, with the Dow around 2300, we had sold all stock funds and placed our clients 100% into money market funds. We did this because we felt the market had risen too far, too fast. The environment had become one of high risk. As the Dow continued to make new highs over the summer months (and everybody "knew" it was going to 3000), we began losing clients to other firms who had no such reservations about risk. Our warnings to our departing clients fell on deaf ears. I'm sure many felt we were out of touch with the realities of the market. In truth, they and their new money managers were the ones out of touch, as the October crash violently demonstrated. In a single day, the Dow Jones dropped more than 500 points, and it did not recover to its former level for two years. The crash vindicated our caution, but it was too late to stabilize our client base. The defections dealt a major blow to our company and required Doug and me to take drastic salary cuts and make other expense-related adjustments.

So there I was facing substantial business and personal financial pressures that I would never have dreamed of a few years earlier. And I was asking . . .

. . . "Lord, why is this happening to me? I travel and speak in Your name. I work and give diligently for Your causes. How come You're treating me like this? Please get me out of this mess. Please reassure me that everything's going to be all right. Please let me know that You're still here with me."

You know what the Lord said to me? Nothing.

I've never heard from the Lord *directly* in all my life. I know some people who have, but I never have. However, the Lord does speak to me by giving me ideas and impressions as I read and meditate in His Word. And, over time, the answer to my pleading question came. It was as if He said:

> "You prayed that you could become mature, didn't you? I'm teaching you how to depend on Me more."

> "You prayed for more faith, didn't you? I'm giving you a chance to trust Me more."

> "You prayed that you could be used to minister to others, didn't you? I'm training you so you can serve Me more."

> "You prayed that you might know Me better, didn't you? I'm helping you to seek Me more."

> "You prayed that you might glorify Me with your life, didn't you? I'm refining you more."

When we pray prayers that contain such "spiritual" requests, we can have confidence we're praying according to God's will. We expect Him to grant us, in His own timing, these qualities of the Christian life we're seeking. But I think that subconsciously we must believe that God answers them with a kind of supernatural lightning bolt. Something like, "Well, bless your heart, child, here's all the faith, love, and Christlikeness you'll ever need." Zap!

Well, unfortunately, it doesn't usually work that way.

Do you want to mature in your Christian walk? Then expect some suffering.

> *Not only so, but we also rejoice in our sufferings, because we know that suffering produces perseverance; perseverance, character; and character, hope. And hope does not disappoint us, because God has poured out his love into our hearts by the Holy Spirit, whom he has given us. (Romans 5:3-5)*

Do you want your to be faith strengthened? Then expect it to be tested.

> *Consider it pure joy, my brothers, whenever you face trials of many kinds, because you know that the testing of your faith develops perseverance. Perseverance must finish its work so that you may be mature and complete, not lacking anything. (James 1:2-4)*

Do you want God to use you to minister to others? Then expect God to first comfort you during your own pain.

> *Praise be to the God and Father of our Lord Jesus Christ, the Father of compassion and the God of all comfort, who comforts us in all our troubles, so that we can comfort those in any trouble with the comfort we ourselves have received from God. (2 Corinthians 1:3-4)*

Do you want to know God better? Then expect to give up the things of this world that are holding you back.

But whatever was to my profit I now consider loss for the sake of Christ. What is more, I consider everything a loss compared to the surpassing greatness of knowing Christ Jesus my Lord, for whose sake I have lost all things. I consider them rubbish, that I may gain Christ and be found in him. . . . I want to know Christ and the power of his resurrection and the fellowship of sharing in his sufferings. (Philippians 3:7-10)

Do you want to glorify Him with your life? Then expect to go through trials.

In this you greatly rejoice, though now for a little while you may have had to suffer grief in all kinds of trials. These have come so that your faith—of greater worth than gold, which perishes even though refined by fire—may be proved genuine and may result in praise, glory and honor when Jesus Christ is revealed. (1 Peter 1:6-7)

Most Christians, at one time or another, will ask God why He allows pain, suffering, and disappointment . . .

. . . to touch His children (in general) and touch *us* (in particular). When we meet the Lord face-to-face, we'll have an opportunity to ask Him in person (although seeing His glory may be all the answer we need). I wouldn't be surprised if part of the answer turns out to be: "Those things happened *because I was answering your prayers, in order to give you what you asked for.*"

As I began to gain an insight into this, I found myself uplifted. Trials are all the more difficult if they seem to be needless or a waste. Once you begin to see that they are purposeful, it's a great thing because then you know that (1) they will come to an end when the purpose is accomplished, (2) you will somehow, in some way, have gained something of great value, and (3) you will have glorified God by trusting Him and giving Him time to work.

A passage that was very encouraging to me during this time was Jeremiah 29:10-14. God was revealing to the Israelites why they were having the excruciating experience of being taken as slaves into the Babylonian captivity.

[10]This is what the Lord says: "When seventy years are completed for Babylon, I will come to you and fulfill my gracious promise to bring you back to this place. [11]For I know the plans I have for you," declares the Lord, "plans to prosper you and not to harm you, plans to give you hope and a future. [12]Then you will call upon me and come and pray to me, and I will listen to you. [13]You will seek me and find me when you seek me with all your heart. [14]I will be found by you," declares the Lord, "and will bring you back from captivity."

Here are the encouraging truths I found in these verses:

• Trials eventually come to an end, and God can be absolutely counted upon to fulfill His promises (verse 10).

• God is still thinking about us, even when we're feeling lonely in our trials (verse 11). He is listening to our heartfelt prayers (verse 12).

• The only thoughts that God has toward us are thoughts of peace that include a future that is hopeful and good (verse 11).

• God allows our trials to come because they are necessary to accomplish His purpose in our lives (verse 11).

• God's purpose is that we would seek Him (verse 13).

• God allows Himself to be found when we search for Him with all our heart. He purposes to ultimately bring about our restoration (verses 13-14).

In this passage, the Israelites have been removed from their land and torn from their possessions, yet God does not tell them to seek the restoration of their land. He does not tell them to seek their possessions. He does not tell them to seek their freedom. He tells them to seek but one thing—Himself. And one way that God has of causing us to seek Him wholeheartedly is by allowing us to lose those other things that we highly prize.

So I knew I needed to seek God, be patient, and wait. I *wanted* to please God; I wanted to trust God. But the circumstances . . .

. . . around me were so utterly discouraging. It's not always easy to expect the best and believe that everything will work out for our good. To the Israelites in exile, seventy years must have seemed like an eternity, and three years can seem like seventy when you're badly hurting.

I concentrated my reading and devotional times in books that gave me hope, and I repeatedly read Job and the Psalms. In addition to Scripture, I read *The God of All Comfort* by Hannah Whitall Smith. I read Amy Carmichael. I read *Disappointment with God* by Philip Yancey. I read *Desiring God* by John Piper. They were all tremendously encouraging.

During this time, I discovered what it means to give to God out of my poverty rather than out of my surplus. The gift of two years of voluntary service in the 1970s paled in comparison to the effort of one week of walking with God during the tough times in the 1980s and saying to Him, "I still love You. I still trust You. I am not offended. I am doing the very best I can to believe You are working everything out together for my good." The two years were offered when I was on top and life was good; the week was given when I was on the bottom and circumstances were bleak. In a fashion similar to the widow and her mite, I believe a single week of "hoping against hope" can be more pleasing and glorifying to God than a two-year missionary journey.

Perhaps you have had occasion to survey the landscape of your life and found very little evidence that God has "plans to prosper you and not to harm you, plans to give you a hope and a future."

May I encourage you to immerse your mind daily in words that will help you to know God more intimately and that will remind you that your God is always present, invariably loving, inevitably faithful, and absolutely worthy of

Recommended Resource

<u>The Pleasures of God</u>:
<u>Meditations on God's</u>
<u>Delight in Being God</u>

by John Piper

Published by
Multnomah Press,
Copyright 1991.

This is one of my very
favorite books! Starting
with Scriptures that
show our God is a
happy God, John Piper
goes on to look at
various aspects of
God's happiness.
Chapters include:

• The Pleasure of God
in His Son,

• The Pleasure of God
in His Creation,

• The Pleasure of God
in the Prayers of the
Upright,

and the one I quote
from on this page,

• The Pleasures of God
in Doing Good to All
Who Hope in Him.

Understanding what
gives God pleasure may
enable you to know our
glorious God better
than you have ever
known Him before.

Visit John Piper's
Desiring God Ministries
website at
<u>www.desiringgod.org</u>.

all your confidence. Consider the promises of God found later in Jeremiah: God is revealing in greater detail what it will be like when the trial His people are going through in Babylon has served its purpose. God declares in Jeremiah 32:

They will be my people, and I will be their God. I will give them singleness of heart and action, so that they will always fear me for their own good and the good of their children after them. I will make an everlasting covenant with them: I will never stop doing good to them, and I will inspire them to fear me, so that they will never turn away from me. I will rejoice in doing them good and will assuredly plant them in this land with all my heart and soul. (Jeremiah 32:38-41)

Those are tremendous promises. In sharing His father's heart, God promises He will "never stop doing good" to you. In *The Pleasures of God*, John Piper looks at the passage this way:

He will keep on doing good. He doesn't do good to his children sometimes and bad to them other times. He keeps on doing good and he never will stop doing good for ten thousand ages of ages. When things are going "bad" that does not mean God has stopped doing good. It means he is shifting things around to get them in place for more good, if you will go on loving him. He works all things together for good "for those who love him" (Romans 8:28). "No good thing does he withhold from those who walk uprightly" (Psalm 84:11). "Lo, it was for my welfare that I had great bitterness" (Isaiah 38:17). "It is good for me that I was afflicted, that I might learn your statutes" (Psalm 119:71). . . .

But the promise is greater yet. Not only does God promise not to turn away from doing good to us, he says, "I will rejoice in doing them good" (Jeremiah 32:41). "The Lord will again take delight in prospering you" (Deuteronomy 30:9). He does not bless us begrudgingly. There is a kind of eagerness about the beneficence of God. He does not wait for us to come to him. He seeks us out, because it is his pleasure to do us good. "The eyes of the Lord run to and fro throughout the whole earth, to show his might in behalf of those whose heart is whole toward him" (2 Chronicles 16:9). God is not waiting for us, he is pursuing us. That, in fact, is the literal translation of Psalm 23:6, "Surely goodness and mercy shall pursue me all the days of my life." God loves to show mercy. He is not hesitant or indecisive or tentative in his desires to do good to his people. His anger must be released by a stiff safety lock, but his mercy has a hair trigger. . . .

But still the promise is greater. First, God promises not to turn away from doing us good. Then he promises that he will do this good with rejoicing. Finally, he promises that this rejoicing over the good of his people will be with all his heart and with all his soul. . . . When God does good to his people it is not so much like a reluctant judge showing kindness to a criminal whom he finds despicable; it is like a bridegroom showing affection to his bride. And add to this, that with God the honeymoon never ends. He is infinite in power and wisdom and creativity and love. And so he has no trouble sustaining a honeymoon level of intensity; he can foresee all the future quirks of our personality and has decided he will keep what's good for us and change what isn't; he will always be as handsome as he ever was, and will see to it that we get more and more beautiful forever; and he is infinitely creative to think of new things to do together so that there will be no boredom for the next trillion ages of millenniums. . . .

When we say that God exults over his people with loud singing, we mean that he exults over those who hope in his love. In this way God maintains his rightful place—the place we love for him to have—at the center of the gospel. There is a condition we must meet in order to know him as our God and be a part of the wonderful covenant in which he never turns away from doing us good but rejoices over us with all his heart and all his soul. That condition is to put our hope in him as the all-satisfying Refuge and Treasure. God takes pleasure in this response with all his heart, because it magnifies the glory of his grace and satisfies the longing of our soul.

As I sought the Lord during those days, I opened my heart to whatever He had purposed for me. I had previously assumed I would continue in the investment advisory profession for the remainder of my career; now I wasn't so sure. Perhaps the Lord was using these difficult circumstances to change the direction of my working life. As long as I was financially comfortable and had a large client base, why would I consider anything else?

So, just in case this was part of the agenda, I surrendered to the Lord all aspects of my professional life. If He wanted to rebuild my company, that would be fine. If He wanted me to take a job working for someone else, that would be fine. If He wanted me to leave the business world and go back into full-time ministry work, that would be fine. I was finally in the best place for a child of God to be: "Whatever You want, Lord, before You even reveal it, the answer is yes." I added a little P.S. "If You think it would be OK, I'd like work that's mentally challenging, emotionally satisfying, and which somehow involves a ministry to people."

The answer came unexpectedly (and unrecognized by me at the time) in October of 1989. I was having lunch with longtime friend Larry Burkett . . .

. . . and his ministry associate in charge of their counseling activities, Steve Humphrey. As we discussed the financial challenges facing the average Christian family, they felt what was lacking was a certain kind of monthly investment newsletter with a truly Christian perspective. Larry said there was a great need for a reliable source of information, written with easy-to-understand, "user-friendly" wording, which would guide readers through the investment process step-by-step with instruction and counsel from a biblical perspective. It would help Christians make the varied and often complex investment decisions they face, as well as continually attempt to help its readers "renew their minds" with God's principles.

My initial response was, "You're right. Sounds great—too bad nobody's doing anything like that." It didn't occur to me that *I* should undertake the task—after all, I was an investment manager, not a writer or publisher. But as the weeks passed, the Lord seemed to keep bringing me back to Larry's comments. The number of investment services and products being offered today is mind-numbing in their variety.

The tendency is to feel overwhelmed. The need was obvious. So I began to pray. Though I agreed he had a great idea, I wondered whether I should be the one to do it.

I began to pray for wisdom: "Lord, do You want *me* to try to do this? Well, it would certainly be mentally challenging—I don't have much experience as a writer and none as a publisher. If I could succeed in encouraging my readers, it would be emotionally satisfying because I know from my own experience how important encouragement is in sustaining our hope during the tough times. And to the extent Christians get their finances and investments straightened out and give more to Your work, it would certainly have a ministry component. But Lord, I don't have the experience or the start-up money or the wisdom to pull this off—*I'd have to depend totally on You.*" Hmm. . . .

After many other closed doors and much prayer, Susie and I felt the Lord was indeed orchestrating events so that I would begin moving in that direction. At a time when I was wondering if I should go into publishing, it "just happened" that Doug and Gena Cobb, two of our best friends, had built a successful publishing business centered on a lineup of monthly computer software journals. Their company was the national leader in its field. Their counsel and prayers were invaluable. The first *Sound Mind Investing* newsletter was issued in July 1990.

SUMMARY OF SECTION SIX

God's wondrous and breathtaking glory
is the greatest theme in all the universe.

God is the sovereign/owner of all His creation, including us.
When we acknowledge His lordship in our lives, as is only reasonable, we
can begin to be transformed into His likeness by the renewing of our minds.

Renewed minds lead to new values.
We see Him as our great Treasure and seek Him as the source of our sufficiency.

Renewed minds lead to new motivations.
We want to invest our lives to see His kingdom built rather than
our own, to see Him receive the glory rather than ourselves.

Renewed minds lead to new ambitions.
We want to live a life worthy of the Lord and to uphold
His righteousness before an unbelieving world.

Renewed minds lead to new sources of wisdom.
We have a new commitment to His written Word and a
new passion for knowing Christ—the Wisdom of God.

Renewed minds lead us to new blessings.
We see Him as the giver of every good gift and learn to be
content with His purposes, which are always
for our good "to give us a future and a hope."

People are often curious as to how a "biblically-based" investment newsletter . . .

. . . differs from a "regular" one. I explain it this way. Society's perspective is that we came into existence strictly by chance. Accordingly, we are just animals seeking to fulfill our needs. Furthermore:

• The goal of work is to do whatever is necessary to achieve success. Indicators of success are the acquisition of money, possessions, and influence.

• Because life is short, lifestyles are geared to immediate gratification — gaining as much pleasure as possible as quickly as possible. This leads to higher consumption now and less saving for the future. A high level of debt and continuous use of credit is considered an acceptable means to this end.

• Investing is geared to get-rich-quick strategies with a short-term time horizon. The recessionary phases of economic cycles are dreaded and pose a constant threat to economic survival.

• Because there is no ultimate purpose or morality, we are free to invent our own. Ethics are relative and personal. They generally play little, if any, role in making spending or investing decisions.

Contrast these views with a Biblical perspective that maintains we came into existence through the creative hand of God. We are essentially spirit beings with an eternal purpose. It follows that:

• The goal of work is to use our God-given talents to serve others or fulfill a calling. Indicators of success are peace with God, showing love for others, contentment in life.

• Because eternal life is possible, a lifestyle of deferred gratification that is focused on eternal issues is appropriate. This leads to less consumption now and more saving for the future and for giving to Christian ministry. A high level of debt and continuous use of credit is discouraged as an unnatural and enslaving lifestyle.

• Investing can be geared to slow-but-sure strategies with a long-term time horizon. Economic cycles are prepared for through a strategy of saving and diversification.

• Because God has a moral purpose for His creation, a law of sowing and reaping prevails. Ethics are based on Biblical wisdom and play an important role in making spending and investing decisions.

Jesus is almost universally regarded as the wisest moral teacher of all time, even by millions who do not consider themselves Christians. After finishing what we call "The Sermon on the Mount," he said, *"Everyone who hears these words of mine and does not put them into practice is like a foolish man who built his house on sand. The rain came down, the streams rose, and the winds blew and beat against that house, and it fell with a great crash."*

Although our society may be building on sand, at the personal and family level we still have the choice of preparing for the inevitable storms of life by following biblical principles. Take a good look around you. Rarely has the truth of the old hymn been so obvious: "On Christ, the solid Rock, I stand. All other ground is sinking sand, all other ground is sinking sand."

More than ten years have now come and gone . . .

. . . since the day I bravely had 500 copies of the first issue printed. The start-up phase was physically demanding, emotionally satisfying, financially unprofitable, and spiritually fulfilling. The way in which events have unfolded have reminded Susie and me on several occasions that our God *"is able to [carry out His purpose and] do superabundantly, far over and above all that we [dare] ask or think—infinitely beyond our highest prayers, desires, thoughts, hopes or dreams—To Him be glory in the church and in Christ Jesus throughout all generations, for ever and ever"* (Ephesians 3:20-21, *Amplified*).

One of the biggest surprises of my new publishing career has been the number of warm and encouraging letters I receive from my readers. They express appreciation for the fact that they are understanding certain financial and investing matters for the first time, and the new hope they have that they can really take control of their investment lives rather than relying on others. Their enthusiasm, and the number of them that say the journal "is an answer to prayer," is quite humbling. I mention this only to point out how wonderfully God answered my prayer that He would give me a ministry as well as a business. He has, and I've never felt so gratified by anything I've done in my professional life.

God is a loving Father to His children. If you're facing challenges, financial or otherwise, He can help you just as He helped me. Trust Him.

The story is told of the young Christian student who was distraught because of an argument he had with his girlfriend. He made an appointment to see the youth minister of his church for advice. When he arrived, his wise friend began their meeting with this prayer:

"Dear God of creation, who created the universe from nothing, scattered billions of stars at a mere word, engineered every favorable condition necessary to support life on this blue planet, populated the oceans and the lands with creatures of unimaginable variety and complexity, orchestrated all of nature and made man its master . . .

"God of Moses, who turned the mighty Nile into a river of blood, sent hordes of frogs, swarms of lice and flies, a plague of disease and boils, devastating hail, locusts that covered the sky, and the death of Egypt's firstborn in order to answer the prayers of his people for freedom. . .

"God of David, who with a river stone dropped a warrior giant to his death and made a shepherd boy a king . . .

"God of the disciples, who on Pentecost received Your power, spoke in other languages so 3,000 were baptized on one day, and then turned the world upside down for Christ . . .

"Father of Jesus, who made the blind see, the lame walk, lepers whole and the dead to rise, and gave His life to rescue those who were hopelessly dead in sin and made them alive to righteousness and eternal life . . .

"God of creation, God of history, God of the Bible, God Almighty . . . could You possibly be of some help with this young man's girlfriend? Amen."

When I heard this story, I couldn't help but smile. How like that young student I can be. Stopping for a moment to reflect on God's sovereign power—and His promise to use it always for my good if I'll put my trust in Him—puts my daily concerns into a whole new perspective.

In truth, my problems are so small, so transitory. And God is so big, bigger than I can possibly imagine. Surely, I trust Him for too little. Perhaps you do, too. If the youth minister had been praying for your concerns, how would he have closed his prayer?

• ". . . could You possibly show this couple how to get out of debt and save for the future as Your word commends?

- ". . . could You possibly lead this man to a job that would be a better fit for the way You've made him and for the financial and family needs that he has?"

- ". . . could You possibly enable this child of Yours to have victory over temptations and live a life that's honoring to You?"

- ". . . could You possibly help this widow to make wise investing decisions as she seeks to be a good steward of Your wealth?"

- ". . . could You possibly show this family how they can give even more to take the saving message of Christ to those who have never heard?"

Could He possibly? We know the answer is, "Of course!" He is the One about whom Jesus said *"with God all things are possible"* (Matthew 19:26).

Our part is to trust Him. We have it on the highest authority that *"Everything is possible for him who believes"* (Mark 9:23). And again, *"If you have faith as small as a mustard seed . . . Nothing will be impossible for you"* (Matthew 17:20).

There is one exception, however, one thing that God *has* declared is impossible for us: *"And without faith it is impossible to please God, because anyone who comes to him must believe that he exists and that he rewards those who earnestly seek him"* (Hebrews 11:6).

So let us seek Him, trusting Him to deliver us through the difficulties of life, remembering that we pray to a God who is too strong to ever lose control of any situation, too wise to ever make a mistake, and too loving to ever abandon us. Just the kind of God we need.

Investing that glorifies God enjoys His blessings.

As I indicated at the beginning of this chapter, it's a tricky matter to accurately discern which experiences in life will ultimately work for our good. The reason for this is not that bad things are necessarily good things in disguise, but rather our God is so great that He can take the bad things and *transform* them into good things. He does this because He purposes to use everything in life that we might "be conformed to the likeness of his Son."

Knowing that what appears good (wealth and success) can actually be bad for us, and that what appears bad ("trials of many kinds") can actually be good for us, gives one a certain humility in praying. This truth is beautifully expressed in the *Prayer of an Unknown Confederate Soldier*:

> I asked God for strength that I might achieve. I was made weak, that I might learn humbly to obey.

> I asked for help, that I might do greater things. I was given infirmity, that I might do better things.

> I asked for riches, that I might be happy. I was given poverty, that I might be wise.

> I asked for power, that I might have the praise of men. I was given weakness, that I might feel the need of God.

> I asked for all things, that I might enjoy life. I was given life, that I might enjoy all things.

> I got nothing that I asked for but everything I hoped for. Almost despite myself, my unspoken prayers were answered.

> I am, among all men, most richly blessed. *(Source Unknown)*

We're all looking for peace in an uncertain world. We don't know what the future holds, but we know who holds the future. Our trust in Him is never misplaced. Paul wrote: "For to me, to live is Christ, and to die is gain." Paul could say that because dying brought him even more of what he was living for. But today, if for us "to live is business success," then to die is loss. If for us "to live is financial riches," then to die is loss. If for us "to live is the praise of men," then to die is loss. Because dying takes all of those things away. On the day that we die, what wealth we may have will be of zero value to us, of no help or comfort whatsoever. But knowing Him will mean everything. And that's why He is our peace.

If you'll aim your life in the direction of God's glory, you'll enjoy His blessings. They may or may not be material blessings. But in whatever form God sends them, you can be sure they will satisfy your deepest longings. *"Praise be to the God and Father of our Lord Jesus Christ, who has blessed us in the heavenly realms with every spiritual blessing in Christ"* (Ephesians 1:3).

To conclude this section and my book, I've collected a few of the hundreds of promises God has made to you in His Word. Consider who you are and what you have, and give thanks!

- You are *a child of God.*
- You are *protected* by the name of Jesus.
- You have *peace* with God.
- You are *free from condemnation.*
- You have been *cleansed* by Christ's blood.
- You are a *joint heir* with Jesus Christ.
- You are *confident* that all things work together for your good.
- You are *inseparable from the love of God.*
- You have *eternal life* in Christ Jesus.
- You are *abiding in Christ;* Christ is abiding in you.
- You are *free of the vicious cycle* of sin and death.
- You are *adequate* for anything because your adequacy comes from God.
- You are *chosen* by God to be holy and blameless.
- You have *wisdom* and insight to know His will.
- You are able to walk boldly *into Christ's presence.*
- You are *strengthened* with His power through His spirit in the inner man.
- You *don't have to be anxious* about anything.
- You are *able to do all things through Christ* who strengthens you.
- You are *indwelt by Him* in whom all fullness dwells.
- You've been presented to God, *holy, blameless, and beyond reproach.*
- You are able to come boldly before His throne of grace and find *mercy* every time.
- *He who is in you is greater* than he who is in the world.
- You have not been given a spirit of fear, but of *power* and of *love* and of *a sound mind.*
- *You are complete in Christ!* ◆

"In your hearts set apart Christ as Lord. Always be prepared to give an answer
to everyone who asks you to give the reason for the hope that you have."
(1 Peter 3:15)

We would not be able to progress very far in our Christian faith apart from the kindnesses
shown to us by others of God's people who were "prepared to give an answer to everyone
who asks." I have been immeasurably helped, encouraged, and inspired along the way by
others who have lived out 1 Peter 3:15 to my benefit. Merely saying thank you, of course, is
an inadequate expression of deep gratitude. But not to say thank you would be to deny the
grace and power of God that reached out through them and changed my view of Him
forever. To the extent this book has been an encouragement to you, you owe thanks as well:

To Claudia Pryor

Thank you, Mom, for taking me to Sunday school at an early age
where I learned about the Savior who loves me.

To Bob McConnell

Thank you for coming and sharing the wonderful discovery
of the Spirit-filled life with us 30 years ago and being an intercessor for us all these years.

To Bill and Vonette Bright

Thank you for modeling the Christian life so powerfully that I knew, beyond ever questioning
again, that the gospel must be true. It is the only explanation for your lives. We love you.

To Arlis Priest

Thank you for taking a fatherly interest in me and showing me that because "the greatest ability is
avail-ability," even ordinary young businessmen can be used by a great God to minister in the world.

To Sim and Mimi Fulcher

Thank you for becoming our beloved extended family in Christ. Susie joins me in praising
our Father for your faithful, creative, and generous love to us and for 25 years of prayers.

To John Piper

(whom I have never met, but would like to)
Thank you for helping me to rediscover that God is breathtaking
and to understand that He is most glorified in me when I am most satisfied in Him.

And Most of All to Susie

Other than our Lord, no one knows you like I do. Others don't know of your tenacity
and faithfulness in prayer. Or of the steadfast trust you have in His goodness even in the
face of crushing disappointments. Or of the deep love you have for His Word and the price
you have paid when standing firm in upholding it. But I know all these things and much more.
And so it is with great insight that I thank the Lord for giving me a wife of noble character.

"A wife of noble character who can find? She is worth far more than rubies.
Her husband has full confidence in her and lacks nothing of value."
(Proverbs 31:10-11)

TOPICAL INDEX

It's reassuring that so many respected leaders gave *Sound Mind Investing* high marks. Equally gratifying were the comments from "everyday ordinary folks" like these who read the first edition and found it a reliable road map as they made important financial decisions.

Your book is one of the best that I've read on financial matters. Your writing was clear and easy to understand. I especially liked the Godly principles that the book was based on. I believe you have helped many people (including me), and have brought honor and glory to God through this book.

Alan Fyfe
Coal Valley, Illinois

SMI is written in an easy-to-read, easy-to-understand, and easy-to-apply manner. I was elated to find the book to fill my needs in a Christian bookstore written by a God-fearing man. God fills our every need, and He has filled a need of mine through Mr. Pryor.

Daniel Rawn
San Diego, California

I want to thank you for writing such a clear, complete guide to investing which incorporates Biblical wisdom. *Sound Mind Investing* has been a tremendous help in sorting out my investment planning for my family.

John Wieloszynski
Buffalo, New York

I have been reading and studying your book *Sound Mind Investing*. What a great help! Before my wife gave me this book, I was in total ignorance about finances. Now I am so grateful that I have this tremendous resource to help me invest wisely and make financial decisions to honor the Lord with all that He has given my family.

Kevin Golde
Cranston, Rhode Island

Awesome, powerful, a masterpiece! I am so grateful that the Lord would lead me to read such a beautiful book as He prepares me to be a steward of His blessings in my life.

George Avila
Miami, Florida

I have never seen so much useful information compiled in one source. Until we found SMI, we had very little information with which to guide ourselves. With the help of your book, we were able to analyze our investments, find several weak areas, and structure an investment plan that I know will help us achieve Godly financial goals.

Becky Kiefer
Rolling Meadows, Illinois

I want to commend you on this book as it is well written, helpfully illustrated, and easily understood. I have read many books and articles about money, investing, etc., and I find that your book tops them all. I want to thank you for giving us a volume written in simple, clear language that is educational, enjoyable, and very practical for those who have any interest in the world of finances.

Richard Kidd
Romulus, New York

I've been reading the SMI book—wow! Praise God that He saw fit to bless you with wisdom that you share so effectively! I was just about to head into the field of investing "blind," but now I understand where I'm going. Thanks!

Pamela Miller
Concord, California

I found SMI to be a wonderful resource manual that I will always be able to refer to. It is so nice to be able to have access to information as important as finances that is backed with a Biblical understanding. I would like to commend you on such a fantastic job.
Paul Fesler
Charleston, South Carolina

Your book has been helpful in enabling me to set up a plan. All of this investing "stuff" was new to me and after talking to three brokers and one CPA it was overwhelming. Your book helped tie it together and give me some confidence and knowledge so I can structure and chart my own plan. Thank you.
Cheryl Guilzon
Westerlo, New York

I have felt so ill-informed in an area that has always appeared to be so intimidating, that of investing. Your book has put the whole notion of investing into a context which I have been able to understand and act upon. I found your book so interesting that I couldn't put it down. I was so delighted to see that you have linked investing with a Christian perspective.
Barbara Apostol
Sutherlin, Oregon

I was planning to start an investment portfolio when I saw your book on the shelf of my local Christian bookstore. It was an answer to my prayers. There were many books dealing with personal and family finances, but only yours on investing. The book was easy and educational reading. Especially interesting were the four investing "risk personalities." They helped my wife and me come to a suitable compromise in our investing strategy. I frequently refer back to SMI as I make purchasing decisions.
Ronald Lee
Miami, Florida

Your book has been very informative. I am the CEO of a Federal Credit Union. I am telling you this to let you know that your book is not only for beginners, but for all levels of investors.
Harry Ovitt
Fredericksburg, Virginia

I just received a copy of your book and wanted you to know how much I'm enjoying it. It's a home run! You have covered the areas that we novices all want to know more about, and you've done it in such a creative way. The charts, graphs, and visual enhancements have made the concepts so easy to understand. Congratulations on a great job!
Lee Ellis
Gainesville, Georgia

Thank you for having developed such a superior educational book as SMI. The book is rich in information from the basics to the subtle elements of investing. The layout of the book has enhanced my understanding and made the subject matter less daunting. For the first time ever, I feel that I have begun to truly understand the operation of investing, instead of parroting the "rules" of investing. Your work has been—for lack of a better word—a blessing to me at this time in my life.
Robert P. Regitano
Albany, New York

First of all, thank you for writing *Sound Mind Investing*! I had stayed away from investing because I believed that the "small investor" did not have a chance these days. I was happy to learn that I was dead wrong. In particular, I appreciate the confidence which you have given me in making my own decisions—a real sense of empowerment! I have purchased multiple copies of your book which I have given to my children, relatives, and friends.
David Goldman
Springfield, Virginia

Sound Mind Investing

THE FINANCIAL NEWSLETTER FOR TODAY'S CHRISTIAN FAMILY

Dear Valued Reader:

I hope this book has been helpful to you! If so, I believe you'd be interested in knowing about my monthly Sound Mind Investing newsletter. Launched in 1990, it has grown to become America's best-selling investment newsletter written from a biblical perspective. Each month, it takes you out into the marketplace and helps you implement the investment philosophy and strategies explained in this book. It offers:

• Biblical goal-setting. Our Four Levels format, based on the priorities taught in Scripture as laid out in this book, helps you do "first things first." In every monthly issue, you get help in four areas.

• In Getting Debt-Free (the Level 1 column), you receive tips on budgeting and money-saving ideas on mortgages, credit cards, and how to cut your living expenses.

• In Saving for Future Needs (Level 2), you'll get information on the best ways and places to save, and primers on interest rates and the various kinds of interest-earning investments most useful to savers.

• In Investing Your Surplus (Level 3), you'll learn basic stock market investing principles and receive specific "getting started" portfolio recommendations.

• In Diversifying For Safety (Level 4), you'll keep up-to-date on the refinements in our Just-the-Basics strategy plus have access to our model Upgrading portfolio of top-performing funds that's updated monthly.

• Mutual fund performance rankings. Each quarter you get a special mutual fund report that ranks over 1,000 mutual funds—stock, bond, special sectors, and global—according to their performance and risk characteristics.

• Instructive feature articles. Each month, our cover article will give you a detailed look at a particular economic, investing, or biblical issue. As you grow in your understanding of investing principles, you'll be better equipped to take charge of your financial life and reach your long-term goals.

• Wealth-creating financial planning ideas. In our "Looking Ahead" column, written by financial planners, insurance agents, and professional accountants, you get a variety of creative planning suggestions.

• Easy to understand format. Check the comments of subscribers on the preceding two pages and you'll see what I mean. SMI makes very few assumptions about your level of understanding of economic and investing matters. That means using everyday, plain-English language (rather than industry jargon) to teach and instruct you.

To learn more about Sound Mind Investing, just send in the postage-paid card located nearby. Or, visit our website at www.soundmindinvesting.com. For less than the cost of a daily cup of coffee, I'll lead you through the financial maze and show you how to make consistently sound investing decisions.

I hope to hear from you soon!

Cordially,